EUROJARGON

A dictionary of European Union acronyms, abbreviations and terminology

7th edition

Compiled and edited by
Eric Davies

eia

Published in the United Kingdom by
European Information Association
Central Library
St Peter's Square
Manchester M2 5PD
Tel: +44 (0)161 228 3691
Fax: +44 (0)161 236 6547
E-mail: eia@libraries.manchester.gov.uk
www.eia.org.uk

ISBN: 0 948272 93 7

Contents

Preface

The internet is invaluable for those of us working with information produced by and about the European Union. The net has not, however, solved one of the basic problems inherent in dealing with 'Europe': deciphering the acronyms, abbreviations and jargon so often used in connection with its structure and activities. Without a key to the language of the EU, much of the material available remains largely unintelligible.

The previous edition of *Eurojargon* was published late in 2000. When I reviewed it in the European Information Association's quarterly journal, *European Information*, I had no idea that I would be editing the next edition. In that review, I identified terms with non-English origins as an Achilles heel for *Eurojargon*. Now in a position to do something about it, I have consciously sought to add French equivalents of English acronyms, abbreviations and names. Whilst the present work can still not be considered multilingual, it should certainly help many - myself included - identify the meaning of many of the more frequently-used French terms used in connection with the EU.

I also argued in the review that "the starting point for a work such as this should surely be ignorance - almost by definition, users are ignorant of the meaning of the term they are seeking." I have therefore also taken the opportunity to include brief profiles of the Union's main bodies, on the basis that even terms such as 'European Commission' will not be readily understood by everyone - and might, indeed, be *misunderstood* by readers of some of the more Euro-phobic press. Despite considerable coverage of European issues by the media, some of its members still display surprising ignorance (perhaps unconscious, perhaps feigned) where the EU is concerned.

This edition of *Eurojargon* includes more than 5,000 entries - some 20% more than its predecessor. To the additions noted above have also been added recently-coined terms (most, but not all, taken from official EU documents) and entries for non-EU terms and organisations which appear in EU-produced or EU-related documents. As in other editions, European Parliament reports have not been included, although their absence is of some concern and that decision will no doubt be reviewed again before the next edition of *Eurojargon* is compiled.

In this volume, the use of **bold** indicates that there is a separate entry for the term in question. Some **bold** terms are preceded by *See* or *See also* references, but others are not - particularly when the emboldened term is simply an expansion of an abbreviation (as, for example, in the entry 'Dir - **Directive**'). URLs are used extensively, often in connection with an organisation - where further details can be found via the corporate website - or to suggest a source of additional information on a topic. In the latter case, most URLs given are for web sites or pages maintained by an EU body, but other sources are occasionally suggested. All URLs were checked for accuracy on 22/23 October 2003.

For the privilege of compiling this volume, I have to thank Anne Ramsay, who compiled all six earlier editions of the work, and who put my name forward as a possible successor once she decided to give up the task. I trust her faith in me proves to have been justified. I must also thank the EIA for publishing this latest edition of *Eurojargon*; I trust it repays their confidence. My heartfelt thanks are extended also to my friend and mentor Freda Carroll, and to Jenny Lawson and Catherine Webb for their invaluable assistance with checking the text and for suggesting improvements. Needless to say, any errors or omissions are my responsibility alone, although anyone noticing such things is invited to contact me with details, so that the next edition can be further improved.

I concluded my review of the previous edition by saying "No EU information collection should be considered complete without a copy of *Eurojargon.*" As editor of this edition, I find myself voicing that opinion even more passionately!

Eric Davies

Foreword

In my role as EU Commissioner, my major responsibilities have been the administrative reform of the Commission and its preparation for enlargement of the European Union in 2004.

As part of this process, the Commission and all other EU institutions, in partnership with Member State Governments, are striving to be more open and transparent in how they work so that all citizens, not just those from the new countries joining us in the future, have a clearer idea of what we do and how we do it.

Recent opinion polls and surveys indicate that there is still much to do. There is widespread ignorance and confusion about the European Union and what it means for the individual citizens living here, as well as the businesses and organisations which operate within the EU. The language often used by policy-makers and the media only increases the feelings of alienation and bafflement. This is why the European Commission launched an initiative in 2002 to work with Member State Governments to improve how we communicate EU policies and initiatives and to inform our citizens more effectively about what is going on.

Anything which helps this process is appreciated. *Eurojargon* is a dictionary of some 5000+ EU terms, acronyms and abbreviations found in EU documents, websites and common parlance. It gives concise descriptions of those terms and points the reader to further information from contact addresses or through website links. As such, it does an excellent job of demystifying some of the more obscure jargon which is sometimes used.

I very much welcome the publication of this, the seventh edition of *Eurojargon*. It has established itself as an essential reference tool for anyone with an interest in the history and development of the EU. I am sure you will find it an invaluable addition to your book shelves.

Rt Hon Neil Kinnock, Vice-President of the European Commission

A

A
Austria

A (point)
A **Council of the European Union** agenda item for formal adoption without discussion. *See also* **B (point)**

A1
Highest rank of **European Commission** official

AA
Agricultural Acreage

AAD
Accompanying administrative document

Aalborg Charter
of European cities and towns towards sustainability. Adopted at a European Conference held in Aalborg 24-27 May 1994

AAMS
Associated African States and Madagascar

Aarhus Convention
'Convention on access to information, public participation and access to justice in environmental matters'. Adopted on 25 June 1998 at the **UN/ECE** Fourth Ministerial Conference, held in Aarhus, Denmark.
www.unece.org/env/pp

AAT
Advanced authoring tools (**DELTA** project)

ABC
A page on **Europa** offering basic factual information on the **European Union**. Now called 'The European Union at a glance'.
http://europa.eu.int/abc/index_en.htm

ABC
Assisting Business Competitiveness. A **Leonardo da Vinci** project involving eight partners from Germany, Ireland, Portugal, Spain and the UK, due to end in December 2003.
www.abcinnovation.com/en/default_en.htm

ABC MALE
Accreditation board of clinical movement analysis laboratories in Europe (a Telematics for Healthcare project within the **Telematics Applications Programme**).
www.ehto.org/ht_projects/html/dynamic/11.html

ABEAM
Across the Borders Effects of **ATM** (an Air Transport project within the **Transport** programme)

ABEL
See **EUDOR**

ABM
Activity-based management

ABSTRACT
External trade statistical domain on the **New Cronos** databank. Also called **EXTTRADE** and available as a CD-ROM from **Eurostat** data shops

AC
Advisory committee

ACACIA
A concerted action towards a comprehensive climate impacts and adaptation assessment for the **European Union** (an **Environment and Climate** project)

ACAFS
Automatic control of an ASIC fabrication sequence as demonstrated in the plasma ETCH area (**ESPRIT** project)

ACC
Article 113 of the **Treaty of Rome** regarding the passage of a **COM** document for Common Commercial Policy legislation

ACCBs
Acceding Country central banks

Acceding Country / Countries
Term used to describe the **10** of 13 Candidate Countries whose accession to the **European Union** was officially agreed at the **Copenhagen European Council**. Also seen as 'Acceding States'

ACCEE
Associated Countries of Central and Eastern Europe

ACCESS
Advanced customer connection: an evolutionary strategy (**RACE** project)

ACCESS
Development platform for unified access to enabling environments (**TIDE** project)

Accession countries
General term for countries preparing to join the **European Union**. *See* also **Acceding Countries**, **Applicant Countries**

Access Directive
Directive 2002/19/EC on access to, and interconnection of, electronic communications networks and associated facilities (**OJ** L108/02)

Accession criteria
In June 1993 the **Copenhagen European Council** recognised the right of the Central and Eastern European Countries to join the **European Union** when they had fulfilled certain political and economic criteria and incorporated the **Acquis Communautaire**. The criteria were confirmed at the Madrid **European Council** in December 1995

Accession Monitoring Program
Set up by the Open Society Institute.
www.eumap.org

Accession partnerships
Part of the pre-accession process set out in **Agenda 2000**, between the **European Commission** and each of the **Applicant Countries**. A framework covering in detail the priorities for adopting the **Acquis Communautaire**

Accession Treaty
Each enlargement of the **European Union** requires an Accession Treaty to be signed, setting out the various agreements between the parties concerned. The first such Treaty came into force on 1 January 1973. The most recent was signed in Athens on 16 April 2003 to enable the EU to welcome **10** new **Member States** in 2004. *See also* **Athens Declaration**

ACCOR
Articulatory-acoustic correlations in coarticulatory processes (**ESPRIT** project)

ACCORD
Computer-aided engineering software for advanced workstations in the **CIM** environment (**ESPRIT** project)

Accounting Directives
Collective term for the **Fourth Company Law Directive** and the **Seventh Company Law Directive**

ACE
Action by the Community relating to the environment (1987-1991) (**OJ** L207/87). Continued as **ACNAT**

ACE
Action Centre for Europe.
Second Floor, 29 Tufton Street, London SW1P 3QL. UK.
www.actioncentreeurope.org.uk

ACE
Action for co-operation in economics. In favour of Poland, Hungary, Yugoslavia, Bulgaria, Romania and Czechoslovakia (within the **Phare** and **Tacis** programmes). *See also* **Phare ACE**.
http://europa.eu.int/comm/economy_finance/publications/phare_ace/ace_en.htm

ACE-2
Aerosol characterisation experiment (**EI** project)

ACEA
European Automobile Manufacturer's Association.
211 rue de Noyer, B–1000 Brussels, Belgium.
www.acea.be

AC-EB
Applicant Countries Eurobarometer. *See* **CCEB**

ACE Quarterly
Magazine produced under **Phare ACE**.
http://europa.eu.int/comm/economy_finance/publications/phare_ace/ace-quarterly_en.htm

ACES
Courseware engineering system (**DELTA** project)

ACI Europe
Airports Council International European Region.
6 square de Meeûs, B-1000 Brussels, Belgium.
www.aci-europe.org

ACKNOWLEDGE
Acquisition of knowledge (**ESPRIT** project)

ACMDP
Advisory Committee on the Management of Demonstration Projects

ACME
Adaptive control of marine engines. One of the eight interrelated Community-funded projects in the field of design, production and operation for safer, more efficient, environmentally friendly and user-friendly ships, coordinated by **NETS**

ACNAT
Action by the Community relating to nature conservation (1992-1993) (**OJ** L370/91). Previously **ACE**, continued as **LIFE**

ACOR
Advisory Committee on Own Resources (Comité consultatif des ressources propres - CCRP)

ACORD
Construction and interrogation of knowledge bases using natural language text and graphics (**ESPRIT** project)

ACP
African, Caribbean and Pacific States: Angola, Antigua and Barbuda, The Bahamas, Barbados, Belize, Benin, Botswana, Burkina Faso, Burundi, Cape Verde, Cameroon, Central African Republic, Comores, Congo, Cook Islands, Côte d'Ivoire, Cuba, Democratic Republic of Congo, Djibouti, Dominican Republic, Equatorial Guinea, Eritrea, Ethiopia, Fiji, Gabon, The Gambia, Ghana, Grenada, Guinea-Bissau, Guinée, Guyana, Haïti, Jamaica, Kenya, Kiribati, Lesotho, Liberia, Madagascar, Malawi, Mali,

Marshall Islands, Mauritania, Mauritius, Micronesia, Federal States of Mozambique, Namibia, Nauru, Niger, Nigeria, Niue, Palau, Papua New Guinea, Rwanda, Saint Kitts and Nevis, Saint Lucia, Saint Vincent & the Grenadines, Samoa, Sao Tome and Principe, Senegal, Seychelles, Sierra Leone, Solomon Islands, Somalia, South Africa, Sudan, Suriname, Swaziland, Tanzania, Tchad, Togo, Tonga, Trinidad and Tobago, Tuvalu, Uganda, Vanuatu, Zambia, Zimbabwe. *See also* **Cotonou Agreement**.
Secretariat: ave Georges-Henri 451, B-1200 Brussels, Belgium.
www.acpsec.org

ACP-ALA-MED
A compendium of short- and long-term macroeconomic indicators of 117 countries. Published by **EUR-OP**. *See also* **Ptiers**

ACPC
Advisory Committee on Procurements and Contracts

ACPM
Advisory Committee on Programme Management

ACQUILEX
Acquisition of lexical knowledge for natural language processing systems (**ESPRIT** project)

Acquired Rights Directive
Directive 77/187/EEC on the approximation of the laws of the Member States relating to the safeguarding of employees' rights in the event of transfers of undertakings, businesses or parts of businesses (**OJ** L61/77). Replaced by Directive 2001/23/EC. Also known as the Transfers Directive. *See also* **TUPE**

Acquis communautaire
A short hand term denoting the whole body of law and policy which has been developed under the **European Community** and **European Union**. One of the objectives specified in Article 2 of the **Treaty on European Union** is "to maintain in full the acquis communautaire and build on it…"

ACRuDA
Assessment and certification rules for digital architecture (a Rail Transport Research project within the **Transport** programme)

ACSTT
Advisory Committee on Scientific and Technical Training

act4europe
A campaign of the Civil Society Contact Group, to lobby on the **Convention on the Future of Europe** and the 2004 Intergovernmental Conference - **IGC**.
www.act4europe.org

ACTA
The study of the use of metaphors as a means for assessment of currently unavailable technology (**CSCW** project).
http://orgwis.gmd.de/projects/ACTA

ACTION
Assisting carers using telematics interventions to meet older persons needs (a Telematics for Disabled and Elderly People project within the **Telematics Applications Programme**)

Action Single Market
See **SMCU**

ACTIP
Animal Cell Technology **Industrial Platform**.
www.actip.org

ACT IT
Application of computer-based systems for training in IT (**TIDE** project)

ACTS
Decision 94/572/EEC for Advanced communications technologies and services (1994-1998) (**OJ** L222/94). Previously **RACE**. Continued as **IST**. *See also* **ICT**

ACTS
High resolution speech recognition (**ESPRIT** project)

ACU
Administration of the Customs Union

ACUSE
Action Committee for the United States of Europe. Set up in 1956 by the architect of the **European Community**, Jean **Monnet**

ACVT
Advisory Committee on Vocational Training

ADAM
Advanced architecture in medicine (**AIM** project)

ADAM
Système Administratif et Documentaire des Achats et Marchés. A **European Commission** Budget **DG** database which contains data on study contracts awarded by the Commission to outside consultants.
http://europa.eu.int/adam/start (in French)

ADAPT
Community Initiative for the adaptation of workers to industrial change (1994-1999) (**OJ** C180/94). Continued as **EQUAL**

ADAPT-BIS
Building the information society (1996-1999) (Guidelines in **OJ** C200/96). *See also* **IS**

ADCIS
Analog-digital CMOS ICS (**ESPRIT** project)

Additionality
The principle that funding received from the **European Union** (e.g. from the **Structural Funds**) should be additional to a **Member State**'s own financial contribution to a project

ADECO
Dismantling workshop for orgel fuels (**JRC** - safety of nuclear materials programme)

ADEOS
Advanced Earth observing satellite

ADEPT
Advanced distributed environment for production technology (**ESPRIT** project)

ADEQUAT
Advanced developments for 0.25 um CMos techniques (**JESSI/ESPRIT** project)

ADEXP
Air traffic services data exchange presentation. One of two **EUROCONTROL** standards adopted by **Directive** 97/15/EC (**OJ** L95/97), which covers the definition and use of compatible technical specifications for the procurement of Air Traffic Management equipment and systems. *See also* **OLDI**

ADF
Additional duty on flour

ADFORA
Advertising in electronic publishing and commerce (a Telematics Information Engineering project within the **Telematics Applications Programme**)

ADKMS
Advanced data and knowledge management systems (**ESPRIT** project)

ADMIN
Personnel and Administration **DG** of the **European Commission**

ADONIS
Analysis and development of new insights into substitution of short car trips by cycling and walking (an Urban Transport project within the **Transport** programme)

Adonnino Report
on a **People's Europe**

ADORA
Analysis and definition of operational requirements for **ATM** (an Air Transport project within the **Transport** programme)

ADOT
Advanced display optimisation tools (**ESPRIT** project)

ADS
Additional duty on sugar

ADVANCE
Network and customer administration systems (**RACE** project)

Adventure
Part of **NEST**, Adventure projects "may be undertaken in any area of research, but are likely to be multidisciplinary" and will feature "ambitious and tangible objectives, with a potential for high impact, but also imply a high risk of failure."

ADVICE
Automatic design validation of integrated circuits using E-beam (**ESPRIT** project)

ADVISER
Added value information service for European research results (**Telematics Applications** project)

AEA
Association of European Airlines.
350 av Louise, B-1050 Brussels, Belgium.
www.aea.be

AEBR
Association of European Border Regions.
AGEG c/o EUREGIO, 362 Enscheder Str, D-48599 Gronau, Germany.
www.are-regions-europe.org/INTERREGIONAL/GB-AEBR.html

AECF
Asia Europe Co-operation Framework. http://europa.eu.int/comm/external_relations/asem/cluster/process.htm

AEDCL
Association of **EDC** Librarians. Became the European Information Association **- EIA**

AEGEE
Association des Etats Généraux des Etudiants de l'Europe (Forum of European Students).
PO Box 72, Etterbeek 1, B-1040 Brussels, Belgium.
www.aegee.org

AEGIS
European air traffic management group for the improvement of scenarios (**EURET** project)

AEIC
European Agency of Information on Consumer Affairs. Appears to have become Centre Européen des Consommateurs (**CEC**)

AEIDL
Association Européenne pour l'Information sur le Développement Local (European Association for Information on Local Development). "A non-profit association specialising in the development and coordination of European networks and the provision of information and methodological tools to local development actors." A support service to European Information networks, run by AEIDL, closed in January 1999. AEIDL was at one time responsible for the LEADER II website (*see* **LEADER+**).
260 Chaussée St Pierre, B-1040 Brussels,

Belgium.
www.aeidl.be

AEIF
Européenne pour l'Intéroperabilité Ferroviaire (European Association for Railway Interoperability).
15 blvd de l'Impératrice, B-1000 Brussels, Belgium.
www.aeif.org

AEJE
Association Européenne des Juristes d'Entreprise (European Company Lawyers' Association - **ECLA**)

AEMI
Advanced environment for medical image interpretation (**AIM** project)

AEOLUS II
Development and construction of two windpower stations (**EUREKA** project)

AEPPC
See **EIPA** (European Insolvency Practitioners Association)

AER
Assembly of European Regions. Immeuble Europe, 20 place des Halles, F-67054 Strasbourg, France.
www.are-regions-europe.org

AER
Assessment of environmental risk related to unsound use of technologies and mass tourism (**Environment and Climate** project)

AER
See **ARE** (Group of the European Radical Alliance)

AERL
Association Européenne pour les Ressources Linguistiques (European Language Resources Association - **ELRA**)

AERONOX
Project on the impact of nitrogen oxide emissions from air traffic in the upper atmosphere (**Environment and Climate** project)

AESOPIAN
Awareness of European solutions and best practices for telematics applications (a telematics Engineering project within the **Telematics Applications Programme**)

AESS
Agencia Europea para la Seguridad y la Salud en el Trabajo (European Agency for Safety and Health at Work - **EU-OSHA**)

AEVG
Asia Europe Vision Group.
http://europa.eu.int/comm/external_relations/asem/cluster/process.htm

AFC
Appropriations for Commitment (in the budget)

AFCO
European Parliament Committee on Constitutional Affairs

AFET
European Parliament Committee on Foreign Affairs, Human Rights, Common Security and Defence Policy

AFFET
Association for European Training of Workers on the Impact of Technologies. Managed by **ETUC**.
155 blvd Emile Jacqmain, B-1210 Brussels, Belgium

AFG
Association des Fabricants de Glucose de l'UE (Association of the Glucose Producers in the EU).

ave de la Joyeuse Entrée 1-5, Boîte 10,
B-1040 Brussels, Belgium

AFIS
Anti-fraud information system (**OLAF**)

AFNOR
Association Francaise de Normalisation. National standards body of France.
www.afnor.fr

AFP
Appropriations for payment (in the budget)

African Union
Organisation of African Unity. Launched 2002; successor to the **OAU**.
www.africa-union.org

AGATA
Advanced gas turbine for automobiles (**EUREKA** project)

AGEFT
Agricultural electronic fund transfer. A project to communicate daily data from the disbursing agencies to the **EAGGF** (**CADDIA** project). Merged with **AGREX**

AFSJ
Area of freedom, security and justice

Agence Europe
Brussels-based publisher, best known for the *Europe Daily Bulletin* (*Bulletin Quotidien Europe*) which is often referred to eponymously as 'Agence Europe'.
www.agenceurope.com

Agencies
In July 2003, there were 15 bodies described as 'Community agencies' - bodies with their own legal personality, governed by European public law, established to fill specific tasks set out in relevant **European Community** legislation. *See* **CEDEFOP**; **CdT**; **CPVO**; **EAR**; **EEA**; **EFILWC**; **EFSA**; **EMCDDA**; **EMEA**; **EMSA**; **EASA**; **ETF**; **EUMC**; **EU-OSHA**; **OHIM**.
http://europa.eu.int/agencies/index_en.htm

Agenda 2000
An initiative for the millennium covering enlargement to Eastern Europe and new provisions for the financing of **European Union** activity. Completed in 1999 (**COM**(97)2000 and also available as *Bulletin of the EU* Supplement 5/1997).
http://europa.eu.int/comm/agenda2000/index_en.htm

Agenda for a Growing Europe
Report on the **European Union**'s efforts to meet the goals of the **Lisbon Strategy**. Presented to the **European Commission** on 18 July 2003, it called for growth to be the Union's first priority. Produced by a High-Level Study Group chaired by André Sapir.
http://europa.eu.int/comm/lisbon_strategy/pdf/sapir_report_en.pdf

AGGEFFECT
Effectiveness of international environmental agreements (**Environment and Climate** project)

AGINFO
An on-line database of the **CAP** and European trade in food and agricultural commodities. Was published by **Agra Europe**, but no longer available.

AGMASCO
Airborne geoid mapping system for coastal oceanography (**MAST III** project)

AGORA
A **CEDEFOP** forum for open, multilateral discussion

AGORA
Network of **SME** networks using telematics (an Education and Training Sector project under the **Telematics Applications Programme**)

Agra Europe
Publisher specialising in European agricultural issues.
80 Calverley Road, Tunbridge Wells, Kent, TN1 2UN, UK.
www.agra-net.com

Agreements Office
of the **Council of the European Union**. Responsible for providing information on agreements and conventions with **Third Countries** and international organisations.
http://db.consilium.eu.int/Accords/default.asp?lang=en

AGREP
A database consisting of a permanent inventory of agricultural research projects in **Member States**

AGREX
Agricultural guarantee fund expenditure. A system to monitor expenditure under the Guarantee Section of the **EAGGF** (**CADDIA** project). Includes **AGEFT**

AGRI
Agriculture **DG** of the **European Commission**

AGRI
European Parliament Committee on Agriculture and Rural Development

AGRIMED
Mediterranean agriculture (1989-1993) (**OJ** L58/90)

AGRI-R
Regional agricultural statistical domain on the **REGIO** database

AGRO-BIOTECH
Applications of biotechnology in agriculture and agro-food industries (**COMETT** project)

AGROMET
A meteorological database within the **CADDIA** programme

AHSEA
Advanced driver assistance systems in Europe (a Telematics for Integrated Applications for Digital Sites project within the **Telematics Applications Programme**)

AI
Artificial Intelligence

AIA
Advanced informed agreement

AIDA
Acquis implementation database (**EFTA**)

AIDA
Advanced integrated circuit design aids (**ESPRIT** project)

AIDA
Alternatives for international document availability (project within Area 5 of the **Telematics Systems Programme**)

AIDMED
Assistant for interacting with multimedia medical databases (**AIM** project)

AIDS
Acquired immune deficiency syndrome. The EU has wide-ranging interests in AIDS. Details of some are presented on **SCADPlus** at:
http://europa.eu.int/scadplus/leg/en/s03000.htm. *See also* **Europe Against AIDS**

Aids
Short form of '**State aids**'

AIEC
See **AEIC**

AILE
Innovative local integration and exchange activities (**HELIOS** project)

AIM
Advanced informatics in medicine in Europe (1988-1990) (**OJ** L314/88). Previously **BICEPS**. Continued as Area 3 of the **Telematics Systems Programme** and **ESPRIT IV**

AIM
AIP application to IBCN maintenance (**RACE** project)

AIMBURN
Advanced intelligent multi-sensor system for control of boilers and furnaces (**ESPRIT** project)

AIMCS
Animal identification and movement control scheme

AIMS
Advanced integrated millimeter wave sub-assemblies (**ESPRIT** project)

AIMS
Aerospace intelligence management and development tool for embedded systems (**EUREKA** project)

AIMS
Assistance to industry mainframe system. A database of information on funding. Replaced by **INFOGRANT**

AIN-ED
The exchange of state aid data (**CADDIA** project)

AIPCEE
EU Fish Processors Association.
Av de Roodebeek, B-1030 Brussels, Belgium

AIR
Agriculture and agro-industrial (including fisheries) research programme (1990-1994) (**OJ** L265/91). Incorporated **ECLAIR**; **FLAIR**; **FOREST**; **JOULE** (Biomass area). Continued as **FAIR**. *See also* **FAP**; **FAR**

AIR
Innovative theme-based rehabilitation activities (**HELIOS** project)

Airbase
Air quality database of the **EEA**

Air borders
See **Green borders**

AIRE Centre
Advice on Individual Rights in Europe.
17 Red Lion Square, London WC1R 4QH, UK.
www.airecentre.org

AISE
Archive of socio-economic information. A **Eurostat** system

AITRAS
An intelligent real-time coupled system for signal understanding (**ESPRIT** project)

AL
Action lines

AL
América Latina (Latin America)

ALA
Asian and Latin American countries

ALAMEDSA
Asia, Latin America, the Mediterranean and South Africa

ALAMOS
Automatic lidar for air monitoring operating system (**EUREKA** project)

AlβAN
Programme of Scholarships for Latin Americans in the **European Union**.

http://europa.eu.int/comm/europeaid/projects/alban/index_en.htm

ALCOM
Algorithms and complexity (**ESPRIT** project)

ALDICT
Access of persons with learning disabilities to information and communication technologies (a Telematics for Disabled and Elderly People project within the **Telematics Applications Programme**)

ALDUV
Algan detectors for low cost solar UV-band monitoring systems (**THESEO** project)

ALE
See **EFA** (European Free Alliance Group)

ALECT
Advanced ceramic materials for aluminium electrolysis technology (**EUREKA** project)

Alexis de Tocqueville Prize
Awarded every two years by the European Institute of Public Administration (**EIPA**).
www.eipa.nl

ALF
Advanced software engineering environment logistics framework (**ESPRIT** project)

ALFA
Amérique Latine-Formation Académique (Latin America Academic Training). Cooperation between higher education establishments in 18 Latin American countries and the **European Union** (1994-1999) (Information in **OJ** C281/96)

ALIM
Future of the food system (**FAST** programme)

AL-INVEST
An initiative to promote co-operation between businesses in the **European Union** and Latin America.
www.al-invest.org

ALIPOR
Autonomous lander instrument packages for oceanographic research. Project to develop a series of instrumentation packages for measurement, monitoring and sampling on the sea floor (**MAST III** project)

ALIS / @LIS
Alliance for the Information Society. Initiative to promote the EU-Latin America partnership in the context of the Information Society. @LIS objectives are: to establish dialogue and cooperation on policy and regulatory frameworks in key areas, and to boost interconnections between research networks and communities in both regions.
http://europa.eu.int/comm/europeaid/projects/alis/index_en.htm

ALL-INN
Allergy innovations (**EUREKA** project)

ALPES
Advanced logical programming environments (**ESPRIT** project)

ALPSOLAR
Field testing and optimisation of photovoltaic solar power plant equipment in alpine regions (**EUREKA** project)

ALTEC
Algorithms for future technologies (**Phare** project)

ALTENER
Alternative energy. Programme to promote renewable energy sources. An initial five-year programme ended in 1997, but was renewed for 1998-2002 as ALTENER II.
http://europa.eu.int/comm/energy/en/pfs_altener_en.html

ALTER
Alternative traffic in towns project. Launched at the first Environment and Transport Ministers' European Council in April 1998. The project aims to create a demand for zero and low emission vehicles among European local and regional authorities

Altmark case
European Court of Justice Case C-280/00 concerning Altmark Trans, a German bus company that claimed it could not survive without public subsidies

ALURE
Regulation 443/92 for financial and technical assistance in the energy sector for developing countries in Asia and Latin America (1995-2003) (**OJ** L52/92).
http://europa.eu.int/comm/europeaid/projects/alure/index_en.htm

AMADEUS
Development, marketing and operation of a European-based global computerised distribution system to meet the future needs of the travel industry (**EUREKA** project)

AMADEUS
Multi-method approach for developing universal specifications (**ESPRIT** project)

AMADIS
Development of advanced training activities and educational software in computational engineering (**COMETT** project)

Amato Reflection Group
on long term implications of EU enlargement. Report presented November 1999

AMBAR
Science park networking (**SPRINT** project)

Amber wastes
See **Wastes**

AMBULANCE
Mobile unit for health care provision via telematics support (a Telematics for Healthcare project within the **Telematics Applications Programme**)

AmCham-EU
EU Committee of the American Chamber of Commerce.
www.eucommittee.be

AMES
Advanced microelectronics educational service (**COMETT** project)

AMES
European network on reactor pressure vessel embrittlement and annealing. A network established by the **JRC**. The **IAM** acts as operating agent and reference laboratory

AMFEP
Association of Manufacturers of Fermentation Enzyme Products.
Av de Roodebeek, B-1030 Brussels, Belgium

AMICE
European computer integrated manufacturing architecture (**ESPRIT** project)

AMIS
Agricultural market intelligence system (a database within the **CADDIA** programme). *See also* **FIS**

AMODEUS
Assimilating models of design, users and systems (**ESPRIT** project)

AMR
Advanced mobile robots for public safety applications (**EUREKA** project)

AMRIE
Alliance of Maritime Regional Interests in Europe.
20-22 rue du Commerce, B-1000 Brussels, Belgium.
www.amrie.org

AMS
Advanced manufacturing system (**ESPRIT** project)

Amsterdam Treaty
See **Treaty of Amsterdam**

AMUE
Association for the Monetary Union of Europe.
26 rue de la Pépinière, F-75008 Paris, France

AMUFOC
Association for Forage Seed Producing Companies. Now part of **ESA**

ANA
Agricultural numerical annexes (**CADDIA** project)

ANCAT
Abatement of Nuisance Caused by Air Transport. A group of experts from within the **ECAC**

ANEC
European Association for the Coordination of Consumer Representation in Standardisation.
36 ave de Tervuren, Boîte 4, B-1040 Brussels, Belgium.
www.anec.org

ANIMA
An office established by the Commission to help with its Community action programme on equal opportunities for women and men, under **Decision** 95/593/EEC (**OJ** L335/95)

Animal Experiments Directive
Directive 86/609/EEC on the approximation of laws, regulations and administrative provisions of the **Member States** regarding the protection of animals used for experimental and other scientific purposes (**OJ** L358/86)

ANIMATE
Added support to strategy, cohesion and dissemination for transport and environment projects (a Telematics for Environment project within the **Telematics Applications Programme**)

Animo
Animal moves management system. Set up under **Decision** 91/398/EEC on a computerized network linking veterinary authorities (**OJ** L221/91)

Ankara Agreement
Association Agreement between the **European Communities** and Turkey, intended to establish a customs union (**OJ** C113/73)

Annex II Bird Species
Those which may be legally hunted under Annex II of the **Birds Directive** (79/409/EEC)

ANNIE
Application of neutral networks for industry in Europe (**ESPRIT** project)

ANTARES
A new traffic approach regarding energy saving (**THERMIE** project).
http://europa.eu.int/comm/energy/en/thermie/antares.htm

Anthem
See **European Anthem**

Antici Group
An informal group composed of the personal assistants to the Permanent Representatives (**COREPER**)

Anti-Raider Directive
Directive 88/627/EEC on rules to inform the public of significant changes in the ownership of shares of companies listed on the Stock Exchange (**OJ** L348/88)

AOCTS
Associated Overseas Countries and Territories

AOIS
Alps Observation and Information System (Système d'Observation et d'Information des Alpes - SOIA). So-called 'Alps Observatory', detailed in **COM**(93)713, "to support, within the frame of the Alpine Convention, the Alpine countries in the management and sustainable development of the rural Alpine space." **European Union** contribution through **JRC**.
www.soia.int/preAC/home.en.htm

AORS
Abnormal occurrences reporting system (a database which forms part of **ERDS**)

AORTICS
Advanced open resources telematics in critical care situations (a Telematics for Healthcare project within the **Telematics Applications Programme**)

APACHIP
Advanced packaging for high performance (**ESPRIT** project)

APACO
Recurrent agricultural acts and management committees (a word processing system within the **CADDIA** programme)

APAS
Preparatory, accompanying and support actions (in the **Fifth Framework Programme**)

APBB
Advanced PROM building blocks (**ESPRIT** project)

APC
A **European Commission** database which monitored Commission Proposals and Communications forwarded to the **Council of the European Union**. Replaced by **PreLex**

APECE
Advanced production engineering continued (sic) education (**COMETT** project)

APECS
Amphibious plant for environmental control and safeguard (**EUREKA** project)

APEP
Association des Producteurs Européens de Potasse (European Potash Producers' Association)

APE-THESEO
Airborne platform for earth observation - third European experiment on stratospheric ozone (**THESEO** project)

APEX
Advanced project for European information exchange: application to the aerospace industry (**EUREKA** project)

APHRODITE
A **PCTE** host-target distributed testing environment (**ESPRIT** project)

API
Association of Producers of Isoglucose of the EU.
1-5 av de la Joyeuse Entrée, Boîte 10, B-1040 Brussels, Belgium

APOLLO
Article procurement with on-line local ordering. A joint project of the **ESA** and the **European Commission** for satellite document delivery (1984-1988)

APPE
Association of Petrochemical Producers in Europe.
4 av Van Nieuwenhuyse, B-1160 Brussels, Belgium

Applicant Countries
By July 2003, 14 countries had formally applied to join the EU: Turkey in April 1987; Cyprus and Malta in July 1990; Hungary in March 1994; Poland in April 1994; Romania and Slovakia in June 1995; Latvia in October 1995; Estonia in November 1995; Lithuania and Bulgaria in December 1995; Czech Republic in January 1996; Slovenia in June 1996; Croatia in February 2003. Of the 14, the **10** joining in 2004 are known as **Acceding Countries** or Acceding States

APPSN
Application pilot for people with special needs (**RACE** project)

APR
Action programme for research

APs
Accession Partnerships

APS
Annual policy strategy. Introduced by the **European Commission** in 2001

APSIS
Application software prototype implementation scheme (**ESPRIT** project)

AQUA
Advanced quantum-well lasers for multi-gigabit transmission (**RACE** project)

AQUACON
A water quality project carried out by the **EI**

Aqua Europa
European Water Conditioning Association. 58 rue de Louvranges, B-1325 Dion-Valmont, Belgium

AQUARELLE
Sharing cultural heritage through multimedia telematics (a Telematics Information Engineering project within the **Telematics Applications Programme**)

AQUARIUS
Aquatic research institutions for the development of user friendly applications in telematics (a Telematics for Education and Training project within the **Telematics Applications Programme**)

AQUARIUS
A project to encourage the safeguarding of the sea (1987). Launched under the **EYE** programme

ARAL
Assistance à la Réforme de l'Administration Libanaise. Also seen as ARLA: Assistance to the Rehabilitation of the Lebanese Administration project

ARAMIS
Advanced runway arrivals management to improve airport safety and efficiency (an Air Transport project within the **Transport** programme)

ARBRE
Arable biomass renewable energy (**THERMIE** project)

ARC
RainbowGroup of the **European Parliament**. From 'Arc-en-Ciel' - French for 'Rainbow'

Arcadia Report
UK House of Lords Select Committee on the European Communities *report on policies for rural areas in the EC*. Published by HMSO as House of Lords paper 1979-80 (129)

Arc Atlantique
See **Atlantic Arc**

ARCDEV
Arctic demonstration and exploratory voyage (**Transport** project). www.cordis.lu/transport/src/arcdev.htm

ARCHEO
EC-funded research project to assess the impact of climate change in Venice by studying some of Canaletto's paintings

ARCHISPLUS
A database of historical archives of the **European Commission**.
http://europa.eu.int/comm/secretariat_general/archisplus/htdocs/en/htm/home.htm

Architects' Directive
Directive 85/384/EEC on the mutual recognition of diplomas, certificates and other evidence of formal qualifications in architecture (**OJ** L223/85)

Architectural Heritage
An annual pilot project to conserve and promote the Union's architectural heritage (incorporated within the **Raphael** programme)

Architecture of Europe
Refers to the various organisations, Institutions, Treaties and traditional relations making up the European area within which members work together on problems of shared interest. An essential part of this is the **Pillars**

ARCHON
Architecture for cooperative heterogenous on-line systems (**ESPRIT** project)

ARCOME
ECHO database of organisations, researchers and publications in the communications field

ARE
Alliance Radicale Européenne. *See also* **ERA**

Area of Freedom, Security and Justice
Established by the **Treaty of Amsterdam**, the concept includes the free movement of people, and appropriate measures concerning external border controls, asylum, immigration and the prevention and combating of crime.
http://europa.eu.int/comm/justice_home/index_en.htm

ARF
ASEAN Regional Forum

ARGO
Action programme for administrative cooperation in the fields of external borders, visas, asylum and immigration.
http://europa.eu.int/comm/justice_home/project/argo_en.htm

ARGOSI
Applications related graphics and **OSI** standards integration (**ESPRIT** project)

ARI
Appraisal of the regional impact

ARIADNE
Access, information and navigation support in the labyrinth of large buildings (a Telematics for Disabled and Elderly People project within the **Telematics Applications Programme**)

ARIADNE
Development of an intelligent driver and navigation support system (**DRIVE** project)

ARIADNE II
Alliance of remote instructional authoring and distribution networks for Europe (a Telematics for Education and Training project within the **Telematics Applications Programme**)

Ariane
Decision 2085/97/EC establishing a programme of support, including translation, in the field of books and reading (1997-1998) (**OJ** L291/97 with an extension to 1999 in OJ L57/99). Replaced by **Culture 2000**

ARIANE
Name of rockets used in the European Space Programme

ARIES
Applied Research and Information-transfer Enhanced Services.
6 rue Jean Calvin, F-75005 Paris, France

ARIN
Advancing rural information networks (a Telematics for Integrated Applications for Digital Sites project within the **Telematics Applications Programme**)

ARION
Actieprogramma: Reizen met een Instructief Karakter voor Onderwijsspecialisten (1978/79-1994). Previously Study visits for education specialists and continued as part of Action 3 within **Socrates**

ARIS
Agriculture and Regional Information Systems Unit (Joint Research Centre, **Institute for the Protection and Security of the Citizen**).
http://ipsc.jrc.cec.eu.int/WS-Agriculture.html

ARIS Network
Action for Research and Information Support in Civilian Demining.
http://demining.jrc.it/aris

ARISE
Anaesthesia risks intelligent supporting environment (**EUREKA** project)

ARISE
A reusability infrastructure for software engineering - off line (**RACE** project)

Aristeion Prizes
European prizes for literature and translation, 1993-2000; funded through the **Ariane** programme

ARLA
See **ARAL**

ARMS
Advanced robotics manipulation system (**ESPRIT** project)

ARP
See **AIR** (Agriculture and Agro-Industrial programme)

ARPS
Agricultural report production system (**CADDIA** project)

ARS
Adverse environment recognition of speech (**ESPRIT** project)

Art
Article - as in 'Article 3 of the Treaty'

ARTEMIS
Application research and testing for emergency management intelligent systems (a Telematics for Environment project within the **Telematics Applications Programme**)

Artemis
European Union military operation in the Democratic Republic of Congo (DRC), launched 12 June 2003.
http://ue.eu.int/pesd/congo/index.asp?lang=EN

ARTERI
Arctic terrestrial ecosystems research initiative: coordination of research in European Arctic and Alpine areas (**TERI** project)

Article 10
of the European Regional Development Fund (**ERDF**) allows financial support for studies or pilot schemes concerning regional development at Community level

Article 6 Committee
European Commission committee to implement financial protocols in Mediterranean countries

Article 55
of the **Treaty of Paris**, concerning technical coal and steel research (1994-1999) (**OJ** C67/94)

Article 56
of the **Treaty of Paris**, concerning Readaptation Grants
Article K.4 Committee
See **K4 Committee**

ARTIFACTS
Advanced robotics in flexible automation: components, tools and strategies (**ESPRIT** project)

ARTISAN
Intelligent framework for the industrial environment (**DELTA** project)

ARTM
Agency for Trans-Mediterranean Networks set up in 1993 for the coordination of **MED-Campus**; **MED-Media** and **MED-Urbs**

ARTMA
Advanced real-time motion analysis (**EUREKA** project)

ARTS-IP
Arts-IP satellite data (**ESPRIT** project)

ASAC
Application specific architecture compilation (**ESPRIT** project)

ASAP
Amsterdam Special Action Programme. Launched by the European Investment Bank (**EIB**) in June 1997 in response to the Amsterdam **European Council**, to step up action in support of job-creating investments (1997-2000) (**OJ** C10/98).
www.eib.org/i2i/en/asap.htm

Asbestos Directive
Directive 2003/18/EC amending Directive 83/477/EEC on the protection of workers from the risks related to exposure to asbestos at work

ASCIS
Behavioural synthesis, partitioning and architectural optimisation for complex systems on silicon (**ESPRIT** project)

ASCOT
Assessment of systems and components for optical telecommunications (**RACE** project)

ASEAN
Association of Southeast Asian Nations.
70-A Jalan Sisingamangaraja, PO Box 2072, Jakarta 12110, Indonesia.
www.aseansec.org

ASEM
Asia Europe Meeting.
http://europa.eu.int/comm/external_relations/asem/cluster/process.htm

ASFALEC
See **EDA**

ASHORED
Adaptable smarter homes for residents who are elderly or disabled (**TIDE** project)

Asia-Invest
A programme to promote and support business co-operation between the **European Union** and Asia. Originally 1996-2000, but extended 2003-2007 as Asia-Invest II.
http://europa.eu.int/comm/europeaid/projects/asia-invest/html2002/main.htm

ASIA-IT&C
Asia Information Technology and Communication Programme. Launched in October 1999 to co-finance mutually beneficial partnerships in ITC between Europe and Asia. Also seen as ASI@ITC.
http://europa.eu.int/comm/europeaid/projects/asia-itc

ASIA-Link
Promotes regional and multilateral networking between higher education institutions in EU **Member States** and 17 countries in South Asia, South-East Asia and China.
http://europa.eu.int/comm/europeaid/projects/asia-link

ASIA Pro Eco
Launched in 2002 "to improve environmental performance and technology partnership in economic sectors, and promote sustainable responsible investment." Based on Asia Eco Best.
http://europa.eu.int/comm/europeaid/projects/asia-pro-eco

Asia Urbs
Funding local government partnerships between the **European Union** and Asia for urban development. Started 1996; extended to December 2003. *See also* **URB-LA**.
http://europa.eu.int/comm/europeaid/projects/asia-urbs/index_en.htm

ASIC
Agricultural Situation in the European Union: the **European Commission**'s annual agricultural report

ASIM
Council of the European Union acronym for reports covering immigration and asylum. *See also* **ENFOPOL**.
www.statewatch.org/eufbi/news4.htm

ASOR
Decision 82/505/EEC regarding the Agreement on the international carriage of passengers by road by means of occasional coach and bus services (**OJ** L230/82). *See also* **Interbus Agreement**

ASP
Advanced sandwich panel (**EUREKA** project)

ASPEC
Association of Sorbitol Producers within the EC.
9 av de Gaulois, B-1040 Brussels, Belgium

ASPIS
Application software prototype implementation system (**ESPRIT** project)

ASSENT
Assessment of telematics programme (a project within the **Telematics Applications Programme**)

Assent procedure
Introduced by the Single European Act (**SEA**) so that the **Council of the European Union** must obtain the approval of the **European Parliament** for **Association Agreements**, Accession Agreements and some legislation

ASSET
Automated support for software engineering technology (**ESPRIT** project)

ASSIFONTE
Association de l'Industrie de la Fonte de Fromage de la CEE (European Association of Manufactures of Processed Cheese).
157 Godesberger Allee, D-53175 Bonn 1, Germany

ASSILEC
See **EDA**

ASSIST
Assessment of information systems and technologies in medicine (**AIM** project)

Association Agreements
cover the **European Union**'s relations with Cyprus, Malta and Turkey in the context of their accession to the Union. The Agreements are similar in scope to **Europe Agreements**, but relations with Cyprus and Malta don't cover political dialogue, and for Turkey the

Agreement aims to achieve a Customs Union

ASSOPOMAC
Association of Potato Breeders. Now part of **ESA**

ASTEP
Advanced software for teaching and evaluation of processes (**EMTF** project)

ASTERISK
System and scenario simulation for testing RTI systems (**DRIVE** project)

ASTRA
Advanced and integrated office systems prototypes for European public administration (**ESPRIT** project)

ASTRID
Amorphous silicon technology for radiological imaging diagnostics (**EUREKA** project)

ASTRID
A socio-technical response to the needs of individuals with dementia and their carers (a Telematics for Disabled and Elderly People project within the **Telematics Applications Programme**)

ASTRON
Applications on the synergy of satellite telecommunications, earth observation and navigation

ATA
Fast prototypeable analogue transistor array development of an analogue ASIC (**EUREKA** project)

ATES
Advanced techniques integration into efficient scientific application software (**ESPRIT** project)

ATEX Directive
From the French 'Atmosphere explosible'. **Directive** 94/9/EC on the approximation of the laws of the **Member States** concerning equipment and protective systems intended for use in potentially explosive atmospheres (**OJ** L100/94). Mandatory from July 2003. Replaced the **Explosive Atmospheres' Directives**.
http://europa.eu.int/comm/enterprise/atex/

Athens Declaration
Made at the signing of the **Accession Treaty** during an informal meeting of the **European Council** in Athens on 16-17 March 2003. The opening paragraphs of the Declaration included: "We the representatives of the citizens and States of the **European Union** meet today on this symbolic site, under the Acropolis, to celebrate an historic event: The signing of the Accession Treaty for Cyprus, the Czech Republic, Estonia, Hungary, Latvia, Lithuania, Malta, Poland, the Slovak Republic and Slovenia."

ATIS
AIT touring information system (**IMPACT** project)

ATLANTEC
An **Interreg II** network which seeks to promote technological co-operation between scientific and industrial players in the regions of the **Atlantic Arc**.

ATLANTIC
The deployment of coherent systems for digital television (**ACTS** project)

ATLANTICA
Developing training methodologies for the European Atlantic regions (**COMETT** project)

Atlantic Arc
A network of 32 regions of the **European**

Union which border the Atlantic together with the islands of the Atlantic and other regions with close economic, ethnic and cultural ties with the Atlantic seaboard regions (**EP DOC** A3-304/92). Map and list in *Innovation and Technology Transfer* 4/1995. A 'Commission' of the **CPMR**. *See also* **CAAC**.
www.arcat.org/Anglais/arcanet.html

Atlantic Area
Cooperation area under **Interreg**, extending from Scotland to Southern Portugal and Andalusia, and comprising: Portugal and Ireland, Galicia, Asturias, Cantabria, Navarre, the Basque Country, Rioja, Castile-Leon, the Canaries and the provinces of Huelva, Cádiz and Sevilla (in Andalusia) in Spain, Aquitaine, Poitou-Charentes, the Loire Region, Upper and Lower Normandy, Limousin, Centre, and Midi-Pyrénées in France, and in the United Kingdom Cumbria, Lancashire, Greater Manchester, Cheshire, Merseyside, Worcestershire and Warwickshire, Avon, Gloucestershire and Wiltshire, Dorset and Somerset, Cornwall and Devon, Staffordshire, Herefordshire, Shropshire, West Midlands, the 22 Welsh unitary authorities, Northern Ireland, the Highlands and Islands and South West Scotland. Total area 856 420 km^2; population 76.1 million.
www.interreg-atlantique.org

Atlantic Axis
Alternative term for **Atlantic Arc**

Atlantic Rim
Alternative term for **Atlantic Area**

ATLAS
A Commission study to integrate communications, navigation and surveillance technologies to support a single air traffic management system for Europe

ATLAS
Study to provide independent information to help determine and prioritise the next steps in terms of **RTD**, demonstration and market stimulation in the energy field (**THERMIE** project)

ATM
Air traffic management

ATMOSPHERE
Advanced techniques and models of system production in a heterogeneous extensible and rigorous environment (**ESPRIT** project)

ATOMOS
Optimisation of manpower in marine transport (**EURET** project)

ATOMS
High densities mass storage memories for knowledge and information storage (**ESPRIT** project)

ATRE
ATM and telecollaboration for research and education (a Telematics for Research project within the **Telematics Applications Programme**)

ATT
Advanced transport telematics

ATTACH
Advanced trans-European telematics applications for Community help (a Telematics for Urban and Rural Areas project within the **Telematics Applications Programme**)

ATTAIN
Applicability in transport and traffic of artificial intelligence (**DRIVE** project)

ATTRACT
Applications in telemedicine taking rapid advantage of cable television network evolution (a Telematics for Healthcare project within the **Telematics Applications Programme**).

www.tid.es/trabajo/attract/home.html

AU
African Union. Successor to the Organisation of African Unity.
PO Box 3243, Roosvelt Street (Old Airport Area), W21K19 Addis Ababa, Ethiopia.
www.africa-union.org

AUDETEL
Audio description of television for the visually disabled and the elderly (**TIDE** project)

AUDIT
Financial control **DG** of the **European Commission**

AULIS
Biomarkers of genotoxicity of urban air pollution, a dose response study (an Environmental Health and Chemical Safety Research project within the **Environment and Climate Programme**)

AUNP
ASEAN-EU University Network Programme. "A Co-operation programme for EU and ASEAN higher education institutions".
http://europa.eu.int/comm/europeaid/projects/aunp

AUSA
Agricultural usable surface area

Australia Group
An informal arrangement aimed at allowing exporting or transshipping countries to minimise the risk of assisting chemical and biological weapon proliferation. The **European Commission** is a member of the Australia Group. *See also* **Missile Technology Control Regime**, **Nuclear Suppliers Group**, **Wassenaar Arrangement**, **Zangger Committee**.
www.australiagroup.net

Authorisation Directive
Directive 2002/20/EC on the authorisation of electronic communications networks and services (**OJ** L108/02)

AUTOCODE
Intelligent system for automatic processing of design codes of practice (**ESPRIT** project)

Auto-Oil
A programme set up in 1993 and resulting in **Directive** 96/44/EC on the measures to be taken against air pollution by emissions from motor vehicles (**OJ** L210/96) and Directive 98/70/EC on fuel quality (OJ L350/98). Auto-Oil II ran from 1997-2000. http://europa.eu.int/comm/environment/autooil

AUTOPOLIS
Automatic policing information system (**DRIVE** project)

AUVIS
Audiovisual information system statistical domain on the **New Cronos** databank

Avant-garde
French term generally meaning 'new', 'unusual', 'experimental'. Used to denote a group of **Member States** which might want to seek greater integration in certain policy areas

AVC
d'Avis Conforme (**Assent procedure**)

AVEC
Association of Poultry Processors and Poultry Import and Export Trade in the EU.
Trommesalen 5, DK-1614 Copenhagen V, Denmark

AV Eureka
Audiovisual Eureka: "a pan-European intergovernmental organization with 35 member countries" which aims to unify "the patchwork of audiovisual markets in Europe so that European citizens can enjoy their neighbours' films."

Secretariat: ave des Arts 44, B-1040 Brussels, Belgium.
Details via: www.aic.sk/workshop/escreen.html

AVIATION
Air transport statistical domain on the **New Cronos** databank

AVICA
Advanced video endoscopy image communication and analysis (**AIM** project)

Avicenne Initiative
Scientific and technical cooperation with **Maghreb** and Mediterranean Basin countries, 1992-1994 (information in **OJ** C173/92 and OJ C106/94)

Avis
See **Opinion**

Avosetta Group
Small informal group of lawyers who aim to promote environmental law in the EU and its **Member States**. From the Latin name of a rare bird which was the subject of a legal case decided by the **European Court of Justice**.
www.avosetta.org

AWG
Permanent Working Group 'Information on Agriculture'

AWU
Annual work unit

B

B
Belgique / Belgium

B (point)
A **Council of the European Union** agenda item which is likely to be discussed at great length, as opposed to **A (point)**

B2B
Business-to-business

B2C
Business-to-consumer

B2Europe
March 2003 initiative "to pool the know-how and resources of Europe's major business support networks so as to deliver basic assistance and advice faster and more efficiently to where businesses need it." See press release IP/03/317

BABEL
Broadcasting Across the Barriers of European Language.
c/o European Broadcasting Union, 17A Ancienne Route, Case Postale 67, Grand-Saconnex, CH-1218 Geneva, Switzerland

BABEL
Integrating cultural differences in telematics engineering (a Telematics Engineering project within the **Telematics Applications Programme**)

BACH
Bank [previously Base] for the Accounts of Companies Harmonised. A **European Commission** database of statistical data on company accounts covering 11 European countries, Japan and the United States.
http://europa.eu.int/comm/economy_finance/indicators/bachdatabase_en.htm

BACIP
Bacillus subtilis genome **Industrial Platform**.
http://europa.eu.int/comm/dg12/biotech/ip2.html#BACIP

BALAI Directive
Directive 92/118/EEC laying down animal health and public health requirements governing trade in and imports into the Community (**OJ** L62/93)

Balladur Plan
Unofficial name for the European **Stability Pact**, originally proposed by French Prime Minister Edouard Balladur in April 1993

Baltic Council
Alternative name for Council of the Baltic Sea States - **CBSS**

Baltic Sea Region Initiative
Prepared at the request of the 1995 Madrid **European Council**. Intended to strengthen political stability and economic development in the Baltic Sea region.
www.cbss.st/documents/euand_baltic_region

Bangemann Challenge
A competition initiated by the city of Stockholm in 1994 calling on all European cities with more than 400,000 inhabitants to present their most interesting information technology applications

Bangemann Report
'Europe and the global information society:

recommendations to the European Council 1994'. Named after the then European Commissioner responsible for information technology, Martin Bangemann. *See also* **Corfu Summit**.
http://europa.eu.int/ISPO/infosoc/backg/bangeman.html

BAP
Biotechnology action programme (1985-1989) (**OJ** L206/88). Previously **BEP**. Continued as **BRIDGE**

Barcelona Convention
for the Protection of the Marine Environment and the Coastal Region of the Mediterranean. A United Nations Environment Programme (**UNEP**) initiative. The **European Community** acceded to the Convention via **Decision** 77/585/EEC (**OJ** L240/77).
www.unepmap.gr and http://europa.eu.int/scadplus/leg/en/lvb/l28084.htm

Barcelona Declaration
Signed at a meeting of the Euro-Mediterranean Conference on 27-28 November 1995, the Declaration is the basis of EU-Mediterranean policy.
http://europa.eu.int/comm/external_relations/euromed/bd.htm

Barcelona Declaration
on Policy Proposals to the **European Commission** on Basic Ethical Principles in Bioethics and Biolaw. Adopted in November 1998 at the last meeting of the **BIOMED II** Project.
www1.umn.edu/humanrts/instree/barcelona.html

Barcelona Process
Alternative name for the **Euro-Mediterranean Partnership**, launched at the Conference of EU and Mediterranean Foreign Ministers in Barcelona on 27-28 November 1995. The 12 Mediterranean countries involved were: Algeria, Cyprus, Egypt, Israel, Jordan, Lebanon, Malta, Morocco, Palestinian Authority, Syria, Tunisia, Turkey

BARFIE
Books and Reading for Intercultural Education. A network set up under **Comenius**, comprising institutions and professionals working with children's books and media.
House of Children's Literature, Kinderliteraturhaus, 6 Mayerhofgasse, A-1040 Vienna, Austria.
www.barfie.net

Barre Plans
for monetary union. Published in *Bulletin of the EC* Supplements 3/69, 2/70. Named after Raymond Barre, then Vice-President of the **European Commission**, and responsible for economic affairs

BARRIER
Development of a multimedia database providing information on the accessibility in public buildings for people with handicaps to their mobility (a Telematics for Disabled and Elderly People project within the **Telematics Applications Programme**)

BARTOC
Bus advanced real time operational control (**DRIVE** project)

BAs
Business Angels

Basel Convention
United Nations Environment Programme (**UNEP**) treaty on hazardous wastes. The **European Community** acceded via **Decision** 93/98/EEC of 1 February 1993 on the conclusion, on behalf of the Community, of the Convention on the control of transboundary movements of hazardous wastes and their disposal (**OJ** L39/93).
www.basel.int

BASELINE
Baseline data for user validation in information engineering (a Telematics Information Engineering project within the **Telematics Applications Programme**)

BASIS
The Barents Sea impact study (**ELOISE** project)

Basle Convention
See **Basel Convention**

BASYS
The Baltic Sea system study (a project within the **MAST III** programme). *See also* **CANIGO**; **MATER**; **OMEX**

BAT
Best available techniques

Bathing Water Directive
Directive 76/160/EEC concerning the quality of bathing water (**OJ** L31/76). An amendment is proposed: **COM**(2002)581 - Proposal for a Directive ... concerning the quality of bathing water.
http://europa.eu.int/water/water-bathing/index_en.html

Batteries Directive
Directive 91/157/EEC on batteries and accumulators containing certain dangerous substances (OJ L78/91)

BBP
Biotechnology for Biodiversity Platform.
http://europa.eu.int/comm/dg12/biotech/ip2.html

BC
Budget Committee

BCC
Biotechnology Coordination Committee

BCC
See **BRE**

BCI
Business climate indicator. A monthly indicator "designed to deliver a clear and early assessment of the cyclical situation within the euro area". Also called the 'common factor'.
http://europa.eu.int/comm/economy_finance/indicators/businessclimate_en.htm

BC-NET
Business Cooperation Network. Set up by the **BCC** to encourage **SME**s to develop links with their counterparts in other **Member States**. Closed 2001

BCR
Bureau Communautaire de Référence (Community Bureau of Reference). Established in 1973 under the aegis of **DG** XII, in connection with Certified Reference Materials (CRMs)

BCR
R&D programme in the field of applied metrology and chemical analysis (1988-1992) (**OJ** L206/88)

BCS
BC-NET central system

BD II
Development of a database for distributed expert systems on low-level computers (**EUREKA** project)

Beacon Europe 1992
An initiative to light beacons throughout the **Member States** to herald the Single European Market (**SEM**) on 1 January 1993

BEAM II
Biomedical equipment assessment and management (a Telematics for Healthcare project within the **Telematics Applications Programme**)

BEC
Broad economic categories

BECOS
A natural language front-end to databases with speech facilities (**EUREKA** project)

BEDA
Bureau of European Designers' Associations. Postbus 91526, NL-2509 EC Den Haag, Netherlands

BEI
Banque européenne d'investissement (European Investment Bank - **EIB**).
www.bei.org

BELMR
Bureau européen pour les langues moins répandues (European Bureau for Lesser Used Languages - **EBLUL**)

BEMA
Biogenic emissions in the Mediterranean area (an **EI** project)

BENE
Business Education Network in Europe.
www.bene-europe.org

Benelux
Benelux Economic Union, comprising Belgium, The Netherlands and Luxembourg

Benelux Memorandum on the Future of Europe
Contribution to the debate on the future of Europe by the governments of Belgium, The Netherlands and Luxembourg, June 2001.
http://europa.eu.int/futurum/documents/other/oth200601_en.htm

BEP
Biomolecular engineering programme (1982-1986) (**OJ** L305/83). Continued as **BAP**

BEPGs
Broad Economic Policy Guidelines.
http://europa.eu.int/comm/economy_finance/publications/broadeconomypolicyguidelines_en.htm

BEQUEST
Building environmental quality evaluation for sustainability through time (**Environment and Climate Programme**)

BERD
Banque européenne pour la reconstruction et le développement (European Bank for Reconstruction and Development - **EBRD**)

BERI
Bog ecostystem research initiative (**TERI** project)

Berlaymont
Until the end of 1991, the star-shaped Berlaymont building was the headquarters of the **European Commission** in Brussels. It was closed when dangerous levels of asbestos were found. Staff were relocated to some 60 locations elsewhere in Brussels, including the **Breydel** building.
www.berlaymont2000.com

Berlin Agreement
concerning the reform of the **CAP**. Adopted by the March 1999 Berlin **European Council**

Berne Convention
Popular name for the **Council of Europe**'s Convention on the Conservation of European Wildlife and Natural Habitats. The **European Community** acceded through **Decision** 82/72/EEC concerning the conclusion of the Convention on the conservation of European wildlife and natural habitats (**OJ** L38/82).
www.nature.coe.int/english/cadres/bern.htm

BERTIE
Changes in the drive behaviour due to the introduction of **RTI** systems (**DRIVE** project)

BEST
Bulletin of European Studies on Time. Published by the **EFILWC**

BEST
Business Environment Simplification Task Force.
http://europa.eu.int/comm/enterprise/enterprise_policy/best

BEST
Methodological approach to **IBC** system requirements and specifications (**RACE** project)

Betel
Interconnection of broadband sites in France and Switzerland: a fibre interconnection initiative to prepare for **TEN-Telecommunications**

BEUC
Bureau Européen des Unions de Consommateurs (European Consumers' Organisation).
36 av de Tervuren, Boîte 4, B-1040 Brussels, Belgium.
www.beuc.org

BEVABS
European office for wine, alcohol and spirit drinks. A special unit at the **EI** in the **JRC** at **Ispra**

BFM
Business feedback mechanism. Launched as a pilot scheme in April 2000, the BFM aims to ensure that EU policy-making takes more account of businesses' experiences of the Internal Market. The pilot was based on feedback from 41 Euro Info Centres (**EIC**s). Replaced by Interactive Policy Making - **IPM**

BIA
Business impact assessment

BIBDEL
Libraries without walls: the delivery of library services to distant users (project within Area 5 of the **Telematics Systems Programme**)

BiblioTECA
Bibliographic texts compositional analysis (project within Area 5 of the **Telematics Systems Programme**)

BIC
Blueprint for interactive classrooms (a Telematics for Education and Training project within the **Telematics Applications Programme**)

BIC
European Business and Innovation Centres. Established 1989, there are now 264 such centres providing integrated support services for the creation of enterprises

BICEPS
See **AIM** (Advanced Informatics in Medicine in Europe)

BICMOS
A high performance cmos-bipolar process for VLSI circuits (**ESPRIT** project)

BINOCULARS
A project to perfect a general system for managing the impact of fertilisers at river basin level (**Environment and Climate Programme**)

BINTERMS
Basic interoperability for terminals for telematic services (**ISIS** Teleworking project)

BIO
Internal briefings of the **European Commission**, at one time available on **RAPID**

BIO COMAC
Biology Concerted Action Committee

BIODEPTH
Biodiversity and ecological processes in terrestrial herbaceous ecosystems: experimental manipulations of plant communities (**TERI** project)

BIOKIT
Clinical diagnosis of gonorrhoea (**EUREKA** project)

BIOLAB
Integrated biomedical laboratory (**AIM** project)

BIOMED II
Decision 94/913/EC for a research and technological development programme in the field of biomedicine and health (1994-1998) (**OJ** L361/94). *See also* **BIOTECH**; **ELSA**; **LST**.
http://europa.eu.int/comm/dg12/biomed1.html

BIOMERIT
Increased innovation and industrial development in the European agro-food sector through biotechnology exploitation (**COMETT** project)

BIOREP
Biotechnology research projects in Europe.
www.niwi.knaw.nl/us/projects/probior.htm

BIOSAFE
Biotechnology information system

BIOSTANDARDS
Establishment of bioinformatic databases and access tools (**ISIS** Bioinformatics project)

BIOTECH
Biotechnology Programme. Part of the **Fourth Framework Programme** under **Decision** 94/912/EC (**OJ** L361/94). Implemented as Quality of Life and Management of Living Resources under the **Fifth Framework Programme**. Previously **BRIDGE**. *See also* **BIOMED**; **LST**.
http://europa.eu.int/comm/research/biot1.html

BIPED
Basic business IBC demonstrator (**RACE** project)

BIPMS
Building industry project management system (**ESPRIT** project)

Birds Directive
Directive 79/409/EEC on the conservation of wild birds (OJ L103/79). Also known as the Wild Birds Directive

BIS
Budget information system

Bistro
The **Tacis** Bistro facility "is designed to respond quickly to requests for support for small scale projects meeting local needs anywhere in Russia, Ukraine, Georgia, Armenia and Kazakhstan."
http://europa.eu.int/comm/europeaid/projects/tacis/bistro_en.htm

BIT
Biotechnology in training (**COMETT** project)

Black List
of dangerous substances discharged into the aquatic environment. **Directive** 76/464 (**OJ** L129/76 - List 1). *See also* **Grey List**

Black Monday
On 30 September 1991, in a diplomatic blunder, the Dutch **Presidency** presented a draft treaty which was rejected by 10 of the 12 **Member States**. The Dutch then had to engage in rapid negotiations on the basis of work done by the previous Luxembourg

Presidency. (The outcome eventually became the **Treaty on European Union**)

Black Monday
Popular term for the stock market crash of 19 October 1987

Black Wednesday
16 September 1992: the day on which the British government, under Prime Minister John Major, suspended sterling's membership of the **ERM**

Blair House Agreement
A November 1992 EU-US agreement intended to protect US exports from animal feed derived from subsidised EU oilseed production, and to provide the basis of an overall **GATT** agricultural agreement

BLEU
Belgium - Luxembourg Economic Union

BLIC
Liaison Office of the Rubber Industries of the EU.
2 av des Arts, Boîte 12, B-1210 Brussels, Belgium

BLNT
Broadband local network technology (**RACE** project)

Block exemptions
are made to exempt certain categories of agreement from Article 85 of the **Treaty of Rome**, which prohibits agreements affecting trade between **Member States**, or which restrict or distort competition e.g. **Know-How Licensing**

Blue Banana
Term coined by French geographer Roget Brunet in 1989. It describes an area (also known as the 'Dorsale') linking London, Brussels, Frankfurt, Zurich and Milan. The name is said to refer to the large concentration of 'blue collar' jobs in the area or, alternatively, to be based on satellite images of a blue, banana-shaped urban conglomeration

Blue borders
See **Green borders**

Blue Flag Campaign
An annual award for bathing beaches in the **Member States** which fulfill certain criteria. An initiative of **FEEE**

BME COMAC
Bio-medical engineering Concerted Action Committee

BOI
Binding origin information (with respect to customs matters)

BookTownNet
European book town network. A telematics application based on a model for sustainable rural development within the cultural heritage (a Telematics for Urban and Rural Areas project within the **Telematics Applications Programme**)

BOP
Balance of payments statistical domain on the **New Cronos** databank

BOPCom
Baltic open port communication (a marine transport project within the **Transport** programme)

BOPS
Back office performance support (**EMTF** project)

Bosman Case
Case C-415/93 in the **European Court of Justice** on the freedom of movement for footballers (Case reported in **ECR** I-1995/12).

http://europa.eu.int/comm/sport/key_files/circ/b_bosman_en.html

BRAIN
Basic research in adaptive intelligence and neurocomputing (part of the **SCIENCE STIMULATION** programme)

Brattle Group
Consultancy firm which prepared the December 2002 report 'The Economic Impact of an EU-US Open Aviation Area' for the **European Commission**. *See also* **TCAA**

BRE
Bureau de Rapprochement des Entreprises (Business Cooperation Centre - BCC). A network of correspondents, promoting cross-border co-operation between **SME**s. Closed 2001

BREVIE
Bridging reality and virtuality with a graspable user interface (**EMTF** project)

Brewers of Europe
Previously CBMC: Confederation of Brewers of the Common Market.
181 ch de la Hulpe, Boîte 20, B-1170 Brussels, Belgium.
www.brewersofeurope.org

Breydel
The main **European Commission** building in Brussels, following the 1991 closure of the **Berlaymont**

BRIC
Biotechnology Regulations Inter-Service Committee

BRIDGE
Biotechnology research for innovation, development and growth in Europe (1990-1994) (**OJ** L360/89). Previously **BAP**; continued as **BIOTECH**

BRITE
Basic research in industrial technologies for Europe. *See* **BRITE/EURAM III**

BRITE/EURAM III
Decision 94/571/EC on industrial and materials technologies (1994-1998) (**OJ** L222/94). Replaced by **GROWTH**. See also **BRITE**; **CRAFT**; **IT**.
www.cordis.lu/brite-euram/home.html

BROKERSGUIDE
Online directory of current information brokers in the EC. Merged with **DIANEGUIDE** to form **I*M GUIDE**

Bruges Group
Established in February 1989 following Prime Minister Margaret Thatcher's September 1988 Bruges speech. The Group's inspiration was her observation that Britain had not rolled back the frontiers of the state in order to have them re-imposed from Brussels.
Suite 216, The Linen Hall, 162-168 Regent Street, London, W1R 5TB, UK.
www.brugesgroup.com

Bruges speech
See **Bruges Group**

Brussels
Capital of Belgium and - due to its being home to numerous European **Institutions** - the self-styled capital of Europe. Used as a (sometimes pejorative) term for '**European Union**', '**European Commission**' etc

Brussels Convention
on jurisdiction and the enforcement of judgments in civil and commercial matters, 27/968 (**OJ** C189/90). Replaced by **Regulation** (EC) No 44/2001 on jurisdiction and the recognition and enforcement of judgments in civil and commercial matters (OJ L12/01). *See also* **Lugano Convention**.
http://europa.eu.int/scadplus/leg/en/lvb/l33054.htm

Brussels Treaty
Treaty amending certain financial provisions of the Treaties establishing the EC and of the Treaty establishing a Single Council of the EC. Signed July 1975; in force 1978

BSC
Biotechnolgy Steering Committee

BSCW
Basic support for cooperative work (**CSCW** project partially funded by the **European Union** under the **Telematics Applications Programme**).
http://bscw.gmd.de

BSE
Bovine spongiform encephalopathy ("mad cow disease"). *See* **ESB1 / ESB2**

BSEC
Black Sea economic cooperation

BSI
British Standards Institution. UK national standards body.
www.bsi.org.uk

BSPF
Baltic Small Projects Facility. Set up in 1995 with **Phare** funding to establish **INTERREG**-type collaboration in Baltic Sea regions

BTI
Binding tariff information. "A central instrument in the implementation process of the Common Customs Tariff".
http://europa.eu.int/comm/taxation_customs/databases/bti_en.htm

BTN
Brussels tariff nomenclature. Replaced by **CCCN**

BTR
Basic technological research

BTWC
Biological and Toxin Weapons Convention. A common position was adopted by the **Council of the European Union** in 1999 (99/346/CFSP, **OJ** L133/99)

BUDG
Budget **DG** of the **European Commission**

BUDG
European Parliament Committee on Budgets

BUILDING 2000
Solar energy pilot project (within the 1985-1988 non-nuclear energy **R&D** programme)

Building Europe Together
A campaign within **PRINCE**

Burden of Proof Directive
Directive 97/80/EC on the burden of proof in cases of discrimination based on sex (**OJ** L14/98)

Business Angels
Entrepreneurs willing to invest time and money to support the creation and development of start-up companies. In 1999, the Enterprise **DG** of the **European Commission** launched a programme to promote networks of Business Angels. *See also* **EBAN**.
http://europa.eu.int/comm/enterprise/entrepreneurship/financing/business_angels.htm

C

CA
Commitment appropriation (in the budget)

CA
Compensatory amounts

CA
Concerted Action

CAAC
Conference of the **Atlantic Arc** Cities. www.arcat.org

Cabinet
A **Commissioner**'s private office. Following the 1999 reform of the **European Commission**, Commissioners are limited to a cabinet of six A-grade staff (nine for the President), including the **Chef de cabinet** and the Deputy Chef de cabinet. There should be at least three different nationalities, with the Chef de cabinet or the Deputy Chef de cabinet preferably being of a different nationality from the Commissioner. Each Commissioner is also expected to ensure a balance of genders in his/her cabinet

Cabotage
A procedure whereby non-resident transport carriers may operate national transport services within another **Member State**

CACOHIS
Computer aided community oral health information system (**AIM** project)

CACTI
Common agricultural customs transmission of information (**CADDIA** project)

CAD
CAD interfaces (**ESPRIT** project)

CAD
Capital Adequacy Directive

CAD
Computer aided design

CADAM
Cancer and aids diagnosis and monitoring (**EUREKA** project)

CAD/CAM
Computer aided design / computer aided manufacturing

CADDIA
Cooperation in automation of data and documentation for imports-exports and agriculture (1985-1992) (**OJ** L96/85 and OJ L145/87)

CADEX CAD
geometry data exchange (**ESPRIT** project)

CADP
Community area development plan

CAF
Common assessment framework. Developed in 1999/2000 by the **Member States** in the context of improving public administration

CAFA
Committee for Administrative and Financial Affairs. Set up in 1998 by the Bureau of the **CoR**

CAFAO
Customs and Fiscal Assistance Office. Established in 1996 by **DG** Taxation and Customs Union to facilitate the implementation of the customs-related provisions of the **Dayton Accords** in Bosnia-Herzegovina

CAFÉ
Clean air for Europe

CAFE
Conditional access for Europe (**ESPRIT** project)

CAFÉ
Conservatives Against a Federal Europe. The group closed down when Iain Duncan Smith became leader of the UK Conservative Party.
www.cafe.org.uk

CAFÉ MONDIAL
Communication applications for education, multi-user open network design, infrastructure and logistics (a Telematics for Urban and Rural Areas project within the **Telematics Applications Programme**)

CAG
Competitiveness Advisory Group. Established in February 1995. Comprises an independent group of eminent people, responsible for producing six-monthly reports on the state of the Union's competitiveness and for advising on economic policy priorities and guidelines with the aim of stimulating competitiveness. CAG II was set up in 1997.
http://europa.eu.int/comm/cdp/cag/index_en.htm

Cajal, Ramón y Scholarships
See **Ramón y Cajal Scholarships**

CAKE
Advanced knowledge-based environments for large database systems (**ESPRIT** project)

CALIES
Computer-aided locomotion by implanted electro-stimulation (**EUREKA** project)

CALYPSO
Computational fluid dynamic in the ship-design process. One of the eight interrelated Community-funded projects in the field of design, production and operation for safer, more efficient, environmentally friendly and user-friendly ships, coordinated by **NETS**. *See also* **CAMELLIA**

CALYPSO
Contact and contact less environments yielding a citizen pass integrating urban services and financial operations (a Telematics for Integrated Applications for Digital Sites project within the **Telematics Applications Programme**)

CAM
Computer aided manufacturing

CAM-A
Customs Assistance Mission to Albania (part of the 1997 **Phare** programme in Albania)

CAMAC
Care-based hospital management and clinical evaluation in Europe (**AIM** project)

CAMAR
Competitiveness of agriculture and management of agricultural resources (1989-1993) (**OJ** L58/90)

CAMARC
Computer-aided movement analyses in a rehabilitation context (**AIM** project)

CAMBI
A research network for market based instruments for environmentally sustainable development (**Environment and Climate** project)

CAMCE
Computer-aided multimedia courseware engineering (**DELTA** project)

CAMELLIA
Environmentally compatible anti-fouling coatings. One of the eight interrelated Community-funded projects in the field of design, production and operation for safer, more efficient, environmentally friendly and user-friendly ships, coordinated by **NETS**. *See also* **CALYPSO**

CAM-ES
Customs Assistance Mission to Eastern Slavonia (part of the **Phare** programme in the Balkans)

CAMILE
Concerted action on management information for libraries in Europe (**Telematics Applications Programme**)

CAN
Committee of an advisory nature. A committee to assist in the management of **DOSES**

CANDI
Combined analogue digital integration (**ESPRIT** project)

Candidate Countries
Alternative term for **Applicant Countries**

CANIGO
Canary Islands Azores Gibraltar Observatories (**MAST III** project). *See also* **BASYS**; **MATER**; **OMEX**

CANS
Citizens access networks and services (a Telematics for Urban and Rural Areas project within the **Telematics Applications Programme**)

CANTOR
Converging agreement by networking telematics for object recognition (a Telematics for Healthcare project within the **Telematics Applications Programme**)

CAOBISCO
Association of the Chocolate, Biscuit and Confectionery Industries of the EU / Association des Industries de la Chocolaterie, Biscuiterie et Confiserie de l'UE.
1 rue Defacqz, Boîte 7, B-1000 Brussels, Belgium.
www.caobisco.com

CAP
Common Agricultural Policy. Established in 1957 by the **Treaty of Rome**, the CAP is one of the Community's oldest 'common' policies, intended to promote and protect the agricultural sector in the **6** original **Member States**. By the 1980s it was increasingly criticised for being expensive and for encouraging over-production. Reforms were agreed in the early 1990s and again in 2003.
http://europa.eu.int/pol/agr/index_en.htm

CAP
Computer assisted production (**EUREKA** project)

CAP
Concerted action programme

CAP 2000
Studies carried out by the Agriculture **DG** of the **European Commission** examining the **CAP**. Reports available on beef, dairy, cereals, wine, rural development.
http://europa.eu.int/comm/agriculture/publi/archive/index_en.htm

Capabilities Commitment Conference
Held in 20 November 2000 in Brussels, to enable **Member States** to review their national commitments to the military capability goals set by the **Helsinki European Council**.
http://ue.eu.int/pesc/military/en/CCC.htm

CAPE
A **Eurochambres** initiative, financially supported by the EU's **Phare** programme. Intended to strengthen Chambers of Commerce and Industry in Central and Eastern Europe and to increase their involvement in the accession process.
www.eurochambres.be/activities/cape.shtml

CAPE 2000
Computer aided post in Europe in the year 2000 (a Telematics for Administrations project within the **Telematics Applications Programme**)

CAPIEL
Coordinating Committee for Common Market Associations of Manufacturers of Industrial Electrical Switchgear and Controlgear.
19 Stresemannallee, D-60591 Frankfurt am Main, Germany

Capital Adequacy Directive
Directive 93/6/EEC on the capital adequacy of investments firms and credit institutions (**OJ** L141/93)

Capital Directive
Directive 88/361/EEC for the implementation of Article 67 of the **Treaty of Rome** (**OJ** L178/88)

CAPRI
Concerted action for transport pricing research integration (**Transport** project)

CAPS
Communication and access to information for persons with special needs (**TIDE** project)

CAPT
Committee on associations with **Third Countries**

CAPTION LIFE
Using telematics to help those suffering with a hearing impairment (a Telematics for Disabled and Elderly People project within the **Telematics Applications Programme**)

CAPTIVE
Collaborative authoring, production and transmission of interactive videos for education (**DELTA** project)

CAR
CAD/CAM for the automotive industry in Europe (**RACE** project)

CARA
Community Association and Reconstruction Assistance to the Western Balkans. Programme adopted by the Commission for assistance to Albania, Bosnia and Herzegovina, Croatia, the Former Yugoslav Republic of Macedonia and the Federal Republic of Yugoslavia (2000-2006) (Guidelines in **COM**(99) 661).
http://europa.eu.int/comm/external_relations/news/12_99/ip_99_963.htm

CARDI-ASSIST
Improving cardiac telediagnosis and surgery enabling technologies and 3D ultrasound imaging (a Telematics for Healthcare project within the **Telematics Applications Programme**)

Cardiff Process
See **Cardiff Report**

Cardiff Report
Annual report from the Internal Market **DG** on the functioning of product and capital markets, produced following a request from the 1998 Cardiff **European Council**. Produced as part of the so-called 'Cardiff Process' and also seen as 'Cardiff report on the functioning of the internal market'.
http://europa.eu.int/comm/internal_market/en/update/economicreform/

CARDIO EUG7
Feasibility study on the European component of the G7 global health care cardiovascular

sub project (a Telematics for Healthcare project within the **Telematics Applications Programme**)

CARDLINK 2
A patient-held portable record for particular application in cases of medical emergency (a Telematics for Healthcare project within the **Telematics Applications Programme**)

CARDS
Community Assistance for Reconstruction, Democratisation and Stabilisation. Programme to provide assistance to the Western Balkans.
http://europa.eu.int/comm/europeaid/projects/cards/index_en.htm

CARE
Decision 93/704/EC on the creation of a Community databank on road accident statistics (**OJ** L329/93)

CARE
Health information network involving **HSSCD** and **HIEMS** (**IDA** project)

CARGOES
Integration of dynamic route guidance and traffic central system (**DRIVE** project)

CARISMA
Coordinated architecture for the interconnection of networks for suitable mobility with telematics applications (**Transport** project)

CARLOS
Communications architecture for layered open systems (**ESPRIT** project)

CARMAT 2000
Car structures using new materials (**EUREKA** project)

CARMINAT
System for the acquisition, transmission, processing and presentation of information to improve the safety of the driver and to make trips easier and more efficient (**EUREKA** project)

Carnegie Group
Forum for ministers of science and research of the **G8** and the **European Commission**; meets biannually

Carnot
Decision 1999/24/EC for a multiannual programme of technological actions promoting the clean and efficient use of solid fuels (1998-2002) (**OJ** L7/99).
http://europa.eu.int/comm/energy/en/pfs_carnot_en.html

Carolus
Infrequently seen alternative spelling of **Karolus**

Carrefour
A network of information centres serving rural communities. From the French 'crossroads'. *See also* **Relays**.
http://europa.eu.int/comm/relays/carrefours/index_en.htm

CART
Community action to promote rural tourism (**COM**(90)438)

Cartagena Agreement
Signed in May 1969, the Cartagena Agreement - also known as the Subregional Integration Agreement, and the Andean Pact - established the Andean Group: Bolivia, Chile, Colombia, Ecuador and Peru (Venezuela joined in 1973; Chile left in 1976)

CARTOON
European Association of Animation Film - **EAAF**

CASA
Cooperative archive of serials and articles

(project within the Telematics for Libraries programme). *See also* **NFP**

CASCADE
Contribution for assessment of common **ATM** development in Europe (an Air Transport project within the **Transport** programme)

CASEIN
Settling of a casein and by-products industrial pilot plant (**EUREKA** project)

CASSIOPE
Computer-aided system for scheduling, information and operation of public transport in Europe (**DRIVE** project)

Cassis de Dijon
Case 120/78 in the **European Court of Justice** which established that any product lawfully produced and marketed in one **Member State** must (in principle) be admitted to the market of any other Member State (Case reported in **ECR** 1979/1)

CASSTM
Commission administrative de la sécurité sociale des travailleurs migrants (Administrative Commission on Social Security for Migrant Workers)

Catalogue of Data Sources
See **CDS**

CATCH II
Citizens advisory system based on telematics for communication and health (a Telematics for Healthcare project within the **Telematics Applications Programme**)

CATDIFF
An online catalogue and ordering tool for official EU publications, developed for **Publications Office** sales agents. Replaced **CATEL**.
http://online.eur-op.eu.int

CATEL
An electronic catalogue containing publicly available documents from **EUR-OP**. Replaced by **CATDIFF**

CAVA
Concerted action on voluntary approaches (coordinated by **CERNA**)

CAVIS
Intelligent automated optical inspection of printed circuit boards (**EUREKA** project)

CBC
Cross-border cooperation between the **NIS** and the **European Union** and between the NIS and **CCE** (**Tacis** programme)

CBMC
Confederation of Brewers of the Common Market. Now **Brewers of Europe**

CBNM
Central Bureau for Nuclear Measurements. Part of the **JRC** at **Geel**

CBP
Cross Border Payments. **Directive** 97/5/EC on cross-border credit transfers (**OJ** L43/97). http://europa.eu.int/scadplus/leg/en/lvb/l24023.htm

CBSS
Council of the Baltic Sea States. Its 12 members are: Denmark, Estonia, Finland, Germany, Iceland, Latvia, Lithuania, Norway, Poland, Russia, Sweden, and the **European Commission**.
Secretariat: Strömsborg, P.O.Box 2010, 103 11 Stockholm, Sweden.
www.cbss.st

CC
Information notes from the **European Court of Auditors**

CC
Chef de Cabinet (Head of **Cabinet**)

CCACE
Comité de coordination des associations coopératives européennes (Coordinating Committee of European Cooperative Associations).
c/o CECOP, 59 rue Guillaume Tell, B-1060 Brussels, Belgium.
www.ccace.org

CCAMLR
Commission for the Conservation of Antarctic Marine Living Resources. The EC acceded through **Decision** 81/691/EEC on the conclusion of the Convention on the conservation of Antarctic marine living resources (**OJ** L252/81).
www.ccamlr.org and http://europa.eu.int/scadplus/leg/en/lvb/l28103.htm

CCBE
Conseil des Barreaux de l'Union européenne / Council of the Bars and Law Societies of the European Union.
45 rue de Trèves, B-1040 Brussels, Belgium.
www.ccbe.org

CCC
Regulation 2913/92 establishing the Community Customs Code. The basic instrument underlying Community customs provision (**OJ** L302/92).
http://europa.eu.int/comm/taxation_customs/law_en.htm

CCC
See **Capabilities Commitment Conference**

CCC
Consumers' Consultative Council. Established in 1973 as an advisory body on consumer policy (**Decision** 73/306/EEC). Replaced in 1995 by the Consumer Committee under Decision 95/260/EC - later repealed by Decision 2000/323/EC (**OJ** L111/00)

CCCC
Community-COST Concertation Committee

CCCN
Customs Cooperation Council Nomenclature. Previously **BTN**. Replaced by **HS**

CCD
Committee on Commerce and Distribution

CCE
Countries of Central Europe

CCE
Cour des comptes européenne (**European Court of Auditors**)

CCEB
Candidate Countries Eurobarometer. A series of surveys launched in 2001 to gauge public opinion in the Candidate Countries (initially called '**Applicant Countries** Eurobarometer').
http://europa.eu.int/comm/public_opinion/cceb_en.htm

CCEE
Countries of Central and Eastern Europe

CCFAC
Codex Committee on Food Additives and Contaminants. Part of the Codex Alimentarius Commission, which was set up by the Food and Agricultural Organisation (**FAO**) and the World Health Organisation (**WHO**).
http://europa.eu.int/comm/food/fs/ifsi/eupositions/ccfac/ccfac_index_en.html

CCFI
Advisory Committee on Training in Nursing

CCFP
Consultative Committee for the Fusion Programme. Set up in 1980

CCFR
Coordinating Committee on Fast Reactors

CCG
Policy Coordination Group for Credit Insurance, Credit Guarantees and Financial Credits

CCL
Common command language

CCN/CSI
Common communications network/commons system interface. The development of common facilities for the transfer of large files and interactive data exchange (**IDA** project)

CCP
Common commercial policy

CCP
Consultative Committee on Publications

CCPC
Consultative Committee on Purchases and Contracts

CCPF
Central Committee of Forest Ownership in the EEC. Now **CEPF**.
47-51 rue du Luxembourg, B - 1050 Brussels, Belgium

CCPI
Advisory Committee for the Management and Coordination of Data Processing programmes

CCPM
Consultative Committee for Programme Management

CCR
Centre Commun de Recherche (Joint Research Centre - **JRC**)

CCRE
Conseil des Communes et Régions d'Europe (Council of European Municipalities and Regions - **CEMR**)

CCRP
Comité consultatif des ressources propres (Advisory Committee on Own Resources - ACOR)

CCT
Common Customs Tariff. *Replaced by* **CN**

CCT
Compulsory Competitive Tendering

CD
Coordinated development of computerised administrative procedures (**CADDIA** project) (**OJ** L33/86)

CD
Chef de délégation (Head of Delegation)

CdC
Chef de Cabinet (Head of a **Cabinet**)

CDBC
Commission Database Committee

CDE
Centre for the Development of Enterprise / Centre pour le Développement de l'Entreprise. Created by the **ACP** and the **European Union** in the context of the **Cotonou Agreement**. *See also* **CDI**

CDI
Centre for the Development of Industry. Now **CDE**. Set up under **LOME I** to facilitate **SME** participation in **EDF** projects.
52 ave Herrmann Debroux, B-1160 Brussels, Belgium.
www.cdi.be

CDIC
Commission Informatics Steering Committee

CDIS
Steering Committee for Statistical Information

CDP
Communiqués de presse (press releases)

CDR
An application editors and software developers workbench for publishing multi-media information using optical read-only storage devices (**ESPRIT** project)

CdR
Comité des regions (Committee of the Regions - **CoR**)

CDS
Catalogue of data sources. A database containing descriptions of authoritative **EEA** and **EIONET** information resources developed by the **ETC/CDS**.
www.mu.niedersachsen.de/system/cds

CdT
Centre de traduction (Translation Centre for the Bodies of the European Union). Set up under **Regulation** 2965/94 (**OJ** L314/94).
Bâtiment Nouvel Hémicycle, 1 rue du Fort Thüngen, L-1499 Luxembourg Kirchberg.
www.cdt.eu.int

CDU
Christlich Demokratische Union / Christian Democratic Union. German political party.
www.cdu.de

CE
Compulsory expenditure

CE
Council of Europe

CE (mark)
Directive 93/465/EEC on Conformity marking (**OJ** L220/93). From Conformité Européenne.
http://europa.eu.int/comm/enterprise/faq/ce-mark.htm

CEA
European Confederation of Agriculture.
23-25 rue de la Science, Boîte 23, B-1040 Brussels, Belgium

CEAC
Conférence Européenne de l'Aviation Civile (European Civil Aviation Conference - **ECAC**)

CEAC
Conference of European Affairs Committees.
See also **COSAC**

CEAS
Citizen's Europe Advisory Service

CEBI
Centre for European Business Information. Name originally given to **EICs**, but no longer used

CEC
Central European countries statistical domain on the **New Cronos** databank

CEC
Centre Européen des Consommateurs (European Consumer Centre).
www.euro-conso.org

CEC
Commission of the European Communities.
See **European Commission**

CEC
Confédération Européenne des Cadres (European Managers' Confederation).
ave Carton de Wiart 148, B-1090 Brussels, Belgium

CEC
Conféderation Européenne de l'industrie de la Chaussure (European Confederation of the Footwear Industry).

53 rue F. Bossaerts, B-1030 Brussels, Belgium.
www.cecshoe.be

CECC
Cenelec Electronic Components Committee.
35 rue de Stassart, B-1050 Brussels, Belgium

CECCs
Central European Candidate Countries

CECC
Communauté Européenne des Coopératives de Consommateurs. *See* **Euro Coop**

Cecchini Report
Published in 1988 (English version by Wildwood House) entitled *The European challenge 1992: the benefits of a Single Market* (plus 16 research volumes published by **OOPEC**). The Report provided a strong incentive for the completion of the **SEM**. A follow-up was published in 1996 as the **Single Market Review**

CECG
Consumers in **European Community** Group. Became **CEG**

CECODE
European Centre of Retail Trade.
c/o HDE, 2 Gothaer Allee, D-50969 Köln, Germany

CECOP
European Committee of Workers Cooperatives, Social Cooperatives and Participative Enterprises.
59 rue Guillaume Tell, B-1060 Brussels, Belgium

CECSO
Comité Européen des Combustibles Solides (European Solid Fuels Association)

CEDB
Component Event Data Bank which forms part of **ERDS**

CEDEFOP
Centre Européen pour le Développement de la Formation Professionnelle (European Centre for the Development of Vocational Training). Set up by **Regulation** 337/75 (**OJ** L39/75).
PO Box 22427, GR-55102 Thessaloniki, Greece.
www.cedefop.gr

CEDI
European Self-employed Confederation.
Oberbexbacherstrasse 7, D-66450 Bexbach, Germany

CEDISYS
Models, languages and logics for concurrent distributed systems (**ESPRIT** project)

CEE
Central and Eastern Europe

CEE
See **UK CEE**

CEEB
Central and Eastern Eurobarometer. Replaced by **CCEB**

CEEC
European Committee for Catholic Education.
19A ave Marnix, Boîte 6, B-1000 Brussels, Belgium

CEEC
Central and Eastern European Countries. Often seen as CEECs

CEEP
Centre Européen de l'Entreprise Publique (European Centre of Public Enterprises). Renamed Centre Européen des Entreprises à Participation Publique et des Entreprises d'Intérêt Economique Général (European Centre of Enterprises with Public Participation and of Enterprises of General Economic Interest).

15 rue de la Charité, Boîte 12, B-1210 Brussels, Belgium.
www.ceep.org

CEEPUS
Central European Exchange Programme for University Studies.
www.adis.at/ceepus

CEES
Central and Eastern European States

CEESA
Central and Eastern European Sustainable Agriculture (**Fifth Framework Programme** project)

CEFES
Creating a European forum in European studies. A virtual seminar in European studies (**SOCRATES** programme)

CEFIC
European Chemical Industry Council.
4 ave E van Nieuwenhuyse, B-1160 Brussels, Belgium.
www.cefic.be

CEFIR
European high temperature fibres (**EUREKA** project)

CEFS
Comité Européen des Fabricants de Sucre (European Committee of Sugar Manufacturers).
182 av de Tervuren, B-1150 Brussels, Belgium.
www.ib.be/cefs

CEFTA
Central European Free Trade Association. Established in 1992 to set up a free trade area and now consists of Poland, Hungary, Czech Republic, Romania, Bulgaria, Slovakia and Slovenia.
www.cefta.org

CEG
Consumers in Europe Group. Merged with the National Consumer Council on 1 April 2001.
20 Grosvenor Gardens, London SW1W 0DH, UK.
www.ncc.org.uk

CEHAPE
Children's Environment and Health Action Plan for Europe

CEI
Central European Initiative. A regional cooperation instrument agreed in 1992 covering the political, cultural and economic fields in **CEEC**, Austria, Italy and Bavaria (as an observer) (**COM**(96)601). *See also* **CEInet**.
www.ceinet.org

CEI-Bois
Confédération Européenne des Industries du Bois (European Confederation of Woodworking Industries).
5 Allée Hof-ter-Vleest, box 4, B-1070 Brussels, Belgium.
www.cei-bois.org

CEIES
European Advisory Committee on Statistical Information in the Economic and Social Spheres (**OJ** L59/91). Secretariat: Unit R-2, BECH A4/124, Statistical Office of the European Communities, L 2920 Luxembourg. Details via Eurostat website under 'Eurostat activities':
http://europa.eu.int/comm/eurostat

CEInet
Internet information pages on **CEI** activities, contacts and projects.
www.ceinet.org

CEJA
European Council of Young Farmers.
23-25 rue de la Science, Boîte 3, B-1040 Brussels, Belgium

CEL
Conseil Européen pour les Langues (European Language Council - ELC).
Freie Universität Berlin ZE, Sprachlabor, 45 Habelschwerdter Allee, D-14195 Berlin, Germany

CELAD
European Committee to Combat Drugs (Council Working Group)

CELEBRATE
Context eLearning with Broadband Technologies. A Cross Programme Action under the **Information Society Technologies Programme**, June 2002-December 2004.
www.eun.org/celebrate/about.html

CELEX
Communitatis Europae LEX. A multilingual database of EU law covering legislation, proposals, opinions, case law and parliamentary questions. Published by **EUR-OP**; available via EUR-OP agents and other information providers.
http://europa.eu.int/celex (password required)

CEMR
Council of European Municipalities and Regions.
Secretariat: 15 rue de Richelieu, F - 75001, Paris, France.
UK contact: 35 Great Smith St, London SW1P 3BJ (where it is known as the Local Government International Bureau - **LGIB**).
www.ccre.org

CEMR-EP
Council of European Municipalities and Regions Employers' Platform

CEN
Comité Européen de Normalisation (European Committee for Standardisation). *See also* **CENELEC**, **CEN-STAR**.
36 rue de Stassart, B-1050 Brussels, Belgium.
www.cenorm.be

CENELEC
Comité Européen de Normalisation Electrotechnique (European Committee for Electrotechnical Standardisation).
36 rue de Stassart, B-1050 Brussels, Belgium.
www.cenelec.org

CEN-STAR
An Action Group on Standards and Research within **CEN**, intended to "increase the co-operation between the researchers and the standardizers, for their mutual benefit"

CENSUS
1990/1991 population census statistical domain on the **New Cronos** databank

CENTAUR
Clean and efficient new transport approach for urban rationalisation (Integrated Quality Targeted Project within the **THERMIE** programme).
http://europa.eu.int/comm/energy/en/thermie/centaur.htm

CENYC
Council of European National Youth Committees.
517-519 de Wavre, B-1040 Brussels, Belgium

CEO
Centre for Earth Observation. Part of the **IPSC** at the **JRC**

CEOS
Conditions of employment of other servants of the EU

CEPF
Central environmental protection fund. Launched within **Phare's** 1997 programme in Hungary to finance a wide range of environmental capital investments

CEPF
Confederation of European Forest Owners.
47-51 rue du Luxembourg, B-1050 Brussels, Belgium.
www.cepf-eu.org

CEPFAR
Centre Européen pour la Promotion et la Formation en milieu agricole (European Training and Development Centre for Farming and Rural Life).
23-25 rue de la Science, Boîte 10, B-1040 Brussels, Belgium

CEPLACA
Assessment of environmental contamination risk by platinum, rhodium and palladium from automobile catalysts (an Environmental Health and Chemical Safety Research project within the **Environment and Climate Programme**)

CEPOL
Collège européen de Police (European Police College). Established in December 2000 by **Decision** 2000/820/JHA (**OJ** L336/00). Secretariat temporarily located in Denmark

CEPS
Centre for European Policy Studies.
1 place du Congrès, B-1000 Brussels, Belgium.
www.ceps.be

CEPT
Conférence européenne des administrations des Postes et Télécommunications (European Conference of Postal and Telecommunications Administrations).
ANACOM, National Communications Authority, 12 av José Malhoa, 1099-017 Lisbon, Portugal.
www.cept.org

CER
Centre for European Reform. Think-tank devoted to improving the quality of the debate on the future of the **European Union**.
29 Tufton Street London SW1P 3QL, UK.
www.cer.org.uk

CER
Community of European Railways.
15 blvd de l'Impératrice, Boîte 11, B-1000 Brussels, Belgium

CERACS
Comparative evaluation of the different radiating cables and systems technologies (**DRIVE** project)

CERAME-UNIE
Liaison Office of the European Ceramic Industries.
18-24 rue des Colonies, Boîte 17, B-1000 Brussels, Belgium

CERD
European **R&D** Committee

CEREC
European Committee for Business, Arts and Culture.
14 Handelskaai, B-1000 Brussels, Belgium

CERES
Cascade environment for the realisation of electronic systems. A project in the microelectronics technology programme (1982-1986)

CERIF
Recommendation 91/337/EEC for a Common European Research Information Format to provide a standard format for European research databases (**OJ** L189/91)

CERISE
European centre for image synthesis: to improve and market computer imaging technology (**EUREKA** project)

CERNA
Centre d'Economie Industrielle.
60 blvd Saint-Michel, F-75272 Paris Cedex

06, France.
www.cerna.ensmp.fr

CERT
Canada-Europe Round Table for Business (FORCCE: Forum sur le commerce Canada-Europe).
www.canada-europe.org

CERTIFIED
Conception and evaluation of roadside testing instruments to formalise impairment evidence in drivers (**Transport** project)

CES
Comité économique et social européen (Economic and Social Committee - **Economic and Social Committee**)

CESAR
Collaboration environments and service architectures for researchers (a **CSCW** Telematics for Research project, partially funded under the **Telematics Applications Programme**).
http://orgwis.gmd.de/projects/CESAR/

CESAR
European Centre for the Support of Rural Activities. A pilot project funded by the **European Commission**

CES Doc
Opinions and reports of the **Economic and Social Committee**

CESE
Comité économique et social européen (European Economic and Social Committee - *see* **Economic and Social Committee**)

CET
Central European Time (Greenwich Meantime + 1 hour)

CET
Common External Tariff. *See also* **CCT** and **CN**

CETIL
Committee of Experts for the Transfer of Information between European Languages

CETIS
European Scientific Data Processing Centre

CEUMC
Chairman of the **EUMC**

CFCU
Central Financing and Coordination Unit (within the **Phare** programme)

CFI
Court of First Instance. Established in 1989, primarily to relieve some of the pressure on the **European Court of Justice**.
Palais de la Cour de justice, Boulevard Konrad Adenauer, Kirchberg, L-2925 Luxembourg.
www.curia.eu.int

CFP
Common Fisheries Policy

CFSP
Common Foreign and Security Policy (Politique étrangère et sécurité européenne - PESC)

CG
Left Unity Group (of the **European Parliament**)

CGC
Decision 84/338/EURATOM, ECSC, EEC for a Management and Coordination Consultative Committee for a Research Action programme (**OJ** L177/84)

CGD
Waste Management Committee

CGF
Credit guarantee fund

CHABADA
Changes in bacterial diversity and activity in Mediterranean coastal waters as affected by eutrophication (**ELOISE** project)

CHAIN
Cultural Heritage Activities and Institutes Network. Development funded by the **Comenius** programme.
www.chain.to

CHAINE
Comprehensive hospital and ambulatory care information networking for episode linkage (a Telematics for Healthcare project within the **Telematics Applications Programme**)

CHAMELEON
Dynamic software migration between cooperating environments (**ESPRIT** project)

Charlemagne Prize
Established in 1949 to recognize "the most meritorious contribution serving European unification and the **European Community**, serving humanity and world peace." Awarded by the city of Aachen, Charlemagne's ancient capital. The Prize was presented for the first time in 1950.
www.aachen.de/EN/city_citizens/charlemagne_prize/index.html

CHARM
Coastal habitats and resources management

CHARME
Correct hardware design towards formal design and verification for provably correct **VLSI** hardware (**ESPRIT** project)

Charter of Fundamental Rights
The objective of the Charter of Fundamental Rights of the **European Union** "is to make more visible and explicit to the Union's citizens the fundamental rights that they already enjoy at European level." The 54-article Charter, which was proclaimed in December 2000 at the Nice **European Council**, covers: dignity, freedoms, equality, solidarity, citizens' rights, justice.
http://europa.eu.int/comm/justice_home/unit/charte/index_en.html

Charter for Peace and Stability
In 1999, EU-Mediterranean Foreign Ministers, meeting in Stuttgart, agreed guidelines for a Euro-Mediterranean Charter for Peace and Stability. The Charter, intended to promote security in the Mediterranean region, has not been signed because of continuing conflict in the Middle East

CHC
Conseiller hors classe

CHEDYN
Advanced dynamic simulator for chemical plants (**EUREKA** project)

CHEF
A kitchen management system for people with mental handicap (**TIDE** project)

Chef de Cabinet
Head of a **Cabinet**

CHEMICON
Chemistry and microphysics of contrail formation (**THESEO** project)

CHEOPS
High order logic supported design for complex data processing (**ESPRIT** project)

CHESS
Climate, hydrochemistry and economics of surface water systems

Cheysson Facility
Funding made available under **ECIP**. Named after Claude Cheysson, Commissioner in Charge of North-South Relations

CHIC
Community health information classification and coding (**AIM** project)

Chicago Convention
Alternative name for the Convention on International Civil Aviation, signed by 52 States on 7 December 1944. The Convention, which established **ICAO**, organises international aviation on the basis of bilateral agreements between signatory countries

CHIEF
Customs handling of import and export freight

CHILIAS
Children in libraries: improving multimedia virtual library access and information skills (project within the **Telematics for Libraries** programme)

ChimEre
Statistical database for chemical products. *See also* **ChimStat**, **RISC**.
http://europa.eu.int/comm/dg03/directs/dg3c/risc/db/plsql/chimere.Main

ChimStat
Statistical database for chemical products. *See also* **ChimEre**, **RISC**.
http://europa.eu.int/comm/dg03/directs/dg3c/risc/db/plsql/chimstat.Main

CHIN
Co-operative health information networks for the community (a Telematics for Healthcare project within the **Telematics Applications Programme**)

CHIP
Chemicals (Hazard Information and Packaging). UK Regulations under Statutory Instrument 1993 No 1746. Amended by CHIP 2: S.I. 1994 No 3247, and again subsequently.
www.hse.gov.uk/lau/lacs/37-7.htm

CHODs
Chiefs of Defence

CHRISTINE
Characteristics and requirements of information systems based on traffic data in an integrated network environment (**DRIVE** project)

CI
Community Initiatives. Previously **NPCI**

CIAA
Confédération des Industries Agro-Alimentaires de l'UE (Confederation of the Food and Drink Industries of the EU).
43 av des Arts, B-1040 Brussels, Belgium.
www.ciaa.be

CICERO
Cultural Information Computer Exchange (a Telematics for Urban and Rural Areas project within the **Telematics Applications Programme**)

CID
Centre for Information and Documentation (**EURATOM**)

CIDAM
CIM system based on a distributed database with individually configurable modules (**ESPRIT** project)

CIDE
Centro nazionale di informazione e documentazione europea (National Centre for European Information and Documentation), Rome. A partnership between the **European Commission** and the Italian Government. *See also* **Jacques Delors European Information Centre**.
www.cide.it

CIDIE
Committee of International Development Institutions on the Environment

CIDREE
Consortium of Institutions for Development and Research in Education in Europe.
Secretariat: Netherlands Institute for Curriculum Development (SLO), PO Box 2041, 7500 CA Enschede, The Netherlands.
www.cidree.org

CIDST
Comité de l'information et de la documentation scientifiques et techniques (Committee for Scientific and Technical Information and Documentation - **CSTID**)

CIF
Cost, insurance, freight

CIM
Computer integrated manufacturing (**ESPRIT** project)

CIMALIVE
Implementation addressing levels of integration in various environments (**ESPRIT** project)

CIMCEE
Comité des industries de la moutarde de la CEE (Committee of the Mustard Industries of the EEC).
30 av de Roodebeek, B-1030 Brussels, Belgium

CIM-PLATO
CIM system planning toolbox (**ESPRIT** project)

CIMSCEE
Committee of the Mayonnaise and Condiment Sauce Industries of the EEC.
30 av de Roodebeek, B-1030 Brussels, Belgium

CIMSTEEL
Computer aided manufacturing for constructional steelwork (**EUREKA** project)

CIN
Changeover Information Network. Initiative to provide up-to-date information on the changeover to the euro in early 2002, when the Single Currency became a reality for many EU citizens.
http://europa.eu.int/comm/economy_finance/publications/euro_related/eurorelated_progress_en.htm

Cinedays
Initiative to celebrate the vitality of European films and raise the profile of Europe's film heritage. Includes TV as well as cinema. Seen also as Cined@ys.
http://europa.eu.int/comm/avpolicy/media/cineday_en.html

CIRCA
Collaborative software used by **Eurostat** and a number of **DG**s. *See also* **CIRCLE**

CIRCA
Communication and Information Resource Centre Administrator.
http://eea.eionet.eu.int:8980/Public/irc/eionet-circle/Home/main

CIRCCE
Confédération Internationale de la Représentation Commerciale des Cadres Européens (European Confederation of Managers in the Commercial Sector).
2 rue d'Hauteville, F-75010 Paris, France

CIRCE
Application and enhancement of an experimental center for system integration in **CIM** (**ESPRIT** project)

CIRCE
European Communities Information and Documentary Research Centre. Replaced by **SII**

CIRCLE
Centre of information resources for

collaboration on environment. A customised version of the **CIRCA** software used on **EIONET**.
http://eea.eionet.eu.int:8980/Public/irc/eionet-circle/Home/main

CIRD
Interservice Committee for **R&D**

CIREA
Centre d'information, de réflexion et d'échange en matière d'asile (Centre for Information, Discussion and Exchange on Asylum). A **Council of the European Union** Working Party, established in 1992

CIREFI
Centre d'information, de réflexion et d'échanges en matière de franchissement des frontières et d'immigration (Centre for Information, Discussion and Exchange on the Crossing of Borders and Immigration). A **Council of the European Union** Working Party

CIS
Commonwealth of Independent States

CIS
Community Innovation Survey. Carried out by **Member States** and coordinated by **Eurostat** on behalf of the **INNOVATION** programme

CIS
Customs information system

CIT
Advisory Committee for Innovation and Technology Transfer

CITE
Centre for Information Technologies and Electronics at the **JRC**. Merged in 1990 to form **ISEI**

CITES
Convention on International Trade in Endangered Species of Wild Fauna and Flora. **Regulation** 338/97 commits **Member States** to the application of the rules prescribed by the Convention (**OJ** L61/97). *See also* **Gaborone Amendment**.
http://europa.eu.int/comm/environment/cites/home_en.htm

CITIES
Cities telecommunications and integrated services (a Telematics for Administrations project within the **Telematics Applications Programme**)

Cities for All
Alternative name for European Urban Observatory - **EUO**

Citizens' Europe
See **People's Europe**

Citizens First
A campaign launched in November 1996 (within the **PRINCE** programme) to enable citizens to obtain information on their EU rights and how to benefit from them.
http://citizens.eu.int/en/en/newsitem-1.htm

Citizens' Network
Proposed in a Communication on public passenger transport in Europe (**COM**(98)431)

Citizens Signpost Service
Free service intended to promote people's rights in the Single Market (**SEM**). Multilingual legal experts offer practical advice and/or signposting to relevant local, national or EU bodies.
http://europa.eu.int/citizensrights/signpost/front_end/signpost_text_en.htm

CITRA
System for the control of dangerous goods

transport in international Alpine corridors (**DRIVE** project)

CIVI
European Parliament Committee on Civil Liberties and Internal Affairs

CIVITAS
City-Vitality-Sustainability. **European Commission** initiative to support urban transport and encourage the use of alternatives to cars in cities.
http://europa.eu.int/comm/energy_transport/en/cut_en/cut_civitas_en.html

CJCE
Cour de justice des Communautés européennes (Court of Justice of the European Communities). Formal name for the **European Court of Justice**

CJE
Court de Justice Europeénne (**European Court of Justice** - ECJ)

CJEC
Court of Justice of the European Communities. More often seen as ECJ - **European Court of Justice**

CJTF
Combined Joint Task Forces. Established by the **NATO** Berlin Summit in June 1996, the CJTF was intended to enable European allies to use NATO resources for operations in which the US did not want to participate

CL4K
Cyberspace learning for kids (a Telematics for Education and Training project within the **Telematics Applications Programme**)

CLAB Europa
European database on case law about unfair contract terms.
http://europa.eu.int/clab/index.htm

CLAIR
Clean air: fluor hydrocarbon replacement in cleaning process during mechadeck production for video recorders (**EUREKA** project)

CLAMOUR
Classifications modelling and utilities research.
www.statistics.gov.uk/methods_quality/clamour/default.asp

CLASET
Electronic format for exchange of classifications. A **Eurostat** initiative to create "an **EDI** message designed to exchange tree structures such as classifications, organisation charts, concept definitions, catalogues, code lists, etc." in a standard format

CLAUDE
Coordinating land use and cover data and analyses in Europe (**Environment and Climate** project)

CLC
CORINE land cover database for the analysis of land use in Europe.
http://dataservice.eea.eu.int/dataservice/metadetails.asp?table=landcover&i=1

CLECAT
Comité Liaison Européen des Commissionnaires et Auxiliares de Transport (European Liaison Committee of Common Market Forwarders). Appears to have become the European Organisation for Forwarding and Logistics:
31 Rue Montoyer, bte 10, B-1000 Brussels, Belgium.
www.clecat.org

CLEF
Cross-language evaluation forum

CLICOFI
Effects of climate induced temperature

change on marine coastal fishes (**ELOISE** project)

CLICS
Categorical logic in computer science (**ESPRIT** project)

CLIMFRESH
Impact of climate change on carbon flux in freshwater ecosystems (a Water, Wetland and Acquatic Ecosystem Research project within the **Environment and Climate Programme**)

CLIMOOR
Climate driven changes in the functioning of heath and moorland ecosystems (**TERI** project)

CLITRAVI
Liaison Centre for the Meat Processing Industry in the EU.
Boulevard Baudouin 18, B-1000 Brussels, Belgium

Club (the)
Institutions of the EC specialising in long-term credit

CLUE
Changing land usage: enhancement of biodiversity and ecosystem development (**TERI** project)

CLUSTER
Cooperative Link between Universities in Science and Technology for Education and Research.
Stichting Cluster, 2 Den Dolech, NL-5612 AZ Eindhoven, Netherlands

CM
Co-ordinators Meeting.
http://europa.eu.int/comm/external_relations/asem/cluster/process.htm

CMAFs
Cooperatives, mutuals, associations, foundations

CME
Compact measure. **Tempus** and **Phare** projects with a one or two year duration

CME
Complementary measures. Technical assistance under **Tempus**

CMEA
Council for Mutual Economic Assistance - popularly known as **COMECON**

CMO
Common Market Organisation. In relation to the **CAP**. Alternative form of 'Common organisation of the market'.
http://europa.eu.int/scadplus/leg/en/s04004.htm

CMR
Substances which are carcinogenic, mutagenic or toxic to reproduction

CMSO
CIM for multi-supplier operations (**ESPRIT** project)

CN
Combined Nomenclature: an 8-digit goods nomenclature which is based on the **HS** and which replaced the **CCT** and **NIMEXE** nomenclatures. Latest update: **Regulation** 1832/2002 amending Annex I to Regulation 2658/87 on the tariff and statistical nomenclature and on the Common Customs Tariff (**OJ** L290/02). Also available on CD through **Eurostat**

CND
United Nations Commission on Narcotic Drugs

CNMA
Communication network for manufacturing applications (**ESPRIT** project)

CNMB
See **CBNM**

CNROP
Centres Nationaux de Ressources pour l'Orientation Professionnelle. *See* **Euroguidance**

CNS
Consultation Procedure

COAST
Coordinated action for seaside towns (a network of coastal tourist areas under **RECITE**)

COAST
See **COASTER**

COASTER
Courseware authoring for scientific training: extended renewal of the original COAST project (a Telematics for Education and Training project within the **Telematics Applications Programme**)

COAT
Coatings for advanced technology development of coatings and fabrication processes for smart windows (**EUREKA** project)

COBIP
Teleworking coordination services for co-operative business processes (a Telematics for Urban and Rural Areas project within the **Telematics Applications Programme**)

Co BRA+
Computerised bibliographic records actions (**Telematics Applications Programme**)

COBROW
Collaborative browsing in information resources (a Telematics for Research project within the **Telematics Applications Programme**)

COBUCO
Cordless business communication system (**ACTS** project)

COCERAL
Comité du Commerce des céréales, aliments du bétail, oléagineux, huile d'olive, huiles et graisses et agrofournitures (Committee of Cereals, Oilseeds, Animal Feed, Olive Oils, Oils and Fats and Agrosupply Trade in the EU).
18 square de Meeûs, Boîte 1, B-1050 Brussels, Belgium.
www.coceral.com

Cockfield White Paper
on plans to complete the Single European Market - **SEM** (**COM**(85) 310 and Commission Document Series *Completing the internal market*. Published by **OOPEC**, 1985

Co-Co
Coordination Committee for European Integration

COCO
Coordination and continuity in primary care: the regional healthcare information network (a Telematics for Healthcare project within the **Telematics Applications Programme**)

CoCoLAF
Comité de coordinación de la lucha contra el fraude (Advisory Committee for the Coordination of Fraud Prevention).
http://europa.eu.int/scadplus/leg/en/lvb/l33161.htm

COCOR
Iron and Steel Nomenclature Coordinating Committee, set up under the **ECSC**. COCOR standardisation activities taken over by **ECISS**

COCOS
Components for future computing systems (**ESPRIT** project)

COD
Co-decision Procedure

CODE
European Parliament Temporary Committee on Conciliation

CODED
Concepts and definitions database (**Eurostat**)

Codecision procedure
Introduced in the **Treaty on European Union**. Where agreement cannot be reached between the **Council of the European Union** and the **European Parliament**, the EP may finally veto the adoption of the measure by an absolute majority of its total membership. The **Treaty of Amsterdam** made this the normal method of legislation involving the EP and the Council (Article 251). *See also* **Conciliation Committee**, **Cooperation Procedure**

CODEPASS
Community complexity and the decomposition process in aquatic systems: an ecosystem approach to manage biodiversity (**TERI** project)

CODEST
Committee for the European Development of Science and Technology. Set up in 1982 by **Decision** 82/835/EEC (**OJ** L350/82)

CODING
Colour desktop publishing (**ESPRIT** project)

CODP
2-D coherent optical dynamic processor (**ESPRIT** project)

CODRO
Council Working Group on Drugs. Part of the **CFSP**

CoE
Council of Europe

CoESS
Confederation of European Security Services.
25 Koningin Fabiolalaan, 1780 Wemmel, Belgium.
www.coess.org

COFACE
Confederation of Family Organisations in the EC.
17 rue de Londres, B-1050 Brussels, Belgium

COFIDEC
Compact CCITT G722 codec for digital telephone set development of a codec compliant … (**EUREKA** project)

COGECA
See **COPA-COGECA**

COGEN III
An EC-ASEAN initiative to support the growth and application of cogeneration in the **ASEAN** countries

COGEN Europe
European Association for the Promotion of Cogeneration.
98 rue Gulledelle, B-1200 Brussels, Belgium.
www.cogen.org

Cohesion
Idea introduced in the **SEA** (additional Title V Articles 130A-130E) to provide economic

and social cohesion and to reduce disparities between the various regions and the backwardness of the Less-Favoured Regions (**LFR**). *See also* **Cohesion Fund**; **Cohesion Report**

Cohesion Fund
Regulation 1164/94 (**OJ** L130/94) set up under the **Treaty on European Union** to establish a financial instrument in the fields of the environment and trans-European transport infrastructure networks in **Member States** with a per capita **GNP** of less than 90% of the EU average. Currently applicable in Greece, Ireland, Portugal, Spain. *See also* **Cohesion**.
http://europa.eu.int/comm/regional_policy/funds/procf/cf_en.htm

Cohesion Report
A triennial report which analyses the contribution of national and EU policies in the reduction of social and economic development gaps (**COM**(96) 542). Previously **Periodic Report**. *See also* **Cohesion**; **Synthetic Index**.
http://europa.eu.int/comm/regional_policy/sources/docoffic/official/repor_en.htm

COHOM
Council Working Group on Human Rights

COINS
Collaborative information acquisition (**CSCW** project partially funded under the **Telematics Applications Programme**).
http://orgwis.gmd.de/projects/Coins/

COINS
Communication and information services statistical domain on the **New Cronos** databank

COINS
Corporate organisations interactive network systems (a Telematics for Education and Training project within the **Telematics Applications Programme**)

COJUR
Council Working Party on Public International Law

COLIPA
Comité de Liaison des Associations Européennes de l'Industrie de la Parfumerie, des Produits Cosmétiques et de Toilette (European Cosmetic, Toiletry and Perfumery Association).
5-7 rue du Congrès, B-1000 Brussels, Belgium.
www.colipa.com

College of Commissioners
The group of **European Commissioner**s

COM
'Commission': as in 'COM doc' ('Commission document') - a working document of the **European Commission**, generally falling into one of three types: proposal for legislation, broad policy document (including 'Green papers' and 'White papers'), report on the implementation of policy. Until early 1998, the number was in the form '(97)123'; since then COMs are numbered as e.g. '(2000)123'. Also seen as 'COM Document', 'COMdoc'. Some can be found under 'Documents of public interest' on **EUR-Lex**:
http://europa.eu.int/eur-lex/en/search/search_dpi.html

COM
Common Organisation of the Market

COMAC
Concerted Action Committee

COMAGRI
European Parliament Committee on Agriculture and Rural Development

COMAH Directive
Directive 96/82/EC on the Control of Major Accident Hazards involving dangerous

substances (**OJ** L10/97). Known as the 'Seveso II' Directive. The original 'Seveso' Directive (82/501/EEC, OJ L230/82) was a response to an accidental release of dioxin from a chemical plant in the Italian town of Seveso, in 1976. Accidents at the Union Carbide factory in Bhopal, India (1984) and the Sandoz warehouse in Basel, Switzerland (1986) led to the scope of the Seveso Directive being broadened by Seveso II

COMANDOS
Construction and management of distributed office systems (**ESPRIT** project)

COMASSO
Association of Plant Breeders of the **European Community**. Now part of **ESA**

COMBAT
Cooperative marketing to overcome the barriers facing disabled teleworkers (**TIDE** project)

COM doc
See **COM**

COMECE
Commission of the Bishops' Conferences of the European Union.
42 rue Stévin, B-1000 Brussels, Belgium

COMECON
Council for Mutual Economic Assistance (CMEA). Established in 1949 to coordinate economic policy between communist states. Original members were: Albania, Bulgaria, Czechoslovakia, Hungary, Poland, Romania, USSR. Other countries joined later: Cuba, East Germany, Mongolia, Vietnam. Abolished in January 1991

COMEDI
Commercial electronic data interchange for the collection, validation, grouping and dissemination of trade statistics (1993-1997) (**OJ** C87/93)

Comenius
Programme for European cooperation on school education. Focuses on pre-school to secondary school education. Part of the **Socrates** programme. Named after the Czech, Johann Amos Comenius "one of the founding fathers of modern education".
http://europa.eu.int/comm/education/programmes/socrates/comenius/index_en.html

COMET
Computerised molecular evaluation of toxicity (an Environmental Health and Chemical Safety Research project within the **Environment and Climate Programme**)

COMETT II
Community programme in education and training for technology (1990-1994) (OJ L13/89). Incorporated into **Leonardo da Vinci**

COMEXT
Eurostat database of trade statistics. Initially external trade, then intra- and extra- EU trade. Retitled *EC Intra & extra EU trade*

COMIC
To investigate the integration of organisational context and notifications of interaction into **CSCW** systems (**ESPRIT** project).
http://orgwis.gmd.de/projects/COMIC/

COMIS
Communication system for cooperative driving (**DRIVE** project)

COMIS
Standard for coding of moving images on digital storage media (**ESPRIT** project)

Comitology
A procedure which allows the **European Commission** to discuss proposed implementing measures with committees of national representatives, under **Decision** 1999/468/EC (**OJ** L184/99).

http://wwwdb.europarl.eu.int/dors/oeil/en/inter51.htm

ComLégi

RISC legislative database covering the chemical industry.
http://europa.eu.int/comm/dg03/directs/dg3c/risc/db/plsql/comlegi.Main

COMMAL

Aluminium matrix composites (**EUREKA** project)

Committee of Independent Experts

Set up by the **European Parliament** to investigate allegations against the Commission. The Committee produced two reports: 'First report on allegations regarding fraud, mismanagement and nepotism in the **European Commission**' and 'Analysis of current practice and proposals for tackling mismanagement, irregularities and fraud'. The first report led to the resignation, on 15 March 1999, of the Commission headed by Jacques **Santer**.
www.europarl.eu.int/experts/press/default_en.htm

Common factor

Alternative term for the business climate indicator (**BCI**)

Common Foreign and Security Policy

Article 11 of the **Treaty on European Union** defines the objectives of the CFSP as being:

- to safeguard the common values, fundamental interests, independence and integrity of the Union in conformity with the principles of the United Nations Charter
- to strengthen the security of the Union in all ways
- to preserve peace and strengthen international security, in accordance with the principles of the United Nations Charter, as well as the principles of the Helsinki Final Act and the objectives of the Paris Charter, including those on external borders
- to promote international cooperation
- to develop and consolidate democracy and the rule of law, and respect for human rights and fundamental freedoms

The CFSP is the second of the **European Union**'s three **Pillars**, and is based on intergovernmental cooperation rather than the **Community method**. It does not include relations of a strictly economic or commercial nature, covered by the Common Commercial Policy

Common Market

Term used (often disparagingly) to refer to the European Economic Community - **EEC**

Common position

The first stage of the **Council of the European Union** adoption of Single Market (**SEM**) legislation prior to the **European Parliament**'s second reading

Communication technologies

See **ACTS** (Advanced communications technologies and services)

Communitisation

The transfer of a matter dealt with under the Intergovernmental Second and Third **Pillars** to the **Community method** of the First Pillar

Community Initiatives

Programmes under the **Structural Funds** to give financial support for EU-wide initiatives. For 2000-2006 they are: **EQUAL**; **INTERREG**; **LEADER+**; **URBAN**.
http://europa.eu.int/comm/regional_policy/funds/prord/prordc/prdc_en.htm

Community method

A decision-making procedure based on the interaction between the **European Commission**, the **European Parliament**, and the **Council of the European Union**. Currently applies only to 'First Pillar' issues (e.g. economy, social affairs, environment, trade) and distinct from the Intergovernmental approach of the Second and Third **Pillars**

Community Patent Court
To be established by 2010, the CPC will be a judicial panel, attached to the **CFI**, set up to hear cases concerning Community Patents

COMMUTE
Common methodology for multimodal transport environmental impact assessment (A Strategic Transport project within the **Transport** programme)

COMNET
Community Network for European Education and Training.
UETP-Toscana, 82 via Cavur, I-50129 Firenze, Italy

COMP
Competition **DG** of the **European Commission**

COMPASS-A
Comprehensive algebraic approach to system specification and development (**ESPRIT** project)

COMPESTELA FORET
Improved emergency services in forested regions (**RECITE** project)

COMPET
Indicators of competitiveness statistical domain on the **New Cronos** database

Competence
What the **European Union** is allowed to do under the Treaties

Competitive and Sustainable Growth
One of four **Thematic Programmes** within the **Fifth Framework Programme** (1998-2002). Also seen simply as 'Growth'.
www.cordis.lu/growth

COMPEX
System of Compensation to offset drops in export earnings for agricultural produce offered by the EU to Least Developed Countries (**LDCs**)

COMPRESIT
Compact reinforced composite development of ultra-high strength compact reinforced composite for civil and structural engineering applications (**EUREKA** project)

COMPRO
Committee for the Simplification of International Trade Procedures in the EC

COM PROGRAMME
New strategic industrial system of communication (**FAST** programme)

COMPULOG
Computational logic (**ESPRIT** project)

Computer Theft Initiative
Fictitious EU initiative invented by a computer security company in the UK. Said to be part of the equally fictitious ECCRI: **European Community** Crime Reduction Initiative

COMQUEST
Oil pipelines statistical domain on the **New Cronos** databank

COMSINE
Communication infrastructure for inland navigation in Europe (**INCO** project)

COMWEB
Comparative analysis of food webs based on flow networks (**MAST III/ELOISE** project)

CONACCOUNT
Coordination of regional and national material flow accounting for environmental sustainability (**Environment and Climate** project)

Concerted Action
Intended to encourage national actors to exchange good practice at European level. Details of CAs concerning business can be seen at:
http://forum.europa.eu.int/irc/sme/euroinformation/info/data/sme/en/cao/

Conciliation Committee
Made up of members of the **Council of the European Union** and the **European Parliament** in equal numbers to attempt to reach agreement on a joint text during the **Co-decision Procedure**.
http://www.europarl.eu.int/code/default_en.htm

CONCIM
Construction computer-integrated manufacturing (**EUREKA** project)

CONCISE
COSINE Network's Central Information Service for Europe

CONCORD I
Concertation coordination (a programme of support actions within the **Telematics Applications Programme**)

CONCORDE EDUCATION
Centre for Organisations and Networks Cooperating in R&D in Education.
60 rue de la Concorde, B-1050 Brussels, Belgium.
http://club.euronet.be/peter.beernaert/main.htm

CONCORDIA
Consensus and Coordination in TA results (a Telematics Engineering project within the **Telematics Applications Programme**)

Concordia
See **Operation Concordia**

CONCUR
Theories of concurrency: unification and extension (**ESPRIT** project)

CONECCS
Consultation, the **European Commission** and Civil Society. A database which provides information about the Commission's formal or structured civil society consultation bodies and offers a directory of pan-European civil society organisations representing a wide range of interests in Europe.
http://europa.eu.int/comm/civil_society/coneccs/index_en.htm

Confidence Pact
See **European Confidence Pact**

Conformity mark
See **CE (mark)**

CONGAS
Biospheric controls on trace gas fluxes in northern wetlands (**TERI** project)

Congress of Europe
A meeting in The Hague, May 1948, attended by more than 1,000 delegates from 20 countries and chaired by Winston Churchill. The aim of the Congress "was to demonstrate the breadth of the movements in favour of European unification, and to determine the objectives which must be met in order to achieve such a union." It paved the way for the creation of the **Council of Europe** in 1949.
www.coe.int

CONNECT
Launched in 1999 "to support European

innovative projects which reinforce synergies and links in the areas of education, training and culture, associated with new technologies." http://europa.eu.int/comm/education/archive/connect/selection_en.html

CONOPS
Concept of operations

CONPRI II
A training project in industrial relations and social dialogue in Europe (Employment and Social Affairs **DG** of the **European Commission**)

CONQUEST
Clinical oncology network for quality in European standards of treatment (a Telematics for Healthcare project within the **Telematics Applications Programme**)

CONSENSUS
A **Phare** programme to support the sustainability of social protection reform in Central and Eastern Europe. Initially 1996/97, but extended to 1998/99 (Consensus II) and then until 30 November 2002 (Consensus III)

Consleg
Consolidated legislation.
http://europa.eu.int/eur-lex/en/consleg/index1.html

CONST
Commission for Constitutional Affairs and European Governance (of the **CoR**)

Construction Products Directive
Directive 89/106/EEC on construction products (**OJ** L40/89)

Consultation procedure
The original method of legislation laid down in the **Treaty of Rome**, requiring only consultation of the **European Parliament** and/or the **Economic and Social Committee**. The most important areas in which it is now used are in relation to **CFSP** and **EMU**

Consumer Committee
See **CCC**

Consumer Credit Directive
Directive 87/102/EEC for the approximation of the laws, regulations and administrative provisions of the **Member States** concerning consumer credit (**OJ** L42/87)

Consumerland
A 'Virtual World' produced by the Health and Consumer Affairs **DG** of the **European Commission** to explain the European aspect of consumer protection.
http://europa.eu.int/ISPO/consumerland

CONT
European Parliament Committee on Budgetary Control

Contractual Netting Directive
Directive 96/10/EC regarding the recognition of contractual netting by the competent authorities (**OJ** L85/96)

CONTROL-C
Concept for transportation and loading of containers. Project coordinated by **NETS**

CONV
Delegation of the **European Parliament** to the **Convention on the Future of Europe** (classed as a 'Temporary committee')

CONVENFL
Development of a new concept of uninterrupted power supply (**EUREKA** project)

Convention on the Future of Europe
Announced at the December 2001 **Laeken Summit**, the 105-member Convention,

Chaired by former French President Valéry Giscard d'Estaing, was officially launched at the end of February 2002. It was responsible for preparing a draft **European Union** Constitution, presented to the Thessaloniki **European Council** on 20 June, which formed the basis for discussions at the **Intergovernmental Conference** which started in October 2003 and which is intended to revise the **European Union**'s structure and decision-making procedures to better equip it for enlargement. Also known as the 'European Convention'.
http://european-convention.eu.int

CONVER
See **KONVER**

Convergence Criteria
for **EMU** as laid down in the **Treaty on European Union**. *See also* **Convergence Report**

Convergence Report
Euro 1999: report on progress towards convergence and recommendation ... to the transition to the third stage of **EMU** (**COM**(98)1999)

Conversion Loans
Job creation loans under Article 56 of the **Treaty of Paris**

Coop
Projects funded under **LIFE**-Nature.
http://europa.eu.int/comm/environment/life/news/life-coop_projects02.htm.

COOPECO
EU-based initiative to facilitate cooperation between European and Latin American companies. *See also* **EUROCENTRES**

Co-operation procedure
Procedure introduced under the **SEA** which extended dialogue between the **Council of the European Union** and the **European Parliament** but, unlike the **Co-decision Procedure**, does not enable Parliament to veto the Council's proposal (Article 252)

COOPECOs
A network of European organisations supporting industrial co-operation and investment promotion in Latin America. A sub-network of **AL-INVEST**.
http://europa.eu.int/comm/europeaid/projects/al-invest/coopecos_en.cfm

Cooperation Procedure
Introduced by the **SEA** and extended under the **Treaty on European Union**, this legislative procedure requires the Council to take into account, at a second reading, any **European Parliament** amendments to a proposal that had been adopted by an absolute majority and accepted by the **European Commission**. Although initially a significant innovation, giving the EP real legislative power, Cooperation has largely been superseded by the **Codecision Procedure** introduced by the **Treaty of Amsterdam**. Proposals considered under the Cooperation Procedure are identified by the code SYN

CoopWWW
Interoperable tools for cooperation support using the world wide web (**CSCW** Telematics Engineering project partly funded by the **Telematics Applications Programme**).
http://orgwis.gmd.de/projects/COOPWWW

COPA
See **COPA-COGECA**

COPA-COGECA
Comité des Organisations Professionnelles Agricoles - Comité Général de la Coopération Agricole de l'Union Européenne (Committee of Agricultural Organisations in the EU -General Committee of Agricultural Cooperation in the EU).

23-25 rue de la Science, Boîte 3, B-1040 Brussels, Belgium.
www.copa-cogeca.be

COPEC
Comité paritaire pour l' Egalité des Chances (Commission Joint Committee for Equal Opportunities)

Coped
Cooperative Programme on Energy and Development. A network of Third World and European research centres in the area of energy economics and planning. Supported by **DG** Energy

Copenhagen Criteria
See **Accession Criteria**

Copenhagen European Council
The December 2002 Copenhagen **European Council** formally concluded enlargement negotiations with the 10. Heralded as an "unprecedented and historic milestone" the Council was particularly symbolic for Denmark, which had also held the Presidency in 1993, when the 'Copenhagen Criteria' (**Accession Criteria**) were established

Copenhagen Report
on political cooperation between the (then **9**) **Member States** 1973. Published in *Bulletin of the EC* 9/1973

Copenur
A Standing Committee of the **Council of the European Union** on Uranium Enrichment

Copernicus
Co-operation in science and technology with Central and Eastern European countries (1992-94). Incorporated into **INCO-Copernicus**.
www.cordis.lu/inco/home.html

Copernicus-PECO
Community of Pan-European Research Networks of Eastern European countries. Replaced by **INCO**

COPERT
Computer programme to calculate emissions from road traffic (**CORINAIR** project)

COPOL
Comparison of national and Community policies

CoR
Committee of the Regions (of the EU). An advisory body set up under the **Treaty on European Union** for consultation on **Cohesion**; trans-European transport networks; health and culture. (Previously the Consultative Council of Regional and Local Authorities of the **AER**).
79 rue Belliard, B-1040 Brussels, Belgium.
www.cor.eu.int

CORDI
Advisory Committee on Industrial **R&D**. Replaced by **IRDAC**

CORDIS
Community Research and Development Information Service.
www.cordis.lu

CORE
Consenus creation and awareness for **R&D** activities in technology for disabled and elderly people (**TIDE** project)

CORECOM
Ad hoc Advisory Committee on the Reprocessing of irradiated nuclear fuels

COREPER
Committee of Permanent Representatives of the **Council of the European Union**. *See also* **UKREP**

COREU
Correspondant Européen. An EU network for

communication between **Member States** to facilitate cooperation in the fields of foreign policy

Corfu Summit
Held 24-25 June 1994. On the basis of the **Bangemann Report**, 'Europe and the global information society', the Summit agreed to establish an Information Society Council and invited the **European Commission** to develop an Action Plan, which was adopted in July 1994 as 'Europe's way to the Information Society'. The Summit also set up a Consultative Commission on Racism and Xenophobia

CORINAIR
Commission Working Group on emission factors for calculating emissions from road transport

CORINE
Decision 85/338/EEC on the Coordination of information on the environment in Europe (1985-1990) (**OJ** L176/85 and OJ L81/90). Work continued under the **EEA**

COSA
Economic accounts for the agriculture and forestry statistical domain on the **New Cronos** databank

COSAC
Conférence des Organes spécialisées dans les affaires communautaires et européennes des Parlements de l'UE (Conference of the Community and European Affairs Committees of Parliaments of the EU). Set up in 1989 to bring together the various committees in the national parliaments of the **Member States** specialising in European affairs. Also known as CEAC - Conference of European Affairs Committees.
www.europarl.eu.int/natparl/cosac/default_en.htm

COSACC
Coordination of security activities between Chambers of Commerce (a Telematics for Administrations project within the **Telematics Applications Programme**)

COSEMCO
Seed Committee of the Common Market. Now part of **ESA**

COSIGA
A concurrent engineering simulation game using advanced multimedia and telecommunication for the education of European engineering students (**EMTF** project)

COSIMA
Control systems for integrated manufacturing: the **CAM** solution (**ESPRIT** project)

COSIMA
Integrated contaminated sites management (a Telematics for Environment project within the **Telematics Applications Programme**)

COSINE
Cooperation for open systems interconnection networking in Europe (**EUREKA** project)

Cosmetics Directive / Cosmetic Products Directive
Directive 76/768/EEC on the approximation of the laws of the **Member States** relating to cosmetic products (**OJ** L262/76). Subject to numerous amendments; for details see:
http://pharmacos.eudra.org/F3/cosmetic/CosmLexUpdates.htm

CosmetLex
Three-volume collection of 'The rules governing cosmetic products in the European Union'. Published by **EUR-OP**.
http://pharmacos.eudra.org/F3/cosmetic/cosmetlex.htm

COSMOS
Cost management with metrics of specification (**ESPRIT** project)

COST
European Cooperation in the field of Scientific and Technical research. Established 1971; participants now drawn from 44 countries, including Australia, Canada and Japan.
Secretariat: Council of the European Union, Justus Lipsius Building, 175 rue de la Loi, B-1048 Brussels, Belgium.
http://ue.eu.int/cost and http://cost.cordis.lu

Costa v Enel
European Court of Justice Case 6/64, which established the supremacy of EC law over national law

COSTEL
Course system for telecommunications training and innovation management (**COMETT** project)

COSYMA
Code system for MARIA (**MARIA** project)

COTANCE
Confédération des Associations Nationales des Tanneurs et Mégissiers de la Communauté Européenne (Confederation of National Associations of Tanners and Dressers of the **European Community**).
3 rue Belliard, B-1040 Brussels, Belgium.
www.euroleather.com

COTER
Commission for Territorial Cohesion Policy (of the **CoR**)

Cotonou Agreement
between the EU and **ACP**, signed in Cotonou, Benin, on 23 June 2000. The 20-year Agreement focuses on reducing poverty via political dialogue, development aid and closer economic and trade cooperation. Successor to the **Lomé Convention**.
http://europa.eu.int/scadplus/leg/en/lvb/r12101.htm

Council of Europe
A 45-member intergovernmental organisation, based in Strasbourg. The CoE is not part of the **European Union**, although all **15** EU **Member States** are CoE members, as are the **10** joining in 2004.
www.coe.int

Council of the European Union
The EU's main decision-making body. Previously called the Council of Ministers; not the same as the **European Council** or the **Council of Europe**. There are nine Council 'configurations':
- General Affairs and External Relations;
- Economic and Financial Affairs;
- Justice and Home Affairs;
- Employment, Social Policy, Health and Consumer Affairs;
- Competitiveness (Internal Market, Industry and Research);
- Transport, Telecommunications and Energy;
- Agriculture and Fisheries;
- Environment;
- Education, Youth and Culture.

Each is comprised of national ministers responsible for the relevant portfolio. Councils meet at different frequencies. There is a Secretariat in Brussels. The Council's responsibilities include: adopting legislation (often in **co-decision** with the **European Parliament**); coordinating the general economic policies of the **Member States**; concluding international agreements; adopting the Community budget (with the European Parliament); defining and implementing the **common foreign and security policy**; police and judicial cooperation in criminal matters).
Secretariat: Rue de la Loi 175, B-1048, Brussels.
http://ue.eu.int

Council of Ministers
Previous name for the **Council of the European Union**

Court of First Instance
See **CFI**, **European Court of Justice**

Court of Justice of the European Communities
See **European Court of Justice**

COUSTO
Integrated optic technologies for real time wide band optical signal processing (**ESPRIT** project)

COVIRA
Computer vision in radiology (**AIM** project)

CP
Community programme

CP
Compact project. **Tempus** and **Tacis** projects which address precisely defined, short-term needs

CP
Cooperation profile (in the **BC-NET** network)

CPA
Classification of products by activity (**OJ** L342/93). The basis for the **CPV**

CPC
Central product classification, published by the **United Nations**

CPC
Community Patent Court

CPC
Council Agreement 89/695/EEC on the Community Patent Convention 1975 (**OJ** L401/89)

CPD
See **Construction Products Directive** 89/106/EEC on construction products (**OJ** L40/89 with latest amendment in OJ L267/96)

CPHS
Technological development in hydrocarbons

CPI
Cour pénale internationale (International Criminal Court - **ICC**)

CPIV
Permanent International Vinegar Committee.
151 Reuterstrasse, D-53113 Bonn, Germany

CPIV
Comité Permanent des **Industries** du **Verre** Européenne (Standing Committee of the European Glass Industries).
89 ave Louise, B-1050 Brussels, Belgium.
www.cpivglass.be

CPMP
Committee for Proprietary Medicinal Products. A scientific committee of **EMEA**

CPMR
Conference of Peripheral Maritime Regions of Europe. Founded in 1973, it now has 149 member regions from 27 countries.
6 rue Saint-Martin, F-35700 Rennes, France.
www.cpmr.org

CPR
Committee of Permanent Representatives - **COREPER**

CPR
Comité de politique régionale (Regional Policy Committee)

CPS
Consumer Policy Service (Health and Consumer Affairs **DG** of the **European Commission**)

CPSA
Standing Committee on Agricultural Structures

CPV
Common (previously Community) Procurement Vocabulary. Previously **CPA**. A classification of goods and services which allocates nine-digit codes to some 6,000 terms commonly used in the procurement process. Published in **OJ** L222/96 (and available via **SIMAP** http://simap.eu.int). Under **Regulation** 2195/2002, a new CPV was to be introduced from late 2003

CPVO
Community Plant Variety Office (Office Communautaire des Variétés Végétales - OCVV). Set up under **Regulation** 2100/94 (**OJ** L227/94).
PO Box 2141, F-49021 Angers Cedex 02, France.
www.cpvo.fr

CPVRO
Community Plant Variety Rights Office. Infrequently-used version of Community Plant Variety Office - **CPVO**

CRAFT
Cooperative Research Action for Technology. Set up in 1989 by **IRDAC** to help **SME**s carry out research. Incorporated into the **Fifth Framework Programme** and **Sixth Framework Programme**

CRE
Association of European Universities / l'association des universités européennes. Merged with the Confederation of EU Rectors' Conferences in March 2001 to create the **EUA**.
www.unige.ch/cre

CREA
Capital Risque pour les Entreprises en phase d'Amorçage (Risk Capital for business start-ups). A Commission initiative 1998-2000

CREATE
Craft enterprises assisting young disabled entrepreneurs. 1998-2001

CREDIT
Capabilities registration, evaluation, diagnosis and advice through internet technologies (**EMTF** project)

CREDO
Cross-border cooperation between **CEC** countries and CEC and **NIS** border regions (**Phare** multi-country programme). 1996-2001.
http://europa.eu.int/comm/enlargement/pas/phare/programmes/multi-bene/credo.htm

CREDSTAT
Credit institutions statistical domain on the **New Cronos** databank

CREST
Clinical rehabilitation using electrical stimulation via telematics (a Telematics for Disabled and Elderly People project within the **Telematics Applications Programme**)

CREST
Comité de la recherche scientifique et technique (Scientific and Technical Research Committee - STRC). Set up in 1974. Previously **PREST**

CREW
Centre for Research on European Women.
25 rue Capouillet, B-1060 Brussels, Belgium

CRIS
Current Research Information Systems in Europe. An umbrella organisation for the advancement of international cooperation among research information systems

CRIT
Cooperative research in information technology (**Phare** programme)

CRL
Co-responsibility levy, under **Regulation** 1079/77 to expand the market in milk and milk products (**OJ** L131/77). Abolished on 1 April 1993

CRM
Certified reference material

CRM
Committee on Medical and Public Health Research. Set up by **PREST** to advise **CREST** on the coordination of national policies

CROCINA
Feasibility study for automated indoor horticulture production and its development (**EUREKA** project)

Crocodile Group / Club
Group of **MEPs** formed in 1980 by Altiero Spinelli, to draw up proposals to reform the Institutions of the EC. The Group met at the Crocodile Restaurant, Strasbourg. Their work eventually resulted in the so-called **Spinelli Treaty**

CROME
Critical Research on Men in Europe.
www.cromenet.org

CRONOS
See **New Cronos**

Cross border payments
See **CBP**

Cross border workers
Workers who live in one EU country but work in another and go home at least once per week

CROW
Conditions of roads and weather (**DRIVE** project)

CRPM
Conférence des Régions Périphériques Maritimes (Conference of Peripheral Maritime Regions of Europe - **CPMR**).
www.crpm.org

CRS
Computerised reservation systems, under **Regulation** 2299/89 (**OJ** L220/89)

CRTDE
Committee on Research, Technological Development and Energy

CSA
Communication systems architecture (**ESPRIT** project)

CSAs
Competitive support activities (part of the **INNOVATION** programme)

CSC
CADDIA Steering Committee

CSCE
Conference on Security and Cooperation in Europe. Now the Organisation for Security and Cooperation in Europe - **OSCE**

CSCM
Conference on Security and Cooperation in the Mediterranean

CSCW
Computer Supported Cooperative Work. A research group of the Institute for Applied Information Technology (FIT). Much of its work has been partially funded by the EU under the **Telematics Applications Programme**. *See also* **BSCW**; **CESAR**; **Coins**; **CSCW-MIKMOD**; **KESO**; **NESSIE**; **POLITeam**.
www.fit.fraunhofer.de/profil/cscw_en.html

CSCW-MIKMOD
Microsimulation models for legislative planning (a **CSCW** project partly funded by the **Telematics Applications Programme**)

CSD
Committee for Spatial Development

C-SET
Interoperable chip-secured electronic transactions (**ISIS** electronic commerce project)

CSF
Community Support Framework under the **Structural Funds**

CSO
COST Committee of Senior Officials

CSP
Cofinancing Support Programme. Launched by the **European Commission** in 1997 to support **NGO**s

CSPs
Country Strategy Papers. Introduced in 2001 to improve the coherence of policy toward **third countries**, particularly, to ensure a match between political priorities and spending on development assistance. CSPs are developed in collaboration with national governments, **Member States**, other donors, and representatives of civil society

CSR
Corporate social responsibility

CST
Comité scientifique et technique (Scientific and Technical Committee)

C-STAR
Coastal sediment transport assessment using SAR (synthetic aperture radar) (**MAST III** project)

CSTEE
Commission Scientific Committee on Toxicity, Ecotoxicity and the Environment. *See also* **SSC**.
http://europa.eu.int/comm/food/fs/sc/sct/index_en.html

CSTID
Committee for Scientific and Technical Information and Documentation

CSU
Christlich-Soziale Union (Christian Social Union). German political party.
www.csu.de

CT
Community transit system

CTA
Centre Technique de Coopération Agricole et Rurale ACP-UE (TCA Technical Centre for Agricultural and Rural Cooperation ACP-EU). Established in 1983 under the **Lomé Convention**.
Postbus 380, NL-6700 AJ Wageningen, Netherlands.
www.agricta.org

CTE
Convention Théâtrale Européenne (European Theatre Convention). A **Kaleidoscope** project.
9 place du Théâtre, L-2613 Luxembourg

CTI
See **Computer Theft Initiative**

CTIC
Trans-border information and consulting centres for consumers. Coordinated by the Consumer Affairs **DG** of the **European Commission**

CTM
Community Trade Mark. Created through

registration at **OHIM**.
http://europa.eu.int/comm/internal_market/en/indprop/tm/

CTM-Online
Community Trade Mark Consultation Service.
http://oami.eu.int/search/trademark/la/en_tm_search.cfm

CTMO
Community Trade Marks Office. Unofficial name for **OHIM**

CTP
Common Transport Policy

CTRs
Common technical regulations

CTS
Conformance testing services

CTS
Continuous Tracking Survey. 1996-1998.
http://europa.eu.int/comm/public_opinion/archives/eo_en.htm

CU
Customs Union. Achieved in the EEC on 1 July 1968

CUBE
Concertation Unit for Biotechnology in Europe

CULT
European Parliament Committee on Culture, Youth, Education, the Media and Sport

Culture 2000
Programme to support cultural co-operation projects. Covers performing arts, visual and plastic arts, literature, heritage, cultural history. **Established by Decision 508/2000 (OJ L63/2000) for the** period 2000-2004. Replaced **Ariane**; **Kaleidoscope**; **Raphael**.
http://europa.eu.int/comm/culture/eac/index_en.html

culture2u
Bulletin of information and intelligence for the cultural sector in Europe, from **Euclid**

Culture-Tracker
Databases of EU and other cultural funding opportunities in the UK and Europe, from **Euclid**

Cupertino
'Co-operation'; as in 'Cupertino agreement' meaning 'co-operation agreement'. Possibly taking its name from a town in California

CUS
Customs Union Service (Taxation and Customs Union **DG** of the **European Commission**)

CUSTODIAN
Conceptualisation for user involvement in specification and tools offering the efficient delivery of system integration around home networks (a Telematics for Disabled and Elderly People project within the **Telematics Applications Programme**)

Customs 2000 / 2002 / 2007
An action programme for Community customs 1996-2000, called Customs 2000, was adopted in 1996 under **Decision** 210/97 (**OJ** L33/97). Customs 2002 ended in December 2002 (Decision 105/2000 (OJ L13/2000), and Customs 2007 runs from January 2003 to December 2007 (Decision 253/2003/EC adopting an action programme for customs in the Community, OJ L36/03).
http://europa.eu.int/comm/taxation_customs/customs/information_notes/c2002/c2002.htm

CVMP
Committee for Veterinary Medicinal Products. A scientific committee of **EMEA**

CVS
CAD for **VLSI** systems (**ESPRIT** project)

CVTS
Continuing vocational training survey

CWASAR
Cooperative wide area service architecture (a Telematics for Urban and Rural Areas project within the **Telematics Applications Programme**)

CYNAMUS
Mass multiplication of virus-free artichoke plants by in-vitro micropropagation (**EUREKA** project)

D

D
Deutschland (Germany) / Deutsch (German)

DA
Dansk (Danish)

DA
Differentiated appropriations

DAB
Digital audio broadcasting. *See also* **WorldDAB**

DAB
Digital audio broadcasting system (**EUREKA** project)

DABLAS Task Force
Danube Black Sea Task Force, whose main objective "is to provide a platform for co-operation for the protection of water and water related ecosystems of the wider Black Sea Region".
http://europa.eu.int/comm/environment/enlarg/dablas_en.htm

DACAR
Data acquisition and communication techniques and their assessment for road transport (**DRIVE** project)

DAFNE III
Data food networking. European food availability databank based on household budget surveys

DAIDA
Advanced interactive development of data-intensive applications (**ESPRIT** project)

DAILY
Make daily life easier (a Telematics for Disabled and Elderly People project within the **Telematics Applications Programme**)

DALI
Delivery and access to local information and services (a Telematics for Urban and Rural Areas project within the **Telematics Applications Programme**)

DAMS
Dynamically adaptable multi-service system (**ESPRIT** project)

Dangerous Preparations Directive
Directive 88/379/EEC relating to the classification, packaging and labelling of dangerous preparations (**OJ** L187/88). *See also* **CHIP**

Dangerous Substances Directive
Directive 67/548/EEC relating to the classification, packaging and labelling of dangerous substances (**OJ** L196/67)

Dangerous Substances and Preparations Directive
Directive 76/769/EEC relating to restrictions on the marketing and use of certain dangerous substances and preparations (**OJ** L262/76)

DAPHNE
Document application processing in a heterogeneous network environment (applied in the **COSINE** project)

DAPHNE
Programme to combat violence against children, young people and women. Currently

funded 2000-2003; initially 1997-1999.
http://europa.eu.int/comm/justice_home/funding/daphne/funding_daphne_en.htm

DAPRO
Data protection in the EU (a Telematics Engineering project within the **Telematics Applications Programme**)

DART
Dynamic awareness raising process regarding telematics in the framework of **NATURA** (a Telematics for Education and Training project within the **Telematics Applications Programme**)

DART
Dynamic response of the forest-Tundra ecotone [sic] to environmental change (**TERI** project)

DARTS
Demonstration of advanced reliability techniques (**ESPRIT** project)

DAS
Déclaration d'assurance. **European Court of Auditors** statement of assurances under Article 188c of the **Treaty on European Union** concerning the reliability of accounts

DASIQ
Distributed automated system for inspection and quality control (**ESPRIT** project)

Dassonville
The **European Court of Justice** judgement in case 8/74 (Procureur du Roi v. Dassonville) established the 'Dassonville Formula': "All trading rules enacted by **Member States** which are capable of hindering, directly or indirectly, actually or potentially, intra-Community trade are to be considered as measures having an effect equivalent to quantitative restrictions"

Data Protection Directive
Directive 95/46/EC of the **European Parliament** and of the **Council of the European Union** of 24 October 1995 on the protection of individuals with regard to the processing of personal data and on the free movement of such data (**OJ** L281/95)

Data Service
Provides access to data sets used in periodical reports of the European Environment Agency (**EEA**).
http://dataservice.eea.eu.int/dataservice

Data Warehouse
Used to maintain the data collected for the EEA's regular *State of the Environment* reports (**EEA** project). Replaced by **Data Service**

David Group
Informal grouping of Euro-sceptic Nordic **MEPs**

Davignon Plan
Guidelines for steel policy issued in 1977 and never published

Dawn raid
Popular term for on-the-spot investigation by **European Commission** staff investigating possible infringements of EC competition law. A company's premises can be visited without prior warning by Commission officials empowered to examine records, take copies of any items required and question staff

Dayton Accords
Formally referred to as the General Framework Agreement for Peace (GFAP), the Dayton Peace Accords / Agreement, negotiated in Dayton, Ohio, in November 1995, sought to end the war in Bosnia and Herzegovina. The Agreement, formally signed in Paris in December 1995, established

the Office of the High Representative (**OHR**). See also **IFOR**, **SFOR**.
www.ohr.int

DCLAA
Developing Countries in Latin America and Asia

DCP
Draft Common Position

DCP
Prefix once used to denote press releases from the Committee of the Regions - **CoR**

DDR
Deutsche Demokratische Republik (German Democratic Republic - the former East Germany)

DDS
Data Dissemination System (as in Tariff Data Dissemination System - **TDSS**)

DE
Deutsch (German)

Dec
Decision

Decibel d'Or
Awarded by the French Conseil National du Bruit. (Presented to the **European Commission** in December 2000 in recognition of its proposal for a directive on the assessment and management of environmental noise - see **Environmental Noise Directive**).

Decision
A type of legal instrument which is used to require named parties (including **Member States** and individuals) to do - or not do - certain things, or to confer certain rights or obligations on them

Declaration of Gmunden
Declaration by the EU Expert Conference 'Crops for a green Industry', Gmunden, 7 October 1998 "for the encouragement of sustainable resources"

DECODE
Dessiner la Commission de Demain. A 'screening exercise' conducted by the **European Commission**, intended to provide a current analysis of all its activities, together with the resources and working methods used. Undertaken from November 1997 to May 1999. Results were published as 'Designing Tomorrow's Commission: A review of the Commission's Organisation and Operation'.
http://europa.eu.int/comm/reform/decode/screening_en.pdf

DECOM 3
Decommissioning of nuclear installations programme (1989-1993) (**OJ** L98/89)

DECT
Digital European cordless telecommunications. **Recommendation** 91/288/EEC (**OJ** L144/91).
http://europa.eu.int/scadplus/leg/en/lvb/l24131.htm

DEDICA
Directory based EDI certificate access and management (a Telematics Engineering project within the **Telematics Applications Programme**)

DEDICS
Distributed environment disaster information and control system (a Telematics for Environment project within the **Telematics Applications Programme**)

Deepening
Term used to describe moves towards greater European integration. Often contrasted to **Widening**

DEFIED
Disabled and elderly people flexible integrate (sic) environment (**TIDE** project)

DEGREE
Diversity effects in grassland ecosystems of Europe (**TERI** project)

Dehaene-von Weizsäcker-Simon Report
on the institutional implications of enlargement, 18 October 1999. Also known as the Three Wise Men Report.
http://europa.eu.int/igc2000/repoct99_en.htm

DEI
Declaration of European interest

Delegations
European Commission offices in **Third Countries**. *See also* **Representations**.
http://europa.eu.int/comm/external_relations/delegations/intro/index.htm

DELILAH
Designing and evaluating learning innovations and learning applications (**TSER** project)

Delors, Jacques
Arguably the most significant President of the **European Commission**, Jacques Delors held the office from January 1985 to December 1994. Amongst the developments during his three consecutive terms as President were the Single European Act (**SEA**), the Single European Market (**SEM**), German reunification, and the **Treaty on European Union**. He also introduced financial reforms popularly known as **Delors I** and **Delors II**, pursued **EMU**, and issued the White Paper **Growth, Competitiveness and Employment**. Delors had a number of conflicts with British Prime Minister Margaret Thatcher, who opposed European integration - favoured by Delors - but who, ironically, had preferred his appointment as President to the original French proposal of Claude Cheysson. *See also* **Delors Report**

Delors I
Making a success of the Single Act (**COM**(87) 100) - a package of financial reforms proposed in 1987 by the **European Commission**, headed by Jacques **Delors**, which provided the basis for decisions taken by the Brussels European Council in February 1988. Also known as the Delors package, Delors plan, Paquet Delors

Delors II
Package of reforms presented by the **European Commission** in February 1992, aimed at securing the Union's medium-term finances. The package was approved by the Edinburgh European Council in December 1992

Delors Package
See **Delors I**

Delors Plan
See **Delors I**

Delors Report
on economic and monetary union in the EC. Published in 1990 by the Committee for the Study of Economic and Monetary Union

Delors White Paper
See **Growth, Competitiveness and Employment**

DELOS
Developing learning organisation models in **SME** clusters (**TSER** project)

DELOS
Network of Excellence on Digital Libraries. Funded by **IST** under the **Fifth Framework Programme**.
www.ercim.org/delos

DELTA
Developing European learning through technological advance (1988-1990) (**OJ**

L206/88). Continued in the **Telematics Systems** and **Telematics Applications Programme**

DELTA-4
A dependable open distributed systems architecture (**ESPRIT** project)

DEMETER
Digital electronic mapping of European territory (**EUREKA** project)

DEMETER
Distance education, multimedia teleservices and telework for farmers (a Telematics for Urban and Rural Areas project within the **Telematics Applications Programme**)

DEMILITARISED
Regions affected by a reduced military presence (**RECITE** project)

DEMO
Demography statistical domain on the **New Cronos** databank

DEMO
Prototype fusion reactor to follow **ITER**

Democratic deficit
The idea that the **EU** system lacks democracy. Of the institutions involved in the decision-making process under the **Community method** only the **European Parliament** is directly elected; **European Commissioners** are appointed by the **Member States**, and the ministers on the **Council of the EU** are elected to serve in national parliaments, not specifically at EU level

DEMON
Design methods based on nets (**ESPRIT** project)

DEMO-R
Demography statistical domain on the **REGIO** database

DEMOS
Distance education and tutoring in heterogeneous telematics environments (a Telematics for Education and Training project within the **Telematics Applications Programme**)

DENEMA
Development of a new market for telematics products in central Asia (a Telematics for Education and Training project within the **Telematics Applications Programme**)

DEP
European Depository Library in major national libraries worldwide. *See also* **Relays**

DEPB
Duty Entitlement PassBook scheme. An export subsidy scheme under which any eligible exporter could apply for credits which were calculated as a percentage of the value of exported finished products. Ended March 1997. Previously **PBS**. *See also* **EOU**; **EPCGS**; **EPZ**; **ITES**

Derogation
A temporary exemption from EU legislation

DESCARTES
Debugging and specification of ADA real-time embedded systems (**ESPRIT** project)

Descartes Prize
An award for scientific excellence, first made in November 2000.
www.cordis.lu/descartes

DESIMA
Decision support for integrated coastal zone management. Project of the **JRC**'s Inland and Marine Water Institute - **IMW**

DESIRE
Development of a European service for information on research and education,

1998-2000 (a Telematics for Research project within the **Telematics Applications Programme**).
www.desire.org

DESIRE
Development of an all dry single-layer photolithography technology for sub-micron devices (**EUREKA** project)

DEsite
is a didactic module, which focuses on the decision-making process within the **EU**.
http://drcwww.kub.nl/dbi/instructie/eu/

DESON
Disorder and electrical properties in silicon oxynitrides (**ESPRIT** project)

DETER
Detection, enforcement and tutoring for driver error reduction (**DRIVE** project)

DETERMINE
Dissemination of environment and transport telematics results and needs analysis in Central and Eastern Europe (a Telematics for Environment project within the **Telematics Applications Programme**)

DEUCE
Electronic university for citizens of Europe (**DELTA** project)

DEV
Development **DG** of the **European Commission**

DEVE
Commission for Sustainable Development within the Committee of the Regions (**CoR**)

DEVE
European Parliament Committee on Development and Cooperation

De Villiers List
Term sometimes used to refer to the Europe of Nations Group, which won 19 seats in the 1994 **European Parliament** elections. The Group was led by the Eurosceptic French politician Philippe de Villiers. For the 1999 EP elections, de Villiers joined forces with Charles Pasqua in the so-called Pasqua-de Villiers list

DFCC
Development Finance Cooperative Committee. Set up under Article 325 of the 4th **Lomé Convention**

DG
Directorate-General - most often encountered in connection with the **European Commission**. The total number of DGs, their names / designated numbers and portfolios have all varied over time, because a new Commission President reorganises the administration and/or because the Commission has been given new responsibilities. Each DG is headed by a **European Commissioner**. Not to be confused with Director General (the senior manager of a DG) or with Directorate (a unit within a DG). In September 2003, the Prodi Commission had the following DGs:
Policies:

Agriculture
Competition
Economic and Financial Affairs
Education and Culture
Employment and Social Affairs
Energy and Transport
Enterprise
Environment
Fisheries
Health and Consumer Protection
Information Society
Internal Market
Joint Research Centre
Justice and Home Affairs
Regional Policy
Research
Taxation and Customs Union

External Relations:
- Development
- Enlargement
- EuropeAid - Co-operation Office
- External Relations
- Humanitarian Aid Office - ECHO
- Trade

The Commission also has a number of supporting **Services**.
Details can be found at: http://europa.eu.int/comm/dgs_en.htm

References are still seen to the numbers used to identify DGs in previous administrations, including:
- DG I External Relations: Commercial Policy and Relations with North America, the Far East, Australia and New Zealand
- DG IA External Relations: Europe and the New Independent States, Common Foreign and Security Policy and External Missions
- DG IB External Relations: Southern Mediterranean, Middle and Near East, Latin America, South and South-East Asia and North-South Cooperation
- DG II Economic and Financial Affairs
- DG III Industry
- DG IV Competition
- DG V Employment, Industrial Relations and Social Affairs
- DG VI Agriculture
- DG VII Transport
- DG VIII Development
- DG IX Personnel and Administration
- DG X Information, Communication, Culture, Audiovisual
- DG XI Environment, Nuclear Safety and Civil Protection
- DG XII Science, Research and Development
- DG XIII Telecommunications, Information Market and Exploitation of Research
- DG XIV Fisheries
- DG XV Internal Market and Financial Services
- DG XVI Regional Policies and Cohesion
- DG XVII Energy
- DG XIX Budgets
- DG XXI Taxation and Customs Union
- DG XXII Education, Training and Youth
- DG XXIII Enterprise Policy, Distributive Trades, Tourism and Cooperatives
- DG XXIV Consumer Policy and Consumer Health Protection

The **European Parliament** has the following DGs:
- DG 1 - Presidency
- DG 2 - Committees and Delegations
- DG 3 - Information and Public Relations
- DG 4 - Research
- DG 5 - Personnel
- DG 6 - Administration
- DG 7 - Translation and General Services
- DG 8 - Finance

The **Council of the European Union** has the following DGs:
- DG A - Personnel and Administration
- DG B - Agriculture - Fisheries
- DG C - Internal market - Competitiveness - Industry - Research - Energy - Transport - Information society
- DG E - External economic relations, common foreign and security policy
- DG F - Press - Communication - Protocol
- DG G - Economic and social affairs
- DG H - Justice and home affairs
- DG I - Protection of the environment and consumers - Civil protection - Health - Foodstuffs - Education - Youth - Culture - Audiovisual

Details of DG structures can be found at: http://europa.eu.int/idea/en/index.htm

DG
Director General. **European Commission** official heading a **DG** - responsible to a **European Commissioner**

DIABCARD 3
Improved communication in diabetes care based on chipcard technology (a Telematics for Healthcare project within the **Telematics Applications Programme**)

DIABCARE Q-NET
Diabcare quality network in Europe (a Telematics for Healthcare project within the **Telematics Applications Programme**)

Dialogue with Business
Initiative from the **European Commission** to help companies make the most of the Single European Market (**SEM**).
http://europa.eu.int/business

Dialogue with Citizens
European Commission initiative to provide people with information about their rights as EU citizens.
http://europa.eu.int/citizens

Dialogue Youth
improvement of information services to young people by developing cooperation between European youth networks (**Youth for Europe** project).
http://europa.eu.int/scadplus/leg/en/cha/c11601b.htm

DIAMOND
Development and integration of accurate operations in numerical data processing (**ESPRIT** project)

DIANE
Automatic integrated system for neutronography (**EUREKA** project)

DIANEGUIDE
An on-line description of databases now merged with **BROKERSGUIDE** to form **I*M GUIDE**

DIAS
Distributed intelligent actuators and sensors (**ESPRIT** project)

DICTUM
Development of an interactive communication training system using teleworkers (**TIDE** project)

DIDAMES
Distributed industrial design and manufacturing of electronic subassemblies (**RACE** project)

DIECAST
Medium pressure die casting (**EUREKA** project)

DIGICULT
Digital heritage and cultural content.
www.cordis.lu/ist/ka3/digicult

DIGISAT
Advanced digital satellite broadcasting and interactivity services (**ACTS** project)

DIME
Development of integrated monetary electronics. This programme never became operational

DIMPE
Distributed integrated multi-media publishing environment (**RACE** project)

DIMUN
Distributed manufacturing using existing and developing public networks (**RACE** project)

DIN
Deutsches Institut für Normung. National standards body of Germany.
www.din.de

DIPECHO
Disaster Preparedness ECHO. An initiative of the European Community Humanitarian Office (**ECHO**) involving natural and manmade disaster preparedness and prevention for the Caribbean. Initially 1996-

1998, extended to cover 2000-2001.
www.disaster.info.desastres.net/dipecho

Diplomas Directives
1st **Directive** 89/48/EEC on the recognition of higher education diplomas awarded on completion of professional education (**OJ** L19/89). 2nd Directive 92/51/EEC…for the recognition of professional education and training (OJ L209/92)

DNS
Domain name system. *See also* **dot.eu**, **EURID**

DIPLOMAT
A 1997-1998 **ACTS** project intended to develop a European Charter for Telework

Dir
Directive

DIRAC
Database for reliability calculations (**RACE** project)

Directive
A form of EU legislation which sets out the objectives to be achieved, but leaves **Member States** to introduce their own implementing legislation

DIRECTORIA
Convention for local and regional authorities. A Regional Policy **DG** initiative of the **European Commission**

DIRTYSUPRA
Study of the influence of impurities on the properties of high TC superconductors (**ESPRIT** project)

DIS
Decentralised implementation system (part of the **Phare** programme)

DIS
Drug information systems (**Phare** project)

DiSCiPl
Debugging Systems for Constraint Programming (partly funded by the **ESPRIT** programme).
http://discipl.inria.fr

DISCUS
Distance information, support and communication for European carers (a Telematics for Disabled and Elderly People project within the **Telematics Applications Programme**)

DISNET
Domain-independent information and services network (**IMPACT** project)

Distance Selling Directive
Directive 97/7/EC on the protection of consumers in respect of distance contracts (**OJ** L144/97)

DISTINCT
Deployment and integration of smartcard technology and information networks for cross-sector telematics (a Telematics for Integrated Applications for Digital Sites project within the **Telematics Applications Programme**)

DIVIDEND
Dealer interactive video (**RACE** project)

DK
Danmark / Denmark

DLM-Forum
DLM stands for 'Données lisibles par machine' (in English - 'Machine-readable data'). The DLM-Forum is based on the conclusions of the June 1994 Corfu European Council concerning cooperation in archiving (**OJ** C235/94).
http://europa.eu.int/historical_archives/dlm_forum/

DMA
Depth and motion analysis (**ESPRIT** project)

DNS
Domain name system. *See also* **dot.eu**, **EURID**

Dobrís Assessment
A report published by the **EEA** in 1995 on *Europe's environment*. A second report was published in 1998. Dobrís Castle is near Prague.
http://reports.eea.eu.int/92-826-5409-5/en

doc
'document'. As in **EP Doc**, **SEC doc**

DOC
Key public documents issued by the **European Commission** and the **Council of the European Union**, available via the **RAPID** database.
http://europa.eu.int/rapid/start/welcome.htm

DOC@HOME
Project to develop diagnosis device under the **IST** programme

DOCED
A programme covering a number of infrastructure activities in the agricultural databases (**CADDIA** project)

Docurama
"Panorama of Community documentation". Originally an internal **European Commission** publication listing libraries, archives and information units in the Commission and other EU bodies. A version is available on the web, but with links to **DG** websites rather than to lists of libraries, archives and information units.
http://europa.eu.int/comm/libraries/docurama/dgs_en.htm

DOEOIS
Design and operational evaluation of distributed office information servers (**ESPRIT** project)

DOM
départements d'outre-mer (French Overseas Departments - FOD: Guadeloupe, French Guiana, Martinique, Réunion)

DOMINC
Advanced control strategies and methods for motorway RTI - system of the future (**DRIVE** project)

DOMIS
ECHO directory of materials data information sources

DOMITEL
Domestic interactive telematic education and learning (a Telematics for Education and Training project within the **Telematics Applications Programme**)

DOMUS
Domestic consumption and utility sectors (**Environment and Climate** project)

Dooge Report
on Institutional affairs presented to the **European Council** in March 1985. Published in the *Bulletin of the European Communities* 3/1985 p102

Doorstep Selling Directive
Directive 85/577/EEC on contracts negotiated away from business premises which protects consumers from high-pressure door-to-door salesmen (**OJ** L372/85)

DORIS
Digital and organisational regeneration initiative for urban and rural sites which are declining (a Telematics for Integrated Applications for Digital Sites project within the **Telematics Applications Programme**)

Dorsale
Alternative term for **Blue Banana**

DOSE
Internal **European Parliament** database for the management of Working Documents. Replaced by **PARDOC**

DOSES
Development of statistical expert systems (1989-1993) (**OJ** L200/89). Continued as **DOSIS**

DOSIS
Development of statistical information systems. A **Eurostat** project within the **Fourth Framework Programme**. Previously **DOSES**

dot.com Summit
See **Lisbon Summit**

dot.eu
The **European Commission** has proposed the introduction of a new internet Top Level Domain (TLD) for Europe: **'.eu'**. It is intended to give European internet users their own identity. *See also* **EURID**.
http://europa.eu.int/information_society/topics/telecoms/internet/eu_domain/index_en.htm

DOUCEUR
Documents Utiles et Communs pour **Eurostat**

DPSIR
Driving forces, pressures, states, impacts, responses: a model for environmental management adopted by the **EEA**

DR
Technical group of the European Right (of the **European Parliament,** 1984-89). Also known as ER

DRACO
Driver and accident coordinated observer (**DRIVE** project)

DRAGON
Distribution and re-usability of ADA R/T applications through graceful and on-line operations (**ESPRIT** project)

DRAMA
Developments for rehabilitation of the arm - a multimedia approach (a Telematics for Disabled and Elderly People project within the **Telematics Applications Programme**)

DRC
Democratic Republic of the Congo. *See* **Artemis**

DREAM
Feasibility study for monitoring driver status (**DRIVE** project)

Drins Report
Proposed legislation on aldrin, dieldrin and endrin discharges (**OJ** C146/79; OJ C341/80; OJ C309/86)

DRIVAGE
Factors in elderly people's driving abilities (**DRIVE** project)

DRIVE
Dedicated road infrastructure for vehicle safety in Europe (1988-1991) (**OJ** L206/88). Continued as Area 2 of the **Telematics Systems** programme

DRUMS
Defeasible reasoning and uncertainty management systems (**ESPRIT** project)

DRYDEL
Dry develop optical lithography for **VLSI** (**ESPRIT** project)

DSDIC
Design support for distributed industrial control (**ESPRIT** project)

DSIS
Distributed statistical information services. A framework which aims to support the Community statistical system (a **Eurostat** initiative sponsored by the **IDA** programme)

DSS
Directorate of Science Strategy. Established in 2001 "to support the **JRC** in the development and implementation of its science strategies". Details via:
www.jrc.cec.eu.int/who_we_are/our_locations.htm

DTCS
Policy analysis and spatial conflicts in transport policy (**Environment and Climate** project)

DTD
Document type definition

DTI Briefings
See **Spearhead**

Dual Pricing Directive
Directive 98/6/EC on consumer protection in the indication of the prices of products offered to consumers (**OJ** L80/98). Also known as Unit Prices Directive

Dual-use Goods
Goods and technologies which are developed for civilian use, but which can have military applications. Subject to **Regulation** 1334/2000 setting up a Community regime for the control of exports of dual use items and technology (**OJ** L159/00). Regulation 149/2003 (OJ L30/03) is a consolidated version, incorporating numerous amendments.
http://europa.eu.int/comm/trade/goods/dualuse/index_en.htm

DubliNET
"A secure electronic network of transmission channels between the national authorities dealing with asylum applications". Became operational on 1 September 2003 in the **Member States**, Norway and Iceland

Dublin Foundation
Name sometimes used for the European Foundation for the Improvement of Living and Working Conditions - **EFILWC**

Dublin Group
An "informal consultation mechanism of major world players": EU **Member States**, **European Commission**, Australia, Norway, Canada, Japan, USA, **UNDCP**

DUFIMESHT
Dust filtration with metal screens at high temperature (**EUREKA** project)

DUMIP
Ultrasonic mechanised devices for internal pipeline inspection (**EUREKA** project)

Dundalk Case
Case 45/87 in the **European Court of Justice** on public works contracts (reported in **ECR** 1988/8)

DUNDIS
ECHO Directory of **United Nations** Databases and Information Systems

Duration Directive
Directive 93/98/EEC harmonising the term of protection of copyright and certain related rights (**OJ** L290/93)

DUS
Distinct, uniform, stable

DVB
Digital video broadcasting

DVBIRD
Digital video broadcasting integrated receiver decoder (**ACTS** project)

DYANA
Dynamic interpretation of natural language (**ESPRIT** project)

DYNAMO
Dynamic models to predict and scale-up the impact of environmental change on biogeochemical cycling (**TERI** project)

DYONISOS
Wine growing regions (**RECITE** project)

E

E
España / Espagne (Spain)

E
Ellas (Greece)

E101
An EU form required when working in another EU country for up to 12 months, either for a home **Member State** employer or as self-employed, to prove cover under the national social protection (national insurance) scheme

E111
An EU form which entitles the holder to free or reduced-cost emergency medical treatment when visiting another **Member State**

E2RC
European Environmental Reference Centre.
http://nfp-gr.eionet.eu.int/epd_eop_en/eks_en/eop_en/e2rc_en/e2rc_en.html

EA
European Association. Proposal for a Statute to enable associations to take advantage of the Single European Market - **SEM (OJ** C236/93).
http://europa.eu.int/scadplus/leg/en/lvb/l26017.htm

EAA
Economic accounts for agriculture

EAAA
European Association of Advertising Agencies. Now European Association of Communications Agencies - **EACA**

EAAF
European Association of Animation Film. Also known as CARTOON.
314 blvd Lambermont, B-1030 Brussels, Belgium.
www.cartoon-media.be

EAB
ESPRIT Advisory Board

EABS
Database of references to the published results of scientific and technical research programmes, wholly or partly sponsored by the EU. Now on **CORDIS** as **RTD-PUBLICATIONS**

EAC
Education and Culture **DG** of the **European Commission**

EAC
European accident code (**JRC** - reactor safety programme)

EAC
European Association for Cooperation. A non profit-making association set up and managed by the Commission; wound up 1998

EAC
Europe Against Cancer. Initially 1996-2000; extended to December 2002.
http://europa.eu.int/comm/health/ph_overview/previous_programme/cancer/cancer_en.htm

EACA
European Association of Communications

Agencies. Previously European Association of Advertising Agencies.
www.eaca.be

EACF
Extension et Accélération de la Confiance Financière (Extension and Acceleration of Financial Confidence). A **Business Angels** project to look into the possibility of setting up a 'virtual community' on the internet where people with new ideas can meet investors and entrepreneurs

EACN
European Association of Community Networking

EACRO
European Association of Contract Research Organisations

EAEC
European Atomic Energy Community - **EURATOM**

EAF
Economic accounts for forestry

EAFR
See **EAR**

EAG
External Advisory Group

EAGGF
European Agricultural Guidance and Guarantee Fund (Fonds européen d'orientation et de garantie agricole - FEOGA). Established in 1962 to finance the Common Agricultural Policy - **CAP**.
http://europa.eu.int/comm/agriculture/fin/index_en.htm

EAGLE
European Association for Grey Literature Exploitation. Set up to manage **SIGLE**.
www.kb.nl/infolev/eagle/frames.htm

EAHIL
European Association for Health Information and Libraries (Association Européenne pour l'Information et les Bibliothèques de Santé).
Secretariat, c/o NVB Bureau, Nieuwegracht 15, 3512 LC Utrecht, The Netherlands.
www.eahil.org

EAP
Environment Action Programme. The EU's sixth EAP ('Environment 2010: Our future, Our choice') covers 2001-2010: **Decision** 1600/2002/EC (**OJ** L242/02). Seen also as 'Environment Action Plan'.
http://europa.eu.int/comm/environment/newprg/

EAPN
European Anti Poverty Network (Le Réseau européen des associations de lutte contre la pauvreté et l'exclusion sociale).
rue du Congrès 37-41 (Bte 2), B-1000, Brussels, Belgium.
www.eapn.org

EAR
European Agency for Reconstruction. Manages **European Union** assistance programmes in Serbia and Montenegro and the former Yugoslav Republic of Macedonia. Established February 2000, with headquarters in Thessaloniki and operational centres in Pristina, Belgrade, Podgorica and Skopje.
www.ear.eu.int

EARN
European Academic and Research Network. Became part of **TERENA**

EARNING
Harmonised earnings statistical domain on the **New Cronos** databank

EARNs
Euro area reference notes. Established by the **EIB** in March 1999, EARNs are EIB benchmark issues in Euros

EARSEC
European airborne remote sensing capabilities (**Ispra** project)

EAS
European Administrative Space

EASA
European Aviation Safety Agency. Set up under **Regulation** 1592/2002 (**OJ** L240/02) and formally came into being 28 September 2003.
www.easa.eu.int

EASE
Education Advanced Search Europe. "EASE will introduce the most powerful education search platform in Europe".
www.cedefop.eu.int/ease

EASE
Project to investigate cross-border sulphur pollution in the Black Triangle area, which is found at the border of the former East Germany, the Czech Republic and Poland (within the **INCO** programme)

EASHW
Sometimes used for European Agency for Safety and Health at Work (**EU-OSHA**)

EASI
European Applications in Surgical Interventions (a Telematics for Healthcare project within the **Telematics Applications Programme**)

EASI-ISAE
Educating authors for simulated interaction: intercommunication software for appreciating educators (**EMTF** project)

EASM
European Automotive Suppliers' Mission to Michigan

EASOE
European Arctic stratospheric ozone experiment

EAST
EUREKA advanced software technology: development of software factories incorporating software engineering (EUREKA project)

EAST
European Assistance for Science and Technology. A **European Parliament** own-initiative proposal (**EP Doc** A3 174/90)

EASYTEX
Aesthetical, adjustable, serviceable and mainstay textiles for disabled and elderly (a Telematics for Disabled and Elderly People project within the **Telematics Applications Programme**)

EAT
European Advertising Tripartite.
267 ave de Tervuren, B-1150 Brussels, Belgium.
www.belgium-info.com/projects/eat/index.htm

EATA
European Association for Telematic Applications.
8-10 Methonis Street, GR-10680 Athens, Greece

EATCHIP
European air traffic control harmonisation and integration programme. Managed by **EUROCONTROL** to implement the **ECAC** strategy to harmonise and integrate European air traffic management services

EATI
European Addiction Training Institute. Part of the five-year Community programme for the prevention of drug dependence (1996-2000) (**OJ** L19/97).
P.O. Box 3907, 1001 AS Amsterdam, The Netherlands.
www.eati.org

EATMS
European air traffic management system

EATS
Efficiency of assistive technology and services (a Telematics for Disabled and Elderly People project within the **Telematics Applications Programme**)

EAVE
Entrepreneurs de l'Audiovisuel Européen (European Audiovisual Entrepreneurs). Set up under the **MEDIA** programme.
14 rue de la Presse, B-1000 Brussels, Belgium.
www.eave.org

EBA
Euro Banking Association (Association bancaire pour l'euro). Previously ECU Banking Association.
4 rue de Galliéra, F-75116 Paris, France.
www.abe.org

EBA
See **Everything but Arms**

EBAN
European **Business Angels** Network.
c/o Eurada, 12 av des Arts, Boîte7, B-1210 Brussels, Belgium.
www.eban.org

EBARBS
Everything But Arms, Rice,Bananas and Sugar

EBAS III
Tacis project aimed at strengthening the commercial banking skills and operations of Russian regional banks

EBES
European Board for EDI Standardisation

EBIC
European Business Information Centre. Little-used alternative term for Euro Info Centre - **EIC**

EBIP
Environmental Biotechnology **Industrial Platform**.
www.ebip.org and www.ebip.org

EBLIDA
European Bureau of Library, Information and Documentation Associations.
PO Box 43300, NL-2504 The Hague, The Netherlands.
www.eblida.org

EBLUL
European Bureau for Lesser Used Languages (BELMR - Bureau européen pour les langues moins répandues).
49 rue Saint-Josse, B-1210, Brussels, Belgium.
www.eblul.org

EBN
European BIC Network. **BIC**s are Business and Innovation Centres.
168 av de Tervuren, Box 25, B-1150 Brussels, Belgium.
www.ebn.be

EBNIC
The European Biotechnology Node for Interaction with China. To facilitate direct contact between European academic and industrial biotechnologists and their Chinese counterparts (an **INCO** activity).

EMBO, 1 Meyerhofstrasse, D-69117 Heidelberg, Germany.
www.ebnic.org

EBO
European Union Baroque Orchestra. Also known as European Community Baroque Orchestra.
Hordley, Wooton, Woodstock, Oxon OX20 1EP, UK.
www.charitiesdirect.com/charity4/ch011384.htm

EBP
European Books in Print (project within Area 5 of the **Telematics Systems** programme)

EBP
European business programme to train management specialists at Business Institutes

EBR
European Business Register. Network providing company information Managed by the EBR **EEIG**.
22 rue de l'Industrie, B-1040 Brussels, Belgium.
www.ebr.org

EBRD
European Bank for Reconstruction and Development. Established in 1991 by **Decision** 90/674/EEC (**OJ** L372/90) to foster the transition towards open market economies and to promote private and entrepreneurial initiatives in the **CEEC** and **CIS**. Operates in 27 countries "from central Europe to central Asia."
1 Exchange Sq, London EC2A 2EH, UK.
www.ebrd.com

EbS
Europe by Satellite. The EU's TV news agency, which provides EU-related information intended primarily for media professionals.
http://europa.eu.int/comm/ebs/index.html

EBT
European Business Trends. Statistical domain on the **New Cronos** database

EBTI
European Binding Tariff Information.
http://europa.eu.int/comm/taxation_customs/dds/en/ebticau.htm

EBTRA II
EC Bureau for Bank Training and Restructuring Advice. A **Tacis** project to develop a network of banking institutions and associations in the **CIS**

EC
European Communities or **European Community**

EC
European Council; sometimes used to mean Council of Ministers - now the **Council of the European Union**

ECA
European Catering Association.
Bourne House, Horsell Park, Woking, Surrey GU21 4LY, UK.
www.eca2.gh0.co.uk

ECA
European Cockpit Association.
39 rue du Commerce, B-1000 Brussels, Belgium.
www.eca-cockpit.com

ECA
European Court of Auditors (Cour des comptes européenne - CCE)

ECAA
European common aviation area

ECAC
European Civil Aviation Conference.
3 bis Villa Emile Bergerat, 92522 Neuilly sur

Seine Cedex, France.
www.ecac-ceac.org

ECAP I / ECAP II
EC/**ASEAN** Patents and Trademarks Programme (ECAP I). Now EC-ASEAN Intellectual Property Rights Co-operation Programme (ECAP II).
www.ecap-project.org/ecap/site/en

ECARDA
European Common Approach for **R&D** in **ATM** (a Telematics for transport project within the **Telematics Applications Programme**)

ECAS
European Citizen Action Service. "Created in 1990 as an international non-profit organization, independent of political parties, commercial interests and the EU Institutions. The association's mission is to enable NGOs and individuals to make their voice heard with the EU."
53 rue de la Concorde, B-1050 Brussels, Belgium.
www.ecas.org

ECAT
Environmental Centres for Administration and Technology. A network of centres involved in environment-related EU policies

ECATA
European consortium in advanced training for aeronautics (**COMETT** project)

ECB
European Central Bank. Established on 1st June 1998 to replace the **EMI**.
29 Kaiserstrasse, D-60311 Frankfurt am Main, Germany.
www.ecb.int

ECB
European Chemicals Bureau. Part of the **IHCP**.
http://ecb.jrc.it

ECBA
European Countries Biologists Association (previously European Communities Biologists' Association).
C/o Institute of Biology, 20 Queensberry Place, London SW7 2DZ, UK.
www.partner4sport.de/ecba/lr/index.html

ECBS
European Committee for Banking Standards.
12 av de Tervuren, B-1040 Brussels, Belgium.
www.ecbs.org

ECC
European Communities Commission. Alternative term for Commission of the European Communities - *see* **European Commission**

ECC
European Consumer Centre. *See* **Euroguichet**

ECCAIRS
European Co-ordination Centre for Aviation Incident Reporting Systems

ECCB
European Committee of Central Balance Sheet Data Offices. Established in 1985 to carry out studies on EU enterprises and to exchange information on methods of financial analysis

ECCN
European Child Care Network

ECCOFEX
European Commission Coordinating Committee of Options and Future Exchanges

ECCRI
European Community Crime Reduction Initiative. *See* **Computer Theft Initiative**

ECDC
European Centre for Disease Prevention and Control.
http://europa.eu.int/comm/health/ph_overview/strategy/ecdc/ecdc_en.htm

ECDIN
Environmental Chemicals Data and Information Network

ECDL
European computer driving licence. Managed by the European Computer Driving Licence Foundation Ltd, which is also responsible for the International Computer Driving Licence (ICDL).
www.ecdl.com

ECDL
European Conferences on Digital Libraries. Organised by **DELOS** since 1997.
http://delos-noe.iei.pi.cnr.it/activities/researchforum/ECDL/ecdl.html?content=ecdl_c.html

ECDPM
European Centre for Development Policy Management (Centre Européen de Gestion des Politiques de Développement). Aims to improve cooperation between Europe and countries in Africa, the Caribbean, and the Pacific.
21 Onze Lieve Vrouweplein, 6211 HE Maastricht, The Netherlands.
www.oneworld.org/ecdpm

ECDVT
European Centre for the Development of Vocational Training. More popularly known as **CEDEFOP** (Centre Européen pour le Développement de la Formation Professionnelle).
www.cedefop.eu.int

ECE
See **UN/ECE**

ECE
See **Eurocentros**

ECERP
EU-China Enterprise Reform Project

ECETOC
European Centre for Exotoxicology and Toxicology of Chemicals.
Michelangelo Building, 4 av E Van Nieuwenhuyse, Boîte 6, B-1160 Brussels, Belgium.
www.ecetoc.org

ECF
European Cyclists' Federation (Fédération Européennes des Cyclistes - FEC).
c/o ADFC, 8-9 Grünenstrasse, 28199 Bremen, Germany.
www.ecf.com

ECFI
European Court of First Instance. Alternative for the more commonly-used **CFI**

ECFIN
Economic and Financial Affairs **DG** of the **European Commission**

ECFTU
European Confederation of Free Trade Unions in the Community. Became **ETUC** in 1973

ECG
European Cooperation Grouping. Now **EEIG**

ECGI
European Corporate Governance Institute.
120 av des Statuaires, B-1180 Brussels, Belgium.
www.ecgi.org

ECHE
European Parliament Temporary Committee on the Echelon interception system.
www.europarl.eu.int/committees/echelon_home.htm

Echelon
Code-name for a communications interception system run by and for the "military-intelligence community". *See also* **ECHE**

ECHO
Electronic case-handling in offices (**RACE** project)

ECHO
European Commission Host Organisation. The ECHO database was closed in Oct 1998

ECHO
European Commission's Humanitarian Aid Office (Office d'Aide humanitaire de la Commission européenne), often referred to as the Humanitarian Aid Office (previously European Community Humanitarian Aid Office).
200 rue de la Loi, B-1049 Brussels, Belgium.
http://europa.eu.int/comm/echo

ECHOES
Educational hypermedia online system (**EMTF** project)

ECHP
European Community Household Panel

ECI
European Cosmetics Inventory. **Decision** 96/335/EC, establishing an inventory and a common nomenclature of ingredients employed in cosmetic products (**OJ** L132/96 - 684 pages!)

ECI
EURATOM classified information

ECIA
European Council of Information Associations.
www.aslib.co.uk/ecia/index.html

ECICS
European Customs Inventory of Chemical Substances: A guide to the classification of chemicals in the combined nomenclature.
http://europa.eu.int/comm/taxation_customs/databases/ecics_en.htm

ECIF
European Construction Industry Federation (Fédération de l'Industrie Européenne de la Construction - FIEC).
66 av Louise, B-1050 Brussels, Belgium.
www.fiec.org

EC-IIP
European Community International Investment Partner

ECIP
European CAD integration project (**ESPRIT** project)

ECIP
European Communities Investment Partners. Intended to promote joint ventures between firms in the **Member States** and those in Latin America, Asia and the Mediterranean. Initially 1992-1994, but extended to 1999

ECIR
European Centre for Industrial Relations.
http://europa.eu.int/scadplus/leg/en/cha/c10709.htm

ECIS
European Centre for Infrastructure Studies. Established 1994 by the European Round Table of Industrialists (**ERT**); closed 1997

ECISS
European Committee for Iron and Steel Standardisation.

c/o **CEN**, 36 rue de Stassart, B-1050 Brussels, Belgium. *See also* **COCOR**

ECJ
European Court of Justice

ECLA
European Company Lawyers' Association (Association Européenne des Juristes d'Entreprise - AEJE).
36 rue Ravenstein, B-1000 Brussels, Belgium.
www.ecla.org

ECLAIR
European collaborative linkage of agriculture and industry through research. (1988-1993) (**OJ** L60/89). *See also* **FLAIR**. Continued as **AIR**

ECLAS
The **European Commission**'s union catalogue, created in 1982. Includes the holdings of the **Réseaubib** library network. Originally 'European Commission Library Automated System'.
http://europa.eu.int/eclas

ECM
European Common Market. *See also* **Common Market**

ECMAST
European Conference on Multimedia Applications, Services and Techniques. Coordinated by **COST** and the **ACTS** programme

ECMM
European Community Monitor Mission. A non-**United Nations** body formed to monitor ceasefires. Operated in the Western Balkans; replaced in December 2000 by the European Union Monitoring Mission (**EUMM**)

ECOBULB
Ecological flower bulb farming and its automated mechanisation (**EUREKA** project)

Eco-Counsellors
Counsellors appointed in 12 **Member State** towns during the 1987 European Year of the Environment (**EYE**) to advise on environmental issues

ECOFIN
Economic and Financial Affairs configuration of the **Council of the European Union**

ECOFLAT
The ECO-metabolism of an estuarine tidal flat (**ELOISE** project)

ECOIN
European core inventory

Eco-label
Award scheme which seeks to encourage companies to market 'greener' (i.e. more environmentally friendly) products. Introduced in 1992; currently governed by **Regulation** 1980/2000 (**OJ** L237/00).
http://europa.eu.int/comm/environment/ecolabel

ECOLE/GRIP
European collaboration in oncology literature evaluation/getting research into practice (a Telematics for Healthcare project within the **Telematics Applications Programme**)

ECOLES
Development of representation in machine learning (**ESPRIT** project)

ECOMAC
Eco-management accounting as a tool of environmental management (**Environment and Climate** project)

ECOMANAGEMENT
Project to help SMEs develop their environmental management (a Telematics for

Environment project within the **Telematics Applications Programme**)

ECOM-IS
Electronic commerce open market for industry sectors.
www.cenorm.be/isss/Workshop/ec/ECOM-IS/default.htm

ECOMONT
Ecological effects of land use changes on European terrestrial mountain ecosystems (**TERI** project)

ECON
European Parliament Committee on Economic and Monetary Affairs

ECON DEV
Network of science centres (**RECITE** project)

ECONET
EU Network for the Implementation and Enforcement of Environmental Law. Renamed **IMPEL**

Economat stores
European Commission's subsidised in-house shops in Brussels and Luxembourg. Closed in 2001

Economic and Social Committee
Officially entitled the European Economic and Social Committee. One of the five EU **Institutions**, the ESC is a consultative forum which represents the interests of socio-economic organisations (employers' federations, trade-unions, consumers).
2 rue Ravenstein, B-1000 Brussels, Belgium.
www.esc.eu.int

ECON-R
Economic accounts statistical domain on the **REGIO** database

ECOPAC
Econometrics of impacts projects (**Transport** project).
www.cordis.lu/transport/src/ecopac.htm

ECOPAVE
Development of a multi-purpose composite pavement system (**BRITE** project)

Ecopoints
Regulation 3298/94, laying down detailed measures concerning the system of Rights of Transit (Ecopoints) for heavy goods vehicles transiting through Austria (**OJ** L341/94)

ECO-R
Regional economic accounts statistical domain on the **REGIO** database

ECOS
European city cooperation scheme. Now within **INTERREG**

ECOS
Commission for Economic and Social Policy within the **CoR**

ECOSA
European Consumer Safety Association.
PO Box 75169, 1070 AD Amsterdam, The Netherlands.
www.ecosa.org

ECOSIM
Ecological and environmental monitoring and simulation system for management decision support in urban areas (a Telematics for Environment project within the **Telematics Applications Programme**)

ECOSOC
Economic and Social Committee

Ecotrim
Eurostat term concerning national accounts: "theoretical analysis of the latest temporal

disaggregation from the national accountants point of view"

ECOTTRIS
European collaboration on transition training for improved safety (**Transport** project)

ECOWAT
Energy efficiency and water supply (**RECITE** project)

ECP
European cooperation programmes for language - teacher training (Action A within **LINGUA**)

ECPC
European Civil Peace Corps

ECPI
European consumer price index. Produced by **Eurostat** and based on the **HCPIs** of the **Member States** (**OJ** C84/95)

ECPRD
European Centre for Parliamentary Research and Documentation. "Set up in 1977 as a network to foster cooperation and exchanges of information between parliamentary libraries and research departments in Europe."
www.ecprd.org/index.asp

ECR
European Centre for the Regions. Barcelona office of the **EIPA**.
20 C/Girona, E-08010 Barcelona, Spain.
www.eipa.nl/barcelona/presentationAWM.htm

ECR
European Commercial Register. A list of companies, maintained by the **European Court of Justice**

ECR
European Court Reports. Reports of Cases before the **European Court of Justice**

ECRE
European Council on Refugees and Exiles. The umbrella organisation for co-operation between European non-governmental organisations concerned with refugees.
Secretariat: Clifton Centre, Unit 22, 3rd Floor, 110 Clifton Street, London EC2A 4HT, UK.
www.ecre.org

ECR-SC
European Court Reports - Staff Cases. *See also* **ECR**

ECS
European Company Statute. *See* **SE** (Societas Europeae)

ECSA
European Community Shipowners' Association.
45 rue Ducale, B-1000 Brussels, Belgium.
www.ecsa.be

ECSA
European Community Studies Association.
www.ecsanet.org

ECSC
European Coal and Steel Community. The first of the Communities to be established, the ECSC entered into force on 23 July 1952 and expired on 23 July 2002. *See also* **Paris Treaty**.
http://europa.eu.int/ecsc/index_en.htm

ECSC Treaty
See **Paris Treaty**

ECSI
European Customer Satisfaction Index.
3 rue du Luxembourg, B-1000 Brussels, Belgium.
www.eoq.org/ECSI.html

ECT
The use of terrestrial model ecosystems to assess environmental risks in ecosystems (an Environmental Health and Chemical Safety Research project within the **Environment and Climate Programme**)

ECTA
European Communities Trade Mark Association.
286 Bisschoppenhoflaan, Box 5, B-2100 Deurne-Antwerpen, Belgium.
www.ecta.org

ECTARC
European Centre for Traditional and Regional Cultures.
Parade Street, Llangollen, Denbighshire, Wales LL20 8RB, UK

ECTI
EU-Canada Trade Initiative.
http://europa.eu.int/comm/trade/bilateral/canada/ecti.htm

ECTN
European Children's Television. A network supported by the **Kaleidoscope** programme

EC Treaty
See **Treaty of Rome**

ECTS
European Community Course Credit Transfer System (established under the **Erasmus** programme)

ECU
European Currency Unit. Replaced by **euro**. *See also* **EMS**

EC-UNRWA
Community contribution to the **United Nations** Relief and Works Agency for Palestine Refugees

Ecup+
European copyright user platform (**Telematics Applications** project)

Ecurie
European Community Urgent Radiological Information Exchange. **Decision** 87/600/Euratom (**OJ** L371/87). Updated by Agreement between the European Atomic Energy Community (**Euratom**) and non-member States of the **European Union** on the participation of the latter in the Community arrangements for the early exchange of information in the event of radiological emergency (OJ C102/03)

ECVAM
European Centre for the Validation of Alternative Methods [to the use of animals in experiments]. Part of the **IHCP** at the **JRC**.
http://ecvam.jrc.it/index.htm

ECVP
European Community's Visitors' Programme. Established by the **European Commission** and the **European Parliament** to enable young leaders from the USA, Canada, Latin American countries, Australia, New Zealand and Japan to visit Europe

ECVP
European Conference on Visual Perception.
www.ecvp.org

ED
European Democrats. Group in the **European Parliament**, 1979-1992. Became part of the **EPP/ED**

ED
European Documentation

EDA
European Dairy Association (Association Laitiere Européenne). Formed from ASSILEC and ASFALEC.

14 rue Montoyer, B-1000 Brussels, Belgium.
http://eda.euromilk.org

EDA
European Democratic Alliance (Rassemblement des démocrates européens - RDE). Group in the **European Parliament** 1988-1994

E-Day
1 January 2002, the date of the final changeover to the **euro**

EDC
European Defence Community. A proposal for a 100,000-strong European army was put to the French National Assembly on 24 October 1950 by French Prime Minister Rene Pleven (hence it being known also as the 'Pleven Plan'). The EDC was created by the 1952 Treaty of Paris, but - along with plans for a European Political Community (**EPC**) - was abandoned in 1954 when the French National Assembly refused to ratify a modified version

EDC
European Documentation Centre. Beginning in 1963 a network of EDCs was set up in universities and higher education institutions to promote the study of European integration. By August 2003 there were 544 Centres (324 in **Member States**). *See also* **Relays**.
http://europa.eu.int/comm/relays/edc/index_en.htm

EDCOMER
European Documentation Centre and Observatory on Migration and Ethnic Relations. Launched in June 1995 with financial support from the Employment and Social Affairs **DG** of the **European Commission**.
Utrecht University, P.O.Box 80.140 - 3508 TC Utrecht, The Netherlands.
www.ercomer.org/edcomer

EDD
Group for a Europe of Democracies and Diversities (of the **European Parliament**).
www.europarl.eu.int/edd

EDDRA
Exchange on Drug Demand Reduction Action. An information system set up by **EMCDDA**.
http://eddra.emcdda.eu.int:8008/eddra

EDF
European Development Fund. Finances programmes in the **ACP** States under the **Cotonou Agreement** (previously the **Lomé Convention**)

EDF
European Disability Forum (Forum européen des personnes handicapées - FEPH).
39-41 rue du Commerce, B-1000 Brussels, Belgium.
www.edf.unicall.be

EDI
Electronic Data Interchange. A European system of electronic links for transborder trade between businesses

EDIC
EC translation service query language on the **Eurodicautom** database

Edicom
Electronic Data Interchange on Commerce. Trans-European network for the collection, production and dissemination of statistics on the trading of goods within the Community and between the Community and non-member countries. **Decision** 507/2001/EC (**OJ** L76/01).
http://europa.eu.int/scadplus/leg/en/lvb/l11034.htm

EDIE
European direct investment in Europe

EDIFACT
"An international multi-sectoral language for exchanging electronic messages".
http://forum.europa.eu.int/irc/dsis/eeg6/info/data/bop/stdEDI.htm

EDIFLOW
Inventory of dataflows exchanged between **Eurostat** and **Member States** (**Eurostat** project)

EDIG
European Defence Industry Group. Members: Austria, Belgium, Denmark, Finland, France, Germany, Greece, Italy, Netherlands, Norway, Portugal, Spain, Sweden, Turkey, UK.
Secretariat: 94 Gulledelle, B5, B-1200 Brussels, Belgium.
www.edig.org

EDIL
Electronic document interchange between libraries (project within Area 5 of the **Telematics Systems Programme**)

EDILIBE
Electronic data interchange for libraries and booksellers in Europe (project within Area 5 of the **Telematics Systems Programme**)

Edinburgh Facility
A temporary lending facility agreed at the December 1992 **Edinburgh Summit** to fund infrastructure projects from **EIB** resources, especially for trans-European transport, telecommunications and energy networks, environmental protection and conservation. *See also* **Edinburgh Growth Initiative**

Edinburgh Growth Initiative
Set up at the December 1992 **Edinburgh Summit** to promote economic recovery in Europe (**COM**(93)54 and COM(93)164). *See also* **Edinburgh Facility**; **EIF**

Edinburgh Summit
Held in December 1992, the Edinburgh European Council discussed: the Danes' rejection of the **Treaty on European Union**; the principle of **subsidiarity**; openness and transparency; Community funding during the 1990s; enlargement (negotiations with EFTA countries); and an initiative to promote growth and to combat unemployment. *See also* **Edinburgh Facility**, **Edinburgh Growth Initiative**

EDI-ROAD
EDI project under the **TEDIS** programme

EDIT
EU Databases Information and Training. UK-based consultancy firm, no longer active

EDITA
European Database for International Trade Activities.
www.edita.org

EDITRANS
EDI project under the **TEDIS** programme

EDITYRE
EDI project under the **TEDIS** programme

EDIUS
European Direct Investment in the USA

EDL
European Day of Languages. Celebrated on 26 September each year. Originally a **Council of Europe** initiative.
http://europa.eu.int/comm/education/policies/lang/languages/day26_en.html and www.ecml.at/edl

EDMC
European Drugs Monitoring Centre. Term occasionally used for the **EMCDDA**

EDN
Europe des Nations (Europe of Nations Group, of the European Parliament). Now **UEN**

EDP
European Development Pole. A transfrontier reconversion zone around Longwy-Aubange-Petange which has received some **Structural Funds** aid

EDPEC
Energy Demonstration Project of the European Communities

EDPS
European Data Protection Supervisor. Established under **Regulation** 45/2001 on the protection of individuals with regard to the processing of personal data by the institutions and bodies of the Community and on the free movement of such data (**OJ** L8/01)

EDPW
European Drug Prevention Week. Held in November 1992, October 1994 and November 1998

EDR
European Document Research.
1100 17th Street, N.W., Suite 301 Washington, DC 200036, USA.
www.europeandocuments.com

EDS
European declarative system (**ESPRIT** project)

E-DSRR
Enhanced digital short range system applications (a Telematics for Education and Training project within the **Telematics Applications Programme**)

EDU
European Democratic Union

EDU
EUROPOL Drugs Unit

EDUC
Commission for Culture and Education within the Committee of the Regions (**CoR**)

EDUCATE
End-user courses in information access through communication technology (project within Area 5 of the **Telematics Systems Programme**)

EEA
European Economic Area. Created in 1992 by an agreement between the European Community and the then seven members of **EFTA**. Membership now comprises the EU Member States plus Iceland, Liechtenstein and Norway.
http://europa.eu.int/comm/external_relations/eea

EEA
European Entertainment Alliance.
C/o UNI-Europa, 31 rue de l'Hôpital, Box 9, B-1000 Brussels, Belgium.

EEA
European Environment Agency. Provides "information to improve Europe's environment". Set up under **Regulation** 1210/90 (**OJ** L120/90).
6 Kongens Nytorv, DK-1050 Copenhagen, Denmark.
www.eea.eu.int

EEA-CC
European Economic Area Consultative Committee. *See also* **EEA**

EEB
European Environmental Bureau.
34 blvd de Waterloo, B-1000 Brussels, Belgium.
www.eeb.org

EEB
European Export Bank

EEC
European Economic Community. Established

by the **Treaty of Rome**, the EEC was the most significant of the Communities set up by the Founding Treaties and became the basis of the **European Community**

EEC Treaty
See **Treaty of Rome**

EEE
Electrical and electronic equipment. *See also* **WEEE**

EEG6
EBES Expert Group 6 - statistics (sponsored by the **IDA** programme)

EEIG
European Economic Interest Group. **Regulation** 2137/85 on (**OJ** L199/85). Previously European Cooperation Grouping (ECG)

EEIS
European Environmental Information Services (a Telematics for Environment project within the **Telematics Applications Programme**)

EEJ-Net
European Extra-Judicial Network.
A network to facilitate access to justice for consumers, especially in cross-border e-commerce disputes.
www.eejnet.org

EEM
Energy efficient electric motors. *See also* **EuroDEEM**

EEMIN
European Environment Monitoring and Information Network (OJ L120/90)

EEMR
Exchange of experience, monitoring and reporting activities (part of the **Phare** programme)

EEMS
European Enterprise Mobility Services

EEO
European Employment Observatory (l'Observatoire européen de l'emploi - OEE). Secretariat: ECOTEC Research and Consulting Ltd, Priestley House, 28-34 Albert Street, Birmingham B4 7UD, UK.
www.eu-employment-observatory.net

EEP
European educational project (within Action 1 of **Comenius**)

EEP
European exchange programme (**Raphael** programme)

EERO
European Environmental Research Organisation.
P0 Box 191, 6700 AD Wageningen, The Netherlands

EES
European Employment Strategy. Launched at the 1997 **Luxembourg Jobs Summit**.
http://europa.eu.int/comm/employment_social/employment_strategy/index_en.htm

EES
European Economic Space. Term sometimes used for the European Economic Area - **EEA**

EESC
European Economic and Social Committee. *See* **Economic and Social Committee**

EESD
Energy, Environment and Sustainable Development. One of the **Thematic Programmes** which form part of the **Fifth Framework Programme**.
www.cordis.lu/eesd

EETP
European educational teleports (a Telematics for Education and Training project within the **Telematics Applications Programme**)

EEU
Eurydice European Unit

eEurope
An initiative launched in December 1999 to bring the benefits of the information society (**IS**) to all Europeans. Specific actions needed to implement the initiative were adopted in the eEurope 2002 Action Plan and subsequently the eEurope 2005 Action Plan.
http://europa.eu.int/information_society/eeurope/2005/index_en.htm

EF
European File. A series of pamphlets published by **OOPEC** which ceased publication with issue 7/92

EF
European Foundation. Shorthand for the **EFILWC**

EFA
European Federation of Agricultural Workers' Unions. Became **EFFAT** in December 2000

EFA
European Film Academy (set up under the **MEDIA** programme)

EFA
European Food Authority. Original name for the European Food Safety Authority (**EFSA**)

EFA
European Free Alliance Group (of the European Parliament). *See* **GREENS/EFA**

EFA
European Federation of Accountants (Fédération des Experts Comptables Européens - **FEE**)

EFAH
European Forum for the Arts and Heritage (Forum Européen pour les Arts et le Patrimoine - FEAP).
10 rue de la Science, B-1000 Brussels, Belgium.
www.efah.org

EFBWW
European Federation of Building and Wood Workers.
45 rue Royale, B-1000 Brussels, Belgium

EFC
Economic and Financial Committee of the EU

EFC
European Foundation Centre

EFCA
European Federation of Engineering Consultancy Associations.
Secretariat: 3-5 av des Arts, B-1210 Brussels, Belgium.
www.efcanet.org

EFCI
European Federation of Cleaning Industries (Fédération Européenne du Nettoyage Industriel - FENI).
www.feni.be

EFER
European Foundation for Entrepreneurship Research

EFEX
European Financial Expertise Network. Identifies European expertise to match the demand for financial sector advice in South East Asia.
200 rue de la Loi, B-1049 Brussels, Belgium.
http://europa.eu.int/comm/internal_market/efex

EFFAS
European Federation of Financial Analysts Societies.
Palais de la Bourse, place de la Bourse, F-75002 Paris, France.
www.effas.com

EFFAT
European Federation of Food, Agriculture and Tourism Workers. Formed December 2000 when the European Federation of Agricultural Workers' Unions (EFA) merged with the European Committee for Food, Catering and Allied Workers' Unions within the IUF (ECF-IUF).
38 rue Fossé-aux-Loups, Boîte 8, B-1000 Brussels, Belgium.
www.effat.org

EFFECT
Environmental forecasting for the effective control of traffic (a Telematics for Environment project within the **Telematics Applications Programme**)

EFFIS
European Forest Fire Information System

EFICS
European Forestry Information and Communications System. Set up by **Regulation** 1615/89. Modified and extended by Regulation 1100/98 - no longer in force (**OJ** L157/98)

EFIEA
European forum on integrated environmental assessment (**Environment and Climate** project)

EFIFC
European Federation of Investment Funds and Companies (**FEFSI** - Fédération Européenne des Fonds et Sociétés d'Investissement)

EFIL
Term sometimes used for the European Foundation for the Improvement of Living and Working Conditions - **EFILWC**

EFILWC
European Foundation for the Improvement of Living and Working Conditions. Set up in 1975 to contribute to the planning and establishment of better living and working conditions (**Regulation** 1365/75, **OJ** L139/75).
Wyattville Road, Loughlinstown, Dublin 18, Ireland.
www.eurofound.eu.int

EFMD
European Foundation for Management Development.
88 rue Gachard, B-1050 Brussels, Belgium.
www.efmd.be

EFN
European Forecasting Network. Established in 2001 to improve the understanding of **euro** area economic developments and to provide economic policy advice.
http://europa.eu.int/comm/economy_finance/efn_en.htm

EFPA
European Food Service and Packaging Association.
Avenue d'Auderghem 67, B-1040, Brussels, Belgium.
www.efpa.com

EFPIA
European Federation of Pharmaceutical Industries and Associations.
108 Rue du Trône, B-1050 Brussels, Belgium.
www.efpia.org

EFPICC
European Fair Practices Copyright Campaign. Organised by **EBLIDA**

EFQM
European Foundation for Quality Management.
15 av des Pléiades, B-1200 Brussels, Belgium.
www.efqm.org

EFSA
European Food Safety Authority. Responsible for providing independent scientific advice on all matters with a direct or indirect impact on food safety. Established January 2002. Originally referred to as the European Food Authority (EFA).
www.efsa.eu.int

EFTA
Electronic Funds Transfer Association.
www.efta.org

EFTA
European Free Trade Association. Currently consists of Iceland, Liechtenstein, Norway and Switzerland. Previous members included Denmark, Finland, Portugal, Sweden, UK.
9-11 rue de Varembé, CH-1202 Geneva 20, Switzerland.
http://secretariat.efta.int/efta

EGE
European Group on Ethics in Science and New Technologies. Previously **GAEIB**.
http://europa.eu.int/comm/european_group_ethics/index_en.htm

EGEO
Environment and Geo-Information Unit. Once part of the Space Applications Institute (**SAI**)

EGLEI
European Group for Local Employment Initiatives (Groupe Européen pour les Initiatives Locales pour l'Emploi). Dissolved 1998

EGNOS
European Geostationary Navigation Overlay Service. A tripartite agreement between the **European Commission**, the European Space Agency (**ESA**) and **Eurocontrol**. EGNOS is the first phase of the EU's policy on a global navigation satellite system, the second phase being the **Galileo** programme. It should be fully operational in 2004.
http://europa.eu.int/comm/dgs/energy_transport/galileo/intro/steps_en.htm

EGPA
European Group of Public Administration (Groupe européen d'Administration publique - GEAP).
A regional group of the International Institute of Administrative Sciences.
1 rue Defacqz, Bte 11, B-1000 Brussels, Belgium.
www.iiasiisa.be/egpa/agacc.htm

EHCR
Electronic health care records support action (a Telematics for Healthcare project within the **Telematics Applications Programme**)

EHLASS
European Home and Leisure Accident Surveillance System. **Decision** 3092/94/EC (1994-1997) (**OJ** L331/94). From 1999 integrated into **INJURY-PREV C**. Previously **HASS**

EHT
Employment in high-tech statistical domain on the **New Cronos** databank

EHTO
European Health Telematics Observatory (a Telematics for Healthcare project within the **Telematics Applications Programme**).
www.ehto.org

EI
Environment Institute. Now Institute for

Environment and Sustainability (**IES**) at the **JRC**

EIA
Environmental Impact Assessment. *See* **Impact Directive**

EIA
European Information Association. Previously **AEDCL**.
Manager: Ms C Webb, Central Library, St Peter's Square, Manchester M2 5PD, UK.
www.eia.org.uk

EIA
Extended impact assessment

EIA Directive
See **Environmental Impact Assessment Directive**

EIARD
European Initiative for Agricultural Research for Development
Executive Secretary: 8 Square de Meeus, B-1050 Brussels, Belgium. *See also* **Infosys**.
www.eiard.org

EIB
European Investment Bank. The Union's long-term financing institution, intended to "contribute towards the integration, balanced development and economic and social cohesion" of the **Member States**.
100 blvd Konrad Adenauer, L-2950 Luxembourg.
www.eib.org

EIB
Evaluation Instruments Bank. Database launched in June 2000 by the European Monitoring Centre for Drugs and Drug Addiction (**EMCDDA**).
http://eibdata.emcdda.eu.int/databases_eib.shtml

EIC
Euro Info Centre. Established in 1987 to help **SME**s take advantage of the Single European Market (**SEM**). Initially 39-strong, the network comprises some 270 Centres which inform, advise and assist businesses. Now part of the **B2Europe** initiative. *See also* **EICC**, **Relays**.
http://europa.eu.int/comm/enterprise/networks/eic/eic.html

EICC
Euro Info Correspondence Centre. Set up, with financial support from the **Phare** programme, to facilitate collaboration between **OCT**s and EU firms, based on the **EIC** network. The network has 14 Centres spread through: Egypt, Gaza, Israel, Jordan, Kosovo, Lebanon, Malta, Switzerland, Syria, Tunisia, Turkey

EICP
European index of consumer prices

EIDHR
European Initiative for Democracy and Human Rights

EIESP
European Institute of Education and Social Policy.
Univerity of Paris, IX-Dauphiné, place du Maréchal de Lattre de Tassigny, F-75116 Paris, France.
www.eiesp.org

EIF
European Internet Forum. An initiative launched by the Information Society **DG** to raise awareness across Europe on internet related questions.
http://europa.eu.int/ISPO/policy/eif/i_Welcome.html

EIF
European Investment Forum. Designed for

companies in the ICT sector seeking private venture capital, the EIF is "Western Europe's leading technology investment event". Partly funded by the **IST** Programme.
Europe Unlimited SA, 7 place E. Flagey, B-1050 Brussels, Belgium.
www.e-unlimited.com

EIF
European Investment Fund. Set up under the **Edinburgh Growth Initiative** to provide financial guarantees to aid economic Growth. **Decision** 94/375/EC (**OJ** L173/94). *See also* **ETF, I-TEC 2**.
43 av J.F.Kennedy, L-2968 Luxembourg.
www.eif.org

Eighth Company Law Directive
Directive 84/253/EEC on the approval of persons responsible for carrying out the statutory audits of accounting documents (**OJ** L126/84).
http://europa.eu.int/scadplus/leg/en/lvb/l26011.htm

EIIA
European Information Industry Association

EIL
European Innovation Loan. A proposed initiative which was never agreed

EIM
Employment Incentive Measures. **Decision** 1145/2002/EC on Community incentive measures in the field of employment (**OJ** L170/02).
http://europa.eu.int/comm/employment_social/incentive_measures/info_en.htm

EIMI
European Innovation Monitoring Initiative. Set up under **SPRINT**, continued as **EIMS**

EIMS
European Innovation Monitoring System. Part of the **INNOVATION** programme. Previously **EIMI**.
www.cordis.lu/eims/home.html

e-Inclusion
Council **Resolution** of 8 October 2001 on "e-Inclusion" - exploiting the opportunities of the information society for social inclusion (**OJ** C292/010)

EINECS
European Inventory of Existing Chemical Substances. *See also* **EINECS-Plus**; **ELINCS**.
http://ecb.jrc.it/existing-chemicals

EINECS-Plus
Version of **EINECS** published by Ovid (previously SilverPlatter) and Croner.CCH

E-INTERFACE
Standardisation of integrated **LAN** services and service access protocols (**ESPRIT** project)

EIOAPP
EIONET telematics application development group (a Telematics for Environment project within the **Telematics Applications Programme**)

EIOL
European infrastructure for open learning (**DELTA** project)

EIONET
European Environment Information and Observation Network. Set up within the **IDA** programme under **Regulation** 1210/90 (**OJ** L120/90). *See also* **MCE**.
www.eionet.eu.int

EIOP
European Integration On-line Papers - "the only peer reviewed E-journal in the field of European integration".
http://eiop.or.at/eiop

EIP
Euro Info Point. *See* **IPE**

EIPA
European Insolvency Practitioners' Association. Now **INSOL**

EIPA
European Institute of Public Administration. Established in 1981, the EIPA is "an independent institute carrying out training and research on public administration and European policies". Satellite offices in Brussels, Luxembourg, Barcelona, Milan.
PO Box 1229, NL-6201 BH Maastricht, The Netherlands.
www.eipa.nl

EIPG
Energy Investment Promotion Group

EIPP
European Innovation Policy Portal

EIPPCB
European IPPC Bureau. Operates within the framework of Article 16(2) of **Directive** 96/61/EC on Integrated Pollution Prevention and Control (**OJ** L257/96). Based at the **JRC**, Seville.
http://eippcb.jrc.es

EIRA
European Industrial Regions Association (Régions Européennes de Technologie industrielle - **RETI**)

EIRENE
European Information Researchers' Network. Secretariat: Charnwood Wing, GRTC, Ashby Rd, Loughborough, Leicestershire LE11 3BJ UK.
www.eirene.com

EIRO
European Industrial Relations **Observatory** at the **EFILWC**. *See also* **EIROnline**

EIROnline
Web database of industrial relations in Europe produced by **EIRO**.
www.eiro.eurofound.ie

EIS
E-mail information service (seen on **DG** Trade website)

EIS
Europe Information Service. Brussels-based publisher, best known for the daily 'European Report'. *See also* **EISnet**.
66-68 av Adolphe Lacomblé, B-1030 Brussels, Belgium.
http://eisnet.eis.be

EIS
European Information Service. A monthly information bulletin published in the UK by the **LGIB**.
www.lgib.gov.uk/eis

EIS
European Information System for customs purposes (**OJ** C316/95)

EIS
European Innovation Scoreboard. Focuses on high-tech innovation and provides 17 main indicators for tracking the EU's progress towards the **Lisbon Strategy**. Part of the European **Trend Chart** on Innovation.
http://trendchart.cordis.lu/Scoreboard2002/index.html

EISBPG
European Information Society Best Practices Gallery. Proposed under the **PROMISE** initiative, but seems to have been dropped

EISnet
Collective term for a web-based information services provided by Europe Information Service (**EIS**)

EISOSH
European information system for occupation safety and health (a Telematics for Healthcare project within the **Telematics Applications Programme**).
www.ehto.org/ht_projects/html/dynamic/29.html

EITC
European IT conference

EJC
European Journalism Centre.
60 Boschstraat, NL- 6211 AX Maastricht, The Netherlands.
www.ejc.nl

EJT
Joint programme to encourage the exchange of young workers within the Community (1985-1991). Continued as **PETRA**

EKORN
EU/Korea **R&D** Network

EL
Elinika (Greek)

ELADIS
European local administrative data integration study (a Telematics for Integrated Applications for Digital Sites project within the **Telematics Applications Programme**)

ELAN
ESPRIT/European local area network (**ESPRIT** project)

ELARG
Enlargement **DG** of the **European Commission**

ELC
Employment and Labour Market Committee. Part of the consultative process for the implementation of employment guidelines across the **European Commission**, **Member State** ministries and social partners

ELC
European Language Council (Conseil Européen pour les Langues - **CEL)**

ELC
Federation of European Food Additives and Food Enzymes Industries. Maintains a list of **E numbers**.
9 av des Gaulois, B-1040 Brussels, Belgium.
www.elc-eu.org

ELCID
European Living Conditions Information Directory. Compiled by the **EFILWC**

ELDONet
European light dosimeter network (an Environmental Health and Chemical Safety Research project within the **Environment and Climate Programme**)

ELDR
Group of the European Liberal Democrat and Reform Party (of the **European Parliament**).
http://eld.europarl.eu.int

ELDRED
European lakes, dams and reservoirs database (**EEA** project)

ELECTRA
Electronic learning environment for continual training and research in Alma (Aachen, Liège, Maastricht and Diepenbeek / Hasselt) (a Telematics for Education and Training project within the **Telematics Applications Programme**)

Electro-Magnetic Compatibility Directive
Directive 89/336/EEC on the approximation of the laws of the **Member States** relating to electromagnetic compatibility (**OJ** L139/89)

ELENA
Power range with fully integrated electronic control system for high efficiency low emission vehicles (**EUREKA** project)

Eleventh VAT Directive
Directive 80/368/EEC of 26 March 1980 on the harmonization of the laws of the **Member States** relating to turnover taxes - exclusion of the French overseas departments from the scope of Directive 77/388/EEC (**OJ** L90/80)

ELGODIPINE
Anti-anginal calcium antagonist (**EUREKA** project)

ELIA
European League of Institutes of the Arts.
105 Keizersgracht, 1015 CH Amsterdam, The Netherlands.
www.elia-artschools.org

eLIG
eLearning Industry Group Recommendations to enhance e-Learning in Europe.
Mr. Barry Brennan, Project Manager, International Co-operation Europe Ltd. - ICEL, 265 av de Fré, Bte 27, 1180 Uccle, Brussels, Belgium.
www.elig.org

ELINCS
European List of Notified Chemical Substances. Supplements **EINECS**.
http://ecb.jrc.it/existing-chemicals

ELIS
Electrical installation system (**EUREKA** project)

ELISE
Electronic library image service for Europe (project within Area 5 of the **Telematics Systems Programme**)

ELISE
European loan insurance scheme for employment. Premiums are linked to loan guarantees from the **EIF**

ELK
EIB's liquid Kronor programme

ELO
Elusive office (**ESPRIT** project)

ELO
European Liaison Officer. Generic term for (usually) a local government employee who deals with European funding issues

ELOISE
European land-ocean interaction studies. Part of an initiative on integrated coastal zone management.
http://europa.eu.int/comm/dg12/eloise/eloise-p.html

ELPRO
Electronic public procurement system for Europe (a Telematics for Administrations project within the **Telematics Applications Programme**)

ELRA
European Language Resources Association (Association Européenne pour les Ressources Linguistiques - AERL).
55-57 rue Brillat Savarin, F-75013 Paris, France.
www.elra.info

ELS
European licensing system. In the context of regulatory procedures associated with marketing authorisation of medicinal products

ELSA
Electronic library SGML applications. Project within Area 5 of the **Telematics Systems Programme**

ELSA
Ethical, legal and social aspects (of the Life Sciences and Technologies of the **Fourth Framework Programme** 1994-1998).
www.cordis.lu/elsa/home.html

ELSA
European Laboratory for Structural Assessment at **Ispra**.
www.elsa.jrc.it

ELSA
European Law Students' Association.
1 rue Defacqz, B-1050 Brussels, Belgium.
www.elsa-online.org

ELSNET
European Network of Excellence in Human Language Technologies.
www.elsnet.org

El Teide Declaration
A joint initiative of the **European Commission** and the Spanish **Presidency**, intended to halt bio-diversity loss by 2010. Presented in Tenerife on 9 May 2002 at a conference organised to mark the 10th anniversary of the **Habitats Directive**

ELTIS
European Local Transport Information Service.
ELTIS Helpdesk, University of the West of England, Room 2Q17, Faculty of the Built Environment, Frenchay Campus, Coldharbour Lane, Bristol BS16 1QY, UK.
www.eltis.org

ELVIL
European Legislative Virtual Library.
http://elvil.sub.su.se/sam/elvil.htm

ELVs
Emission limit values

ELVs
End of life vehicles

ELWW
European laboratory without walls. Also seen as European Laboratories without walls

Elysée Treaty
Popular name for the Treaty of Friendship and Reconciliation, signed in Paris in 1963 by French President de Gaulle and West German Prime Minister Adenauer

Elysée Treaty
Proposed name for what became the **Dayton Accords**

EM
European Movement (Mouvement Européen). Founded in 1948, to «contribute to the establishment of a united, federal Europe founded on the respect of basic rights, peace principles, democratic principles of liberty and solidarity, and citizens' participation».
25 square de Meeûs, B-1000 Brussels, Belgium.
www.europeanmovement.org

EMAIL
Environmental management architecture for information delivery (a Telematics for Environment project within the **Telematics Applications Programme**)

EMAS
Eco-Management and Audit Scheme. "A voluntary scheme for organisations willing to commit themselves to evaluate and improve their environmental performance." Launched 1995, revised 2001.
http://europa.eu.int/comm/environment/emas

EMBA
Management of technology in a European environment (**COMETT** project)

EMBO
European Molecular Biology Organization.
1 Meyerhofstraße, D-69117 Heidelberg,

Germany.
www.embo.org

EMC
Electromagnetic compatibility. *See also* **EMC Directive**

EMC
ESPRIT Management Committee

EMC
European Managers' Confederation (Confédération Européenne des Cadres - **CEC**)

EMC Directive
Directive 89/336/EEC on the approximation of the laws of the **Member States** relating to electromagnetic compatibility (**OJ** L139/89)

EMCC
European Monitoring Centre on Change. Established in 2001 by the European Foundation for the Improvement of Living and Working Conditions (**EFILWC**).
www.eurofound.eu.int/emcc/emcc.htm

EMCDDA
European Monitoring Centre for Drugs and Drug Addiction. Set up by **Regulation** 302/93 (**OJ** L36/93).
23-25 rua da Cruz de Santa Apólina, PT-1149-045 Lisbon, Portugal.
www.emcdda.eu.int

EMCEF
European Mine, Chemical and Energy Workers' Federation.
109 av Emile de Béco, B-1050 Brussels, Belgium.
www.emcef.org

EMCF
European Monetary Cooperation Fund. Dissolved - assets and liabilities passed to the European Monetary Institute (EMI)

EMEA
European Agency for the Evaluation of Medicinal Products. Set up by **Regulation** 2309/93 (**OJ** L214/93).
7 Westferry Circus, Canary Wharf, London E14 4HB, UK.
www.emea.eu.int

EMEP
Co-operative Programme for Monitoring and Evaluation of the Long-Range Transmission of Air Pollutants in Europe. **Decision** 86/277/EEC (**OJ** L181/86).
www.emep.int

EMF
European Monetary Fund. Created by '**Resolution** of the European Council of 5 December 1978 on the establishment of the European Monetary System (**EMS**) and related matters', following a proposal in the **Stuttgart Declaration**

EMF
European Multimedia Forum.
9 rue du Moniteur , B-1000 Brussels, Belgium.
www.e-multimedia.org

EMI
European Monetary Institute. Established under the **Treaty on European Union**. Forerunner of the **ECB**

EMIRE
Online version of the European Employment and Industrial Relations Glossaries. Compiled by the **EFILWC**.
www.eurofound.eu.int/emire/emire.html

EMiReC
European Mineral Resources RTD Council. Details via:
www.euromines.org

EMMA
European marine motorways (**Transport**

project).
www.cordis.lu/transport/src/emma.htm

EMMA
Integrated environmental monitoring, forecasting and warning systems in metropolitan areas (a Telematics for Environment project within the **Telematics Applications Programme**)

EMMI
Euregional multimedia information exchange (a Telematics for Administrations project within the **Telematics Applications Programme**).
www.cs.unimaas.nl/res/otherres/pubserv/pro/emmi.htm

EMMIS
Evaluation of man/machine interaction (**DRIVE** project)

EMOT
European masters programme in management of technology (**COMETT** project)

EMP
European Database of Medicinal Products. Available via **EudraNet**.
http://eudraportal.eudra.org

EMPL
Employment and Social Affairs **DG** of the **European Commission**

EMPL
European Parliament Committee on Employment and Social Affairs

EMPLOY
Employment statistical domain on the **New Cronos** databank

EMPLOY
European multimedia pedagogic local support network organisation for the social integration of unemployed young Europeans (a Telematics for Urban and Rural Areas project within the **Telematics Applications Programme**)

EMPLOYMENT
A **Community Initiative** on employment and the development of human resources (1994-1999) (Guidelines in **OJ** C180/94). Consisted of four strands: **HORIZON**; **INTEGRA**; **NOW** and **YOUTHSTART**. Continued as **EQUAL**

Employment Confidence Pact
Alternative term for **European Confidence Pact**

Employment, Growth and Competitiveness
White Paper on growth, competitiveness, and employment: The challenges and ways forward into the 21st century (**COM**(93)700).
http://europa.eu.int/en/record/white/c93700/contents.html

EMS
Enzymatic modification of soy proteins (**EUREKA** project)

EMS
European Monetary System. A system of fixed, but adjustable exchange rates, introduced in March 1979 as a precursor to **EMU** (**OJ** L379/78)

EMSA
European Maritime Safety Agency. Set up following the **Erika** disaster.
http://europa.eu.int/agencies/emsa/index_en.htm

EMTF
Educational Multimedia Task Force. Set up by the **European Commission** to study and develop educational and cultural products

across Europe.
www.ecotec.com/mes

EMU
Economic and Monetary Union. A process which resulted in the adoption of the Single European Currency (the **euro**) in January 1999.
See also **Convergence Criteria**; **Convergence Report**; **EMS**; **'ins'**; **'pre-ins'**; **Stability and Growth Pact**; **Werner Report**.
http://europa.eu.int/scadplus/leg/en/lvb/l25007.htm

EMU
Economic and Monetary Union campaign (within **PRINCE**)

EMUA
European monetary unit of account

EMUNET
Early website on **EMU**. Was at www.euro-emu.co.uk, but no longer available

EN
English

EN
Euronorm

ENABLE
Enabler for access to computer-based vocational tasks with language and speech (a Telematics for Disabled and Elderly People project within the **Telematics Applications Programme**)

ENAM
European North Atlantic margin: quantification and modelling of large-scale sedimentary processes and fluxes (**MAST III** project)

ENAR
European Network Against Racism (Réseau européen contre le racisme).
43 rue de la Charité, B-1210 Brussels, Belgium.
www.enar-eu.org

ENCATA
European network of centres for the advancement of telematics in urban and rural areas (a Telematics for Urban and Rural Areas project within the **Telematics Applications Programme**)

ENCORE
European network of catchments organised for research on ecosystems (**STEP** project)

END
Environmental Noise Directive: 2002/49/EC relating to the assessment and management of environmental noise (**OJ** L189/02)

ENDEF
European Non-Destructive Evaluation Forum. An expert group, managed by the Energy **DG** of the **European Commission**

ENDHASP
European Network of Drug and HIV/AIDS Services in Prisons. Part of the five-year Community programme for the prevention of drug dependence (1996-2000)

ENDOC
On-line directory of environmental information and documentation centres in the **Member States**. Ceased in June 1989

ENDS
European nuclear documentation system

ENDS Report
A publication from Environmental Data Services:
www.ends.co.uk

ENER
Energy **DG** of the **European Commission**

ENER
European Parliament Committee on Energy, Research and Technology

Energetic Friends
Project set up as part of **European Science Week** 2001.

ENERGIE
The Energy subprogramme within the **EESD** programme (1999-2002). Successor to **JOULE-THERMIE**.
www.cordis.lu/eesd/home.html

ENERGY
Regional energy statistical domain on the **REGIO** database

Energy Charter
See **European Energy Charter Treaty**

Energy Star
The United States registered certification mark, owned by the United States Environmental Protection Agency. Adopted by the EU in an agreement with the US on the coordination of energy-efficient labelling programmes (**COM**(99)328).
http://europa.eu.int/comm/energy/en/ener-star-prog.html

ENFOPOL
According to Statewatch, a **Council of the European Union** acronym "for hundreds of reports concerning "Police cooperation" in the EU". See: www.statewatch.org/eufbi/news4.htm

Engineers' Directive
Proposed **Directive** (first presented in 1969) for the mutual recognition of diplomas in engineering

ENIG
Environment Information Group: a permanent Working Group

ENIP
European Neuroscience **Industrial Platform**. Seen also as E.NIP and E-NIP.
http://europa.eu.int/comm/dg12/biotech/ip2.html#ENIP

ENIQ
European Network for Inspection Qualification. A network established by the **JRC** on the verification of the effectiveness and performance of inspection techniques in nuclear plants. www.jrc.nl/eniq

ENIVD
European Network for Diagnostics of 'Imported' Viral Diseases.
www.enivd.org

Enlargement
Term used for the growth of the **European Community / European Union** as more countries join. Since 1952, the **6** original **Member States** have been joined by:

1973: Denmark, Ireland, United Kingdom
1981: Greece
1986: Portugal, Spain
1995: Austria, Finland, Sweden
2004: Cyprus, Czech Republic, Estonia, Hungary, Latvia, Lithuania, Malta, Poland, Slovakia, Slovenia.

See also **Applicant Countries**.
http://europa.eu.int/comm/enlargement/index_en.html

ENLIST
European network for legal information, study and training (**EMTF** project).
www.ecotec.com/mes/projects/enlist.html

ENMP
European Network Male Prostitution.
159 Stadhouderskade, 1074 BC, Amsterdam, The Netherlands.
www.enmp.org

ENN
European Neurological Network (a Telematics

for Healthcare project within the **Telematics Applications Programme**)

ENOS
European network of ocean stations (**COST** action project)

ENOW
European Network of Women (also seen as ENW)

Enrich
European network for research into global change. Part of the **Environment and Climate Programme** to provide networking and to promote regional cooperation with developing countries in the global environment field (**OJ** C306/96)

ENS
European Nervous Systems (project within the **Telematics Systems Programme**)

ENS
European network and services. A project under the **INNOVATION** programme

ENSR
European Network for **SME** Research.
Founded by EIM Netherlands, 33 Italiëlaan, P.O. box 7001, 2701 AA Zoetermeer, The Netherlands.
www.eim.nl

ENTA
European Network for the Treatment of **AIDS**.
Prof N Clumeck, Hôpital St Pierre, 322 rue Haute, B-1000 Brussels, Belgium

ENTP
European network of training partnerships (under the **PETRA** programme)

ENTR
Enterprise **DG** of the **European Commission**

E numbers
Code numbers for additives (antioxidants, colourants, preservatives) in foodstuffs and animal feed. No complete list is published officially, but one is maintained by the **ELC**: www.elc-eu.org/default.htm

ENV
Environment **DG** of the **European Commission**

ENV
Environment and Climate Programme

ENVI
European Parliament Committee on the Environment, public health and consumer policy

ENVIB
Development of integrated systems for environmental mechanical vibration testing (**EUREKA** project)

ENVINET
Group of **EUREKA** projects

ENVIREG
Regional environment. A **Structural Funds** initiative to protect the environment and to promote economic development (1990-1993) (Guidelines in **OJ** C115/90)

ENVIROCITY
Public environmental information services (a Telematics for Environment project within the **Telematics Applications Programme**)

ENVIRONET
Transfer of expertise in urban planning and environmental protection from developed cities to disadvantaged ones (**RECITE** project)

ENVIRONMENT
Activity 3 of the **Fourth Framework Programme**

Environment 2010
The Union's 6th Environment Action Programme (**EAP**)

Environment and Climate Programme
Set up by **Decision** 94/911/EC for an **Environment and Climate Programme** (1994-1998) (**OJ** L361/94). Replaced by **EESD**. Previously **EPOCH**; **STEP**.
www.cordis.lu/env/home.html

Environmental Impact Assessment Directive
Directive 85/337/EEC of 27 June 1985 on the assessment of the effects of certain public and private projects on the environment (OJ L175/85)

Environmental Noise Directive
Directive 2002/49/EC relating to the assessment and management of environmental noise (OJ L189/02)

EnviroWindows
An "information marketplace for businesses, local authorities and their stakeholders", developed by the European Environment Agency (**EEA**).
http://ewindows.eu.org

ENVISION
Environmental vision. Part of the Annual Work Programme of the European Environment Agency (**EEA**)

ENVISYS
Environmental monitoring warning and emergency system (a Telematics for Environment project within the **Telematics Applications Programme**)

ENW
European Network of Women (also seen as ENOW)

EOCS:HSC
European occupational case studies in health and social care (a Telematics for Healthcare project within the **Telematics Applications Programme**)

EOCTP
European Developing Countries Clinical Trials Partnership.
http://edctp.cineca.org

EOD
Enseignement ouvert et à distance (open and distance learning - **ODL**)

EODS
European occupational diseases statistics

EOI
European organ index (**Raphael** programme)

EoI
Expression of interest

EON 2000
A research project to implement the **Habitats Directive**

EORCU
European Ozone Research Coordinating Unit.
14 Union Road, Cambridge CB2 1HE, UK.
www.ozone-sec.ch.cam.ac.uk

EOTA
European Organisation for Technical Approvals.
40 av des Arts, B-1040 Brussels, Belgium.
www.eota.be

EOTC
European Organisation for Conformity Assessment (previously European Organisation for Testing and Certification).
36 rue de Stassart, B-1050 Brussels, Belgium.
www.eotc.be

EOU
Export Orientated Units. An export subsidy scheme. *See also* **DEPB**; **EPCGS**; **EPZ**; **ITES**

EOWM
Equal Opportunities for Women and Men.
http://europa.eu.int/comm/employment_social/equ_opp/index_en.htm

EP
European Parliament

EPA
European Parents' Association (Association Européenne des Parents d'Élèves).
1A rue du Champ de Mars, B-1050 Brussels, Belgium.
www.epa-parents.org

EPADES
Forerunner of the **EUROPARL** website

EPBN
European Plant Biotechnology Network. Launched in 1998 to promote the networking, exploitation and dissemination of the results of pan-European projects in this field (part of the **BIOTECH** programme)

EPC
European Patent Convention. Council Agreement 89/695/EEC (**OJ** L401/89)

EPC
Economic Policy Committee

EPC
Environmental Policy Centre. Established 1992. Also seen as EPCE. Taken over by Enhesa.
15 rue du Mail, B-1050 Brussels, Belgium.
www.epce.com

EPC
European Policy Centre. A Brussels-based think-tank.
Residence Palace, 155 rue de la Loi, B-1040 Brussels, Belgium.
www.theepc.be

EPC
European Political Cooperation. Informally introduced in 1970 and incorporated into the **SEA**

EPCE
Alternative for Environmental Policy Centre (**EPC**)

EPCGS
Export Promotion Capital Goods Scheme. An export subsidy scheme. *See also* **DEPB**; **EOU**; **EPZ**; **ITES**

EP Doc
'European Parliament document'. Reports of the **European Parliament**

EPE
Environmental Protection Expenditure

EPER
European Pollutant Emission Register. **Decision** 2000/479/EC on the implementation of a European pollutant emission register (**OJ** L192/00).
http://europa.eu.int/comm/environment/ippc/eper

EPHOS
European Procurement Handbook for Open Systems. Version 7 published 1992 as EUR 14021. *Replaced by* **SPRITE-S2**

EPI
Environmental policy integration

EPI
Institute of Professional Representatives before the European Patent Office.
P.O.Box 260112, D-80058 München, Germany.
www.patentepi.com

EPIAM
Knowledge-based system for epidemiology (**AIM** project)

EPIC
Early process design integrated with controls (**ESPRIT** project)

EPIC
Electronic Privacy Information Center. US organisation established in 1994 "to focus public attention on emerging civil liberties issues".
www.epic.org

EPIC
European prospective investigation of cancer

EPIC
European prototype for integrated care. An **AIM** project.
www.ehto.org/aim/volume2/epic.html

EPIC
European Public Information Centre. A network in UK public libraries established by the Commission **Representation** in the UK. Previously Public Information Relay (**PIR**). *See also* **Relays**

EPICENTRE
Proposed centralised **European Parliament** library service to be housed in the EP building in Brussels. Once completed, however, it became known as the Parliamentary Documentation Centre

EPID COMAC
Epidemiology Concerted Action Committee

EPIOPTIC
European project: investigation of optical probe techniques for interface characterisation (**ESPRIT** project)

EPI-RAID
Evaluation of prototype and improvement to RAID workstation (**TIDE** project)

EPIs
Electronic payment instruments.
http://europa.eu.int/comm/internal_market/payments/index_en.htm

Epistel
See **OVIDE/Epistel**

EPITELIO Network
Excluded people integration by the use of telematic innovative opportunities - network (a Telematics for Urban and Rural Areas project within the **Telematics Applications Programme**)

EPLOT
Enhanced performance lasers for optical transmission (**RACE** project)

EPO
European Patent Office. Set up in 1973. Not an EU body.
27 Erhardtstrasse, D-80331 München, Germany.
www.european-patent-office.org

EPOC
Employee direct participation in organisational change. An **EFILWC** project to stimulate debate between the social partners and the EU **Institutions**

EPOCH
European Programme on Climatology and Natural Hazards (1989-1993) (**OJ** L359/89). Continued as **Environment and Climate Programme**

E-POLL
Electronic polling system for remote voting operations (**IST** project)

EPOQUE
EP on-line query. A restricted access documentary database covering the work of the **European Parliament** and Sessional documents. *Replaced* **PARDOC** and **PARQ**

EPOS
European PTT open learning service (**DELTA** project)

EPP/ED
European People's Party / European Democrats. Group in the **European Parliament**.
http://epp-ed.europarl.eu.int/home/en/default.asp

EPPIC
Thematic research network for the paper and pulp industry under the **Sixth Framework Programme**

EPQ
European Parliamentary Question

EPRD
European Programme for Reconstruction and Development. **Decision** 94/822/EC (1996-1999) established an agreement between the EU and the Republic of South Africa for the support of specific projects (**OJ** L341/94)

EPROM
Study and development and industrialisation of integrated circuit non-volatile memory having storage capacity of 16 Mbit (**EUREKA** project)

EPSECC
Environmental policy, social exclusion and climate change (**Environment and Climate** project)

EPSILON
Advanced knowledge base management system (**ESPRIT** project)

ePSO
Electronic Payment Systems Observatory. Run by the European Central Bank (**ECB**). Publishes a monthly electronic newsletter ePSO-N.
www.e-pso.info/epso/index.html

EPSO
European Communities Personnel Selection Office (Office européen de sélection du personnel - OESP). Established July 2002.
http://europa.eu.int/epso/

EPSO
European Plant Science Organisation.
927 Technologiepark, 9052 Gent, Belgium.
www.epsoweb.org

ePSO-N
See **ePSO**

EPSP
European peer support project. Part of the five-year Community programme for the prevention of drug dependence (1996-2000)

EPSU
European Federation of Public Service Unions (Fédération Syndicale Européenne des Services Publics - FSESP).
45 rue Royale, B-1000 Brussels, Belgium.
www.epsu.org

EPTA
European Parliamentary Technology Assessment. A network linking the **STOA** Unit with parliamentary technological assessment bodies in Denmark, France, Germany, the Netherlands and the UK. *See also* **ETAN**

EPU
European Payments Union

EPU
European Political Union

EPZ
Export processing zones. An export subsidy scheme. *See also* **DEPB**; **EOU**; **EPCGS**; **ITES**

EQUAL
Electronic services for a better quality of life (a Telematics for Integrated Applications for Digital Sites project within the **Telematics Applications Programme**)

EQUAL
Transnational cooperation to combat all forms of discrimination and inequalities in the labour market (2000-2006). A **Community Initiative**.
http://europa.eu.int/comm/employment_social/equal/index_en.html

Equal Pay Directive
Directive 75/117/EEC on the approximation of the laws of the **Member States** relating to the application of the principle of equal pay for men and women (**OJ** L45/75)

Equal Treatment Directive
Directive 76/207/EEC of 9 February 1976 on the implementation of the principle of equal treatment for men and women as regards access to employment, vocational training and promotion, and working conditions (**OJ** L39/76)

EQUALITY
Extending quality urban service for added-value living using interactive telematic systems (a Telematics for Urban and Rural Areas project within the **Telematics Applications Programme**)

Equal Opportunities for Women
Abbreviated form of 'Equal Opportunities for Women and Men' (**EOWM**)

EQUASIS
Established in 2000 by the **European Commission** and the French Maritime Administration, Equasis is an information system intended to collect and disseminate quality and safety-related information on merchant ships.
www.equasis.org

EQUATOR
Environment for qualitative temporal reasoning (**ESPRIT** project)

EQUICERA
Thermomechanical ceramic heating equipment (**EUREKA** project)

EQUUS
Efficient qualitative and quantitative use of KBSs in financial management (**ESPRIT** project)

ER
Technical group of the European Right (of the **European Parliament,** 1984-89). Also known as DR

ERA
European Radical Alliance (Group in the **European Parliament**, 4th parliamentary term 1994-1999). Seen also as ARE: Alliance Radicale Européenne

ERA
European Regions Airline Association.
Baker Suite, Fairoaks Airport, Chobham, Woking, Surrey G024 8HX, UK.
www.eraa.org

ERA
European Research Area.
http://europa.eu.int/comm/research/era/index_en.html

Erasmus
European Community action scheme for the mobility of university students (1987-1994) (**OJ** L395/89). Continued within the **Socrates** programme

ERB
ESPRIT Review Board

ERB
Enterprise Rapprochement Bureau

ERC
European Radiocommunications Committee. Sub-committee of **CEPT**

ERC
European Reference Centre. A now defunct network which supplied primarily free EU information; based primarily in colleges and public libraries

ERC
European Research Council

ERC
European Resource Centre for Schools and Colleges. An initiative of the Commission **Representation** in the UK to provide EU information direct to schools and colleges. Some disbanded when Commission funding ceased. A type of **Relay**

ERCOM
Solution to the recycling problems due to the use of reinforced plastics in the industry (**EUREKA** project)

ERCSC
European Resource Centres for Schools and Colleges. *See* **ERC**

ERDF
European Regional Development Fund (Fonds Européen de Développement Régional - FEDER). Intended to promote economic and social cohesion in the **Member States**. One of the **Structural Funds**.
http://europa.eu.int/scadplus/leg/en/lvb/l60015.htm

ERDS
European Reliability Data System (**JRC** - reactor safety). *See also* **AORS**; **CEDB**; **GRPDS**; **OUSR**

ERF
European Research Forum. Advises on EU Science and Technology policy. Created by **Decision** 98/611/EC on the creation of the European Research Forum (**OJ** L290/98). Superseded **ESTA**.
http://europa.eu.int/comm/research/erf.html

ERGO
European research gateway on-line. **R&D** project involving the creation of a website covering around 71,000 research projects.
www.cordis.lu/ergo

ERGO II
Action programme for the long-term unemployed (1993-1996)

ERICA
European Research into Consumer Affairs.
www.net-consumers.org/erica/index.htm

Erika I, Erika II
Two packages of legislative proposals adopted in response to the December 1999 disaster in which a single-hull oil tanker, the Erika, broke in two off the southern tip of Brittany. The resulting pollution affected some 400 kilometres of French coastline. In March 2000 the **European Commission** adopted a series of proposals (Erika I) intended to address some of the environmental issues, and in December 2000 agreed a second set of measures (Erika II).
http://europa.eu.int/comm/transport/maritime/safety/erika_en.htm

ERIO
European Roma Information Office

ERIS@
European Regional Information Society Association.
19 rue de Pavie, B-1000 Brussels, Belgium.
www.erisa.be

ERIT
Federation of European Professionals Working in the Field of Drug Abuse. Part of the five-year Community programme for the prevention of drug dependence (1996-2000).
www.erit.org

ERLAP
European Reference Laboratory for Air Pollution. Part of the **IES**

ERM / ERM2
Exchange Rate Mechanism / New Exchange Rate Mechanism (of the **EMS**)

ERMES
European Radio Messaging System (**OJ** L310/90)

EROMM
European register of microform master (project within Area 5 of the **Telematics Systems Programme**)

EROS 2000
European river ocean system (**MAST/STEP** programme)

ERRAC
European Rail Research Advisory Council.
www.errac.org

ERRF
European Rapid Reaction Force. Expanded form of Rapid Reaction Force - **RRF**

ERS
European Safety Reporting System. Electronic reporting system for transmission and management of safety reports in pharmacovigilance. Now **EudraVigilance**

ERSTI
European Report on Science and Technology Indicators

ERT
European Round Table of Industrialists.
113 av Henri Jaspar, B-1060 Brussels, Belgium.
www.ert.be

ERTA case
European Court of Justice Case 22/70, Commission v Council, concerning a proposed European Road Transport Agreement, which established Community competence in external relations

ERTICO
Intelligent Transport Systems Europe.
Blue Tower, 326 av Louise, B-1050 Brussels, Belgium.
www.ertico.com

ERTIS
European road transport information services (**EUREKA** project)

ERTMS
European rail traffic management system (**EURET** project)

ERW
An office system research workstation for Europe (**ESPRIT** project)

ES
Español / Espagnol (Spanish)

ES2
Automatic design and production of custom chips using direct printing on silicon (**EUREKA** project)

ESA
Employment and Social Affairs. A series of periodicals which replaced the series *Social Europe*

ESA
European Seed Association. Established 2000, by merging AMUFOC, ASSOPOMAC, COMASSO, COSEMCO.
11 av Michel Ange, B-1000 Brussels, Belgium.
www.euroseeds.org

ESA
European Space Agency.
8-10 rue Mario Nikis, F-75738 Paris Cédex 15, France.
www.esa.int

ESA 95
Regulation 2223/96 on the European system of national and regional accounts in the Community (**OJ** L310/96)

ESAC
ECVAM Scientific Advisory Committee

ESAM
European Seals Administration Manager

ESATT
European Science and Technology Transfer Network (**Copernicus** project). *See also* **RICE**

ESAVS
European School for Postgraduate Veterinary Training and Continuing Education (**COMETT** project)

ESAW
European Statistics on Accidents at Work. A **Eurostat** and Employment and Social Affairs **DG** project to establish comparable EU statistics on accidents at work

ESB
European Soil Bureau. A project at the Institute for Environment and Sustainability (**IES**).
http://ies.jrc.cec.eu.int/Projects/ESB/

ESB1 / ESB2
Temporary **European Parliament** committees of inquiry into BSE (bovine spongiform encephalopathy). ESB2 was specifically to monitor action taken in response to recommendations on BSE

ESBG
European Saving Banks Group (Groupement Européen des Caisses d'Epargne).
11 rue Marie Thérèse, B-1000 Brussels, Belgium.
www.savings-banks.com

ESC
Economic and Social Committee - popular term for European Economic and Social Committee

ESCAPE
Entangled sulphur and carbon cycles in phaeocystis dominated ecosystems (**ELOISE** project)

ESCAPE
Group of **EUREKA** projects

ESCB
European System of Central Banks. Comprises the **ECB** and **NCB**s.
www.ecb.int

ESCF
European Seed Capital Funds

ESD
Protection for submicron technologies (**ESPRIT** project)

ESDA
European Security and Defence Assembly. Proposed by the **WEU** Assembly to monitor the activities of EU security bodies. The proposal was made in March 2000 in Lisbon, and is known as the 'Lisbon Initiative'

ESDEP
European steel design education programme (**COMETT** project)

ESDI
European Security and Defence Identity. The Declaration on Western European Union annexed to the 1992 **Treaty on European Union** noted the "need to develop a genuine European security and defence identity"

ESDIS
Employment and Social Dimension of the Information Society (**IS**)

ESDP
European Security and Defence Policy

ESDP
European Spatial Development Perspective. Adopted by the informal **Council of the European Union** responsible for spatial planning, at its meeting in Potsdam in May 1999

ESF
EUREKA software factory (**EUREKA** project)

ESF
Europe sans frontiers (Europe without frontiers). Term used to describe the concept of the Single European Market (**SEM**)

ESF
European Science Foundation.
1 quai Lezay Marnésia, F-67080 Strasbourg, France.
www.esf.org

ESF
European Social Fund. One of the **Structural Funds**.
http://europa.eu.int/comm/employment_social/esf2000/index.htm

ESI
Economic sentiment indicator

ESIF
European security and intelligence force

ESIF
European Service Industries Forum.
26 Markt, B-9700 Oudenarde, Belgium

ESIG
European Solvents Industry Group.
www.esig.org

ESIMEAU
Information technologies for the modeling of water resources in semi-arid zones. Partly funded by **INCO-DC** and **ESPRIT**.

ESIS
European Survey of Information Society Projects and Actions. An inventory of European Information Society (**IS**) projects and actions, initially running for two years from February 1997 (**ISPO**-led project).
http://europa.eu.int/ISPO/esis/default.htm

ESLA
Ethical, social and legal aspects of human genome analysis. Continued by **HEF**

ESmail
E-mail bulletin from the Employment and Social Affairs **DG**. Previously 5mail.
http://europa.eu.int/comm/dgs/employment_social/esmail_en.htm

ESM-BASE
Author support for student modelling in multimedia learning processes (**DELTA** project)

ESOP II
European sub Polar ocean programme phase II: the thermohaline circulation in the Greenland sea (**MAST III** project)

ESP
Ebit service project (**RACE** project)

esp@cenet
EPO service to provide enterprises with free patent information.
www.european-patent-office.org/espacenet

ESPITI
European software process improvement training initiative (part of the **ESSI** project)

ESPO
European Sea Ports Organisation.
6 Treurenberg, B-1000 Brussels, Belgium.
www.espo.be

ESPOIR
European shoe programme on instant response (**SPRINT** project)

ESPON
European Spatial Planning Observatory Network (part of the **ESDP**)

ESPRIT
Information technologies programme. Part of the **Fourth Framework Programme**. Continued as **IST**.
www.cordis.lu/esprit/home.html

ESQUIRE
Education science and quality assurance in radiotherapy in Europe

ESRO
European Space Research Organisation. Now **ESA**

ESS
European statistical system

Essen Priorities
Five key areas for action on employment, established at the 1994 **Essen Summit** (**COM**(95)250).
www.europarl.eu.int/factsheets/4_8_3_en.htm

Essen Summit
The December 1994 Essen **European Council** included discussions on a European employment strategy; preparing Central and Eastern European countries for EU accession; extending the **LEONARDO** and **SOCRATES** programmes to the associated countries; and establishing Trans European Networks

ESSENTIAL
European systems strategy for evolution of new technology in advanced learning (**DELTA** project)

ESSI
European software and systems initiative (**ESPRIT** project)

ESSN
European senior service network which is designed to help the management of enterprises in **Tacis** countries

ESSOR
Essais Orgel - a 25 MW experimental reactor constructed in the mid-1960's at **Ispra**

ESSPROS
European system of integrated social protection statistics

ESTA
European Science and Technology Assembly. Established 1994 to assist the **European Commission** implement EU research. Replaced in 1998 by the European Research Forum (**ERF**). http://europa.eu.int/comm/dg12/esta/index.html

ESTAT
Eurostat **DG** of the **European Commission**

Ester
European source term code system. A Community initiative in the analysis of **LWR** to stimulate collaboration between laboratories. Coordinated by the **JRC**

ESTI
European Society of Transport Institutes

ESTI
European solar test installation at **Ispra**

ESTO
European Science and Technology Observatory. Developed by **IPTS** and part of the **JRC**.
http://esto.jrc.es

ESTPER
European severe trauma perspective (**EMTF** project).
www.ecotec.com/mes/projects/estper.html

ESTRI
Electronic standard for the transfer of regulatory information

ESU
European size unit

ET
Education in the transport sector (**COMETT** project)

ETA
European Technical Approval (for construction products) under **Decision** 94/23/EC (**OJ** L17/94)

ETAG
EURONET Technical Aspects Working Group

ETAN
European Technology Assessment Network. Succeeded by **STRATA**.
www.cordis.lu/etan/home.html

ETAP
A programme of desk research relating to energy policy within the EU (1998-2002)

ET-ASSIST
European telemedicine for medical assistance (a Telematics for Healthcare project within the **Telematics Applications Programme**)

ETC
European Technology Community

ETC
European Topic Centre. Contracted by the European Environment Agency (**EEA**) to lead the development in European environmental information. In August 2003 there were five ETCs: Air and Climate Change (**ETC/ACC**), Nature Protection & Biodiversity (**ETC/NPB**), Terrestrial Environment (**ETC-TE**), European Topic Centre on Waste and Material Flows (**ETC/WMF**), European Topic Centre on Water (**ETC/WTR**). Details at:
www.eionet.eu.int/Topic_Centres

ETC
Eurotech Capital

ETC/ACC
European Topic Centre on Air and Climate Change.
http://air-climate.eionet.eu.int

ETC/AEM
European Topic Centre on Air Emissions. Replaced by **ETC/ACC**

ETC/AQ
European Topic Centre on Air Quality. Replaced by **ETC/ACC**

ETC/CDS
European Topic Centre on Catalogue of Data Sources. Ceased, but website still available:
www.mu.niedersachsen.de/cds/etc-cds_neu/information.html

ETC/IW
European Topic Centre on Inland Waters. Replaced by **ETC/WTR**

ETC/LC
European Topic Centre on Land Cover. Replaced by **ETC/TE**

ETC/MC
European Topic Centre on Marine and Coastal environment. Replaced by **ETC/WTR**

ETC/NC
European Topic Centre on Nature Conservation. Replaced by **ETC/NPB**

ETC/NPB
European Topic Centre on Nature Protection & Biodiversity.
http://nature.eionet.eu.int

ETC/S
European Topic Centre on Soil. Replaced by **ETC-TE**

ETC/TE
European Topic Centre on Terrestrial Environment.
http://terrestrial.eionet.eu.int

ETC/W
European Topic Centre on Waste. Replaced by **ETC/WMF**

ETC/WMF
European Topic Centre on Waste and Material Flows.
http://waste.eionet.eu.int

ETC/WTR
European Topic Centre on Water.
http://water.eionet.eu.int

ETD
European Telework Development. "An Initiative supported by the **European Commission** (DGXIII) as part of the Advanced Communications Technologies and Services (**ACTS**) Programme."
www.eto.org.uk/etd

ETEE
Educational technologies for European enterprises (**DELTA** project)

ETEMA
European terrestrial ecosystem modelling activity (**TERI** project)

eTEN
New name for **TEN-Telecommunications**

ETF
European Technology Facility for **SME**s, set up by the **EIB** under the Amsterdam Special Action Programme (**ASAP**) and managed by the **EIF** (1998-2002) (**OJ** C302/98)

ETF
European Training Foundation. Set up by **Regulation** 1360/90 (**OJ** L131/90) to give technical assistance under **Phare** and **Tacis**.
Villa Gualino, 65 Viale Settimio Severo, I-10133 Turin, Italy.
www.etf.eu.int

ETF
European Transport workers' Federation (Fédération Européenne des Travailleurs des Transports).
165 rue du Midi, B-1000 Brussels, Belgium.
www.itf.org.uk/ETF/be/welcome.htm

ETHEL
European Tritium Handling Experimental Laboratory (**JRC** project)

ETHNIC
European Union co-funded project to raise public awareness of science and technology amongst ethnic minorities

ETHOS
European Telematics Horizontal Observatory Service (a Programme Support Actions project within the **Telematics Applications Programme**)

eTIP
Electronic form of Technology Implementation Plan - **TIP**.
http://etip.cordis.lu/overview.htm

ETIS
e- and telecommunications information services (previously European Telecommunications Informatics Services). Brings together telecommunications operators, suppliers and content providers.
331 av Louise, BE-1050 Brussels, Belgium.
www.etis.org

ETK
Exchange of Technology and Knowhow. Conference organised by **Eurostat** and **ISIS** in 1999.
http://europa.eu.int/en/comm/eurostat/research/conferences/etk-99

ETL
European Test Laboratory at **Petten**

ETMP
European Technology Market Place. Alternative for **Technology Marketplace**.
www.cordis.lu/marketplace

ETNO
European Telecommunications Network Operators' Association.
54 av Louise, B-1050 Brussels, Belgium.
www.etno.be

ETOMEP
European Technical Office for Medicinal Products at the **EMEA**

ETOP
European technology for optical processing

ETP
Executive Training Programme. Started in 1979 for Japan, later extended to Korea.
www.etp.org

ETR
Electrothermal ribbon (**ESPRIT** project)

ETS
European Trusted Services. Set up to establish security of information services.
www.cordis.lu/infosec/src/ets.htm

ETSA
European Textile Services Association.
24 rue Montoyer, B-1000 Brussels, Belgium.
www.etsa-europe.org

ETSI
European Telecommunications Standards Institute.
650 route de Lucioles, F-06921 Sophia Antipolis Cédex, France.
www.etsi.org

ETTI
European Technology Transfer Initiative. Launched in 1998 to accelerate the exploitation of research results emerging from the **JRC**

ETTN
European Technology Transfer Network, coordinated by the **JRC**

ETUC
European Trade Union Confederation. *Previously* **ECFTU**.
5 blvd Roi Albert II, B-1210, Brussels, Belgium.
www.etuc.org

ETUCO
European Trade Union College.
5 blvd du Roi Albert II, Bte 7, B-1210 Brussels, Belgium.
www.etuc.org/etuco

ETUDE
European trade union distance education (**EMTF** project)

ETUE-Net
European trade union education network (a Telematics for Education and Training project within the **Telematics Applications Programme**)

ETUF:TCL
European Trade Union Federation of Textiles, Clothing and Leather (Fédération Syndicale Européenne du Textile, de l'Habillement et du Cuir).
8 rue J Stevens, B-1000 Brussels, Belgium

ETUI
European Trade Union Institute.
5 blvd du Roi Albert II, box 4, B-1210 Brussels, Belgium.
www.etuc.org/ETUI

ETV
Electronic Training Village. A **CEDEFOP** initiative launched in 1998.
www.trainingvillage.gr

ETY
European Tourism Year (1990). Alternative for European Year of Tourism - **EYT**

EU
Euronorm

EU
European Union

EUA
European Unit of Account. *See* **ECU**

EUA
European University Association. Founded March 2001 as the result of a merger between the Association of European Universities and the Confederation of EU Rectors' Conferences.
10 rue du Conseil Général, CH-1211, Genève 4, Switzerland.
www.unige.ch/eua

EUAM
EU Administration Mostar. **Decision** 94/308/CFSP (**OJ** L134/94)

EU Aware
Web-based information service from Ellis Publications. www.ellispub.com

EUBIMA
Mass spectrometric analysis of biologically active macromolecules (**EUREKA** project)

EUC
European universal classroom. An **ISPO** funded project to "demonstrate the usefulness and added European value of using multimedia and ICT in education" (part of the **EUN** programme).
www.medianet.org/euc

EU-CHIP
Euro-Chinese information point. An online information service for Chinese and European IT companies, partly funded by the **European Commission**

EUCLID
European and international information, news and analysis for the arts and cultural sector.
1st Floor, 46-48 Mount Pleasant, Liverpool L3 5SD, UK.
www.euclid.co.uk

EUCLIDES
European standard for clinical laboratory data exchange between independent information systems (**AIM** project)

EUCOFEL
European Union of the Fruit and Vegetable Wholesale, Import and Export Trade / Union européenne du commerce de gros,

d'expédition, d'importation et d'exportation de fruits et legumes.
29 rue Jenneval, B-1000 Brussels, Belgium

Eucolait
"The European Union of Dairy Trade" (also seen as European Union of Importers, Exporters and Dealers in Dairy Products).
26 av Livingstone, Boîte 5, B-1000 Brussels, Belgium.
www.eucolait-dairytrade.org

EUCREA
European Association for Creativity by Disabled People. Became EUCREA International in 1999.
c/o Cemaforre, 115 rue de Ménilmontant, F-75020 Paris, France.
www.eucrea-international.org

EUCREX
European cloud and radiation experiment (**EPOCH** project)

EUDAT
European Association for the Development of Databases in Education and Training

EUDIF
Women's European Network of Documentation and Information.
8 Sentier du Presbytère, B-1630 Linkebeek, Belgium.
www.eurplace.org/orga/eudif

EU Direct
A current awareness service on EU information, available from UK publisher Butterworths.
www.butterworths.co.uk

EUDISED
European Documentation and Information System for Education.
Published by the **Council of Europe**

EUDoc
European Integration Online Documentation. Available on the ECSA website:
www.ecsanet.org

EUDOR
European document repository. An online document delivery service from **EUR-OP**. Ceased June 2001

EudraLex
A nine-volume collection of rules governing medicinal products in the EU. *See also* **EudraNet**.
http://pharmacos.eudra.org/F2/eudralex/index.htm

EudraMat
A database of economic information on pharmaceutical products

EudraNet
A network to disseminate information on pharmaceutical products.
www.eudra.org

EudraTrack
A tracking system for regulatory procedures for pharmaceutical products

EudraVigilance
"The European data-processing network and database management system for the exchange, processing and evaluation of Individual Case Safety Reports (**ICSR**s) related to medicinal products authorised in the European Economic Area (**EEA**)." Previously **ERS**.
www.eudravigilance.org

EUDUG
EU Databases User Group. Formerly the UK Eurobases User Group. Contact: Sue Hopkins, Wills Memorial Library, Queens Road, University of Bristol, Bristol BS8 1RJ, UK.
www.eudug.org

EuE
End use Equipment

EUFMD
European Commission for the Control of Foot and Mouth Disease. Established in 1954 by the **United Nations** Food and Agriculture Organisation.
www.fao.org/ag/AGA/AGAH/EUFMD/default.htm

EUI
European University Institute.
Badia Fiesolana, 5 via dei Roccettini, I-50016 San Domenico di Fiesola, Florence, Italy.
www.iue.it

EU Infodisk
A bibliographic legal database published by ILI.
www.ili.co.uk

EU interactive
A web-based EU information service published by LAWTEL, but now ceased

EUKIOSK
A service for citizens via information kiosks (**ISIS** multimedia systems project)

EUL
European United Left (group in the **European Parliament**). Also seen as European Unitary Left. *See* **GUE/NGL**

EULEGIS
European user views to legislative information in structured form (a Telematics for Administrations project within the **Telematics Applications Programme**)

EULIT
Effects of eutrophicated seawater on rocky shore ecosystems studied in large littoral mesocosms (**ELOISE** project)

EUL/NGL
Confederal Group of the European United Left - Nordic Green Left (of the **European Parliament**). *See* **GUE/NGL**

EUMC
European Monitoring Centre on Racism and Xenophobia. Established by the EU in 1997 to combat racism, xenophobia and anti-semitism throughout Europe.
3 Rahlgasse, A-1060 Vienna, Austria.
www.eumc.eu.int

EUMC
European Union Military Committee. The highest military body established within the **Council of the European Union**.
http://ue.eu.int/pesc/military/en/EUMC.htm

EUMED
EU-Mediterranean countries

EUMEDIS
Euro-Mediterranean Information Society (part of **MEDA**'s regional cooperation programme)

EUMM
European Union Monitoring Mission. Operated in the Western Balkans under Joint Action (2000/811/CFSP). Replaced the European Community Monitor Mission (**ECMM**) in December 2000

EUMS
European Union Military Staff

EUN
European Schoolnet. Project to establish a European school information network. Funded by the **EMTF** and coordinated by the **SOCRATES** programme.
http://eunbrux02.eun.org/portal/index-en.cfm

EUNET
Experimental network funded by

INNOVATION, linking national technology transfer schemes to transfer technology from research institutions to industry

EUnetART
European network of art organisations for children and young people.
PO Box 15884, 1001 NJ Amsterdam, The Netherlands.
www.eunetart.org

EUNIS
European Nature Information System.
http://eunis.eea.eu.int/eunis3/eunis.jsp

EUO
European Urban Observatory. Also known as 'Cities for All', EUO investigates the quality of life of people with disabilities in European cities.
www.bcn.es/ciutat-disminucio/angles/a_proj03.html

EU-OSHA
European Agency for Safety and Health at Work. Set up in 1994.
33 Gran Via, E-48009 Bilbao, Spain.
http://europe.osha.eu.int

EUHPID
European Health Promotion Indicators Development.
Secretariat, Faculty of Health, University of Brighton, Falmer, Brighton BN1 9PH, UK.
www.brighton.ac.uk/euhpid

EUICs
European Union Information Centres. Set up "in all capitals of central European candidate countries between October 1998 (Prague) and September 2001 (Sofia)"

EuLA
European Lime Association.
c/o Bundesverband der Deutschen Kalkindustrie e.V., 67-71 Annastr, D-509 Köln, Germany

euLISnet
European Union Legal Information Sources on Internet.
www.eulisnet.be

EUPEPT
Synthetic Peptides for clinical nutrition (**EUREKA** project)

EUPHORE
European photo-reactor (**EI** project)

EUPOL
European Union Police Mission. *See also* **Operation Concordia**, **Proxima**

EUPRIO
European University Public Relations and Information Officers Association.
www.tue.nl/csc/euprio

EUR
Series of scientific and technical reports published by **EUR-OP** and some commercial publishers

EUR1, EUR2
denominations of **euro** coins.
http://www.euro.ecb.int/en/section/euro0/coins.html

EUR 6 … EUR 25
Shorthand for number of **Member States**. Can be seen as EUR 6, EUR 9, EUR 10, EUR 12, EUR 15, EUR 25. For details of countries concerned, see listing of numbers (**6**, **9** etc) at the start of this volume

EURAB
European Research Advisory Board. A high-level, independent advisory committee which advises the **European Commission** on the design and implementation of research policy. Set up in 2001.
http://europa.eu.int/comm/research/eurab/index_en.html

EURADA
European Association of Development Agencies (Association des Agences Régionales de Développement).
12 av des Arts, Boîte 7, B-1210 Brussels, Belgium.
www.eurada.org

EURAM
See **BRITE/EURAM**

EURAMIS
European Advanced Multilingual Information System. A computer system to develop and integrate multilingual tools into multilingual services for translators

EURASHE
European Association of Institutions in Higher Education.
38-2 Wolvengracht, B-1000 Brussels, Belgium.
www.eurashe.be

EURATEX
European Apparel & Textile Organisation.
24 rue Montoyer, Bte 10, B-1000 Brussels, Belgium.
www.euratex.org

EURATHLON
A programme to encourage sports projects and programmes with a European dimension 1995-1999 (**OJ** C222/96)

EuRaTIN
European Research and Technology Information Network

EURATN
European Aeronautical Telecommunication Network (**EURET** project)

EURATOM
European Atomic Energy Community.
46 rue du Luxembourg, B-1000 Brussels, Belgium

EURATOM Treaty
Signed by Belgium, France, Germany, Italy, Luxembourg and the Netherlands on 25th March 1957. Came into force 1st January 1958. The lesser-known of the two **Treaties of Rome**

EUREAU
European Union of National Associations of Water Suppliers and Waste Water Services / Union Européenne des Associations Nationales de Distributeurs d'Eau et de Services d'Assainissement.
127 rue Colonel Bourg, B-1140 Brussels, Belgium.
http://users.skynet.be/eureau

EUREED-II
Dynamics and stability of reed-dominated ecosystems in relation to major environmental factors that are subject to global and regional anthropogenically-induced changes (**Environment and Climate** project)

EUREKA
A database of projects financed under the **EUREKA** programme.

EUREKA
European Research and Coordination Agency." Brussels-based pan-European network for market-oriented, industrial R&D." 1985 French initiative for non-military industrial research in advanced technology in Europe.
www3.eureka.be

EURENEW
European Charter for Sustainable Energy. In a **Resolution** of 18 June 1998, the **European Parliament** called for a charter on Renewable Energy Sources to be drawn up (**OJ** C210/98)

EURES
European Employment Services. A network

enabling public employment services of the **Member States** to exchange data relating to employment opportunities. Established by **Decision** 93/569/EEC (**OJ** L274/93). Previously **SEDOC**.
http://europa.eu.int/eures

EURESCO
European Research Conferences.
www.esf.org/euresco

EURESPOIR
See **Europe Against Cancer**

EURET
European Research and Technical Development programme in the field of Transport (1990-1993) (**OJ** L8/91). Continued as **Transport**

EUREX EUREKA
Research Expert System (**EUREKA** project)

EURHISTAR
An on-line database of EU historical archives, produced by the European University Institute (**EUI**).
www.iue.it/ECArchives

EUR*id*
European Registry of Internet Domain names. A consortium chosen to manage the **dot.eu** Top level domain.
http://eurid.org

EURILIA
European Initiative in Library and Information in Aerospace (project within Area 5 of the **Telematics Systems Programme**)

EURISLE
Economic integration of islands (**RECITE** project)

Euristote
On-line directory of University theses and studies on research into European integration.
http://europa.eu.int/comm/dg10/university/euristote/index_en.html

EUR-Lex
"The portal to European law"- an official EU website which includes free access to legislation, proposals, **European Court of Justice** case law and the full text of the **OJ**.
http://europa.eu.int/eur-lex

euro
EU currency from 1 January 1999. Replaced the **ECU**. **Regulation** 974/98 on the introduction of the euro (**OJ** L139/98). *See also* **EMS**; **euro-11**; **euro-12**; **Stability Pact**.
www.euro.ecb.int/en.html

EURO
Statistics for the EU from quarterly national statistics. A statistical domain on the **New Cronos** databank

euro-11 / euro-12
The 11 **Member States** which initially joined **EMU** (Austria; Belgium; Finland; France; Germany; Ireland; Italy; Luxembourg; The Netherlands; Portugal; Spain). They were later followed by Greece, thus turning the euro-11 into the euro-12. Also referred to as euroland and eurozone

EURO<26 card
A European youth card giving access to discounts, services and information throughout Europe to promote youth mobility and access to culture and information. Managed by **EYCA**.
www.eyca.org

EuroACE
European Alliance of Companies for Energy Efficiency in Buildings.
375 av Louise, Bte 4, B-1050 Brussels, Belgium.
www.euroace.org

EURO-AIM
European Organisation for an Audiovisual Independent Market

EUROAIRNET
European Air Quality Monitoring Network established under the aegis of the **ETC/AQ**

Eurobarometer
Public opinion surveys undertaken for the **European Commission**. The first Eurobarometer interviews were conducted in 1973.
http://europa.eu.int/comm/public_opinion

EUROBASES
Former database distribution service of the **European Commission** operated by **EUR-OP**

EUROBIO
Group of **EUREKA** projects

EUROBORDER
The port as a hub in the intermodal transport chain (**Transport** project)

EUROBOT
Group of **EUREKA** projects

EUROCARE
Group of **EUREKA** projects

EUROCASE
European case initiative (**EUREKA** project)

EUROCAT
A bibliographic database of EU materials. Published by Chadwyck-Healey (now Proquest).
www.proquest.co.uk

EUROCAT
European catchments: catchment changes and their impact on the coast.
www.iia-cnr.unical.it/EUROCAT/project.htm

EUROCAT
European Surveillance of Congenital Anomalies.
Room 1F08, University of Ulster, Newtonabbey, Co Antrim Northern Ireland, BT37 OQB, UK.
www.eurocat.ulster.ac.uk

EuroCAUCE
European Coalition Against Unsolicited Commercial Email.
www.euro.cauce.org

Eurocentres
See **Eurocentros**

Eurocentros
Eurocentros de Cooperación Empresarial (Eurocentres for Enterprise Co-operation). A network of Latin American organisations responsible for the promotion and organisation of activities taking place within the **AL-INVEST** programme. Also seen as Eurocentres

EUROCERAM
RECITE project linking ceramics industry regions.
www.euroceram.org

Eurochambres
Association of European Chambers of Commerce and Industry.
5 rue d'Archimède, Boîte 4, B-1000 Brussels, Belgium.
www.eurochambres.be

EUROCHEMOMETRICS
Chemometrics and qualimetrics for the chemical, pharmaceutical and agro-alimentary industry (**COMETT** project)

EUROCIEL
Observatory networks comprising wide-field visible and infra-red sensing instruments (**EUREKA** project)

EURO-CIETT
European arm of the Confédération Internationale des Entreprises de Travail Temporaire (International Confederation of Temporary Work Businesses).
2 place de Luxembourg, B-1050 Brussels, Belgium.
www.ciett.org

EUROCIM
Flexible automated factory for electronic cards, including preparation of circuits and quality control of products (**EUREKA** project)

EUROCITIES
European Association of Metropolitan Cities. A network set up in 1986 to bring together major municipal authorities in Europe to share ideas and resources.
18 square de Meeûs, B-1050, Brussels, Belgium.
www.eurocities.org

EUROCODES
Reference documents for the preparation of product standards in the construction field

EUROCOM
Group of **EUREKA** projects

EUROCOMP
European structural polymeric composites group (**EUREKA** project)

EUROCONTROL
European Organisation for the Safety of Air Navigation.
96 rue de la Fusée, B-1130 Brussels, Belgium.
www.eurocontrol.be

Euro Coop
European Community of Consumer Cooperatives (Communauté Européenne des Coopératives de Consommateurs).
17 rue Archimède, Boîte 2, B-1000 Brussels, Belgium.
www.eurocoop.org

Eurocorps
European Corps. So-called 'European Army' established in 1992. Operational since November 1995, with military contributions from Belgium, France, Germany, Luxembourg and Spain. *See also* **Euroforce**, **Euromarfor**.
BP 82 E, F-67020 Strasbourg Cedex 1, France.
www.eurocorps.org

Eurocost
Project to install a telematic service for Greek micro-enterprises in the automobile repairs sector. 1998-2000

Eurocoton
Committee of the Cotton and Allied Textile Industries of the EU.
24 rue Montoyer, B-1000 Brussels, Belgium

Eurocracy
"The EU President game" - a board game about the **European Union**.
www.eu-president.com

Eurocracy
Term - often used disparagingly - to denote the bureaucracy associated with the EU and its institutions

EUROCOUNSEL
Action research programme focusing on ways to improve guidance and employment counselling services for the long term unemployed (an **EFILWC** programme)

EUROCRON
A Eurostat databank containing general economic statistics (**EurostatISTICS**), some regional data (**REGIOSTAT**) and some farm structure survey information

Eurodac
A computer-based fingerprint recognition system, initially used in the context of asylum seekers, but extended to cover illegal immigrants. Launched 15 January 2003.
http://europa.eu.int/comm/justice_home/news/information_dossiers/wai/news_eurodac_index_en.htm

EuroDEEM
European database of efficient electric motors.
http://energyefficiency.jrc.cec.eu.int/eurodeem/index.htm

EURODELPHES
Device for electronic learning and pedagogy of history in European schools (**EMTF** project)

EURODEMO
European telematics demonstration centre (a Telematics for Research project within the **Telematics Applications Programme**)

Eurodesk
A European network for the dissemination of EU information to young people and those who work with them. Supported by the Education and Culture **DG**.
Brussels Link: Scotland House, 6 Rond-Point Schuman, B-1040 Brussels, Belgium.
www.eurodesk.org

Eurodiaconia
"A federation of churches, non-statutory welfare organizations and NGOs in Europe operating at national and international level … within the traditions of the Reformation as well as in the Anglican and Orthodox traditions".
166 rue Joseph II, B-1000 Brussels, Belgium.
www.eurodiaconia.org

Eurodicautom
Online database of EU terminology.
http://europa.eu.int/eurodicautom

Eurodisc Directive
See **Eurovignette Directive**

Eurodoc
"An e-mail discussion list for European Documentation Centres and Depository Libraries worldwide. It provides a forum for those who work in **EDC**s or **DEP**s to exchange information, seek help with enquiries, and track down references as well as discuss weightier policy issues. It has been instrumental in improving provision for EDCs, but it is also there to offer practical help, support, commiseration and encouragement".
www.jiscmail.ac.uk/lists/eurodoc.html

EURODYN
High technology gas turbine engine demonstrator programme (**EUREKA** project)

EUROEDUCA
Group of **EUREKA** projects

EUROENERGY
Group of **EUREKA** projects

EUROENVIRON
Group of **EUREKA** projects

EUROFAN
European network for the functional analysis of yeast genes discovered by systematic sequencing (**BIOTECH** project)

EUROFAR
Group of **EUREKA** projects

EUROFARM
A database on the structure of agricultural holdings developed by **Eurostat**

EUROFARM
Structure of agricultural holdings statistical domain on the **New Cronos** databank (a summary of the **EUROFARM** database)

EUROFER
European Confederation of Iron and Steel Industries.
211 rue du Noyer, B-1030 Brussels, Belgium.
www.eurofer.org

Eurofile
European Legislation & Standards Service CD-ROM, available from Technical Indexes.
www.tionestop.com

Eurofinas
European Federation of Finance House Associations.
267 av de Tervuren, B-1150 Brussels, Belgium.
www.eurofinas.org

EUROFLUX
A study of exchanges of carbon dioxide, water and energy in 17 forests throughout Europe (**Environment and Climate** project)

EUROFOR
Automation and computerisation of a drilling apparatus for the petroleum industry (**EUREKA** project)

Eurofor
Euroforce - military force answerable to the **WEU**. Established in November 1995 by France, Italy, Spain and Portugal, the Euroforce HQ is in Florence. Intended to provide "a rapid-reaction land capability, equipped with easily deployable light forces with a level of availability adapted to the mission it is to carry out." See also **Eurocorps**, **Euromarfor**

EUROFORM
The improvement of employment opportunities and new qualifications through vocational training and employment. A **Structural Funds i**nitiative (1990-1993) (Guidelines in **OJ** C327/90). Continued under **EMPLOYMENT**

EUROFRET
European system for international road Freight Transport operation (**DRIVE** project)

EUROGAME
European regions game (**EMTF** project)

EUROGATHERER
Personalised information gathering system (a Telematics Information Engineering project within the **Telematics Applications Programme**)

EUROGI
European Umbrella Organisation for Geographic Information.
PO Box 9046, NL-7300 BA Apeldoorn, The Netherlands.
www.eurogi.org

Eurogroup
Informal group within **NATO**, consisting of European Defence Ministers

Euroguichet
Network of consumer advice centres, launched in the early 1990s. *See also* **Relays**.
http://europa.eu.int/comm/consumers/redress/compl/euroguichet/index_en.htm

Euroguidance
The 'working title' for a network of LEONARDO National Resource Centres for Vocational Guidance (NRCVG; Centres Nationaux de Ressources pour l'Orientation Professionnelle - CNROP) which "act as a link between the guidance services of each

country, exchanging information about work, study and training opportunities throughout Europe".
www.euroguidance.org.uk

EUROHELP
Intelligent help for information systems users (**ESPRIT** project)

EUROHOT
Design, development, evaluation and dissemination of an open, flexible, distance learning scheme ... for the European highway construction and maintenance industry (**COMETT** project)

Euro Info Centre
See **EIC**

Euro Info Point
See **EIP**

EURO-JUS
A service offering free legal advice from a lawyer. Available via **Representations** of the **European Commission**

Eurojust
Intended to facilitate cooperation between national prosecuting authorities and to improve coordination of criminal investigations and the exchange of information. Set up in 2002, it comprises national prosecutors, magistrates, and/or police officers seconded from each **Member State**.
174 Maanweg, 2516 AB The Hague, The Netherlands.
www.eurojust.eu.int

EUR OK
Pronounced "you're okay". Slogan of an initiative to give a new image to Europe in Northern Ireland

EuroKom
Electronic mail and computer conferencing service established in 1983 as an **ESPRIT** project. One-time provider of e-mail services to the **EIC** network.
EuroKom House, Unit A2, Nutgrove Office Park, Rathfarnham, Dublin 14, Ireland.
www.eurokom.ie

Euroland
See **Euro-11**, **Euro-12**

EUROLASER
Group of **EUREKA** projects

Eurolaw
A database of EU law, published by ILI.
www.ili.co.uk

EUROLEADERS
Training programme for young European entrepreneurs to study the management implications of the Single Market (**SEM**).
Managed by the European Business and Innovation Centre Network.
168 av de Tervuren, B-1150 Brussels, Belgium.
www.ebn.be

EUROLIB
European Community and Associated Institutions Library Co-operation Group. Met for the first time in June 1988.
www.eurolib.net

Eurolib-Per
An online database of periodicals in the libraries of the **EUROLIB** group

Eurolibraries
A network operating in Denmark, Spain, Sweden and the UK, intended to make EU information available to the general public. The network is managed by the **European Commission** Representation in the Member State concerned. In the UK, it is more popularly known as the **EPIC** network

Eurolibraries
European Database of Libraries Limited. Provides direct mailings to librarians and information specialists in Western Europe.
www.eurolibraries.com

EUROLILIA
European Initiative in Library and Information in Aerospace (**Telematics Applications** project)

Eurolist Directive
Directive 80/390/EEC coordinating the requirements for the drawing up, scrutiny and distribution of the listing particulars to be published for the admission of securities to official stock exchange listing (**OJ** L100/80)

EUROLITH
New protective coatings for the protection of marbles and carbonate stones of ancient monuments and statues (**EUREKA** project)

EUROM
Quarterly CD-ROM of Community Trade Mark (**CTM**) applications and registrations since 1997

EUROM
European Federation of Precision, Mechanical & Optical Industries.
Thornton Heath, CR7 7JG, UK

Euromanagement
A pilot action of standardisation, certification, quality and safety: measures to provide advisory services to **SME**s in the Single Market (**SEM**)

EUROMAR
Group of **EUREKA** projects

Euromarfor
European Maritime Force. A "non-standing, preconfigured, multinational maritime force having both maritime and amphibious capabilities" established in May 1995 by France, Italy, Spain and Portugal under the aegis of the **WEU**. *See* also **Eurocorps**, **Eurofor**

EUROMART
European Cooperative Measures for Aeronautical Research and Technology. A report on the European aeronautical industry requested by the **European Commission** and published in November 1988

EUROMAT
Group of **EUREKA** projects

EUROMATERIAUX
A university/enterprise network for materials set up in 1988 under the **COMETT** programme

EUROMATH
Communications software between mathematicians (**SCIENCE** project)

EUROMATIC
Group of **EUREKA** projects

EUROMECUM
An information package containing data on European higher education and research institutions. Details via keyword search on:
www.raabe.de

EUROMED
Euro-Mediterranean Partnership. Established by the Conference of Foreign Ministers held in Barcelona in November 1995. A joint initiative by the 27 Partners on both sides of the Mediterranean: the 15 member States of the EU plus Algeria, Cyprus, Egypt, Israel, Jordan, Lebanon, Malta, Morocco, Syria, Tunisia, Turkey and the Palestinian territories. Financed under the **MEDA** programme. *See also* **Barcelona Declaration**, **Barcelona Process**.
http://europa.eu.int/comm/external_relations/euromed/index.htm

EUROMED
Standards for processing and visualising medical images (**ISIS** bioinformatics project)

EUROMED HERITAGE
Regional programme for a Euro-Mediterranean cultural **HERITAGE**. Financed under the **MEDA** programme

Euro-Mediterranean Partnership
See **EUROMED**

EUROMET
European meteorological education and training (a Telematics for Education and Training project within the **Telematics Applications Programme**)

Euro-*Meth*work
European Methadone Network. A forum "for those who are active in the substitution treatment field". Part of the five-year Community programme for the prevention of drug dependence (1996-2000).
Q4Q, 77 Vijzelstraat, 1017 HG Amsterdam, The Netherlands.
www.euromethwork.org

EUROMOD
An integrated European benefit-tax model (**TSER** project)

EUROMODEL
Hydrodynamic modelling of the Western Mediterranean (**MAST** project)

Euromonitor
A market research publisher.
60-61 Britton Street, London EC1M 5UX, UK.
www.euromonitor.com

Euromosaic
Publishes reports on the status of minority languages throughout the EU. The website is based in Catalonia and is available in Catalan, English and French.
www.uoc.edu/euromosaic

EUROMOTOR
Training modules for innovation in motor vehicle design and manufacture (**COMETT** project)

EuronAid
European Association of Non-Governmental Organisations/NGOs active in Food Security and Food Aid programmes.
60 Houtweg, NL-2514 BN The Hague, The Netherlands.
www.euronaid.nl

EURONETT
Evaluating user reaction on new European transport technologies (**DRIVE** project)

EURONICE
A database set up by **OHIM** "for the storage and reuse of translations of the most frequently used expressions by Community trade mark applicants to describe the goods and services covered by their marks."
http://oami.eu.int/en/mark/marque/euronice.htm

Euronorm
Basic European Standard, published by **CEN** and **CENELEC**. Commonly abbreviated to EN, sometimes to EU

EUR-OP
'Popular' name adopted by the Office for Official Publications of the European Communities (**OOPEC**). Since changed to Publications Office

Europa
"The European Union online". Managed by the **European Commission**, it "provides up-to-date coverage of **European Union** affairs and essential information on European integration. Users can also consult

all legislation currently in force or under discussion, access the websites of each of the EU institutions and find out about the policies administered by the European Union under the powers devolved to it by the Treaties." *See also* **EUROPAplus**, **Europateam**.
http://europa.eu.int or www.europa.eu.int

EuroPa
European Network for Parkinson's Disease.
www.europarkinson.net

eurOPAC
Online public access catalogues of the members of **EUROLIB**

Europa-Campus
A website of information on education and training. Was at http://europa.eu.int/campus, but no longer available

EUROPAGATE
European SR-Z39.50 Gateway (project within Area 5 of the **Telematics Systems Programme**)

Europa Nostra
Pan-European Federation for Heritage / Fédération pan-européenne du Patrimoine.
35 Lange Voorhout, NL-2514 EC The Hague, The Netherlands.
www.europanostra.org

EUROPAplus
European Commission Intranet, consisting of **EUROPA** plus additional internal information. *See also* **Europateam**

EUROPARI
Group of **EUREKA** projects

EUROPARL
The website of the **European Parliament**. *Previously* **EPADES**.
www.europarl.eu.int

Europartenariat
An EU initiative to stimulate and create cooperation and partnership agreements between companies. Held in different locations each year. Discontinued 2001

Europass
Decision 99/51/EC on the promotion of European pathways in work-linked training, including apprenticeship (**OJ** L17/99).
http://europa.eu.int/comm/education/europass/index_en.html

Europateam
An internal **European Commission** website, available to the Union's **Institutions** and consisting of selected information from **EUROPAplus**

EUROPATH
European pathology assisted by telematics for health (a Telematics for Healthcare project within the **Telematics Applications Programme**)

EuropaWorld
Web-based service produced by EuropaWorld Limited, which reports on development issues from a European perspective.
www.europaworld.org

EuroPAWS
European Public Awareness of Science. Project set up as part of **European Science Week** 2001.
www.europaws.org

Europe 2000
Document on land use and physical planning (**COM**(91)452). *See also* **Europe 2000+**

Europe 2000+
Europe 2000+: cooperation for European territorial development. Published in 1994 by **EUR-OP** as an update to **Europe 2000**

Europe Against AIDS
was an action plan adopted under **Decision** 91/317/EEC, initially spanning 1991-1993, but extended 1994-1995 by Decision 1729/95/EC. That was followed by Decision 96/647/EC adopting a programme of Community action on the prevention of **AIDS** and certain other communicable diseases within the framework for action in the field of public health (1996-2000) (**OJ** L95/96)

Europe Against Cancer
Decision 646/96/EC for a programme of action against cancer (1996-2000) (**OJ** L95/96). Previously EURESPOIR

Europe Agreements
Signed by 10 **Applicant Countries** (Bulgaria, Czech Republic, Estonia, Hungary, Latvia, Lithuania, Poland, Romania, Slovakia, Slovenia), Europe Agreements form the basis for bilateral relations between the EU and those countries in the context of accession. Issues covered are: trade, political dialogue, law, industry, environment, transport, customs. Relations with Cyprus, Malta and Turkey are covered by **Association Agreements**.
http://europa.eu.int/comm/enlargement/pas/europe_agr.htm

European Administrative Space
A term used in connection with administrative reform in **CEECs** in the context of EU enlargement. Defined by **SIGMA** as **an "evolving process of increasing convergence between national administrative legal orders and administrative practices" of the Member States**

EuropeAid
Set up the in January 2001, the EuropeAid Co-operation Office is responsible for managing external aid provided under the Community budget and the European Development Fund (**EDF**). It does not deal with **Phare**, **Ispa**, **Sapard**, humanitarian activities, macro-financial assistance, the **CFSP** or the **Rapid Reaction Facility**.
http://europa.eu.int/comm/europeaid/index_en.htm

European Anthem
The Union's anthem, adopted in 1986 by the **European Community**, is the 'Ode to Joy' from the 4th movement of Beethoven's Ninth Symphony. Only the music is used - not the lyrics. In 1972 the piece was adopted as the anthem of the **Council of Europe**.
http://europa.eu.int/abc/symbols/anthem/index_en.htm

European Briefings
See **Spearhead**

European Charter for Small Enterprises
Adopted at the June 2000 **Feira Summit**, the Charter called upon **Member States** and the **Commission** to support and encourage small enterprises in 10 key areas.
http://europa.eu.int/comm/enterprise/enterprise_policy/charter

European Coal and Steel Community Treaty
See **Treaty of Paris**

European Commission
The Commission is the 'civil service' of the **European Union**. Although formally called the 'Commission of the **European Communities**', it had long been popularly termed 'European Commission' and on 17 November 1993 the Commission unilaterally decided to refer to itself as such. The Commission's responsibilities include initiating and implementing legislation, helping ensure that Community law is properly applied (in its role as 'Guardian of the Treaties'), and representing the Union on the international stage. It has some 24,000 staff. *See also* **Delegations**, **DG**, **European**

Commissioner, Kinnock reforms, Representations.
200 rue de la Loi, B-1049 Brussels, Belgium.
http://europa.eu.int/comm/index_en.htm

European Commissioner
The **European Commission** is managed by a group of Commissioners, headed by a Commission President, each responsible for one or more **DG**s and/or **Services**. The President is appointed by the Heads of State or Government of the **Member States** and then appoints the other Commissioners from candidates nominated by the national governments. Appointments must be ratified by the **European Parliament**.
http://europa.eu.int/comm/index_en.htm

European Communities
European Coal and Steel Community (**ECSC**), European Economic Community (**EEC**; renamed European Community - **EC**), European Atomic Energy Community (**EAEC**)

European Community
Under the **Treaty on European Union** the European Economic Community (**EEC**) became the European Community. The Community has a legal personality, with **Member States** agreeing to abide by its laws. It is thus different from the **European Union**, which is based on intergovernmental cooperation. *See also* **Community Method, Pillars**

European Community Crime Reduction Initiative
See **Computer Theft Initiative**

European Conference
A forum for the EU **Member States** and **Applicant Countries** to discuss political issues of mutual interest. Established by the 1997 **Luxembourg Summit**, the Conference meets twice a year - once at the level of Heads of State or Government and the President of the **European Commission**, and once at the level of foreign ministers. It first met in London in March 1998

European Confidence Pact
Launched in June 1996 by Jacques **Santer** to create jobs. It had four pillars: macro-economic policy, the single market, employment systems and structural polices (**COM**(96)507). Also seen as 'Employment Confidence Pact'

European Consumer Centres
See **Euroguichet**

European Co-operative Statute
Adopted by the **Council of the European Union** on 22 July 2003. Also seen as Societas Cooperativa Europaea - SCE.
http://europa.eu.int/comm/enterprise/entrepreneurship/coop/statutes/statutes-coop.htm

European Council
Meetings of Heads of State which usually take place twice yearly at the end of the rotating six-month **Presidency** of each **Member State**. Popularly termed 'European Summits', 'Summits', 'Summit meetings'

European Court
In an EU context, this usually means the **European Court of Justice**, but it is often used in the media to refer to the European Court of Human Rights (a **Council of Europe** institution)

European Court of Auditors
Established in 1977, the ECA is the Union Institution responsible for auditing the Union's revenue and expenditure. *See also* **DAS**.
12 rue Alcide de Gasperi, L-1615 Luxembourg.
www.eca.eu.int

European Court of Justice
Popular term for Court of Justice of the European Communities. Often referred to as "the European Court".
Palais de la Cour de Justice, Boulevard Konrad Adenauer, Kirchberg, L-2925 Luxembourg.
www.curia.eu.int

European Defence Community
See **EDC**

European Digital Cities
The provision of an open cooperation network for a concerted urban development through telematics (a Telematics for Urban and Rural Areas project within the **Telematics Applications Programme**)

European District
The area of **Brussels** which houses the EU **Institutions**

European Documentation
A series of information pamphlets issued by **EUR-OP**; partly replaced by more substantial booklets in the **Europe on the Move** series

European Energy Charter Treaty
Decision 94/998/EC to join Western technology and capital with resources in Eastern Europe (**OJ** L380/94). The Treaty entered into force in 1998.
www.encharter.org

European Fast-Stream
A scheme to encourage recruitment into the **European Union** from the British civil service

European Food Safety Authority
See **EFSA**

European Investment Bank
See **EIB**

European Ombudsman
The person appointed by the **European Parliament** to investigate complaints concerning maladministration in any EU **Institution** or activity. Introduced in the **Treaty on European Union**. The first Ombudsman was Jacob Söderman (1995-2003). Professor P. Nikiforos Diamandouros took over the post on 1 April 2003.
1 av du Président Schuman, BP 403, F-67001 Strasbourg, France.
www.euro-ombudsman.eu.int

European Parliament
Often seen as 'EP'. The Union's only democratically-elected Institution. First direct elections held in 1979; latest in 1999; next in 2004. Role changed by the **Maastricht Treaty** and **Amsterdam Treaty**, from a consultative assembly into a legislative body (see **Co-decision Procedure**). At the end of 2001, there were 626 Members of the European Parliament (MEPs), who sit in political, not national, groups, which are subject to change. Those in the 1999-2004 Parliament are:
PPE-DE Group of the European People's Party (Christian Democrats) and European Democrats;
PSE Group of the Party of European Socialists;
ELDR Group of the European Liberal, Democrat and Reform Party;
Verts/ALE Group of the Greens/European Free Alliance;
GUE/NGL Confederal Group of the European United Left/Nordic Green Left;
UEN Union for Europe of the Nations Group;
EDD Group for a Europe of Democracies and Diversities;
NI Non-attached.
The Parliament maintains three homes:
Alleé du Printemps, BP 1024/F, F-67070 Strasbourg Cedex, France; Plateau du

Kirchberg, BP 1601, L-2929 Luxembourg; rue Wiertz, BP 1047, B-1047 Brussels, Belgium.
www.europarl.eu.int

European Relays
See **Relays**

European Science and Technology Week
"Demonstrates and explains the impact of science, its uses, and its applications in the daily lives of European citizens".
www.cordis.lu/scienceweek/home.htm

European Social Fund
See **ESF**

European Stability Pact
See **Stability Pact**

European Summit
Popular term for a meeting of the **European Council**

European Topic Centres
See **ETCs**

European Union
Term introduced in the **Treaty on European Union**. Officially used for matters concerning the 'external' functions of the European Communities i.e. the Second and Third Pillars of the Three **Pillars**. However, it is popularly used to refer to the European Community / European Union with no distinction between them

European Union Publishers' Forum
A partnership between EU **Institutions** and publishers intended to improve access to EU-related information.
http://publications.eu.int/general/en/forum_en.htm

European Update
A database produced by Deloitte Touche Europe Services

European Voluntary Service
See **EVS**

European Youth Forum
"An international organisation established by national youth councils and international non-governmental youth organisations to represent the interests of young people from all over Europe".
120 rue Joseph II, B-1000 Brussels, Belgium.
www.youthforum.org

Europe Biotech
Project set up as part of **European Science Week** 2001

EUROPECHE
Association of National Organisations of Fishing Enterprises in the EU.
23-25 rue de la Science, Boîte 15, B-1040 Brussels, Belgium

Europe Daily Bulletin
See **Agence Europe**

Europe Day
9 May is celebrated as Europe Day. On 9 May 1950, the French Minister for Foreign Affairs, Robert **Schuman**, made a speech in which he proposed that the coal and steel industries of France and Germany should be pooled. His proposal led to the creation of the European Coal and Steel Community (**ECSC**) - the first institution of what is now the **European Union**. Also known as Schuman Day.
http://europa.eu.int/abc/symbols/9-may/index_en.htm

Europe Direct
An enquiry service on EU issues which offers: a single Freephone number from anywhere in the **Member States** (00 800 6 7 8 9 10 11); a normal telephone number from anywhere in the world (+32 2 299 96 96); an e-mail enquiry service; and an interactive, real-time

Web-Assistance service.
http://europa.eu.int/europedirect

EUROPE MMM
Remote and on-line publication of multimedia (a Telematics Information Engineering project within the **Telematics Applications Programme**)

EUROPEN
European Organization for Packaging and the Environment.
Le Royal Tervuren, 6 av de l'Armée, B-1040 Brussels, Belgium.
www.europen.be

Europe on the Move
A series of information pamphlets issued by **EUR-OP** which began in 1991. Some are available online at:
http://europa.eu.int/comm/publications/booklets/move/index_en.htm

Europe's 500
A programme launched by **EFER** to promote entrepreneurship in the EU

EUROPIC
European development of post-secondary training of students and trainers in integrated circuit fabrication techniques (**COMETT** project)

EUROPICON
European process intelligent control (**EUREKA** project)

Europinion
Contains results of the European Continuous Tracking Survey (**CTS**).
http://europa.eu.int/comm/public_opinion/archives_en.htm

EUROPMI
European Committee for Small and Medium-Sized Independent Companies. Merged Secretariats with **UEAPME** in 1999

EUROPOL
European Police Office. Established by the EUROPOL Convention (**OJ** C316/95).
47 Raamweg, NL-2509 The Hague, The Netherlands.
www.europol.eu.int

EUROPOLIS
New intelligent control systems to aid urban and inter-urban traffic and advanced metropolitan information control and monitoring (**EUREKA** project)

EUROPROMS
European Production and Market Statistics. A database produced by Eurostat

Euroqualification
A joint initiative to establish a permanent partnership of training organisations in the **Member States** (1989-)

Euroquest
An information system on sources of European finance produced by **EBN**

EUROREF
A bibliographic database published by ELLIS. Now ceased.
www.ellispub.com

EUROROUTES
Road routes designated by the **UN/ECE**

EUROS
Proposed Community Shipping Register, originally put forward in 1989, amended 1992 (**OJ** C19/92)

Eurosclerosis
Generally taken to mean a period of little or no progress towards European integration. The term was coined in the period following the 1973 oil crisis and the Community's first **enlargement**, when **Member States** suffered high unemployment, high inflation and low growth

EUROSCOLA
Programme of meetings between sixth-form classes from **Member States**. Details from national offices of the **European Parliament**

EuroSIDA
A **BIOMED** study to assess the impact of antiretroviral drugs on the outcome of the general population of HIV-infected patients living in Europe.
www.cphiv.dk/eurosida

EUROSILVA
Cooperation on tree physiology research (**EUREKA** project)

EUROSSAM
European salt marshes modelling (**ELOISE** project)

EUROSTARS
System for the thematic analysis of remote sensed data (**EUREKA** project)

Eurostat
A **DG** of the **European Commission** which provides the Union's statistical service. Eurostat focuses on presenting statistics in a consolidated, harmonised format. Adopted in 1973, when Denmark, Ireland and the UK joined the **European Communities**, the name 'Eurostat' was chosen to avoid having to translate the formal 'Statistical Office of the European Communities' (SOEC) into the six official languages.
Jean Monnet Building, rue Alcide de Gasperi, L-2920 Luxembourg.
http://europa.eu.int/comm/eurostat/

EUROSTATISTICS
Paper copy of the main economic and social statistics domains published monthly by Eurostat and also loaded on the **New Cronos** databank

EUROSTATUS
Main indicators statistical domain on the **New Cronos** databank

EUROSTEP
European Association of Satellites in Training Education Programmes (**DELTA** project)

EUROSYNET
Cooperation in public procurement and promotion of **SMEs** (**RECITE** project)

Eurotalk
E-mail discussion group for members of the European Information Association (**EIA**).
www.jiscmail.ac.uk/files/EUROTALK/Intro.doc

Euro-TAP-Viet
A technical assistance programme to assist Vietnam towards a market economy

EuroTechAlert
European information service for the results of public research. Set up under the **SPRINT** programme

Eurotech Capital
European Technology Private Capital. A financial device for **SMEs** to promote transnational high-technology projects (**OJ** C192/89).
www.cordis.lu/finance/src/euro-cap.htm

EUROTECNET II
European technical network: Community action programme in the field of vocational training and technological change (1990-1994) (**OJ** L393/89). Continued as part of the **Leonardo da Vinci** programme

EUROTEXT
A web-based teaching and learning resource of key EU documents, developed by the Universities of Hull and Ulster, under the e-Lib programme. Password-controlled access; also available as part of **KnowEurope**.
http://eurotext.ulst.ac.uk:8017

EUROTOLL
European project for toll effects and pricing strategies (**Transport** project)

EUROTOPP
European transport planning process (**DRIVE** project)

EUROTRA
Decision 90/664/EEC for a European Translation System of advanced design (1990-1992) (**OJ** L358/90). Project discontinued

EUROTRAC
European experiment on transport and transformation of environmentally relevant trace constituents in the troposphere over Europe (**EUREKA** project)

EUROTRANS
Group of **EUREKA** projects

EURO-TRIANGLE
Transl/retrieval-oriented information base adapting data from 'native speaking' grammmatical/lexicograph (**EUREKA** project)

EUROTRIP
European trip planning system (**DRIVE** project)

EUROTUNNEL
Standardised segmental lining for fully mechanised continuous tunnel operation with new waterstop system (**EUREKA** project)

Euro Units
A UK national network to support providers of vocational education and training. Some were subsumed within the **ERC** network

Euro Velo
A network of 12 long-distance European cycle routes promoted by the European Cyclist Federation (**ECF**) with the help of the EU.
www.eurovelo.org

EURO VIEW
Pilot directory service for European telematics applications (a Telematics for Administrations project within the **Telematics Applications Programme**)

Eurovignette Directive
Directive 1999/62/EC on the charging of heavy goods vehicles for the use of certain infrastructures (**OJ** L187/99). Sometimes seen as 'Eurodisc Directive'

EUROVISE
European vision system economic (**EUREKA** project)

Eurovoc
A multilingual thesaurus which "provides a means of indexing the documents in the documentation systems of the European institutions and of their users."
http://europa.eu.int/celex/eurovoc

EURO-WATERNET
A water resources information and monitoring network for Europe, designed and tested by the **ETC/IW**

Euro-X
The Euro-X Council comprises Finance Ministers of the **eurozone** who meet informally to discuss the single currency.

eurozone
See **euro-11**, **euro-12**

EURYBASE
"The information database on education systems in Europe". Maintained by **EURYDICE**.
www.eurydice.org

EURYCLEE
Network of national information centres specialising in new information technologies and education in the **Member States**

EURYDICE
"The Information Network on Education in Europe." Continued as part of the **Socrates** programme.
EURYDICE European Unit, 240 av Louise, B-1050 Brussels, Belgium.
www.eurydice.org

EU-SEASED
Internet database of seafloor samples held at European research institutions (product of a **MAST III** project).
www.eu-seased.net

EUSF
See **Solidarity Fund**

EUSIDIC
European Association of Information Services.
Secretariat: c/o Fachinformationszentrum Karlsruhe, 76344 Eggenstein-Leopoldshafen, Germany.
www.eusidic.org

EUSIS
European soil information system (**ESB** project)

EUSRs
European Union's Special Representatives - under the **CFSP**. For details see:
http://ue.eu.int/pesc/envoye.asp?lang=en

EUSTAT
Empowering users through assistive technology (a Telematics for Disabled and Elderly People project within the **Telematics Applications Programme**)

EUTERPE
Exploitation unifiée de la terminologie au Parlement européen (European Parliament one-stop terminology management system).
www.europarl.eu.int/terminology/default_en.htm

EUVAS
Environmental ultraviolet action spectroscopy (an Environmental and Chemical Safety Research project within the **Environment and Climate Programme**)

EUW
European Union of Women

EVA
Evaluation process for road transport informatics (**DRIVE** project)

EVALUE
Evaluation and self-evaluation of universities in Europe (**TSER** project)

EVCA
European Private Equity and Venture Capital Association.
4 Minervastraat, B-1930 Zaventem, Belgium.
www.evca.com

EVE
Environmental valuation in Europe (within the **Environment and Climate Programme**)

EVE
Espace Video Européen (**MEDIA** project)

EVENET
Eurovillage on the European information infrastructure (a Telematics for Urban and Rural Areas project within the **Telematics Applications Programme**).
www.tweuro.com/tura/tourism/html/evenet.html

EVEREST
Three dimensional algorithms for robust and efficient semiconductor simulator (**ESPRIT** project)

Everything but Arms
Initiative to grant duty-free access to imports, except arms and munitions, from least developed countries (**LDCs**). **Regulation** 416/2001 (**OJ** L60/01). Special provisions applied to rice, bananas and sugar - *see* **EBARBS**.
http://europa.eu.int/comm/trade/issues/global/gsp/eba/index_en.htm

EVIDENT
European versatility in deaf education using new technologies (**EMTF** project)

Evimar
European Virtual Maritime Institute. A network of 17 partners from 11 **Member States**, Evimar is intended to address the main challenges facing the European shipping industry

EVS
European Voluntary Service for young people. An informal education programme providing young people with work opportunities abroad (1998-1999). Replaced by **Youth**

EWC
European Works Council, under **Directive** 94/45/EC (**OJ** L254/94).
http://europa.eu.int/scadplus/leg/en/cha/c10805.htm

EWC
European waste catalogue (**OJ** L5/94)

EWGRB
European Working Group on Research and Biodiversity (within the **Environment and Climate Programme**)

E-Windows
See **EnviroWindows**

EWL
European Women's Lobby.
18 rue Hydraulique, B-1210 Brussels, Belgium.
www.womenlobby.org

EWON
European Work Organisation Network. Set up by the Commission to support and speed up the modernisation process in EU enterprises.
http://europa.eu.int/comm/employment_social/soc-dial/workorg/ewon/index_en.htm

EWS
Euroworkstation (**ESPRIT** project)

EXAP
Exceptional Assistance Programme (to Azerbaijan)

EXCISE
Excise control. Automation of access to SEED (System for exchange of excise data) (**IDA** project)

EXCLUSION I
See **Poverty**

EXE
Extranet education (**EMTF** project)

Executive Agencies
On 14 December 2000, in the context of its reform, the **European Commission** approved a proposal for a Regulation to set up 'Executive Agencies' - external organisations which would implement Community programmes.
http://europa.eu.int/comm/reform/2002/chapter04_en.htm

EXLIB
Expansion of European systems for the visually disadvantaged (project within Area 5 of the **Telematics Systems Programme**)

EXMAN
Experimental manipulations of forest ecosystems in Europe (**STEP** project)

EXPERTS
EDI/XML procurement enabling real trade standards (**ISIS** Electronic Commerce project)

Experts Group on Trafficking in Human Beings
Set up under **Decision** of 25 March 2003 setting up a consultative group, to be known as the 'Experts Group on Trafficking in Human Beings' (**OJ** L79/03).
http://europa.eu.int/comm/justice_home/fsj/crime/trafficking/wai/fsj_crime_human_trafficking_en.htm

Explosive Atmospheres Directives
Directives 76/117/EEC and 79/196/EEC on electrical equipment for use in potentially explosive atmospheres (**OJ** L24/76; OJ L43/79). Replaced by **ATEX Directive**

EXPOLIS
Air pollution exposure distribution of adult urban population in Europe (an Environmental Health and Chemical Safety Research project within the **Environment and Climate Programme**)

EXPROM
Promotion of Community Exports to Japan. *See also* **ETP**.
http://europa.eu.int/comm/external_relations/japan/intro/exprom.htm

Extensification
A policy of farming less intensively in order to balance lower output by savings in expenditure on feedingstuffs, fertilisers and pesticides

EXTRA
A service which provides interested parties in the EU and Central and Eastern Europe with information on results from across the whole of the EU's Transport **RTD** programme. Started January 1998.
http://europa.eu.int/comm/transport/extra/home.html

EXTRA2
Euromethodologies X travel assessment to assess European travel behaviour (a **Transport** project)

EXTRACOM
Telematics in foreign trade statistics (**IDA** project)

EXTRAMINT
Extranet, multicast intranet (a Telematics Information Engineering project within the **Telematics Applications Programme**)

EXTTRADE
External trade. A database within **New Cronos**

EXVOC
Expert system contribution to vocational training (**DELTA** project)

EYAR
European Year Against Racism (1997).
http://europa.eu.int/scadplus/leg/en/cha/c10410.htm

EYCA
European Youth Card Association. *See also* **EURO<26** card.
Leidsestraat 59 II, 1017 NV Amsterdam, The Netherlands.
www.eyca.org

EYE
European Year of the Environment (1987-1988) (**OJ** C63/86)

EYE
European Youth Exchange network.
Tiefendorfergasse 11/32, A-1140 Vienna, Austria

EYES

European Year of Education through Sport 2004.
http://europa.eu.int/comm/sport/key_files/annee_eur/a_2004_en.html

EYL

European Year of Languages. A joint EU-**Council of Europe** initiative in 2001.
http://culture.coe.fr/AEL2001EYL

EYLL

European Year of Lifelong Learning (1996) under **Decision** 2493/95/EC (**OJ** L256/95)

EYT

European Year of Tourism (1990) (**OJ** L17/89). Also seen as European Tourism Year - ETY

F

F
France

FABULA
Bilingual multimedia educational material for children (**EMTF** project)

FAC
Foreign Affairs Council (of the **Council of the European Union**)

FACE
Federation of Associations for Hunting and Conservation of the EU (Fédération des Associations de Chasse et Conservation de la Faune Sauvage de l'UE).
82 rue F Pelletier, B-1030 Brussels, Belgium.
www.face-europe.org

FACE
Framework for Academic Cooperation in Europe (**Erasmus** project)

FACILE
Support tools for housing design and management, integrated with telematics systems and services (a Telematics for Disabled and Elderly People project within the **Telematics Applications Programme**)

FACIT
Fast Automatic Conversion with Integrated Tools (project within Area 5 of the **Telematics Systems Programme**)

FACT
Feasibility studies for the creation of global cardiovascular multimedia databases (a Telematics for Healthcare project within the **Telematics Applications Programme**)

FACT Fund
Created by **DG** VIII (now DG Development) and approved by the **CDI** in 1996, to support the development of **ACP** companies

FADN
Farm Accountancy Data Network. Set up in 1965 (**OJ** 1859/65), it is "an instrument for evaluating the income of agricultural holdings and the impacts of the Common Agricultural Policy."
http://europa.eu.int/comm/agriculture/rica/index_en.cfm

FAEP
Fédération des Associations d'Éditeurs de Périodiques de la CE (European Federation of Magazine Publishers).
15 rue d'Arlon, B-1050 Brussels, Belgium.
www.faep.org

FAIP
Farm Animal Industrial Platform.
www.faip.dk

FAIR
Decision 94/805/EC for Fisheries, Agriculture and agro-Industrial Research (1994-1998) (**OJ** L334/94). Previously **AIR**.

FAIR
Forecast and assessment of socio-economic impact of advanced communications and recommendations (part of the **ACTS** programme).
www.databank.it/dbc/fair/page04.htm

Falcone Council
Joint Action 98/245/JHA on a programme of exchanges, training and cooperation for

persons responsible for action to combat organised crime (1998-2002) (**OJ** L99/98).
http://europa.eu.int/comm/justice_home/project/falcone_en.htm

FAME
Fate and activity modelling of environmental pollutants using structure-activity relationships (an Environmental Health and Chemical Safety Research project within the **Environment and Climate Programme**)

FAMIMO
Fuzzy algorithms for the control of multi-input, multi-output processes (supported by the **ESPRIT** programme).
http://iridia.ulb.ac.be/~famimo/index.html

FAMOS
Group of **EUREKA** projects

FANS
Finland, Austria, Norway and Sweden

FAOR
Functional analysis of office requirements (**ESPRIT** project)

FAP
Final abandonment premium

FAP
Forestry action programme (within the Renewable Raw Materials programme) (1989-1992) (**OJ** L359/89). Continued in **AIR**

FAR
Fisheries and Aquaculture Research (1988-1992) (**OJ** L314/87). Continued in **AIR**

Farm to fork strategy
The concept of ensuring food safety at all stages of the food supply chain. Also seen as 'Farm to table'.
http://europa.eu.int/comm/food/fs/intro/index_en.html

FARO
Fuel melting and release oven (**JRC** - reactor safety programme)

FASDE
Future alarm and awareness services for the disabled and elderly (**TIDE** project)

FASE
European Parliament Committee on Foreign Affairs, Security and Defence policy

FASP
Flexible automation in ship prefabrication (**EUREKA** project)

FASS
Fast ships safety (**Transport** project)

FASSEL
Diagnostic procedure through selective and specific filtration of antigens on labelled antibodies (**EUREKA** project)

FAST
Forecasting and assessment in the field of science and technology (part of the **MONITOR** programme)

FASTCAT
High speed multilingual computer assisted translation system (**EUREKA** project)

FASTDOC
Fast document ordering and document delivery (project within Area 5 of the **Telematics Systems Programme**)

Fast-Stream
See **European Fast-Stream**

FATHTS
Fatigue-based design rules for the application of high-tensile steels in ships (**BRITE/EURAM** project)

FAUDIT
EAGGF auditing system (**CADDIA** project)

FAWEU
Forces answerable to **WEU**.
See also **Eurocorps**, **Eurofor**, **Euromarfor**

FBE
Fédération Bancaire de l'Union Européenne (European Banking Federation).
10 rue Montoyer, B-1000 Brussels, Belgium.
www.fbe.be

FBF
A database of **EAGGF** budget forecasting (**CADDIA** project)

FBS
Family budget survey

FCB
Fuel cell bus (**EUREKA** project)

FCNM
Framework Convention for the Protection of National Minorities (of the **Council of Europe**).
http://conventions.coe.int/Treaty/EN/Treaties/Html/157.htm

FCPN
Factory customer premise network (**ESPRIT** project)

FCTC
Framework Convention on Tobacco Control. A **United Nations** initiative, which the **European Union** did much to promote.
www.fctc.org

FEANTSA
Fédération Européenne d'Associations Nationales Travaillant avec les Sans-Abri (European Federation of National Organisations Working with the Homeless).
194 Chaussée de Louvain, B-1210 Brussels, Belgium.
www.feantsa.org

FEAP
Forum Européen pour les Arts et le Patrimoine (European Forum for the Arts and Heritage - **EFAH**)

FEC
Fédération Européennes des Cyclistes (European Cyclists' Federation - **ECF**)

FED
Fond Européen de Développement (European Development Fund - **EDF**)

FEDARENE
European Federation of Regional Energy and Environment Agencies.
11 rue du Beau-Site, B-1000 Brussels, Belgium.
www.fedarene.org

FEDER
Fonds Européen de Développement Régional (European Regional Development Fund - **ERDF**)

FEDIOL
EU Seed Crushers' and Oil Processors' Federation.
168 av de Tervuren (bte 12) - 1st floor, B-1150 Brussels, Belgium.
www.fediol.be

Fédolive
Federation of the Olive Oil Industry of the EC

FEE
Fédération des Editeurs Européens (Federation of European Publishers - FEP).
204 av de Tervuren, B-1150 Brussels, Belgium.
www.fep-fee.be

FEE
Fédération des Experts Comptables Européens (European Federation of Accountants).
83 rue de la Loi, B-1040 Brussels, Belgium.
www.fee.be

FEE
Foundation for Environmental Education. Previously Foundation for Environmental Education in Europe - FEEE.
PO Box 3022, Norwich NR5 8ZU, UK.
www.fee-international.org

FEEE
Foundation for Environmental Education in Europe. Now **FEE**

FEFAF
Fédération Européenne des Femmes Actives aux Foyer (European Federation of Women Working in the Home).
76 av Père Damien, B-1150 Brussels, Belgium.
www.fefaf.org

FEFSI
Fédération Européenne des Fonds et Sociétés d'Investissement (European Federation of Investment Funds and Companies - EFIFC).
18 square de Meeûs, B-1050 Brussels, Belgium.
www.fefsi.org

FEIP
Front-end for echograph image processing (**AIM** project)

Feira Summit
Meeting in Santa Maria da Feira, Portugal, on 19-20 June 2000, the **European Council**: confirmed its commitment to establishing a Common European Security and Defence Policy; confirmed the importance of the **Lisbon Strategy**; endorsed the **e-Europe** 2002 Action Plan and called for a knowledge-based economy to close the numeracy gap and to encourage '**info-inclusion**'; welcomed the **European Charter for Small Enterprises**; reached agreement on the **Tax Package**; and welcomed the decision of Greece to become the 12th member of the **eurozone**

FELICITA
Development of ferroelectric liquid crystal devices for information technology applications (**ESPRIT** project)

FEMIP
Facility for Euro-Mediterranean Investment and Partnership. Launched in October 2002, primarily to increase support to the private sector. The **Council of the European Union** was due to decide in October 2003 on whether to convert the Facility into an **EIB** subsidiary Euro-Mediterranean Bank

FEMIRCs
Fellow Members to the Innovation Relay Centres. Members of the Innovation Relay Centres (**IRC**) network based in the **CEEC**s

FEMISE
Forum Euro-Méditerranéen des Instituts Economiques (Euro-Mediterranean Forum of Economic Institutes).
58 blvd Charles Livon, Palais du Pharo, 13007 Marseille, France.
www.femise.org

FEMM
European Parliament Committee on Women's Rights and Equal Opportunities

FENI
Fédération Européenne du Nettoyage Industriel (European Federation of Cleaning Industries - EFCI).
www.feni.be

FEOGA
Fonds Européen d'Orientation et de Garantie Agricole (European Agricultural Guidance and Guarantee Fund - **EAGGF**)

FEOPAY
A project to review the payment system for the Guidance section of the **EAGGF** (**CADDIA** project)

FEORI
A project to establish a database for aid applications under the Guidance section of the **EAGGF** (**CADDIA** project)

FEP
Federation of European Publishers (Fédération des Editeurs Européens - **FEE**)

FEPF
European Federation of the Industries of Earthenware and China Tableware and Ornamental Ware (Fédération Européenne des industries de Porcelaine et de Faïence de table et d'ornementation).
18-24 rue des Colonies, Bte 17, B-1000 Brussels, Belgium

FEPH
Forum européen des personnes handicapées (European Disability Forum - **EDF**)

FESAT
Fondation Européenne des Services d'Accueil Téléphonique Drogues et Toxicomanies (European Foundation of Drug Help Lines). Part of the five-year EU programme for the prevention of drug dependence (1996-2000).
19 rue du Marteau, B-1000 Brussels, Belgium.
www.fesat.org

FESTIVAL
Functional electrical stimulation to improve value ability and lifestyle (**TIDE** project)

FFI
Family farm income

FI
Finnish (Suomi)

FIABCI
International Real Estate Federation.
23 av Bosquet, F-75007 Paris, France.
www.fiabci.com

FIABEX
Expert system for the automatic calculation and presentation of fault tree analysis (**EUREKA** project)

FIAP
European Parliament Temporary Committee on Foot and Mouth Disease

Fiche d'impact
A brief note attached to an EU proposal for legislation, which indicates the likely effect of that proposal on a small firm or on the environment

FIDE
Formally integrated data environment (**ESPRIT** project)

FIDES
Fisheries data exchange system. The telematic exchange of catch reports, fleet register data and fishing licences (**IDA** project)

FIDESY
Fire detection system based on intelligent processing of infrared and visible images (**EUREKA** project)

FIEC
Fédération de l'Industrie Européenne de la Construction (European Construction Industry Federation - ECIF)

FIELDBUS
Communications architecture based on local area networks for real time control of industrial processes and machines (**EUREKA** project)

FIESTA
Facility for the implementation of effective

sectoral and technical assistance (a Polish programme set up under **Phare**)

FIFG
Financial Instrument for Fisheries Guidance. One of the **Structural Funds**.
http://europa.eu.int/comm/fisheries/doc_et_publ/factsheets/facts/en/pcp5_2.htm

Fifth Company Law Directive
Term used to refer to a 1972 proposal (**COM**(1972)887) which aimed to harmonise the structure and management of public limited liability companies. The proposal was amended a number of times before being withdrawn in December 1991

Fifth Framework Programme
for research, technological development and demonstration (RTD) activities for the period 1998-2002. It included four thematic programmes (Quality of life and management of living resources; User friendly information society; Competitive and sustainable growth; Energy, environment and sustainable development) and three horizontal programmes (Confirming the international role of community research; Promotion of innovation and encouragement of participation of SMEs; Improving human research potential and the socio-economic knowledge base). Often seen as 5FP or FP5. Succeeded by **Sixth Framework Programme**.
http://europa.eu.int/comm/research/fp5.html

FINATLANTIC
Development of a risk capital fund in the Atlantic region (**RECITE** project)

Finet, Paul
See **Paul Finet Foundation**

Fin-net
Consumer Complaints Network for Financial Services. An out-of-court complaints network for financial services to help businesses and consumers resolve disputes in the Internal Market. Launched February 2001.
http://finnet.jrc.it

FINREAD
Financial transactional IC card reader (**ISIS** Electronic Commerce project)

FIORE
Funding and investment objective for road transport informatics in Europe (**DRIVE** project)

FIP
Fungal Industrial Platform.
http://europa.eu.int/comm/dg12/biotech/ip2.html#FIP

FIRES
Facility for investigating runaway events safety (**JRC** project)

FIRST
Friendly interactive robot for service tasks (**EUREKA** project)

FIRST
Fundamentals of intelligent reliable robot systems (**ESPRIT** project)

FIRST
Project to merge the web for schools project and the **EUN** (supported by the **ESPRIT** programme)

First Banking Directive
Directive 77/780/EEC on the coordination of the laws, regulations and administrative provisions relating to the taking up and pursuit of the business of credit institutions (**OJ** L322/1977). No longer in force

First Pillar
See **Pillars**

FIS
Fast information system to establish a computer infrastructure for the horizontal utilisation of the **AMIS** database (**CADDIA** project)

FISCALIS
Decision 888/98/EC for a multiannual programme of Community action to reinforce the functioning of the indirect taxation systems of the Single Market - **SEM** (1998-2002) (**OJ** L206/98). Extended 2003-2007 by Decision 2235/2002/EC (OJ L341/02). Previously **MATTHAEUS TAX**.
http://europa.eu.int/comm/taxation_customs/taxation/fiscalis/index_en.htm

FISH
Annual catches by fishing zone statistical domain on the **New Cronos** databank

FISH
European Parliament Committee on Fisheries. Renamed **PECH**

FISH
Fisheries **DG** of the **European Commission**

FIS-IDES
Fast information system - interactive data exchange system. A telematic application for the management of the Common Agricultural Policy (**IDA** project)

FIT
Finance for innovative technology

FITCE
Federation of Telecommunications Engineers of the European Community.
80 Reyerslaan, Blvd Reyers, B-1030 Brussels, Belgium.
www.fitce.org

FIWG
Financial Issues Working Group. Part of the Electronic Commerce actions of the Information Society **DG** of the **European Commission** and the G8-10 pilot project

FLAIR
Food-linked agro-industrial research (1989-1993) (**OJ** L200/89). *See also* **ECLAIR**. Continued as **AIR**

FLEET
Freight and logistics efforts for European traffic (**DRIVE** project)

FLEX
Flexible learning environment experiment (**EMTF** project)

Flexicurity
A balance of labour market flexibility and social security

FLEXPLAN
Knowledge-based planning and control in manufacturing environments (**ESPRIT** project)

Florence process
In 1998 the **European Commission** set up the Electricity Regulatory Forum of Florence. The Forum convenes twice a year and consists of national regulatory authorities, **Member States**, the **European Commission**, transmission system operators, electricity traders, consumers, network users, and power exchanges

Florence Summit
The June 1996 **European Council**: confirmed that stage 3 of **EMU** would start on 1 January 1999; invited Member States to ratify the **EUROPOL Convention**; approved the establishment of a European Monitoring Centre on Racism and Xenophobia (**EUMC**); in the context of the 1996 **IGC**, asked the incoming Irish Presidency to prepare a general outline for a draft revision of the Treaties; discussed **BSE** in the United Kingdom

FLUIDS
Future lines of user interface decision support (a Telematics Engineering project within the **Telematics Applications Programme**)

FLUSTRIN
Fluid structure interaction (**EUREKA** project)

FMD
Foot and mouth disease. *See also* **EUFMD**, **FIAP**

FMM
Foreign Ministers Meeting . In the context e.g. of the Asia-Europe Meeting (**ASEM**): http://europa.eu.int/comm/external_relations/asem/cluster/process.htm

FNVA
Farm net value-added

FoB
Free on board. Contract term meaning that the seller is required to deliver and load goods on board a ship in the port of shipment specified in the sale contract

FoB
Friends of Bruges. *See* **Bruges Group**

FOCUS
Front-ends for open and closed user systems (**ESPRIT** project)

FOD
French Overseas Departments: Guadeloupe, French Guiana, Martinique, Réunion (Territoires d'outre-mer - TOM; départements d'outre-mer - DOM)

FoEE
Friends of the Earth Europe.
29 rue Blanche, B-1060 Brussels, Belgium.
www.foeeurope.org

FOF
Towards an integrated theory for design, production and production management of complex, one-of-a-kind products in the factory of the future (**ESPRIT** project)

FOI
Freedom of information

Fontainebleau Summit
The main decisions taken at the Fontainebleau **European Council** in June 1984 were to reduce the UK's contributions to the Community budget, and to increase the Community's resources by raising the **VAT** ceiling from 1% to 1.4%. The Summit also set up the **Dooge** committee and the **Adonnino** committee on a People's Europe

Footbridge
See **Passerelle**

FOPS
Falling-object protective structures relating to wheeled agricultural or forestry tractors

FORATOM
European Atomic Forum.
15-17 rue Belliard, 8e étage, B-1040 Brussels, Belgium.
www.foratom.org

FORCCE
Forum sur le commerce Canada-Europe (Canada-Europe Round Table for Business - CERT).
57 rue Froissart, B-1040 Brussels, Belgium.
www.canada-europe.org

FORCE
Formation Continue en Europe (Development of continuing vocational training in Europe) (1990-1993) (**OJ** L156/90). Continued as part of the **Leonardo da Vinci** programme

Force Catalogue
List of **Member States**' national contributions to the Union's rapid reaction capabilities. *See also* **Headline Goal**

FORES
Forestry statistical domain on the **New Cronos** databank

FOREST
Forestry sector research and technology (Subprogramme of the Raw Materials and Recycling programme) (1990-1992) **(OJ** L359/89). Continued as **AIR**

Forest Focus
Proposal for a **Regulation** concerning monitoring of forests and environmental interactions in the Community. **COM**(2002)404 - issued July 2002; still under discussion July 2003.
http://europa.eu.int/comm/environment/nature/forest-regulations.htm

Forest Trees
The study of genetic diversity in forest species (a **BIOTECH** project)

FORFUN
Formal description of arbitrary systems by means of functional languages (**ESPRIT** project)

FORMAST
Formal methods for asynchronous system technology (**ESPRIT** project)

FORMENTOR
Expert system for dealing with major plant failures and security control (**EUREKA** project)

FOR-ME-TOO
Formalisms, methods and tools (**ESPRIT** project)

FORMEX
Formalised exchange of electronic publications. An **OOPEC** programme to store multi-lingual publications in machine-readable format. Details published in 1984

FORNET
European Foreign Policy Research Network. "Represents the first formal attempt to structure and co-ordinate a network of researchers across Europe focusing on foreign policy governance".
www.fornet.info

Fortress Europe
Phrase used by US businesses in the run-up to the Single Market (**SEM**) to refer to Europe's perceived protectionist stance. Since used in other contexts, including enlargement and immigration

FORTUNE
Forum of user-organisations training for usability and networking in Europe (a Telematics for Disabled and Elderly People project within the **Telematics Applications Programme**)

Forty Eight Hour Directive
See **Working Time Directive**

FORUM
A pan-European network for language courses (a Telematics for Education and Training project within the **Telematics Applications Programme**)

Fouchet Plan
Produced between March 1961 and April 1962 by a committee chaired by Christian Fouchet, French Ambassador to Denmark. The Plan sought to enhance the **Member States**' roles in foreign and defence policy by creating a 'union of states' based on intergovernmental co-operation

of **Enlargement**. Published in the *Bulletin of the EC* Supplement 1/78

FRG
Federal Republic of Germany (West Germany)

FRIDA
Framework for integrated dynamic analysis of travel and traffic (**DRIVE** project)

FRIENDS
Farming and rural information, expertise and news dissemination service (a Telematics for Urban and Rural Areas project within the **Telematics Applications Programme**)

FRSWG
Fast Reactor Safety Working Group

FRUCTUS
Orchards statistical domain on the **New Cronos** databank

FRY
Federal Republic of Yugoslavia (sometimes Former Republic of Yugoslavia)

FSA-HSC
Formal safety assessment of high-speed craft. Project in the field of design, production and operation for safer, more efficient, environmentally friendly and user-friendly ships (coordinated by **TN-NETS**)

FSAP
Financial Services Action Plan.
http://europa.eu.int/comm/internal_market/en/finances/actionplan

FSE
Fonds Social Européen (European Social Fund - **ESF**)

FSESP
Fédération Syndicale Européenne des Services Publics (European Federation of Public Service Unions - **EPSU**)

FSGP
Financial Services Policy Group of personal representatives of EU Finance Ministers

FSSRS
Farm survey support reference system

FSU
Forward Studies Unit. A **European Commission** unit set up in 1989 to monitor and evaluate European integration.
http://europa.eu.int/comm/cdp/index_en.htm

FTAA
Free Trade Area of the Americas

FTSC
Fusion Technology Steering Committee

Fuel Gap Programme
A **Tacis** initiative to help compensate Ukraine for the deficit in electricity production which resulted from the closure of the Chernobyl nuclear plant in December 2000

FUNCODE
Coding, service and interoperability for high-quality videotelephones and high-definition television (**RACE** project)

FURS
Functional urban regions

FUSION
Decision 1999/175/Euratom adopting a **Key Actions** programme in the field of nuclear energy (1998-2002) (**OJ** L64/99).
http://europa.eu.int/comm/dg12/fusion1.html

Fusion Treaty
Another name for the **Merger Treaty**

FVA
Food and Veterinary Agency. Predecessor of the **FVO**

Founding Treaties
Collective term for the **Treaty of Paris** and **Treaties of Rome**

FOURCOM
Network for information exchange on competition policy (**IDA** project)

Four Freedoms
The free movement of goods, services, people and capital - the base on which the Single Market (**SEM**) is built

Fourth Framework Programme
Covered EU research and technological development activities 1994-1998. Seen also as 4FP and FP4. *See also* **Framework Programme, Fifth Framework Programme, Sixth Framework Programme**.
http://europa.eu.int/comm/research/fp4.html

Fourth Motor Insurance Directive
Directive 2000/26/EC on the approximation of the laws of the **Member States** relating to insurance against civil liability in respect of the use of motor vehicles and amending Directives 73/239/EEC and 88/357/EEC (**OJ** L181/00)

FOWM
Fibre optic well monitoring system (**EUREKA** project)

FP
Flash profile (within **BC-NET**)

FP
Framework Programme

FP4
Fourth Framework Programme

FP5
Fifth Framework Programme

FP6
Sixth Framework Programme

FR
Français (French)

FRAMES
European agreement on the radio access system for third generation multi-media mobile communications (**ACTS** project)

Framework Directive
A term sometimes used to denote a **Directive** which sets out a framework for action, within which specific points are addressed by individual legislative acts (e.g. Water Framework Directive - **WFD**)

Framework Programme
A broad programme of activity, within which specific actions take place. Used especially in the context of research and technological development (RTD). *See also* **Third framework Programme, Fourth Framework Programme, Fifth Framework Programme, Sixth Framework Programme, Third framework Programme**.

Francovich v Italy
Case C-6/90, in which the **European Court of Justice** held that an individual can claim damages directly against a state for loss suffered because of the state's failure to implement a **Directive**

FRCC
Fast Reactors Coordinating Committee

Free movement
One of the **Four Freedoms** on which the Single Market (**SEM**) is based

Free Mover
Student who does not participate in an **ICP** of the **Erasmus** and **Socrates** programmes, but who may apply for a grant under the programme

Fresco Report
on the general considerations of the problems

FVO
Food and Veterinary Office. Part of the **European Commission**'s Health and Consumer Protection **DG**. Based at Grange, County Meath, Ireland.
http://europa.eu.int/comm/food/fs/inspections/index_en.html

FWP
Framework Programme

FYROM
Former Yugoslav Republic of Macedonia (also seen as fYROM)

G

G
Greece (sometimes used for Germany)

G5
Group of Five major industrial democracies: France, Germany, Japan, UK, US

G6
Group of Six major industrial democracies: France, Germany, Italy, Japan, UK, US

G7
Group of Seven major industrial democracies: Canada, France, Germany, Italy, Japan, UK, US

G7 GLOPHIN
Global public health information network feasibility study / accompanying measure (a Telematics for Healthcare project within the **Telematics Applications Programme**)

G8
Group of Eight major industrial democracies: Canada, France, Germany, Italy, Japan, Russia, UK, US.
www.g7.utoronto.ca [sic]

G20
Group of 20. Members are the **G7** plus: Argentina, Australia, Brazil, China, India, Mexico, Russia, Saudi Arabia, South Africa, South Korea, Turkey, EU and IMF/World Bank.
www.hacienda.gob.mx/g20-2003

G24
Intergovernmental Group of Twenty-Four on International Monetary Affairs. Algeria, Argentina, Brazil, Colombia, Congo, Côte d'Ivoire, Egypt, Ethiopia, Gabon, Ghana, Guatemala, India, Iran, Lebanon, Mexico, Nigeria, Pakistan, Peru, Philippines, South Africa, Sri Lanka, Syria, Trinidad and Tobago, Venezuela.
www.g24.org

G77
Group of 77. Afghanistan, Algeria, Angola, Antigua and Barbuda, Argentina, Bahamas, Bahrain, Bangladesh, Barbados, Belize, Benin, Bhutan, Bolivia, Bosnia and Herzegovina, Botswana, Brazil, Brunei Darussalam, Burkina Faso, Burundi, Cambodia, Cameroon, Cape Verde, Central African Republic, Chad, Chile, China, Colombia, Comoros, Democratic Republic of the Congo, Republic of the Congo, Costa Rica, Côte d'Ivoire, Cuba, Cyprus, Djibouti, Dominica, Dominican Republic, Ecuador, Egypt, El Salvador, Equatorial Guinea, Ethiopia, Fiji, Gabon, Gambia, Ghana, Grenada, Guatemala, Guinea, Guinea-Bissau, Guyana, Haiti, Honduras, India, Indonesia, Iran, Iraq, Jamaica, Jordan, Kenya, Democratic People's Republic of Korea, Republic of Korea, Kuwait, Lao People's Democratic Republic, Lebanon, Lesotho, Liberia, Libya, Madagascar, Malawi, Malaysia, Maldives, Mali, Malta, Marshall Islands, Mauritania, Mauritius, Micronesia, Mongolia, Morocco, Mozambique, Myanmar, Namibia, Nepal, Nicaragua, Niger, Nigeria, Oman, Pakistan, Panama, Papua New Guinea, Paraguay, Peru, Philippines, Qatar, Romania, Rwanda, St. Kitts and Nevis, St. Lucia, St. Vincent and the Grenadines, Sao Tome and Principe, Saudi Arabia, Senegal, Seychelles, Sierra Leone, Singapore, Solomon Islands, Somalia, South Africa, Sri Lanka, Sudan, Suriname,

Swaziland, Syrian Arab Republic, Tanzania, Thailand, Togo, Tonga, Trinidad and Tobago, Tunisia, Uganda, United Arab Emirates, Uruguay, Vanuatu, Venezuela, Vietnam, Western Samoa, Yemen, Yugoslavia, Zambia, Zimbabwe, Palestine Liberation Organization (PLO).
www.g77.org

Gaborone Amendment
Allows regional economic integration organisations to accede to the **CITES** Convention. Adopted 1983 in Gaborone, Botswana

GAC
General Advisory Committee of the **JRC**

GAEIB
Group of Advisers on the Ethical Implications of Biotechnology. Replaced by **EGE**.
http://europa.eu.int/comm/european_group_ethics/index_en.htm

GAERC
General Affairs and External Relations Council (of the **Council of the European Union**)

GAG
General Affairs Group (of the **Council of the European Union**)

GALA
Global access to local applications and services (a Telematics for Integrated Applications for Digital Sites project within the **Telematics Applications Programme**)

GALENO 2000
Development of automatic non-invasive medical diagnostic equipment based on new sensors and artificial intelligence (**EUREKA** project)

GALILEO
Satellite navigation technology project (a project within the **GNSS** programme).
http://europa.eu.int/comm/dgs/energy_transport/galileo/index_en.htm

GALILEO time
Extremely precise time measurement provided via the GALILEO programme.
http://europa.eu.int/comm/dgs/energy_transport/galileo/applications/time_en.htm

GAMES
General architecture for medical expert systems (**AIM** project)

GAMMA-EC
Gaming and multimedia applications for environmental crisis management training (**EMTF** project)

GAP
Analysis and forecasting group. A sub-group of **SOG-T**

GASTER
Gastrointestinal endoscopy applications for standards in telecommunications and research (a Telematics for Healthcare project within the **Telematics Applications Programme**)

GAT
General air traffic. In the context of managing civilian airspace

Gate2Growth
European Commission-supported initiative to help projects or companies find investors, under the **Innovation/SMEs** programme. Successor to **LIFT**.
www.gate2growth.com

GATS
General Agreement on Trade in Services.
http://europa.eu.int/comm/trade/issues/sectoral/services/index_en.htm

GATT
General Agreement on Tariffs and Trade (1948-1994). *See* **WTO**

GAUCHO
General distributed architecture for unified communication in heterogeneous OSI-environments (**ESPRIT** project)

GB
Great Britain

GBDe
Global Business Dialogue on Electronic Commerce.
www.gbde.org

GCAC
General Concerted Action Committee

GDP
Gross domestic product

GDR
German Democratic Republic (Deutsche Demokratische Republik - DDR; the former East Germany)

GEAP
Groupe Européen d'Administration Publique (European Group of Public Administration - **EGPA**)

GEBC
Groupement Européen des Banques Coopératives (European Association of Co-operative Banks).
26-38 rue de l'industrie, B-1040 Brussels, Belgium.
www.gebc.coop

Geel
A **JRC** establishment.
Steenweg op Retie, B-2440 Geel, Belgium

GEIE
Groupemement Européen d'Intérêt Economique (European Economic Interest Group - **EEIG**)

GELOS
Global Environmental Information Locator Service

GEMET
General multilingual environmental thesaurus.
www.mu.niedersachsen.de/cds/etc-cds_neu/software.html#GEMET

GEN
Global European ntwork agreement for digital telecommunication links between the **Member States**

GENDA
General case handling database (**EFTA**)

GENE
European Parliament Temporary Committee on Human Genetics and Other New Technologies of Modern Medicine

GENEDIS
Real-time generation of the 2.5D sketch for moving scenes (**ESPRIT** project)

GENELEX
Generic lexicon (**EUREKA** project)

GENESIS
Development of distributed memory **MIMD** system for very high performance numerical computing (**ESPRIT** project)

GENESIS
A general environment for formal systems development (**ESPRIT** project)

GENIS
Standardisation support for GEN (an Electronic Commerce project within **ISIS**)

GENIUS ZEUS
Integrated system to promote advanced tourist services in Europe (a Telematics for Urban and Rural Areas project within the **Telematics Applications Programme**)

Genscher-Colombo Plan
A 1981 initiative by the German and Italian Foreign Ministers, Hans-Dietrich Genscher and Emilio Colombo, to include security and defence within European Political Cooperation (**EPC**)

GEO
Application of robotics to the construction industry to eliminate laborious and dangerous tasks as well as improving productivity (**EUREKA** project)

GEOMED
Geographical mediation system (a Telematics Information Engineering project within the **Telematics Applications Programme**)

GEONOM
Nomenclature of countries and territories for the external trade statistics of the Community and statistics of trade between **Member States**.
http://europa.eu.int/comm/eurostat/ramon/geonom/geonom_en.html

GEOSERVE
Geo-data access services (a Telematics for Administrations project within the **Telematics Applications Programme**)

GEOSTAR
Geophysical and oceanographic station for abyssal research. A deep sea observatory (**MAST III** project)

GEOTEL
Application pilot in the petroleum and chemicals industry (**RACE** project)

GESAC
Groupement Européen des Sociétés d'Auteurs et Compositeurs (European Grouping of Societies of Authors and Composers).
23 rue Montoyer, B-1000 Brussels, Belgium.
www.gesac.org

GESMES
Generic statistical message: an **Edifact** message

GETS
Global emergency telemedicine service (a Telematics for Healthcare project within the **Telematics Applications Programme**)

GFAP
See **Dayton Accords**

GFCF
Gross fixed capital formation

GIDS
Generic intelligent driver support system (**DRIVE** project)

GINGER 2000
Improvement of communications between European public engineering works sites … (**EUREKA** project)

GINTRAP
Guide to industrial trading regulations and practice. CD-ROM database of EC and national legislation concerning consumer protection and trading standards, published in the early 1990s by **ELLIS**

Giovannini Group
Formed in 1996 to advise the **European Commission** on financial market issues. Chaired by Alberto Giovannini, Deputy General Manager of Banca di Roma.
http://europa.eu.int/comm/economy_finance/giovannini_en.htm

GIPE
Generation of interactive programming environments (**ESPRIT** project)

GIRP
Groupement International de la Répartition Pharmaceutique Européenne (European Association of Pharmaceutical Wholesalers).
40avdeBroqueville,B-1200Brussels,Belgium

GISCO
Geographic information system of the **European Commission** (topographical data from **EUROSTAT**)

GISEDI
Electronic trade for geographical information (a Telematics Information Engineering project within the **Telematics Applications Programme**)

GISELA
Groupe Interservice Elargissement (Interservice Group on Enlargement)

GLOBAL HORIZON
Feasibility study on the implementation of the European component of the **G7** global cancer network sub-project (a Telematics for Healthcare project within the **Telematics Applications Programme**)

GLOBE
Global Legislators Organization for a Balanced Environment. A group of European and American legislators formed to improve the global environment.
www.globeinternational.org

GLOBIS
Global change and biodiversity in soils (**TERI** project)

GLP
Good laboratory practice

GMES
Global monitoring for environment and security. Project to deliver satellite processed data and geographic information.
www.gmes.info

GMMs
Genetically modified micro-organisms. **Directive** 90/219/EEC (**OJ** L117/90)

GMOs
Genetically Modified Organisms. **Directive** 90/220/EEC (**OJ** L117/90) no longer in force - replaced by Directive 2001/18/EC (OJ L106/01) which was amended by **Regulation** 1830/2003, concerning the traceability and labelling of genetically modified organisms and the traceability of food and feed products produced from genetically modified organisms (OJ L268/03)

Gmunden
See **Declaration of Gmunden**

GNP
Gross national product

GNSS
Global navigation satellite system

GoDigital
A promotional campaign by **DG** Enterprise to encourage **SME**s to use the internet.
http://europa.eu.int/ISPO/ecommerce/godigital/Welcome.html

Go East/Go West
A **European Parliament** initiative to enable researchers from the West to spend time in **CEEC** and vice versa (**EP Doc** A3 174/90)

Golden Banana
Term for the area linking Madrid and Barcelona with Northern Italy via Provence

Goldplating
A term used (especially in the UK) to describe the over-zealous interpretation of EU legislation by national officials

GOPA
Group of Policy Advisers.
http://europa.eu.int/comm/dgs/policy_advisers/index_en.htm

Gov
Government

GOV
Government accounts statistical domain on the **New Cronos** databank

GPIC
CADDIA policy interservice group

GPPC
General purpose portable communicator (**TIDE** project)

GPRMC
European Composites Industry Association. Diamant Building, 80 blvd A. Reyerslaan, B-1030 Brussels, Belgium.
www.gprmc.be

GPSD
General Product Safety Directive. **Directive** 92/59/EEC on general product safety (**OJ** L228/92)

GR
Greek / Greece

GRADIENT
Graphics and knowledge-based dialogue for dynamic systems (**ESPRIT** project)

GRAMINAE
Biosphere atmosphere interactions of ammonia with grasslands across Europe (**TERI** project)

GrantPoint
Database of grants and other support available for individuals and small firms in the UK. Published by EPRC Ltd.
www.eprcltd.strath.ac.uk/grantpoint

GRASP
Global retrieval access and information system for property items (a Telematics for Administrations project within the **Telematics Applications Programme**)

GRASPIN
Personal workstation for incremental graphic specialisation and formal implementation of non-sequential systems (**ESPRIT** project)

GRECO
Groupement Européen pour la Circulation des Oeuvres (**MEDIA** project).

GREEN
General Research on Environment for Eastern European Nations. A **European Parliament** own-initiative proposal (**EP Doc** A3 174/90)

'Green G8'
A group of eight environmental non-governmental organisations (NGOs) which presents an annual scorecard on the **European Commission**'s environmental performance. The Group comprises: BirdLife International, Climate Action Network, European Environmental Bureau, Friends of the Earth Europe, Friends of Nature International, Greenpeace European Unit, European Federation for Transport and Environment, WWF European Policy Office.
www.foeeurope.org/links/g8.htm

Green borders
Land borders. Usually seen used in conjunction with 'blue' borders (sea) and 'air' borders

Green Currency
See **Green Rate**

Green Diplomacy
The idea of integrating the environment into the Union's external relations by promoting diplomacy on environment and sustainable development

GreenLight
A voluntary programme in which non-residential electricity consumers commit themselves to installing energy-efficient lighting technologies. Launched in February 2000.
www.eu-greenlight.org

Green Paper
A discussion paper which is widely circulated for comment. Precedes a **White Paper**.
http://europa.eu.int/comm/off/green/index_en.htm

Green Pound
See **Green Rate**

Green Rate
An artificial exchange rate used to convert **CAP** support prices into national currencies. Also seen as Green Currency, Green Pound

Greens/EFA
Greens and European Free Alliance group (of the **European Parliament**). Previously **EFA**, Greens, **V**.
www.greens-efa.org/en

Green wastes
See **Wastes**

GRETA
Co-fired green-tape ceramics as a three-dimensional hybrid component (CC-3D) (**EUREKA** project)

Grey List
of dangerous substances discharged into the aquatic environment under **Directive** 76/464/EEC (**OJ** L129/76 - List 2). *See also* **Black List**

GRIM
Groupe Réglementation, Information et Management. Set up in 1987 by **DG** III of the **European Commission**

GRIP
Greenland ice core project (**EPOCH** project)

GRIPS
General relation-based information processing software

Grotius
Programme aimed at legal practitioners, to promote judicial cooperation between **Member States**, 1996-2000. Superseded by the Grotius II criminal programme for judicial cooperation in criminal matters (**Decision** 2001/512/JHA; **OJ** L186/2001).
http://europa.eu.int/comm/justice_home/project/grotius_genpenal_en.htm

Grotius Civil Programme
Programme of incentives and exchanges for legal practitioners in the area of civil law, 1996 to 2000. Extended to 31 December 2001.
http://europa.eu.int/comm/justice_home/project/grotius_civil_en.htm

GroupDesk
A **CSCW** project to provide support for cooperation and awareness in distributed working groups.
http://orgwis.gmd.de/projects/GroupDesk

Groupeuro
Network of conference speakers specialising in **EMU** affairs

GROUPISOL
Groupement des Producteurs de l'UE de Céramiques Techniques (Association of the European Manufacturers of Technical Ceramics for Electronic, Electrical, Mechanical and other Applications)

GROW
Global real order web (a Telematics for Urban and Rural Areas project within the **Telematics Applications Programme**)

GROWTH
Specific programme for **RTD** and demonstration on competitive and sustainable growth (1998-2002). **Decision** 1999/169/EC (**OJ** L64/99). One of the **Thematic Programmes** which form part of the **Fifth Framework Programme**. Previously **BRITE/EURAM III**, **SMT**

Growth, Competitiveness and Employment
White Paper on growth, competitiveness, employment: the challenges and ways forward into the 21st Century (**COM**(93)700 and *Bulletin of the EC* Supplement 6/93 - in 2 parts).
http://europa.eu.int/en/record/white/c93700/contents.html

GRPDS
Generic reliability parameter data system. Part of **ERDS**

GRULA
Grupo Regional Latin / Grupo Latinoamericano. Seen variously as Group of Latin American countries / Group of Latin American and Caribbean countries / Informal group of Latin-American members of the **WTO**

GRUNDTVIG
Adult education and lifelong learning programme (within the **Socrates** programme)

GSP
Generalised system of preferences. Preferential import duties into the EU from developing countries

GTS
Galileo technical support

GUE/NGL
Groupe Confédéral de la Gauche Unitaire Européenne / Gauche Verte Nordique (Confederal Group of the European United Left / Nordic Green Left in the **European Parliament**).
www.europarl.eu.int/gue

GUIB
Textual and graphical user interfaces for blind people (**TIDE** project)

GUIDE
Telematics applications for education and training documentation guide support (a Telematics for Education and Training project within the **Telematics Applications Programme**)

GUTENBERG
A programme to promote access to books and reading (**OJ** C183/89 and OJ C160/93)

GVA
Gross value added

Gymnich
An informal weekend meeting of EU Foreign Ministers in the country holding the Presidency. Named after a castle in Germany where the first such meeting was held

H

HAA
Development of hybrid antibodies of the anthracycline group (**EUREKA** project)

Habitats Directive
Directive 92/43/EEC on the conservation of natural habitats and of wild fauna and flora (**OJ** L206/92). See also **Natura 2000**

HACCP
Hazard analysis critical control point

HAE2000
Healthy Ageing Europe **Industrial Platform**.
http://europa.eu.int/comm/dg12/biotech/ip2.html#HAE

Hague Report
on the Common Fisheries Policy, July 1976. Not published, but associated Council **Resolution** published in **OJ** C105/81

Hague Summit
At their December 1969 meeting in The Hague, leaders of the **6** EC **Member States** agreed to start membership negotiations with Denmark, Ireland, Norway and the UK. They also discussed political unification, agreed **to** adopt definitive arrangements for the **CAP**, and that the Community should have its **own resources**.

HALIOS
Development of technologies for future fishing vessels (**EUREKA** project)

Hallstein Doctrine
A principle of foreign policy under which the Federal Republic of Germany (West Germany) claimed to be the sole representative of Germany in international relations, and would not establish or maintain diplomatic relations with countries which recognised the German Democratic Republic (DDR - East Germany)

HALOMAX
Mid and high latitude stratospheric distribution of long and short lived halogen species during the maximum chlorine loading (**THESEO** project)

HAMPIIS
Hearing aids and mobile phones immunity and interference standards (**ISIS** Multimedia Systems project)

HANDYAIDS
An index of technical aids available in Europe for disabled people. A module of **HANDYNET**

HANDYCE
An EU information system for disabled people consisting of **HANDYLEX** and **HANDYCOM**. Not developed

HANDYCOM
Any document of EU origin relating to disabled people which does not appear in **HANDYLEX**. Not operational

HANDYLEX
EU and national legislation concerned with the disabled. Not operational

HANDYNET
An EU information system containing descriptions of technical aids for disabled

people set up by **Decision** 89/658 (**OJ** L393/89). No longer in force

HANDYSEARCH
Index of current research on technical aids for disabled people in the EU. Not operational

HANDYTEC
An information system on technical aids for the disabled within **HANDYNET**

HANDYVOC
A multi-lingual thesaurus on technical aids for the disabled. Not operational

HANDYWHO
A European index of organisations associated with technical aids for the disabled within **HANDYNET**

HANSA
Healthcare advanced networked system architecture (a Telematics for Healthcare project within the **Telematics Applications Programme**)

HARD
Hardware resources for development (**CADDIA** project)

HARDIE
Harmonisation of roadside and driver information in Europe (**DRIVE** project)

HARP
An autonomous speech rehabilitation system for hearing impaired people (**TIDE** project)

HASS
Home accident surveillance system (1976-1986). Continued as **EHLASS**, which in turn became **INJURY-PREV C**

HASTE
Health and Safety in Europe. A report and off-line database published in 1995 by **EFILWC**

HATS
Hands assessment and treatment system (a Telematics for Disabled and Elderly People project within the **Telematics Applications Programme**)

HAWK
Knowledge-based open publication model for intelligent media services (a Telematics Information Engineering project within the **Telematics Applications Programme**)

HBS
Household budgets survey statistical domain on the **New Cronos** databank

HCM
Human capital and mobility programme (1990-1994) (**OJ** L107/92). Previously **SCIENCE**. Continued as **TMR**

HCPI
Harmonised consumer price index. Produced by each **Member State** (**OJ** C84/95)

HC-REMA
Health care resource management (a Telematics for Healthcare project within the **Telematics Applications Programme**)

HD
Harmonised document. Issued by **CEN / CENELEC** when details of a European standard cannot be agreed

HDG
Horizontal Drugs Group which coordinates the drugs activities of the EU. Set up in 1997 by **COREPER**

HDTV
High-definition television. Compatible high-definition television system (**EUREKA** project)

Headline Goal
The EU's military capability to be achieved by 2003. Essentially being able "to deploy rapidly and then sustain forces capable of the full range of **Petersberg Tasks** as set out in the Amsterdam Treaty." Also seen as Helsinki Headline Goal.
http://ue.eu.int/pesc/Military/en/HeadGoal.htm

HEALTHBENCH
Health information and decision support workbench (**AIM** project)

HEALTHLINE
Securing the success of health telematics projects implementation of the telehealth through information dissemination and training (a Telematics for Healthcare project within the **Telematics Applications Programme**)

HEALTHPLANS
A concerted action to support national and regional health authorities in developing plans for the introduction of healthcare telematics (a Telematics for Healthcare project within the **Telematics Applications Programme**)

HEALTHWATCH
Healthwatch database (a Telematics for Healthcare project within the **Telematics Applications Programme**)

HEARDIP
Hearing aid research with digital intelligent processing (**TIDE** project)

HEART
Horizontal European activities in rehabilitation technology (**TIDE** project)

Hebdos
Weekly meetings of **European Commissioners**' chief advisors

HECTOR
Health emergency management and coordination through telematics operational resources (a Telematics for Healthcare project within the **Telematics Applications Programme**)

HEF
Human embryo and foetus group. Working group in the field of bioethics. Replaced **ESLA** and **HER**

HELEN
Investigation into Greek language transliteration problems (project within Area 5 of the **Telematics Systems Programme**)

Helena Prize
European Parliament prize for women achievers in art; industry and commerce; science and scientific research and for outstanding contributions to public life

HELIOS
Hospital environment language within an information object system (**AIM** project)

HELIOS II
Handicapped people in the European Community living independently in an open society (1993-1996). **Decision** 93/136/EEC (**OJ** L56/93)

HELP'ME
Handicapped elderly lonely person's multimedia equipment (**TIDE** project)

Helsinki Convention
on the protection of the marine environment of the Baltic Sea area (**OJ** L73/94)

Helsinki Declaration
of the **Economic and Social Committee**, concerning the **Convention on the Future of Europe**.
www.esc.eu.int/CESlink/docs/Dec_Helsinki_EN.pdf

Helsinki Group
Alternative name for the **Helsinki Six**

Helsinki Group
Comprises national civil servants involved in promoting the participation of women in science. The Group, which assists the **European Commission** in preparing comparable European statistics and indicators, first met in Helsinki in November 1999.
www.cordis.lu/improving/women/activities.htm

Helsinki Headline Goal
See **Headline Goal**

Helsinki Six
The group of countries with which the **European Union** started accession negotiations in February 2000: Bulgaria, Latvia, Lithuania, Malta, Romania, Slovakia. The decision to open negotiations was made at the 1999 **Helsinki Summit**. Also known as the Helsinki Group

HEPATITIS C
Development of diagnostic screening and confirmation assays for detection of hepatitis C virus infection: cloning (**EUREKA** project)

HER
Human embryo research. *See* **HEF**

HERCULE
Application of robotics to the construction industry (**EUREKA** project)

HEREIN
Heritage information network (a Telematics for Administrations project within the **Telematics Applications Programme**)

HERITAGE
Historic environment for integrated telematics application programmes in Europe (a Telematics for Integrated Applications for Digital Sites project within the **Telematics Applications Programme**)

HERMES
Harmonised European research on models of energy systems. A European model which analyses the inter-relationships between energy and the economy

HERMES
Message handling survey and trends for the IES user community (**ESPRIT** project)

HERMES
Telematic healthcare, remoteness and mobility factors in common European scenarios (a Telematics for Healthcare project within the **Telematics Applications Programme**)

HERODE
Handling of mixed text/image/voice documents based on a standardised office document architecture (**ESPRIT** project)

HESSILSIL
Heterostructure of semiconducting silicides on silicon-applications to SI compatible optoelectronic devices (**ESPRIT** project)

HFR
High flux reactor at **Petten**

HICP
Harmonised index of consumer prices. Alternative version of **HCPI**

HIDCIM
Holographic labelling techniques for automatic identification in CIM-environments (**ESPRIT** project)

HIEMS
Health information exchange and monitoring system (**IDA** project)

High Authority
The original executive body of the **ECSC**. Together with the **EEC** and **EURATOM** Commissions, it was merged into a single **European Commission** by the **Merger Treaty**

High Representative
for the Common Foreign and Security Policy (**CFSP**). Doubles as Secretary-General of the Council. The current post holder, Javier Solana Madariaga, is also Secretary-General of the Western European Union (**WEU**).
http://ue.eu.int/solana/index.asp

HIPACS
Hospital integrated picture archiving and communication system (**AIM** project)

HIPC
Highly indebted poor countries. Also seen as heavily indebted poor countries.
http://europa.eu.int/scadplus/leg/en/lvb/r12401.htm and www.worldbank.org/hipc

HIPM-FAMILY
Publishing model for family home entertainment (a Telematics Information Engineering project within the **Telematics Applications Programme**)

HIPPOKRATES
A multi-annual programme of incentives and exchanges, training and cooperation for the prevention of crime in the EU, adopted in June 2001. Also seen as Hippocrates.
http://europa.eu.int/comm/justice_home/project/hippokrates/en/index-en.htm

HISTA 3
Therapeutic development of histamine H3 receptor agonist (**EUREKA** project)

HIVITS
High-quality videophone and **HDTV** systems (**RACE** project)

HLEG
High Level Expert Group

HLP
High Level Panel

HLWG
High Level Working Group

HOME
Highly optimised microscope environment (**AIM** project)

HOME
Home applications optimum multimedia/multimodal system for environment control (a Telematics for Disabled and Elderly People project within the **Telematics Applications Programme**)

HOMEBRAIN
Design for all (a Telematics for Disabled and Elderly People project within the **Telematics Applications Programme**)

HOMER-D
Home rehabilitation treatment and dialysis (a Telematics for Healthcare project within the **Telematics Applications Programme**)

HONLEA
Heads of national drugs law enforcement agencies-Europe

HOPE
Humanitarian office programme environment. A financial management database used by **ECHO** to monitor contracts and financial information

HOPES
Horizontal project for the evaluation of trafficsSafety and man-machine interaction (**DRIVE** project)

Horeca
Hotels, restaurants, cafés

Horeca-ta
Hotels, restaurants, cafés, travel agents

HORIZON
Part of the **Community Initiative EMPLOYMENT** (1994-1999), HORIZON sought to improve the employability and job prospects of disabled people.
http://europa.eu.int/comm/employment_social/esf/en/public/sr_hor/sr_hor.htm

HORIZON 2000
on development cooperation in the run-up to 2000 (**SEC**(92)915)

HORIZON ACTION
Horizontal accompanying measure for the action cluster for telematics-assisted cooperative work for healthcare professionals (a Telematics for Healthcare project within the **Telematics Applications Programme**)

Horizontal Programmes
Wide-ranging programmes to ensure coordination, support and coherence within the EU's research policy. A component of the **Fifth Framework Programme**. *See* **IMPROVING**, **INCO II**, **INNOVATION/SMEs**. *See also* **Thematic Programmes**

HOSCOM
Hospitals comparisons: medical and financial data (**AIM** project)

Hotrec
Hotels, restaurants and cafés in Europe

HPC-Vision
Interconnection of broadband sites in France and Germany: a fibre interconnection initiative to prepare for **TEN-Telecommunications**

HPPWB
High performance printing wiring boards (**EUREKA** project)

HPV
Diagnosis of human papilloma virus infection (**EUREKA** project)

HRTP
Japan industry insight programme (now known as Japan industry insight programme).
www.eujapan.com/europe/hrtp.html

HS
Harmonised system (Système harmonisé - SH). Internationally recognized list of commodities which forms the basis for trade negotiations. Managed by the World Customs Organisation.
http://forum.europa.eu.int/irc/dsis/coded/info/data/coded/en/gl000081.htm

HS-ADEPT
Home systems-access for disabled and elderly people to this technology (**TIDE** project)

HSD
Human and social development

HSPRO-EU
Health and safety promotion in the **European Union** (a Telematics for Healthcare project within the **Telematics Applications Programme**)

HSR COMAC
Health service research concerted action committee

HSSCD
Health surveillance system for communicable diseases (**IDA** project). See also **CARE**

HTCOR-DB
A high temperature corrosion database, accessed via the **JRC** at **Petten**

HTDS
Host target development system (**ESPRIT** project)

HTM-DB
High temperature materials databank containing information on engineering materials with high temperature applications. Access via the **JRC** at **Petten**

HTPV
Group of **EUREKA** projects

HUFIT
Human factor laboratories in information technologies (**ESPRIT** project)

Human Capital and Mobility
See **HCM**

HYACE
Hydrate autoclave coring equipment system (**MAST III** project)

HYDRE
Improved water facilities in the Mediterranean area (project)

HYETI
High yield and high reliability ULSI system (project)

HYPDOC
Hypermedia publishing and cooperation (a Telematics Information Engineering project within the **Telematics Applications Programme**)

HYPERLIB
Hypertext interfaces to library information systems.
www.cordis.lu/libraries/en/projects/hyperlib.html

HyperMuseum
The European cultural network (a Telematics for Administrations project within the **Telematics Applications Programme**)

HYPIT
Human resources and management product interface (project)

HYPRO
Establishment of new, advanced treatment of waste water (project)

I

I
Italia (Italy)

i2i
Innovation 2000 Initiative. European Investment Bank (**EIB**) initiative to fund innovation. Initial programme ended 2003; extended to 2010 as the Innovation 2010 Initiative.
www.eib.org/i2i/en/index.htm

I4C
Integration and communication for the continuity of cardiac care (a Telematics for Healthcare project within the **Telematics Applications Programme**)

I&T Magazine
Industry and Telecommunications Magazine which ceased publication in 1997. Previously XIII Magazine

IACIS
Intelligent area communication and information system (**ESPRIT** project)

IADS
Integrated applications for digital sites (**Telematics Applications** project)

IAEVA
A distributed multimedia database and environment for virtual walks of 3D models of human organs (a Telematics for Healthcare project within the **Telematics Applications Programme**)

IAM
Institute for Advanced Materials. Part of the **JRC** at **Petten** and **Ispra**

IAP
Integrated action programme

IAP
Internet Action Plan

IAS
Internal Audit Service (within the **European Commission**).
http://europa.eu.int/comm/dgs/internal_audit/index_en.htm

IBASS
Intelligent business applications support system (**ESPRIT** project)

IBBS
Electronic identification of blood bags in connection with autologous blood banking (**EUREKA** project)

IBC
Integrated broadband communications (**RACE** project)

IBEX
International buyers exhibitions. Ended Spring 2002

IBPP
See **Tacis IBPP**

IBSFC
International Baltic Sea Fishery Commission

ICAN
Integrated communication and control for all needs (a Telematics for Disabled and Elderly People project within the **Telematics Applications Programme**)

ICAO
International Civil Aviation Organization. *See also* **Chicago Convention**.
www.icao.int

ICARE
Industrial characterisation of an advanced resonant etcher (**ESPRIT** project)

ICARE 9000
ISO9000 on-demand consulting and remote electronic training for **SME**s in urban and rural areas (a Telematics for Urban and Rural Areas project within the **Telematics Applications Programme**)

ICAROS
Integrated computational assessment via remote observation system. A three-year project led by the **European Commission** with 10 partners from Greece, Germany, Hungary and Italy to develop an innovative system for monitoring and managing urban air quality and the related health risks.
http://mara.jrc.it/icaros.html

ICARUS
EDI project under the **TEDIS** programme

ICARUS
Incremental construction and reuse of requirements specifications (**ESPRIT** project)

ICARUS
Interurban control and roads utilisation simulation (**DRIVE** project)

ICATT
International Commission for the Conservation of Atlantic Tuna

ICC
International Criminal Court (Cour pénale internationale - CPI). The first permanent international tribunal established to try cases of war crimes, crimes against humanity and genocide. Set up by the signatories of the 1998 Rome Treaty.
www.icc-cpi.int

ICCP
Inter-governmental Committee of the Cartagena Protocol

ICD
Multiview VLSI-design system (**ESPRIT** project)

ICDL
International computer driving licence. *See also* **ECDL** - European computer driving licence

ICE-CAR
Interworking public key certification infrastructure for commerce administration and research (a Telematics for Research project within the **Telematics Applications Programme**)

ICE-TEL
Interworking public key infrastructure for Europe (a Telematics for Research project within the **Telematics Applications Programme**)

ICI
Intelligent communication interface (**ESPRIT** project)

ICP
Information and communication policy

ICP
Inter-university cooperation programmes (within the **Erasmus** programme)

ICSIC
Integrated communication system for intensive care (**AIM** project)

ICSR
Individual case safety reports

ICT
Information and communication technologies

ICTDAS
Integrated CAE [Computer Aided Engineering] techniques for dynamic analysis of structures (**ESPRIT** project)

I-Cubed
Innovation and incubation initiative. Funded under the **Leonardo da Vinci** programme

IDA
Interchange of data between administrations. To become the IDAbc (Interoperable delivery of pan-European eGovernment services to public administrations, businesses and citizens) in 2005.
http://europa.eu.int/ISPO/ida/jsps/index.jsp

IDAbc
See **IDA**

IDEA
Indicators and data for European analysis (funded by the **TSER** programme)

IDEA
Integrated development environment for ADA (**EUREKA** project)

IDEA
Electronic directory of the European **Institutions**. Previously the Inter-institutional Directory of the EU. Created 1996. Also known as 'Who's Who in the European Union?' and sometimes called the 'Organigramme'.
http://europa.eu.int/idea/en/index.htm

IDEAL
Interactive dialogues for explanation and learning (**ESPRIT** project)

IDEAL-IST
Information dissemination and European awareness launch for the **IST** programme

IDEALS
Integration of dedicated for advanced training linked to small and medium enterprises and Institutes of higher education [sic] (a Telematics for Education and Training project within the **Telematics Applications Programme**)

IDEE
Social insertion in urban regions (**RECITE** project)

IDEHA
Integrated electric drive for automation (**EUREKA** project)

IDES
Interactive data entry system (**CADDIA** project)

IDMS
Integrated data management system

IDO
Integrated development operations in urban and industrial areas (within the framework of the **Structural funds**) (1979-1999). *See also* **IDP**

IDP
Integrated development programmes in rural areas (within the framework of the **Structural Funds**) (1979-1999). *See also* **IDO**

IDPS
Integrated design and production system (**ESPRIT** project)

IDRIS
Intelligent drive for shop floor systems (**ESPRIT** project)

IDST
Scientific and technical information and documentation

IE
Ireland

IEAR
European Communities Institute for Economic Analysis

I-EDN
Group of Independents for a Europe of Nations, in the **European Parliament** (4th parliamentary term 1994-1999)

IEEP
Institute for European Environmental Policy. 18 av des Gaulois, B-1040 Brussels, Belgium.
www.ieep.org.uk

IES
Institute for Environment and Sustainability. Part of the **JRC**.
http://ies.jrc.cec.eu.int

IES-DC
European Commission Host Organisation (**ECHO**) database on Information exchange systems - data collections. Directory and reference services on European information technology projects

IESERV2
Information engineering support services (a Telematics Information Engineering project within the **Telematics Applications Programme**)

IETM
Informal European theatre meetings. A **Kaleidoscope** project to facilitate information exchanges amongst people working in the performing arts. 19 square Sainctelette, B-1000 Brussels, Belgium.
www.ietm.org

IFOR
NATO-led Implementation Force in Bosnia and Herzegovina. Also called Operation Joint Endeavour. Spanned 20 December 1995-20 December 1996. Superseded by **SFOR**. *See also* **Dayton Accords**.
www.nato.int/ifor/ifor.htm

IGC
Intergovernmental Conference. A process - not a single meeting - during which representatives of EU governments negotiate on significant issues. *First*: (1950-1951) resulting in the **Paris Treaty**; *Second*: (1955-1957) resulting in the Treaties establishing the **EEC** and **EURATOM**; *Third*: (1985) resulting in the **SEA**; *Fourth/Fifth*: (1990-1991) resulting in the **Treaty on European Union**; *Sixth*: (1996-1997) resulting in the **Amsterdam Treaty**; *Seventh*: (2000-2001) resulting in the **Treaty of Nice**. *Eighth*: (2003-2004) to discuss the proposed **EU** Constitution

IGI
Inter-Institutional Group on Information

IGLO
See **EuRaTIN**

IGO
Intergovernmental organisation

IGOS
Image guided orthopaedic surgery (a Telematics for Healthcare project within the **Telematics Applications Programme**)

IGS
Inspectorate General **DG** of the **European Commission**

IHCP
Institute for Health and Consumer Protection. Created by the **JRC** in 1998 and based at **Ispra**.
http://ihcp.jrc.cec.eu.int

IHS
Integrated home systems: development of a communications system for use inside the home (**EUREKA** project)

IIP
International Investment Partners. *See* also **EC-IIP**

IKAROS
Intelligence and knowledge aided recognition of speech (**ESPRIT** project)

ILE
Isotopic lead experiment (environmental research programme)

ILOs
Immigration Liaison Officers. The 2003 Greek **Presidency** proposed an 'Initiative of the Hellenic Republic with a view to adopting a Council **Regulation** on the creation of an immigration liaison officers network' (**OJ** C140/03)

ILO
International Labour Organization. A **United Nations** body.
4 route des Morillons, CH-1211 Geneva 22, Switzerland.
www.ilo.org

I'M
Information Market

IMACE
International Margarine Association of the Countries of Europe.
168 av de Tervuren, Boîte 12, B-1150 Brussels, Belgium.
www.imace.org

IMAGINE
Integrated multimedia applications generating innovative networks in European digital towns (a Telematics for Integrated Applications for Digital Sites project within the **Telematics Applications Programme**)

IMATE
Innovative multimedia application for textile education (**EMTF** project)

IMAURO
Integrated model for the analysis of urban route optimisation (**DRIVE** project)

I*M EUROPE
Information Market Europe.
www.echo.lu

I*M FORUM
Information Market Forum. A database of organisations and individuals specialising in consultancy on the electronic information market and the identification of partners for calls for research proposals related to the Information Market

IMG
Individual mobility grants to fund individual visits by higher education staff, senior Ministry Officers and education planners within Europe (part of the **Phare** programme)

I*M GUIDE
Information market guide database. Previously **BROKERSGUIDE** and **DIANEGUIDE**

IMMUNITY
Impacts of increased and multiple use of inland navigation and identification of tools to reduce negative impacts (**Transport** project)

IMMUNOSCREEN
Development of two categories of rapid immunoassays based on membrane technology (**EUREKA** project)

IMO
Information Market Observatory. Established under **IMPACT2**. Now ceased.

IMO
International Maritime Organization.
4 Albert Embankment, London SE1 7SR, UK.
www.imo.org

IMP
Integrated Mediterranean Programmes (1985-1993) (**OJ** L197/85)

IMP
Telematic exchange of information on medicinal products (**IDA** project)

IMPACS
Integrated manufacturing planning and control system (**ESPRIT** project)

IMPACT
Implementation aspects concerning planning and legislation (**DRIVE** project)

IMPACT
Increasing the impact of assistive technology (a Telematics for Disabled and Elderly People project within the **Telematics Applications Programme**)

IMPACT 2
Programme for an information services market (1992-1995) (**OJ** L377/91). Continued by **INFO 2000**

Impact Directive
See **Environmental Impact Assessment Directive**

IMPEL
Implementation and enforcement of environmental law: an informal network of the environmental authorities.
http://europa.eu.int/comm/environment/impel

IMPLUS
Improved plastic pipe systems (**EUREKA** project)

IMPPACT
Integrated modelling of products and processes using advanced computer technologies (**ESPRIT** project)

IMPRIMATUR
Intellectual multimedia property rights model and terminology for universal reference (**ESPRIT** project)

IMPROFEED
Development of new methods for the improvement of the feed value of raw materials and feeds (**EUREKA** project)

Improving
Decision 99/173/EC adopting a specific programme for Improving Human Research Potential and the Socio-Economic Knowledge Base (1998-2002) (**OJ** L64/99). One of the **Horizontal programmes** which form part of **Fifth Framework Programme**. Formerly **TMR**, **TSER**.
www.cordis.lu/improving

IMPULSE
Interoperable modular pilot plants underlying logistic system in Europe (**Transport** project).
www.cordis.lu/transport/src/impulse.htm

IMPW
Integrated management process workbench (**ESPRIT** project)

IMRI
Improved magnetic resonance imaging system (**EUREKA** project)

IMSE
Integrated modelling support environment (**ESPRIT** project)

IMT
Industrial and materials technologies programme. Alternative term for **BRITE/ EURAM III**

IMT
Innovation management techniques. A strand of the **INNOVATION** programme. www.cordis.lu/imt/home.html

IMU
Image and movement understanding (**ESPRIT** project)

IMW
Inland and Marine Water Institute at the **JRC**

INAS
Advisory services to the Russian insurance industry. A **Tacis** project

INCA
Integrated network architecture for office communications (**ESPRIT** project)

INCA
Standardised interface for sensors and actuators (**EUREKA** project)

INCARNATION
Efficient inland navigation information system (**Transport** project)

INCIPIT
Bibliographic records and images: a CD-ROM of incunabula editions (project within Area 5 of the **Telematics Systems Programme**)

INCLUDE
Inclusion of disabled and elderly in telematics (a Telematics for Disabled and Elderly People project within the **Telematics Applications Programme**)

INCO
International cooperation. Specific Research and Technological Development Programme in the Field of Cooperation with **Third Countries** and International Organisations, 1994-1998. Superseded by **INCO II**.
http://europa.eu.int/comm/research/intco/achieve/index_en.html

INCO II
Decision 99/171/EC adopting a specific programme confirming the international role of Community research (1998-2002) (**OJ** L64/99). One of the **Horizontal programmes** which form part of **Fifth Framework Programme**. Previously **Copernicus-PECO**; *See also* **INCO**, **INCO-Copernicus**; **INCO-DC**; **INCOPOL**.
www.cordis.lu/inco2/home.html

INCO-Copernicus
Scientific & Technical cooperation with the **CCE** and with the **NIS** (1994-1998). *See also* **Copernicus**; **INCO II**

INCO-DC
Cooperation with **Third Countries** and international organisations - developing countries. *See* also **INCO II**

INCOPOL
International cooperation policies. A series of seven studies commissioned by **INCO** on the cooperation activities of the 18 **EEA** countries (15 **Member States** plus Iceland, Liechtenstein and Norway) in the field of international **RTD** cooperation

IND
Non-attached. Group of the **European Parliament**. Now **NI**

INDAC
Integral nuclear data information centre

INDICES
Interfacing disabled people with industry standard computing environments (**TIDE** project)

INDIS
Information dissemination in European **RTD** (**Phare** project). *See also* **RICE**

INDOC
Intelligent documents production demonstrator (**ESPRIT** project)

Industrial Platform
An industrial grouping established on the initiative of industry around biotechnology **RTD**. *See* **ACTIP**; **BACIP**; **BBP**; **EBIP**; **ENIP**; **FAIP**; **FIP**; **HAE2000**; **IPM**; **IVTIP**; **LABIP**; **PIP**; **SBIP**; **TSE IP**; **YIP**.
http://europa.eu.int/comm/dg12/biotech/ip1.html

IN-EMERGENCY
Integrated incident management, emergency healthcare and environment monitoring in road networks (a Telematics for Integrated Applications for Digital Sites project within the **Telematics Applications Programme**)

INFEO
Earth observation data and information exchange system. Launched by the **CEO** in 1998

INFO 92
A database produced by the Secretariat-General of the **European Commission** which covered progress on the legislation contained in the Single Market (**SEM**) and the **Social Charter**

INFO 2000
Decision 96/339/EC for a multiannual programme to stimulate the development of a European multimedia content industry (1996-1999) (**OJ** L129/96). Previously **IMPACT 2**

InfoCARE
Interactive information system for health/social care (a Telematics for Healthcare project within the **Telematics Applications Programme**)

Infodisk
See **EU Infodisk**

INFOEURO ACCESS
European wide access to information about the **European Union** and its **Member States** (**IMPACT** project)

InfoGrant
Database of grants and other financial assistance schemes available to businesses in the UK. *Successor to* **AIMS**. Published by EPRC Ltd.
www.eprcltd.strath.ac.uk/infogrant

Info-inclusion
The idea of ensuring that the benefits of the Information Society are felt by all EU citizens. The **Feira Summit** endorsed the eEurope 2002 Action Plan, requesting "the institutions ... to ensure its full and timely implementation by 2002 and to prepare longer term perspectives for a knowledge-based economy encouraging info-inclusion and closing the numeracy gap"

INFOLOG
Intermodal information link for improved logistics (**Transport** project)

INFOMALL
Full-cycle information mall (a Telematics Information Engineering project within the **Telematics Applications Programme**)

Infoplanet
Project set up as part of **European Science Week** 2001

InfoPoint Europe
See **EIP**

Inforegio
Term adopted by the **European Commission** for material giving information about the Union's regional policy. More recently a

dedicated regional policy website; now the website of the Commission's **DG** for Regional Policy.
http://europa.eu.int/comm/regional_policy

INFORM
Information management and decision support in high dependency environments (**AIM** project)

Information Relays
See **Relays**

Information Society
See **IS**

Information Society Technologies Programme
See **IST**

Information Technology
See **IST**

InfoRules
Database of business regulations and services. Successor to **STARS**. Published by EPRC Ltd.
www.eprcltd.strath.ac.uk/inforules

INFOS
Assessment of policy instruments for efficient ozone abatement strategies in Europe (**Environment and Climate** project)

INFOSAFE
Information system for road user safety and traffic performance (**DRIVE** project)

INFOSOND
Information and service on demand (a Telematics for Urban and Rural Areas project within the **Telematics Applications Programme**)

INFOSTAT
Information systems project to prepare **ETIS** (**Transport** project)

Infosys
Information and communication system. A gateway to databases on agronomic research for development, established by the **EIARD**

INFSO
Information Society **DG** of the **European Commission**

Initiatives
See **Community Initiatives**

INJURY-PREV C
Decision 372/1999/EC adopting a programme of Community action on injury prevention in the framework for action in the field of public health (1999-2003) (**OJ** L46/99). *See also* **EHLASS**

INLANDWW
Inland waterways transport statistical domain on the **New Cronos** databank

Innobarometer
An opinion poll carried out in 2001 and 2002 under the **Eurobarometer** system, to gauge attitudes towards innovation in Europe.
www.cordis.lu/innovation-smes/src/innobarometer.htm

INNOVAT
Survey on innovation in EU enterprises statistical domain on the **New Cronos** databank

Innovation
Decision 94/917/EC for the dissemination of the results of RTD activities: Activity 3 of the **Fourth Framework Programme** (1994-1998) (**OJ** L361/94). Previously **SPRINT**; **VALUE**. Replaced by **INNOVATION/SMEs**. See also **IMT**; **IRC**.
www.cordis.lu/innovation/home.html

Innovation 2010
See **i2i**

Innovation Relay Centres
See **IRC**

Innovation/SMEs
Decision 1999/172/EC adopting a programme of research, technological development and demonstration to promote innovation and encourage the participation of **SME**s (1998-2002) (**OJ** L64/99). One of the **Horizontal Programmes** which form part of the **Fifth Framework Programme**. Previously **INNOVATION**.
www.cordis.lu/innovation-smes/home.html

INNOVEX
Study and analysis of five **INNOVATION** projects dealing with the management of water in urban and rural regions

INNVEST
A confidential database to provide commercial and technical information on high-tech projects to **EUROTECH CAPITAL** members

INOGATE
Interstate oil and gas transport to Europe. A **Tacis** programme in the field of energy to stimulate cooperation and help ensure the security of supplies of oil and gas from the Caspian and Central Asia regions to European markets

INPARD
Innovative participatory rural development. Initiative proposed in 2002 to help **Applicant Countries** create jobs and improve incomes in rural areas

INPART
Inclusion through participation (**TSER** project)

Ins
Member States participating in **EMU**. *See also* **Outs**

INSCAD
Development of a **CAD/CAM** system for manufacturing customised insoles for shoes (**TIDE** project)

INSEM
Inter-institutional service of electronic mail

INSIGHT
One of three types of activities supported under **NEST**. INSIGHT projects "are designed to investigate and evaluate new discoveries or phenomena which may bring new risks and potential problems for European society. Their aim will be to generate and consolidate scientific understanding, as well as to assist in formulating responses to address such problems."
http://www.cordis.lu/nest/insight.htm

INSIS
Inter-institutional integrated services information system (1983-1992) (**OJ** L368/82)

INSOL Europe
"The European organisation of insolvency professionals". Previously European Insolvency Practitioners Association (EIPA).
www.insol-europe.org

Insolvency Directive
Directive 2002/74/EC amending Directive 80/987/EEC on the approximation of the laws of the **Member States** relating to the protection of employees in the event of the insolvency of their employer (**OJ** L270/02)

INSPIRE
Innovation ship pilot research (**Transport** project)

INSPIRE
Infrastructure for spatial information in Europe. Aims "to make available relevant, harmonised and quality geographic informa-

tion to support formulation, implementation, monitoring and evaluation of Community policies with a territorial dimension or impact."
www.ec-gis.org/inspire

INST
European Parliament Committee on Institutional Affairs

INSTIL
Integration of symbolic and numeric learning techniques (**ESPRIT** project)

Institutions
Officially the European Union has five 'Institutions', identified in the Treaty of Rome: European Parliament, Council of the European Union, European Commission, European Court of Justice, European Court of Auditors. The term is often used, however, to include other EU bodies, as in this order of protocol given in the 'Interinstitutional style guide' issued by the Publications Office: European Parliament, Council of the European Union, European Commission, Court of Justice and Court of First Instance (CFI) of the European Communities, European Court of Auditors, European Economic and Social Committee, Committee of the Regions (CoR), European Investment Bank (EIB), European Central Bank (ECB)

INTAS
International Association for the Promotion of Cooperation with Scientists from the NIS. It consists of the **Member States**, the 12 **NIS**, Switzerland, Norway and Israel.
58 av des Arts, Boîte 8, B-1000 Brussels, Belgium.
www.intas.be

INTEGRA
European manufacturing interface (**EUREKA** project)

INTEGRA
One of the four strands of the **Community Initiative EMPLOYMENT**. Covered homeless, long-term unemployed, gypsies, ex prisoners and drug abusers (1994-1999)

Integrated Project
An instrument under the **Sixth Framework Programme**

INTEGRATION
Integrating the foundations of functional, logic and object-orientated programming (**ESPRIT** project)

IN-TELE
Internet-based teaching and learning (**EMTF** project)

IN#TEL#EC
Integrated telecommunications training for the European Community (**COMETT** programme)

INTER
Project to develop a communications network in the interests of harmonising European railways (within the **Telematics Applications Programme**)

INTERACT
An information system to coordinate measures at local level to achieve the social and economic integration of disabled and old people. Now part of the **HELIOS** network

Interbus Agreement
Decision 2002/917/EC on the international occasional carriage of passengers by coach and bus (**OJ** L321/02). *See also* **ASOR**

INTERCARE
The interworking and interoperability of networked services for healthcare using internet-based technology (a Telematics for Healthcare project within the **Telematics Applications Programme**)

Interconnection Directive
Directive 97/33/EC on interconnection in telecommunications with regard to ensuring universal service and interoperability through application of the principles of **ONP** (**OJ** L199/97)

Interinstitutional style guide
Gives «rules and conventions» intended to produce a uniform publications style across the Union's **institutions** and **official languages**. Published by the **Publications Office**.
http://eur-op.eu.int/general/en/code_en.htm

INTERLAINE
Committee of the Wool Textile Industry in the EEC (Comité des Industries Lainières de la CEE).
www.interlaine.org

INTERMAPS
Interactive multimedia access publishing services (**DELTA** project)

International Partnership for the Hydrogen Economy
Intended to "provide a mechanism to organize, evaluate and coordinate multinational research, development and deployment programs that advance the transition to a global hydrogen economy."
The EU and US announced agreement on the IPHC at the June 2003 EU-US Summit.
www.eere.energy.gov/hydrogenandfuelcells/partnerships.html

Internal Market
Alternative term for Single European Market (**SEM**)

Interprise
Decision 93/379/EEC for initiatives to encourage partnerships between industries and services in Europe (1993-1996) (**OJ** L161/93). Discontinued 2001

Interreg
A **Community Initiative** to stimulate interregional cooperation in the EU. Financed under the European Regional Development Fund (**ERDF**). Interreg III runs from 2000-2006. Incorporated **RECITE**. *See also* **LACE**.
http://europa.eu.int/comm/regional_policy/interreg3

INTERREG Atlantic Area
See **Atlantic Area**

INTERSUDMED
An **IPTS** activity involving cooperation with countries around the Mediterranean in the field of renewable energies

Intervention Price
The minimum guaranteed price for agricultural produce. Intervention Boards in each **Member State** buy farm produce from the market at this agreed price and store it. Prices are published for individual commodities in the **OJ**

INTRA-SEAS
Integrated management of multimodal traffic in ports (**Transport** project)

INTRASTAT
System for collecting intra-Community trade statistics under **Regulation** 3330/91 (**OJ** L316/01). Developed by **Eurostat**, operational January 1993. Intrastat involves collecting information directly from businesses and value added tax records

INUSE
Information engineering usability support centres (a Telematics Information Engineering project within the **Telematics Applications Programme**)

INVAID
Integration of computer vision techniques for automatic incident detection (**DRIVE** project)

INVAS
Capital markets investment advisory services (a **Tacis** project)

Investment Services Directive
Directive 93/22/EEC on investment services in the securities field (**OJ** L141/93). Amendment proposed in **COM**(2000)729

Ioannina Compromise
on voting rules within the **Council of the European Union** (**OJ** C105/94)

IOLE
IBC on-line environment (**RACE** project)

IOP
Integrated operational programme

IOT
Input-output tables of the national accounts. *See* **TES/IOT**

IP
Indicative programme

IP
Industrial platform

IP
Information à la presse. A series of press releases issued by the **European Commission**. Access via **RAPID**:
http://europa.eu.int/rapid/start/cgi/guesten.ksh

IP
See **Integrated Project**

IP
Internet protocol

IPAP
Investment Promotion Action Plan

IPCES
Intelligent process control by means of expert systems (**ESPRIT** project)

IPDES
Integrated product design system (**ESPRIT** project)

IPE
Info-Points Europe. Network of 140 information centres, set up in 1991, «that can serve as your first port of call for any request for information.» Also known as Euro Info Points. *See also* **Relays**.
http://europa.eu.int/comm/relays/ipe/index_en.htm

IPG
Information providers guide. Aimed at authors of pages on **Europa**. Covers editorial, technical and graphic aspects.
http://europa.eu.int/comm/ipg/index_en.htm

IPHE
See **International Partnership for the Hydrogen Economy**

IPM
Industrial Platform for Microbiology.
http://europa.eu.int/comm/dg12/biotech/ip2.html#IPM

IPM
Interactive policy making. An initiative launched by the **European Commission** in 2001 to improve governance in the **European Union** by using the internet to collect and analyse reactions from consumers, business and citizens and to use them in EU policy-making. Replaced **BFM**.
http://europa.eu.int/yourvoice/ipm

IPPC Directive
Directive 96/61/EC concerning integrated pollution prevention and control (**OJ** L257/96).
http://europa.eu.int/comm/environment/ippc/

IPR
Inward processing relief (in relation to customs matters)

IPR
Intellectual property rights

IPSC
Institute for the Protection and Security of the Citizen. Part of the **JRC**, its role is to "provide research-based, systems-oriented support to EU policies so as to protect the citizen against economic and technological risk."
http://ipsc.jrc.cec.eu.int

IPSI
Improved port/ship interface (**Transport** project)

IPSNI
Integration of people with special needs by the **IBC** (**RACE** project)

IPTF
International Police Task Force

IPTS
Institute for Prospective Technological Studies. Part of the **JRC** at Seville.
www.jrc.es

IPv6
Internet protocol version 6. **COM**(2002)96: Communication on next generation internet - priorities for action in migrating to the new Internet protocol IPv6.
www.ipv6.org

IQ
Intelligent quattro to develop intelligent mechatronic automation and a remote control system for hydraulically operated vehicles which gives possibilities to wide range applications (**EUREKA** project)

IQSG
Inter-service Quality Support Group. Established by the European Commission in September 2000 to monitor the consistency and quality of external aid programming documents. Also seen as iQSG

IRC
Innovation Relay Centre. A network of 68 Centres set up originally under the **VALUE** programme to promote innovation and the exchange of research results. Contined under the **INNOVATION** and **INNOVATION/SMEs** programmes. *See also* **Relays**.
www.cordis.lu/irc/home.html

IRDAC
Industrial R&D Advisory Committee. Previously **CORDI**. Replaced by European Research Forum (**ERF**).
http://europa.eu.int/comm/dg12/irdac.html

IRDSS
Integrated regional development support system (a Telematics for Urban and Rural Areas project within the **Telematics Applications Programme**)

IRE
Innovating regions in Europe. A network of 200-plus members.to facilitate the exchange of experience between regions interested in regional innovation policies, strategies and schemes, and to improve access to good practice.
www.innovating-regions.org

IREFREA
A European network for research and evaluation on drug prevention, which "develops professional partnerships with European experts in the field of youth hardships, drug prevention and drug demand reduction."
www.irefrea.org

IRELA
Institute for Relations between Europe and Latin America

IRENA
Industrial requirements engineering based on nets for added applications (**EUREKA** project)

IRENE
Integrated modelling of renewable natural resources (**FAST** project)

IRENIE
Improved reporting of environmental information using **EIONET** (a Telematics for Environment project within the **Telematics Applications Programme**)

IRHIS
Intelligent adaptive information retrieval systems as hospital information system front end (**AIM** project)

IRIMS
Ispra risk management support system (**JRC** project)

IRIS
European network for the training of women, established 1987. From July 1995 it became an independent association

IRIS
Initiative pour Régions isolées. Continued as **REGIS**

IRIS
Integrated road safety information and navigation system (within the **DRIVE** programme)

IRISI
Inter-Regional Information Society Initiative. A pilot action, started 1994 and funded by **DG**s XIII and XVI, involving six European regions: the North West of England, Sachsen in Germany, Nord Pas-de-Calais in France, Valencia in Spain, Central Macedonia in Greece and Piemonte in Italy. The regions committed themselves to developing the **Information Society** from a regional perspective. Led to the creation of **RISI**

IRL
Ireland

IRMM
Institute for Reference Materials and Measurements. Part of the **JRC** at **Geel**.
www.irmm.jrc.be

IRNU
Information Relays and Networks Unit (of the **European Commission**'s Education and Culture **DG**). *See also* **Relays**

IRSA
Institute for Remote Sensing Applications at the **JRC**. Now part of the Institute for Environment and Sustainability (**IES**)

IS
Information Society. *See also* e-Europe, Information Society Technologies Programme, IS Action Plan, ISPO, IST.
http://europa.eu.int/information_society/index_en.htm

ISA
Integrated systems architecture (**ESPRIT** project)

ISAAC
Integration system architecture for advanced primary care (**AIM** project)

ISABEL
Interconnected broadband islands between Spain and Portugal: a fibre interconnection initiative to prepare for **TEN-Telecommunications**

ISAC
Information Society Activity Centre

IS Action Plan
'Europe's way to the **Information Society**: an Action Plan' (**COM**(94) 347).
http://europa.eu.int/ISPO/docs/htmlgenerated/i_COM(94)347final.html

ISAEUS
Speech training for deaf and hearing-impaired

people (a Telematics for Disabled and Elderly People project within the **Telematics Applications Programme**)

ISAM
Integrated system for small airport management (a Telematics for Integrated Applications for Digital Sites project within the **Telematics Applications Programme**)

ISAR-T
Integration system architecture telematics (a Telematics for Healthcare project within the **Telematics Applications Programme**)

ISCONIS
Improving scientific cooperation with the **NIS** (**INCO** programme)

IS-CORE
Information systems: correctness and reusability (**ESPRIT** project)

ISD
Investment Services Directive

ISDN
Integrated services digital network

ISEI
Institute for Systems Engineering and Informatics. Once part of the **JRC** at **Ispra**. Previously **CITE**

ISEM
IT support for emergency management (**ESPRIT** project)

ISG
Internal Steering Group

ISHTAR
Implementing secure healthcare telematics application in Europe (a Telematics for Healthcare project within the **Telematics Applications Programme**)

ISIDE
Advanced model for integration of DB and KB management systems (**ESPRIT** project)

ISIS
Implementation and feasibility study for integrated services (a Telematics for Integrated Applications for Digital Sites project within the **Telematics Applications Programme**)

ISIS
Information Society Initiative in Standardisation. Set up under **Decision** 87/95/EC (**OJ** L36/87)

ISIS
Institute for Systems, Informatics and Safety. Once Part of the **JRC** at **Ispra**

ISLAND
Information system linking applications in a network demonstrator (a Telematics for Administrations project within the **Telematics Applications Programme**)

ISLED
Influence of rising sea level on ecosystem dynamics of salt marshes (**ELOISE** project)

ISLIL
Integrated system for long distance intercultural learning (**EMTF** project)

ISMAP
Integrated system for management of agricultural production (**EUREKA** project)

Isoglucose Case
Case 138/79 in which the **European Court of Justice** declared a **Regulation** invalid because the **European Parliament** had not been consulted - thus confirming the EP's role in the legislative process

ISOTOPE
Improved structure and organisation for urban

transport operations of passengers in Europe (**Transport** project)

ISPA
Instrument for Structural Policies for Pre-Accession. **Regulation** 1267/1999 establishing an Instrument for Structural Policies for Pre-accession (**OJ** L161/99).
http://europa.eu.int/comm/regional_policy/funds/ispa/ispa_en.htm

ISPO
Information Society Promotion Office (previously Information Society Project Office). Subsumed within the Information Society **DG**

Ispra
Headquarters of the Joint Research Centre - **JRC**.
1 Via E. Fermi, I-21020 Ispra (VA), Italy

ISSUE
IBCN systems and services useability engineering (**RACE** project)

ISSS
Information society standardisation system

IST
Information Society Technologies. **Decision** 1999/168/EC adopting a specific Information Society Technologies programme (1998-2002) (**OJ** L64/99). One of the Thematic Programmes which formed part of the **Fifth Framework Programme**. Previously **ACTS**; **ESPRIT**; **Telematics Applications**.
www.cordis.lu/ist/home.html

IST
Institute for Safety Technology. Once part of the **JRC** at **Ispra.** Now part of the Institute for Health and Consumer Protection - **IHCP**

ISTAG
IST programme Advisory Group

ISTC
International Science and Technology Centre. Set up under **Regulation** 500/94 (**OJ** L64/94).
www.istc.ru

ISTECH
EC-funded project to develop a new method of reinforcing monuments located in seismic areas, using a 'shape memory alloy'

IT
Industrial Technologies. Activity 1.2 of the **Fourth Framework Programme**. *See* **BRITE/EURAM III**; **SMT**

IT
Information technology

IT
Italiano (Italian)

ITACA
IBCN testing architecture for conformance assessment (**RACE** project)

ITCG
Illegal traffic of cultural goods. Protecting the cultural heritage of **Member States** through telematics (**IDA** project)

ITDNS
Integrated tour operating digital network service (**IMPACT** project)

ITEA
Information technology European awards - to recognise innovative products which have market potential (under the **ESPRIT** programme)

I-TEC
Innovation and technology equity capital. A scheme to help private capital investment in **SMEs**; managed by the **EIF**.
www.cordis.lu/finance/src/i-tec.htm

IT EDUCTRA
Information technologies education and training (a Telematics for Healthcare project within the **Telematics Applications Programme**)

ITER
International thermonuclear experimental reactor. Successor to **JET** (**EURATOM** with Japan, USA, Union of Soviet Socialist Republics). **Decision** 92/439/Euratom (**OJ** L244/92)

ITES
Income Tax Exemption Scheme. An export subsidy scheme. *See also* **DEPB**; **EOU**; **EPCGS**; **EPZ**

ITEX
Information technology for the textile and clothing industry (**ESPRIT** project)

ITHACA
Integrated toolkit for highly advanced computer applications (**ESPRIT** project)

ITHACA
Telematics for integrated client centred community care (a Telematics for Healthcare project within the **Telematics Applications Programme**)

ITIS
IBC terminal for interactive services (**RACE** project)

ITMA
I&T Magazine

ITRE
European Parliament Committee on Industry, External Trade, Research and Energy

ITS
Evaluation: intelligent tutoring system shell for industrial/office training (**ESPRIT** project)

ITS
Intelligent transport systems

ITSAEM
Integrated telematics system for administrations environmental management (a Telematics for Environment project within the **Telematics Applications Programme**)

ITS City Pioneers
Planning for intelligent transport in Europe's cities. Project to support the deployment of telematics applications in cities and to manage links with systems on the Trans-European Transport Network (**ERTICO** initiative)

ITSEC
Information technology security evaluation criteria. Council **Recommendation** 95/144/EC (**OJ** L93/95)

ITSIE
Intelligent training systems in industrial environments (**ESPRIT** project)

ITU
Institute for Transuranium Elements. Part of the **JRC** at **Karlsruhe**.
http://itu.jrc.cec.eu.int

ITUC 99
Integrated territorial & urban conservation workshop (**Raphael** programme)

IUCLID
International uniform chemical information database. Covers the classification and evaluation of existing chemical substances. Available from the European Chemicals Bureau, **JRC**.
http://ecb.jrc.it/Iuclid

IUE
l'Institut Universitaire Européen (European University Institute - **EUI**).
www.iue.it

IUI
Prospects for construction techniques creation of an industrialised urban infrastructure applicable on an identified site, using building techniques for the years 2000 to 2020 (**EUREKA** project)

IULA
International Union of Local Authorities.
IULA World Secretariat, P.O. Box 90646, 2509 LP The Hague, The Netherlands.
www.iula.org

IVICO
Integrated video codec (**RACE** project)

IVIS
Integrated vacuum instrumentation system (**EUREKA** project)

IVTIP
In Vitro Testing **Industrial Platform**.
http://europa.eu.int/comm/dg12/biotech/ip2.html#IVTIP

IWS
Intelligent workstation (**ESPRIT** project)

J

Jacques Delors European Information Centre
Located in Lisbon. One of a number of centres providing information about the EU, funded by national governments. *See also* **CIDE**.
www.cijdelors.pt

JAF
COST working party on legal, administrative and financial questions

JAI
Justice et des Affaires Intérieures (Justice and Home Affairs - **JHA**)

JAMES-RN
Joint ATM experiment on European services (a Telematics for Research project within the **Telematics Applications Programme**)

JANUS
Community information system for health and safety at work (**OJ** C28/88). Title of a journal on same topic, 1989-1998

JANUS
Joint academic network using satellite for European distance education and training (**DELTA** project)

Jean Monnet
See **Monnet, Jean**

Jean Monnet Project
to develop European studies, courses and modules in universities. Extended to **CEEC** from 1998.
http://europa.eu.int/comm/dg10/university/ajm/index_en.html

JED
Junior Experts in **Delegation** Programme. Provides graduates from **Member States** with work experience in the **European Commission**'s Delegations in developing countries. http://europa.eu.int/comm/external_relations/jed/index.htm

JEN
Joint European Networks (within the **Tempus** programme)

JENDRPC
Joint **EURATOM** Nuclear Data and Reactor Physics Committee

JEP
Joint Educational Project (under Action IV and E of the **LINGUA** programme)

JEP
Joint Environment Programme

JEP
Joint European Project (under the **Tempus** and **Tacis** programmes). *See also* **Pre-JEP**

JEPS
Bootstrap project for joint European print server (**ESPRIT** project)

JESSI
Joint European submicron silicon initiative (**EUREKA** project). Continued as **MEDEA**

JESSI-JTTT
JESSI transnational technology training (**COMETT** project)

JET
Joint European Torus. Established June 1978 (**OJ** L151/78). *See also* **ITER**.
www.jet.efda.org

JETDLAG
Joint European development of tunable diode laser absorption (**EUREKA** project)

JET-SB
Joint European Supervisory Board

JEV
Joint European Venture scheme. **Decision** 97/761/EC for financial support to **SMEs** for transnational joint ventures (1998-2000) (**OJ** L310/97; incorporated into Decision 98/347/EC in OJ L155/98)

JHA
Justice and Home Affairs (Justice et des Affaires Intérieures - JAI). Also a **DG** of the **European Commission**.
http://europa.eu.int/comm/justice_home/index_en.htm

JI
Joint implementation

JIA
Justice and Internal Affairs. Alternative form of **JHA** (Justice and Home Affairs)

JMPA
Joint production and marketing agreement

JNRC
Joint Nuclear Research Centre

Jobs Summit
See **Luxembourg Jobs Summit**

JOP
Joint Venture Programme, under **Phare** and **Tacis**. Project to help companies to establish joint ventures in Eastern and Central Europe. Discontinued 1999.
www.cordis.lu/finance/src/jop.htm

JOULE II
Joint opportunities for unconventional or long-term energy supply (1990-1994) (**OJ** L257/91). The biomass area was continued within the **AIR** programme. *See* **JOULE-THERMIE**

JOULE-THERMIE
Decision 94/806/EC for research in non-nuclear energy (1994-1998) (**OJ** L334/94). Replaced by **ENERGIE**.
http://europa.eu.int/comm/dg12/joule1.html

JRC
Joint Research Centre. A Directorate-General (**DG**) of the **European Commission**, which provides scientific and technical support for the conception, development, implementation and monitoring of EU policies. The JRC has seven associated Institutes: Institute for Reference Materials and Measurements - **IRMM**; Institute for Transuranium Elements - **ITU**; Institute for the Protection and the Security of the Citizen - **IPSC**; Institute for Environment and Sustainability - **IES**; Institute for Health and Consumer Protection - **IHCP**; Institute for Energy - **IE**; Institute for Prospective Technological Studies - **IPTS**. The Institutes are spread among JRC sites at **Geel**, **Ispra**, **Karlsruhe**, **Petten**, **Seville**.
www.jrc.cec.eu.int

JSP
Joint Study Programme (established under the **Erasmus** programme)

JSTCC
Joint Science and Technology Cooperation Committee. Administers the EU/Canada Agreement for scientific and technological cooperation

JTMP
Joint technology management plan. A contract concluded between participants involved in joint research

Judit
A legal lexicon available from the **European Court of Justice**

JUKE-BOX
Applying telematics technology to improve public access to audio/archives (project within Area 5 of the **Telematics Systems Programme**)

Jumbo Council
Term in which 'Jumbo', meaning 'big', is used to refer to a meeting involving two or more **Councils of the European Union** and hence two or more sets of Ministers. For example, the Jumbo Council of Finance, Interior and Justice Ministers, of 16 October 2001

June Movement
Danish Euro-sceptic group.
www.junibevaegelsen.dk

JURI
European Parliament Committee on Legal Affairs and the Internal Market

Justus Lipsius building
Headquarters of the **Council of the European Union**.
175 rue de la Loi, B-1048 Brussels, Belgium.
http://ue.eu.int/en/info/JUSTUSL.HTM

JV
Joint venture

JWP
Joint working party

K

K4 Committee
Based within the **Council of the European Union**, the K4 Committee was established under Title IV of the **Treaty on European Union** (TEU) to promote co-operation between **Member States** on Justice and Home Affairs (**JHA**). Under the **Treaty of Amsterdam**, K4 was replaced by a new co-ordinating committee established under Article 36 of the TEU

KADS
A methodology for the development of knowledge-based systems (**ESPRIT** project)

Kalanke
Case C-450/93 in the **European Court of Justice** on quotas in favour of employment for women (Case reported in **ECR** I-1995/9-10)

Kaleidoscope
Decision 719/96/EC to support artistic and cultural activities with a European dimension (1996-1998) (**OJ** L99/96). Previously **Platform Europe**. Replaced by **Culture 2000**

KALIMEDIA
Regional promotion of electronic commerce standards for **SME**s (**ISIS** project)

KAMP
Knowledge assurance in multimedia publishing (a Telematics for Education and Training project within the **Telematics Applications Programme**)

Kangaroo Group
"The movement for free movement".
c/o European Parliament, 60 rue Wiertz, EAS 260, B-1047 Brussels, Belgium.
www.kangaroogroup.org

Karlsruhe
A site of the **JRC**.
Linkenheim, Postfach 2340, D-76125 Karlsruhe, Germany

KAROLUS
Action plan for the exchange between **Member State** administrations of national officials engaged in the implementation of the Single Market (**SEM**). Initially 1993-1997, but extended to 1993-1999. **Decision** 92/481/EEC (**OJ** L286/92 and OJ L8/93)

KAU
Kind-of-activity-unit

KAUDYTE
Acquisition and use of knowledge in the control of dynamic systems (**ESPRIT** project)

KAVAS
Knowledge acquisition visualisation and assessment study (**AIM** project)

KB-MUSICA
Knowledge-based multi-sensors systems In **CIM** applications (**ESPRIT** project)

KBS
Knowledge-based systems

KBS-SHIP
Shipboard installation of knowledge-based systems - conceptual design (**ESPRIT** project)

KESO
Knowledge extraction for statistical offices. A **CSCW** project to construct a data mining system that satisfies the needs of providers of large-scale databases (partially funded under the **Telematics Applications Programme**).
http://orgwis.gmd.de/projects/KESO/

Key Actions
Groupings of research projects directed towards common European challenges or problems. A component of the **Fifth Framework Programme**. *See also* **Thematic Programmes**

KEYCOP
Key coastal processes in the mesotrophic Skagerrak and the oligotrophic Northern Aegean: a comparative study (**ELOISE** project)

KEYMARK
A voluntary quality mark launched by **CEN** in 1995

KIMSAC
Kiosk based integrated multimedia service access for citizens (**ACTS** project)

Kinnock reforms
Popular term for a strategy for reforming the **European Commission** developed by Vice-President Neil Kinnock, following the fall of the Santer Commission. The March 2000 White Paper on Reform focused on three main areas of change: Balancing tasks with resources; Achieving a thorough overhaul of management and human resources policies; Improving financial management, efficiency and accountability to ensure that taxpayers get value for money. *See also* **Santer, Jacques** and entries under '**Reform** …'
http://europa.eu.int/comm/reform/index_en.htm

Kirchberg Declaration
Issued by the **WEU** Council of Ministers following their meeting in Luxembourg on 9 May 1994, it gave the nine Central and Eastern European Countries which had signed **Europe Agreements** with the EU the status of Associate Partners in the WEU.
www.weu.int/documents/940509en.pdf

KISS
Knowledge-based interactive signal monitoring system (**AIM** project)

KIWI
KBS user friendly system for information bases (**ESPRIT** project)

KLEX
Development of a knowledge-based system to support operators of waste water treatment plants (**EUREKA** project)

KNOSOS
Knowledge-base environment for software system configuration reusing components (**ESPRIT** project)

KnowEurope
A web-based EU information service produced by ProQuest Information and Learning Company (previously Chadwyck-Healey).
www.knoweurope.net

Know-how Licensing
Regulation 240/96 on the application of Article 85 (3) of the Treaty to certain categories of technology transfer agreements (**OJ** L31/96)

KOMBLE
Communication aids for the handicapped (**TIDE** project)

KONVER
A **Community Initiative** to assist regions affected by the conversion of the defence industry and military bases (1994-1997)

(Guidelines in **OJ** C180/94). Successor to **PERIFRA**

Kralowetz affair
Kralowetz is an international road haulage company, registered in Luxembourg. In January 2002 the company was alleged to have illegally employed hundreds of drivers from central and eastern European countries. Details can be found via:
www.eiro.eurofound.eu.int/2002/02/feature/LU0202104F.html

KRITIC
Knowledge representation and inference techniques in industrial control (**ESPRIT** project)

KWICK
Knowledge workers intelligently collecting/coordinating /consulting knowledge (**ESPRIT** project)

Kyoto
Usually used as shorthand for the Protocol to the **United Nations** Framework Convention on Climate Change, adopted in the Japanese city of Kyoto in December 1997. The Protocol contains legally binding emissions targets for developed countries, which are bound to cut their collective emissions of six key greenhouse gases. It will enter into force 90 days after ratification by at least 55 countries, but that number must include developed countries representing a minimum 55% of the total 1990 carbon dioxide emissions of their peers. The **European Union** and the **Member States** ratified the Protocol in May 2002, but the USA withdrew from the Treaty in March 2001 and in September 2003 Russia refused to ratify it.
http://unfccc.int/resource/convkp.html

L

L
Luxembourg

LAA
Latin American and Asian countries

LAB
Legal Advisory Board. Set up under the **IMPACT** programme to advise the **European Commission** on legal issues raised by the development of the information market

Labelling Directive
Most often seen in connection with **Directive** 2000/13/EC on the approximation of the laws of the **Member States** relating to the labelling, presentation and advertising of foodstuffs (**OJ** L109/00).
The term is also used (sometimes within a particular industry) as a shorthand for other Directives, including:
Directive 98/6/EC on consumer protection in the indication of the prices of products offered to consumers (OJ L80/98).
Directive 1999/45/EC concerning the approximation of the laws, regulations and administrative provisions of the Member States relating to the classification, packaging and labelling of dangerous preparations (OJ L200/99).
Directive 1999/94/EC relating to the availability of consumer information on fuel economy and CO2 emissions in respect of the marketing of new passenger cars (OJ L12/00).
Directive 2001/37/EC on the approximation of the laws, regulations and administrative provisions of the Member States concerning the manufacture, presentation and sale of tobacco products (OJ L194/01)

LABIP
Lactic Acid Bacteria **Industrial Platform**.
http://europa.eu.int/comm/dg12/biotech/ip2.html#LABIP

LABORTEL
Latin American business opportunities for telematics applications projects (a Telematics for Education and Training project within the **Telematics Applications Programme**)

LAC
Latin America and Caribbean

LACE
Linkage assistance and cooperation for the European border regions (within the **INTERREG** programme). *See also* **LACE-Phare**

LACE-PHARE
A programme relating to border regions in **CEEC**. *See also* **LACE**

LACOSTS
Labour costs statistical domain on the **New Cronos** databank

Laeken Group
A group which advised Belgian Prime Minister Guy Verhofstadt on the future of Europe debate in the run-up to the 2001 **Laeken Summit** (the members were Giuliano Amato, Jean-Luc Dehaene, Jacques Delors, Bronislaw Geremek, David Miliband)

Laeken Summit
In the 'Declaration of Laeken', the December 2001 **European Council** in Laeken (Brussels) warned that enlargement had

brought the Union to "a crossroads, a defining moment in its existence" and gave details of the **Convention on the Future of Europe**. The meeting also confirmed that accession negotiations with the 10 most **Applicant Countries** should be completed by the end of 2002; reviewed the Union's action following the terrorist attacks in the USA on 11 September 2001; and issued a Declaration on the European Security and Defence Policy

LAG
Local action group (within the **LEADER** programme)

LAHYSTOTRAIN
Integration of virtual environments and intelligent training systems for laparoscopy/ hysteroscopy surgery training (**EMTF** project)

LAKES
Long distance dispersal in acquatic key species (**TERI** project)

LAMA
Large manipulators for CIM (**ESPRIT** project)

LAMA
Very large optical telescopes (**EUREKA** project)

Lamfalussy Committee / Report
Committee chaired by Alexandre Lamfalussy on the regulation of European securities markets. Also known as the 'Committee of Wise Men', it presented its report in February 2001.
http://europa.eu.int/comm/internal_market/en/finances/general/lamfalussy.htm

LAMP
Laser mouse (**TIDE** project)

LAN
Local area network

LAPIN
Labour policies information network (a Telematics for Administrations project within the **Telematics Applications Programme**)

LASCAR
Large scale reprocessing project. A joint **EURATOM**, International Atomic Energy Agency, French, German, UK, Japanese, USA project

LASFLEUR
Remote sensing of vegetation by monitoring laser-induced chlorophyll fluorescence (**EUREKA** project)

LAT
Learning by advanced telecommunications (**DELTA** project)

LATMIC
Lateral microstructures (**ESPRIT** project)

LCP
Large combustion plant

LDA
Less developed area. *See also* **LFA**

LDCs
Least developed countries. The world's poorest countries, currently numbering 49, identified by **UNCTAD**: Afghanistan, Angola, Bangladesh, Benin, Bhutan, Burkina Faso, Burundi, Cambodia, Cape Verde, Central African Republic, Chad, Comoros, Democratic Republic of Congo, Djibouti, Equatorial Guinea, Eritrea, Ethiopia, Gambia, Guinea, Guinea Bissau, Haiti, Kiribati, Lao People's Democratic Republic, Lesotho, Liberia, Madagascar, Malawi, Maldives, Mali, Mauritania, Mozambique, Myanmar, Nepal, Niger, Rwanda, Samoa, Sao Tome and Principe, Senegal, Sierra Leone, Solomon Islands, Somalia, Sudan, Togo, Tuvalu, Uganda, United Republic of Tanzania, Vanuatu, Yemen, Zambia. The majority are

members of the **ACP**. Previously called Less Developed Countries. The list is reviewed every three years. Sometimes seen as LLDCs. Details of LDCs are available from:
www.unctad.org

LDCs
Less developed countries. Term now replaced by Least developed countries (**LDCs**)

LDEI
Local development and employment initiative

LDR
Liberal, Democratic and Reformist Group (of the **European Parliament**)

LDS
MBE and VPE growth of low dimensionality structure for future quantum semiconductor devices (**ESPRIT** project)

LDTF
Large dynamic test facility (**JRC** - reactor safety programme)

LEA
Local Enterprise Agency to provide technical assistance to **SME**s as part of the **Phare** 1997 programme in Hungary

LEADER +
Liaison Entre Actions de Développement de l'Economie Rurale (Links between Actions for the Development of the Rural Economy). A **Community Initiative** (2000-2006) (**COM**(99) 475). Continuation of LEADER II, which itself followed LEADER.
http://europa.eu.int/comm/agriculture/rur/leaderplus/index.htm

League of Nations
Forerunner to the **United Nations**; established 1920, dissolved 1946

Leased Lines Directive
Directive 92/44/EEC on the application of the **ONP** to leased lines (**OJ** L165/92). No longer in force

LEAST
Learning systems standardisation (**DELTA** project)

LEDA
Local Employment Development Action. Research programme set up by **DG** V (now DG Employment) of the **European Commission**

LEGA
European Parliament Committee on Legal Affairs and Citizen's Rights

Légichim
Legislative database of chemical substances cited in the **OJ**.
http://europa.eu.int/comm/dg03/directs/dg3c/risc/db/plsql/legichim.Main

LEI
Local employment initiative

LEMMA
Methods and architectures for logic engineering in medicine (**AIM** project)

Leonardo da Vinci
Action programme on vocational training policy. Started 1994; second phase (2000-2006) covered by **Decision** 1999/382/EC (**OJ** L146/99). Combines **COMETT**; **EUROTECNET**; **FORCE**; **LINGUA**; **PETRA**.
http://europa.eu.int/comm/education/programmes/leonardo/leonardo_en.html

LEPE
Laboratoire Européen pour la Protection des Eaux (European Reference Laboratory for Water Pollution). Established 1998 and now

part of the **JRC**'s Institute for Environment and Sustainability (**IES**)

Let's go East
See **Go East/Go West**

LFA
Less favoured area. Defined in **Regulation** 1257/1999 on support for rural development from the European Agricultural Guidance and Guarantee Fund (**EAGGF**) (**OJ** L160/99). LFAs include: mountain areas (Article 18), other less-favoured areas (Article 19), areas affected by specific handicaps (Article 20)

LFR
Less favoured region. Defined as having high unemployment, low domestic product per capita and low levels of economic prosperity

LFS
Labour force survey statistical domain on the **New Cronos** databank

LFS-R
Regional labour force survey statistical domain on the **REGIO** database

LG
Liaison group

LGIB
Local Government International Bureau. Publishes European Information Service (EIS).
35 Great Smith Street, London SW1P 3BJ, UK.
www.lgib.gov.uk

LIB-2
Studies on the impact of new information technologies in libraries

LIBE
European Parliament Committee on Citizens' Freedoms and Rights, Justice and Home Affairs

LIBER
Ligue des Bibliothéques Européennes de Recherche (League of European Research Libraries).
Secretariat: Susan Vejlsgaard, Det Kongelige Bibliotek, P.O. Box 2149, DK-1016 Copenhagen K, Denmark.
www.kb.dk/liber

LIDAR
Light detection and ranging (environmental research programme)

LIEN
Link inter-European **NGO**s. *See* **Phare LIEN**; **Tacis LIEN**

LIFE
Financial instrument for the environment.(Instrument financier pour l'environnement). Initially 1992-1995; LIFE II 1996-1999; LIFE III 2000-2004. Consists of three components: LIFE-Environment; LIFE-Nature; LIFE-Third Countries. Replaces **ACNAT**; **MEDSPA**; **NORSPA**.
http://europa.eu.int/comm/life/home.htm

Life in the Universe
Project set up as part of **European Science Week** 2001.
www.lifeinuniverse.org

LIFT
Linking innovation finance and technology. A helpdesk to guide high tech entrepreneurs to obtain funding. Set up under the **INNOVATION/SME**s programme. Now **Gate2Growth**

LILIENTHAL
Multimedia off- and on-line distance learning for European pilot training (**EMTF** project)

LINAC
Linear accelerator at **Geel**, a **JRC** establishment

LINES
Learning information support networks in Europe for **Socrates** (a Telematics for Education and Training project within the **Telematics Applications Programme**)

LINGUA
Action programme to promote foreign language competence (1990-1994) (**OJ** L239/89). Continued as part of the **Leonardo da Vinci** and **Socrates** programmes

LION
Local integrated optical network (**ESPRIT** project)

LIRN
Library information enquiry and referral network (project within Area 5 of the **Telematics Systems Programme**)

Lisbon Initiative
See **ESDA**

Lisbon Strategy
The March 2000 Lisbon **European Council** decided to make the EU "the most competitive and dynamic knowledge-based economy in the world, capable of sustainable economic growth with more and better jobs and greater social cohesion" by 2010. The Lisbon Strategy was intended to meet that objective by: preparing for the transition to a knowledge-based economy and society by enhancing relevant policies, including the information society, research and development, structural reform, and the internal market; modernising the European social model, by investing in people and combating social exclusion; sustaining the current economic outlook and growth prospects by applying appropriate macro-economic policies. *See also* **Lisbon Summit**.
http://europa.eu.int/comm/lisbon_strategy/index_en.html

Lisbon Summit
Also known as the 'dot.com' Summit, the March 2000 **European Council** in Lisbon was devoted to tackling unemployment and promoting economic reform and social cohesion by developing a digital, knowledge-based economy. The **Council of the European Union** and the **European Commission** were asked to draw up an '***e*Europe** Action Plan'. *See also* **Lisbon Strategy**

LISCOM
Listening comfort system for hearing-instruments and telephone (a Telematics for Disabled and Elderly People project within the **Telematics Applications Programme**)

LISTEC
Database of the technical services in the **Member States** having the competence to carry out testing of motor vehicles in accordance with the type approval framework **Directive** 70/156/EEC

LIUTO
Low impact urban transport water omnibus. Project in the field of design, production and operation for safer, more efficient, environmentally friendly and user-friendly ships (**BRITE-EURAM III** project)

LLDCs
Least and less developed countries. *See also* **LDCs**

Loads Directive
Little-used variant of **Manual HandlingDirective**

LOBI
Loop blowdown investigation (**JRC** - reactor safety programme)

Local Content
In the context of attempts to avoid anti-dumping measures, **Regulation** 384/96 (**OJ**

L56/96) specifies the amount of work which must be carried out by a non-EU firm set up in a **Member State** to assemble imported components into a finished article. *See also* **Screwdriver plants**

Local KAU
Local kind-of-activity unit

Local UHP
Local unit of homogeneous production

LOCIN
Database on local initiatives to combat social exclusion in Europe.
http://locin.jrc.it

LOCSTAR
Technological development programme for a system of radio determination by satellites with European coverage (**EUREKA** project)

LOGIMAX
Development of a 2nd generation information and transport network throughout Europe (**EUREKA** project)

LOKI
Logic oriented approach to knowledge and databases supplying natural use interaction (**ESPRIT** project)

Lomé Convention
An agreement between the **European Union** and African, Caribbean and Pacific (**ACP**) States for trade and other forms of co-operation. (*Lomé I* published in **OJ** L25/76; *Lomé II* in OJ L347/80; *Lomé III* in OJ L86/86; *Lomé IV* (1990-2000) in OJ L229/91). Replaced by the **Cotonou Agreement**

London Report
on *European political cooperation* 1981. Published in the UK by HMSO as Command Paper 8424

LOOP
Low-cost optical components (**RACE** project)

LORAN - C
A radionavigation system (**OJ** L59/92)

LORINE
Limited rate imagery network elements (**RACE** project)

Low Voltage Directive
Directive 73/23/EEC on the harmonization of the laws of **Member States** relating to electrical equipment designed for use within certain voltage limits (**OJ** L77/73)

LRE
Linguistic research and engineering (Area 6 of the **Telematics Systems Programme**)

LRRD
Linkages between relief, rehabilitation and development. Initiatives carried out by **Member States** in **Third Countries**

LSIF
Large scale infrastructure facility. Part of the **Phare** investment strategy for Central Europe

LST
Life Sciences and Technologies: Activity 1.4 of the **Fourth Framework Programme**. *See* **BIOMED II**; **BIOTECH II**; **FAIR**

LSVI
Large size visual interface design for multimedia workstation terminals (**ESPRIT** project)

LU
Left Unity Group in the **European Parliament**

LU
Livestock unit

LUCIFER
Land use change interactions with fire in Mediterranean landscape (**TERI** project)

LUCIOLE
Multi-function integrated optical circuits and fibres for sensors and sensor arrays (**EUREKA** project)

Lugano Convention
Extended the **Brussels Convention** to members of **EFTA**. Signed 16 September 1988. *See also* **Luxembourg Convention**

LUIC
Local urban initiative centre. To provide EU information for sustainable development in cities. *See also* **Relays**

Luns-Westerterp Procedure
Intended to ensure that the **Council of the European Union** consults the **European Parliament** on any international agreement conducted by the **European Community** (consultation had previously been restricted to **Association Agreements**)

LUPINPUR
Processing of better lupins into high protein feed components (**EUREKA** project)

Luxembourg Agreement / Compromise
on majority voting, agreed by the **Member States** in 1966

Luxembourg Convention
European Convention on Recognition and Enforcement of Decisions concerning Custody of Children (**Council of Europe**).
http://conventions.coe.int/Treaty/EN/WhatYouWant.asp?NT=105

Luxembourg Convention
on the Community Patent (1975, revised 1989: 89/695/EEC, **OJ** L401/89). A further revision was proposed in **COM**(2000)412: Proposal for a Council **Regulation** on the Community patent

Luxembourg Jobs Summit
An extraordinary **European Council** was held in November 1997 to discuss (un)employment in the EU. Also known as the 'jobs Summit'.
http://europa.eu.int/comm/employment_social/elm/summit/en/home.htm

Luxembourg Process
Agreed at the November 1997 **Luxembourg Summit**, the Process coordinates **Member States**' employment policies in the form of employment guidelines and National Action Plans

Luxembourg Report
on political union, approved in 1970. Published in the *Bulletin of the EC* 11/1970

Luxembourg Six
The group of countries with which the **European Union** started accession negotiations in March 1998: Cyprus, Czech Republic, Estonia, Hungary, Poland, Slovenia. The decision to open negotiations was made at the 1997 **Luxembourg Summit**.

Luxembourg Summit
The December 1997 **European Council** in Luxembourg launched a new round of enlargement and was said to mark "a moment of historic significance for the future of the Union and of Europe as a whole"

LWR
Light water reactor

M

M3S
Intelligent interface for the rehabilitation environment (**TIDE** project)

MAAS Group
An independent expert group appointed in 1994 to examine practical issues relating to the **euro**. Produced the report 'Introduction of the ecu as legal tender'

Maastricht Treaty
See **Treaty on European Union**

MAC
Multi-purpose anti-pollution craft (**EUREKA** project)

MACPOP
Modelling and automatic control of the polishing process (**BRITE** project)

MACRO
Multimedia application for clinical research in oncology (a Telematics for Healthcare project within the **Telematics Applications Programme**)

MACS
Maintenance assistance capability for software (**ESPRIT** project)

MacSharry Reform
1992 reform of the Common Agricultural Policy (**CAP**) which followed from the 1991 MacSharry Plan, named after **European Commissioner** Ray MacSharry

MADAME
Methods for access to data and metadata in Europe.

MADMUD
Digital museums administration and museumsdidaktik (a Telematics Information Engineering project within the **Telematics Applications Programme**)

MADRAS
Modular approach to definition of RACE subscriber premises network (**RACE** project)

MADS
Message passing architectures and description systems (**ESPRIT** project)

MAF
Multimedia applications in furniture (a Telematics Information Engineering project within the **Telematics Applications Programme**)

MAG
Mutual assistance group

MAGEC
Modelling agroecosystems under global environmental change (**TERI** project)

Maghreb countries
Algeria, Libya, Mauritania, Morocco and Tunisia. *See also* **Mashreq countries**

MAGIC
Methods for advanced group technology integrated with **CAD/CAM** (**ESPRIT** project)

MAGICA
Multimedia agent-based interactive catalogues (a Telematics Information Engineering project within the **Telematics Applications Programme**)

MAGNETS
Museum and galleries new technology study (a Telematics for Administrations project within the Telematics Application programme)

MAGP
Multi-annual guidance programme (Programme d'Orientation Pluriannuelle - POP). In the context of **Regulation** 4028/86 on Community measures to improve and adapt structures in the fisheries and aquaculture sector (1987-1993) (**OJ** L376/86). No longer in force

MAHB
Major Accident Hazards Bureau. Based in the **JRC** at **Ispra**

MAID
Multimedia assets for industrial design (a Telematics Information Engineering project within the **Telematics Applications Programme**)

Mail Order Sales Directive
Alternative name for the **Distance Selling Directive**

MALTED
Multimedia authoring for language tutors and educational development (**EMTF** project)

Mandelkern Group
on Better Regulation. A High Level Advisory Group on the quality of regulatory arrangements. The report, issued November 2001, can be seen at:
www.cabinet-office.gov.uk/regulation/europe/Successes/mandelkern.htm

MANICORAL
Multimedia and network in cooperative research and learning (a Telematics for Research project within the **Telematics Applications Programme**)

MANSEV
Market authorisation by network submission and evaluation (a Telematics for Healthcare project within the **Telematics Applications Programme**)

Mansholt Plan
on the reform of agriculture 1970-1980. Published in the *Bulletin of the EC* Supplement 1/1969

Manual Handling Directive
Directive 90/269/EEC on the minimum health and safety requirements for the manual handling of loads where there is a risk particularly of back injury to workers (**OJ** L156/90)

MANUS
Modular anthropomorphous user-adaptable hand prosthesis with enhanced mobility and force feedback (a Telematics for Disabled and Elderly People project within the **Telematics Applications Programme**)

MAP
Mediterranean Action Plan

MAP
Multi-annual programme

MAPS
Mobile applications pilot scheme (**RACE** project)

MAPSCORE
Mapping of polar stratospheric clouds and ozone levels relevant to the region of Europe (an Energy, Environment & Sustainable Development project under the **Fifth Framework Programme**).
www.leos.le.ac.uk/mapscore

MAP-TV
Memory-archives-programmes TV (**MEDIA** project)

MARBEF
Marine Biodiversity and Ecosystem Functioning. A Network of Excellence under the **Sixth Framework Programme**

Marco Polo
Adopted July 2003, the programme "intends to help the transport and logistics industry to achieve sustained modal shifts of road freight to short sea shipping, rail and inland waterway." **Regulation** 1382/2003 on the granting of Community financial assistance to improve the environmental performance of the freight transport system (**OJ** L196/03). Succeeded **PACT**.
http://europa.eu.int/comm/transport/marcopolo/index_en.htm

MARCU
Manipulative automatic reaction control and user supervision (**TIDE** project)

MARGRITE
Marrow graft: integrated telematics in Europe (a Telematics for Healthcare project within the **Telematics Applications Programme**)

MARIA
Methods for assessing the radiological impact of accidents (**AIM** project)

MARIA
Multimedia applications for regional and international access (**AIM** project)

MARIE
Mobile autonomous robot in an industrial environment (**ESPRIT** project)

MARIN
Marine industry applications of broadband communications (**RACE** project)

MARIS
Maritime Information Society. A **G8** initiative.
http://europa.eu.int/ISPO/maris

MARKT
Internal Market **DG** of the **European Commission**

Marlia Reports
A device whereby the President of the **Council of the European Union** presents the General Affairs Council with a progress report on outstanding business from other Councils

MARNET
Inter-regional maritime information network (**Transport** project)

MARNET CFD
Computational fluid dynamics for the marine industry (**BRITE/EURAM III** project)

MAROPT
Marine optical recording system (**EUREKA** project)

MARPOWER
Concepts of advanced marine machinery systems with low pollution and high efficiency (**BRITE/EURAM III** project)

Marques
Association of European Trade Mark Owners.
840 Melton Rd, Thurmaston, Leicester LE4 8BN, UK.
www.marques.org

MARS
Highly secure office information systems - definition phase (**ESPRIT** project)

MARS
Major Accident Reporting System, based at **Ispra**

MARS
Monitoring agriculture with remote sensing (**Ispra** project).
http://mars.jrc.it

MARS
Multimedia access relying on standards (**ISIS** multimedia project)

Marseilles Declaration
In November 2000, **WEU** Ministers agreed a number of measures concerning the changing roles of the WEU and the **European Union**

MARSIS
Marine remote sensing information system for regional European seas (**EUREKA** project)

MART
Definition of an environment to maximise the market for telecommunications-based RT (**TIDE** project)

MARTRANS
Project to create an information system for intermodal transport and supply chain management, within **MARIS**.
www.euromar-eeig.com/initiat/martrans-6/index.htm

MASCOT
Multi-environment advanced system for colour treatment (**ESPRIT** project)

Mashreq countries
Egypt, Jordan, Lebanon and Syria. *See also* **Maghreb countries**

MASIS
Human factors in the man/ship system for the European fleets (**EURET** project)

MASQUES
Medical application software quality enhancement by standards (**AIM** project)

MAST III
Decision 94/804/EC for a Marine Science and Technology **R&D** programme (1994-1998) (**OJ** L334/94). Replaced by **EESD**.
www.cordis.lu/mast/home.html

MATER
Mass transfer and ecosystem response. One of the four major regional RTD projects of **MAST III**. MATER covers the Mediterranean. *See also* **BASYS**; **CANIGO**; **OMEX**.
http://europa.eu.int/comm/research/marine/mtp-mater.html

MATHS
Mathematical access for technology and science for visually disabled users (**TIDE** project)

Mathurin Report
Study of responsibilities, guarantees and insurance in the construction industry with a view to harmonisation at Community level. Final report (condensed version) published 1989

MATIC
Multi-strategy authoring toolkit for intelligent courseware (**DELTA** project)

MATISSE2000
Metropolitan area tourist information support system for Europe 2000 (a Telematics for Integrated Applications for Digital Sites project within the **Telematics Applications Programme**)

MATTHAEUS
Programme for the vocational training of customs officials. **Decision** 91/341/EEC (**OJ** L187/91). Incorporated into **Customs 2000**

MATTHAEUS-TAX
Decision 93/588/EEC for an action programme for the vocational training of indirect taxation officials (1993-1997) (**OJ** L280/93). Replaced by **FISCALIS**

MAUVE
Mini autonomous underwater vehicle (**MAST III** project)

MAWP
Multiannual work programme

MAX
Metropolitan area communication system (**ESPRIT** project)

MBLN
Multimedia as business option for local newspapers (a Telematics Information Engineering project within the **Telematics Applications Programme**)

MC
Management Committee

MCA
Monetary compensatory amounts

MCAC
Management and Coordination Advisory Committee

MCACE
Measurement characterisation and control of ambulatory care in Europe (**AIM** project)

MCBRIDE
Development of a multi-chamber batch reactor for the production of multilayer interpoly dielectrics (**ESPRIT** project)

MCDA
Military and civil defence assets. *See also* **Oslo Guidelines**

MCE
Main component elements. National environmental information bodies appointed as units in the **EIONET** by **Member States**

MCPR
Multi-media communication processing and representation (**RACE** project)

MDSC
Multidisciplinary Scientific Committee. Replaced by the Scientific Steering Committee - **SSC**

ME
Mouvement Européen (European Movement - **EM**)

ME
Mutualité européenne (European Mutual Society)

M-E
See **Mercator Education**

MEA
Multilateral environmental agreement

MEANS
Methods and tools for evaluating structural assistance from the Community in order to ensure greater effectiveness in the use of EU funds

Measurements and Testing
Research and technological development programme in the field of measurements and testing (1990-1994) (**OJ** L126/92). Continued as **SMT**

Meat Labelling Directive
Directive 2000/13/EC on the approximation of the laws of the **Member States** relating to the labelling, presentation and advertising of foodstuffs (**OJ** L109/00)

MECANO
Mechanism of automatic comparison of CD-ROM answers with **OPAC**s (project within Area 5 of the **Telematics Systems Programme**)

MECCANO
Multimedia education and conferencing collaboration over ATM networks and others (a Telematics for Research project within the **Telematics Applications Programme**)

MECCS
Modular environmental control and communications system (**TIDE** project)

MECDIN
Expert system on portable CD-ROM terminal (**EUREKA** project)

MECU
Million **ECU** (European Currency Units)

MED
Mediterranean

MED 12
Algeria, Cyprus, Egypt, Israel, Jordan, Lebanon, Malta, Morocco, Palestinian Territory, Syria, Tunisia, Turkey

MEDA
A programme of financial and technical measures to accompany reforms to the economic and social structures in the Mediterranean non-member countries. The acronym possibly means 'Mediterranean Development Assistance' or 'Mediterranean Assistance'. **Regulation** 1488/96 for a Mediterranean Special programme (1995-1999) (**OJ** L189/96 with guidelines in OJ L325/96). MEDA II covers 2000-2006 (Regulation 2698/2000, OJ L311/00). *See also* **EUMEDIS**; **EUROMED**; **EUROMED HERITAGE**; **MED-Campus**; **MED-Invest**; **MED-Media**; **MED-Techno**; **MED-Urbs**.
http://europa.eu.int/comm/external_relations/euromed/meda.htm

MEDALUS
Mediterranean desertification and land use impacts (**EPOCH** project)

MED-Avicenne
See **Avicenne Initiative**

MED-Campus
Cooperative networks between higher education institutions in the EC and Mediterranean **Third countries**. Started 1992 (**OJ** C161/95) but suspended 1997 because of administrative problems. Activities incorporated into **Tempus**. *See also* **MEDA**

MEDEA
Micro electronics development for European applications (**EUREKA** project). Previously **JESSI**

MEDIA
Programme intended to improve the competitiveness of the European audiovisual industry. Initially 1991-1995; MEDIA II 1996-2000; MEDIA Plus, 2001-2005 (**Decision** 2000/821/EC, **OJ** L13/2001).
http://europa.eu.int/comm/avpolicy/media/index_en.html

MediaAge
Electronic European news service on ageing issues (MediaAge.net), supported by the **European Commission**. No longer available

MEDIAKIDS
Multimedia for kids (**EMTF** project)

MEDICA
Multimedial medical diagnostic assistant (**AIM** project)

MEDICI Framework
Multimedia for education and employment through integrated cultural initiative (**IS** initiative)
www.medicif.org

MEDICINE
Medical data interchange in Europe (**EUREKA** project)

MEDICO
Multimedia education datasystem in clinical oncology (a Telematics for Healthcare project within the **Telematics Applications Programme**)

MEDIMEDIA
Medical images integration for multimedia European databases interconnection and common access (a Telematics for Healthcare project within the **Telematics Applications Programme**)

MED-Invest
Cooperation for the development of **SMEs** in the EU and Mediterranean **Third countries**. Started 1992; apparently later subsumed within 'Euro-Mediterranean SMEs Co-operation': http://europa.eu.int/comm/europeaid/projects/med/regional/smecooperation_en.htm. *See also* **MEDA**

MED-Media
A programme to enhance and create networks between media professionals in the EU and Mediterranean Third countries. Started 1992; apparently later subsumed into 'Euromed Audiovisual': http://europa.eu.int/comm/europeaid/projects/med/regional/audiovisual_en.htm. *See also* **MEDA**

MED-Migration
A sub-topic of **MED-Urbs** (Information in **OJ** C180/95)

MEDREP
ECHO database of biomedical and health care research projects in the EC

MEDSEC
Healthcare security and privacy in the information society (**ISIS** healthcare networks project)

MEDSPA
Mediterranean special programme of action for the protection of the environment (1991-1996) (**OJ** L63/91). Replaced by **LIFE**

MED-Techno
Improvement of efficient technologies in 12 Mediterranean countries. (Information in **OJ** C161/95). *See also* **MEDA**, **MED 12**

MED-Urbs
Cooperation between local authorities in the EU and Mediterranean **Third countries**. Started 1992; suspended 1995 after financial irregularities. Relaunched 1998, but apparently no longer running. *See also* **MEDA**

MEET
Methodologies for estimating air pollutant emissions from transport (**Transport** project)

MEGATAQ
Methods and guidelines for the assessment of telematics applications quality (a Telematics Engineering project within the **Telematics Applications Programme**)

MEIP
Market economy investor principle

MEL
Microelectronics technology programme (1982-1985) (**OJ** L376/81)

Member States
Countries which are members of the **European Union**. *See* **6**, **9**, **10**, **12**, **15**, **25**

MEMCARE
Development of mobile self-supporting emergency hospitals for immediate medical attendance for victims of calamities (**EUREKA** project)

MEMO
A type of press release which gives background information. Available via **RAPID**: http://europa.eu.int/rapid/start/cgi/guesten.ksh

MENTOR
Expert system for dealing with major plant failures and security control (**EUREKA** project)

MENTOR
Multimedia education network for teaching, output and research (**EMTF** project)

MEP
Member of the **European Parliament**

MEPP
Middle East peace process

MERA
MARS-monitoring of agriculture by remote sensing (**Phare** project)

Mercator
A network of three research and documentation centres dealing with the regional and minority languages of the EU. Sometimes referred to as Mercator Central. *See also* the following three entries.
www.mercator-central.org

Mercator Education
European network for regional or minority languages and education.
Contact: Fryske Akademy, PO Box 54, Coulonhus, NL-8900 DX Leeuwarden, The Netherlands.
www.mercator-education.org

Mercator Legislation
A database of legal and/or normative documents concerning European languages. Managed for Mercator by CIEMEN (International Escarré Centre for the Ethnic Minorities and Nations).
Rocafort, 242 bis, 08029, Barcelona, Spain.
www.ciemen.org/mercator/index-gb.htm

Mercator Media
Covers regional and minority languages in radio, television, film, newspapers, magazine and book publishing, archives and libraries and electronic data storage and networks.
Adran Ast. Theatr Ffilm a Theledu, Prifysgol Cymru Aberystwyth
Y Buarth, Aberystwyth SY23 1NN, UK.
www.aber.ac.uk/~merwww

MERCHANT
Methods in electronic retail cash handling (**RACE** project)

MERCI
Multimedia European research conferencing integration (a Telematics for Research project within the **Telematics Applications Programme**)

Mercosur
Mercado Comun del Sur (Marché Commun du Pôle Sud / Southern Cone Common Market). Created 1991. Members: Argentina, Brazil, Paraguay, Uruguay. Also known as the Southern Cone Common Market.
www.mercosur.org.uy

MERGE
Media economic research group of Europe (**EUREKA** project)

Merger Control Regulation
Regulation 4064/89 on the control of concentrations between undertakings (**OJ** L257/90)

Merger Treaty
establishing a single Council and a single Commission. Signed by Belgium, France, Germany, Italy, Luxembourg and The Netherlands on 8 April 1965. Came into force 1 July 1967. Sometimes referred to as the Fusion Treaty. *See also* **Council of the European Union**, **European Commission**

MERIT
Municipal economic and social reform initiative of **Tacis**

MERMAID
Marine environmental remote-controlled measuring and integrated detection

(**EUREKA** project)

MERMAID
Medical emergency aid through telematics (a Telematics for Healthcare project within the **Telematics Applications Programme**)

MERMAID
Metrication and resource modelling AID (**ESPRIT** project)

MERMAIDS
Mediterranean eddy resolving modelling and interdisciplinary studies (**MAST** project)

MESA group
Mutual ECU settlement account. Financial agencies operating in **ECU**s

MESH
Possible mechanisms for high-TC superconductivity and phenomenological approaches (**ESPRIT** project)

META
Multimedia educational telematics applications (a Telematics for Education and Training project within the **Telematics Applications Programme**)

METAP
Mediterranean environmental technological assistance programme financed by the **EIB** and the World Bank

METARAIL
Methodologies and actions for rail noise and vibration control (**Transport** project).
www.cordis.lu/transport/src/metarail.htm

METASA
Digital Towns: Multimedia European experimental Towns with A Social pull Approach (a Telematics for Urban and Rural Areas project within the **Telematics Applications Programme**)

METEOR
An integrated formal approach to industrial software development (**ESPRIT** project)

METKIT
Metrics education tool kit (**ESPRIT** project)

METRE
Measurements, standards and reference techniques (**JRC** research programme)

Metric Martyrs
A UK-based pressure group formed after traders in Sunderland, UK, were accused in February and March 2000 of illegally weighing produce in UK imperial (pounds and ounces) rather than metric measures.
The Steve Thoburn (Metric Martyr) Defence Fund, PO Box 526, Sunderland SR1 3YS, UK.
www.metricmartyrs.sageweb.co.uk

METR-ICS
High precision (**ESPRIT** project)

Metropolis
Metrology in support of precautionary sciences and sustainable development policies. A network of 38 scientific institutions in 17 European countries, developing an interdisciplinary approach to measurements and their reliability in environmental monitoring.
http://europa.eu.int/comm/research/growth/gcc/projects/metropolis.html

MEUA
Million European Units of Account. *See also* **MECU**

MFA
Multi-fibre agreement (1974-1994). MFA I published in **OJ** L118/74; MFA II in **OJ** L348/77; MFA III in OJ L83/82; MFA IV in OJ L341/86 and extended to December 1994 in OJ L124/94. Replaced by the **WTO**

Agreement on Textiles and Clothing (1995-2004)

MFIs
Monetary financial institutions

MGP
Mediterranean guidance programme

MGS
Multi guarantee scheme

MIAC
Multipoint interactive audiovisual communication (**ESPRIT** project)

MIAS
Multipoint interactive audiovisual system (**ESPRIT** project)

MIC
Mobile information centre. Essentially an articulated lorry used as a base for supplying information about the EU and its policies. An initiative started and managed by the **European Commission**'s London **Representation**

MICA
Met improvements for controller aids (**Transport** project)

MICOFF
Microwave conservation of fast food (**EUREKA** project)

MICROMARE
Development of micro-sensors for use in the marine environment (**MAST III** project).
www.dmu.dk/LakeandEstuarineEcology/Micromare

MIDAS-NET
Multimedia information, demonstration and support network. 1997-1999 (**INFO2000** initiative)

MIF
Maritime Industries Forum.
www.mif-eu.org

MIGRAT
International migration statistical domain on the **New Cronos** databank

MILIEU
Environment statistical domain on the **New Cronos** databank

MILREPs
Military representatives

MIMD
Multiple instruction-mutiple data

MIME
Development of emulators and simulators (**RACE** project)

MIMEH
Models of innovative management of European heritage (**Raphael** project)

MIMI
Medical workstation for intelligent interactive acquisition and analysis of digital medical images (**AIM** project)

MINE
Microbial information network Europe (**BAP** project)

MINERVA
Education and multimedia initiative (part of the **Socrates** programme)

MINIFLOATER
Low cost oil and gas production facility in deep water (**EUREKA** project)

Mini Schengen
Term sometimes used to refer to the Nordic Passport Union, whose members are

Denmark, Finland, Iceland, Norway, Sweden. *See also* **Schengen Agreement**

MINSTREL
New information models for office filing and retrieval (**ESPRIT** project)

MINT
Managing the integration of new technology (**SPRINT** project)

MINTOUR
Multimedia information network for tourists (a Telematics for Administrations project within the **Telematics Applications Programme**)

MINWAGES
Minimum wages statistical domain on the **New Cronos** databank

MIOCA
Monolithic integrated optics for customer access applications (**RACE** project)

MIP
Multi-annual indicative programme

MIPEX
Message based industrial property (a Telematics for Administrations project within the **Telematics Applications Programme**)

MIRAGE
Combined multimedia development environment for TV, radio and on-line production and delivery (a Telematics Information Engineering project within the **Telematics Applications Programme**)

MIRAGE
Migration of radioisotopes in the geosphere (Radioactive waste programme)

MIRIAM
Model scheme for information on rural development initiatives and agricultural markets. Proposal rejected 1991

MIRS
Musical information retrieval system (project within Area 5 of the **Telematics Systems Programme**)

MIRTI
Models of industrial relations in telework innovation (a Telematics Engineering project within the **Telematics Applications Programme**)

MIRTO
Multimedia interaction with regional and transnational organisations (a Telematics for Administrations project within the **Telematics Applications Programme**)

MIS
Multilingual information system (**ESPRIT** project)

MISEP
Mutual information system on employment polices. A database on employment policy and unemployment measures. Now part of the European Employment Observatory (**EEO**). Associated magazine, InforMISEP, renamed European Employment Observatory Review

MISSCEEC
Mutual information system on social protection in the Central and Eastern European Countries

Missile Technology Control Regime
An "informal and voluntary association of countries which share the goals of non-proliferation of unmanned delivery systems for weapons of mass destruction, and which seek to coordinate national export licensing efforts aimed at preventing their proliferation." *See also* **Australia Group**, **Nuclear Suppliers**

Group, **Wassenaar Arrangement**, **Zangger Committee**.
www.mtcr.info

Miss Model
Term used to calculate the benefits (or otherwise) of an EC / **GATT** agreement

MISSOC
Mutual information system on social protection in the **Member States** of the **European Union**.
http://europa.eu.int/comm/employment_social/soc-prot/missoc98/english/f_main.htm

MITHRA
Development, industrialisation and the sale of mobile robots for tele-surveillance (**EUREKA** project)

MITI
Multilingual intelligent interface (**IMPACT** project)

MLIS
Multilingual information society. **Decision** 96/664/EC (**OJ** L306/96). Ended November 1999. *See also* **ELRA**

MLT
Machine learning toolbox (**ESPRIT** project)

MLTS
Medium and long-term translation service

MM12
A multi-modal interface for man-machine interaction with knowledge-based systems (**ESPRIT** project)

MMOMS
Multi-modal organ modelling system (**AIM** project)

MNC
Mediterranean non-member countries: Algeria; Cyprus; Egypt; Israel and the Occupied Territories; Jordan; Lebanon; Malta; Morocco; Syria; Tunisia; Turkey (Cyprus and Malta will become EU **Member States** in 2004)

MNE
Multinational enterprise

MNY
Banking and financial statistical domain on the **New Cronos** databank

MOBCARE
Home/ambulatory healthcare services based on mobile communication (a Telematics for Healthcare project within the **Telematics Applications Programme**)

MOBIC
Mobility of blind and elderly people interacting with computers (**TIDE** project)

MOBIDICK
Multivariable on-line bilingual dictionary kit (**EUREKA** project)

MOBIL
Intelligent mobility and transportation aid for elderly people with combined motor and mental impairment (a Telematics for Disabled and Elderly People project within the **Telematics Applications Programme**)

MOBILE
Extending European information access through mobile libraries (project within Area 5 of the **Telematics Systems Programme**)

MODA SPECTRA
Motor disability assessment specialists training (**EMTF** project)

MODEM
Modelling of emission and consumption in urban areas (**DRIVE** project)

MODEM
Multimedia optimisation demonstration for education in microelectronics (a Telematics for Education and Training project within the **Telematics Applications Programme**)

MODEMA
Modelling for the disabled in working environments (**TIDE** project)

MODESTI
Mould design and manufacturing optimisation by development, standardisation and integration of **CAD/CAM** procedures (**BRITE** project)

MODULATES
Multimedia organisation for developing the understanding and learning of advanced technologies in European schools (**EMTF** project)

MOHAWC
Models of human actions in work context (**ESPRIT** project)

MOLAND
Monitoring land use / cover dynamics. Research project carried out at the **JRC**s Space Applications Institute (**SAI**; now the Institute for Environment and Sustainability - **IES**).
http://moland.jrc.it

Molitor Group
of independent experts on legislative and administrative simplification. Report published as **COM**(95)288

MOLCOM
Exploration of electronic properties in conducting organic materials as a function of structural modifications (**ESPRIT** project)

MOLSWITCH
Evaluation of molecular switch type devices … (**ESPRIT** project)

MOMEDA
Mobile medical data (a Telematics for Healthcare project within the **Telematics Applications Programme**)

Money Laundering Directive
Directive 91/308/EEC on prevention of the use of the financial system for the purpose of money laundering (**OJ** L166/91)

MONICA
System integration for incident-congestion detection and traffic monitoring (**DRIVE** project)

MONITOR
Strategic analysis, forecasting and evaluation in matters of research and technology programme (1989-1993) (**OJ** L200/89). *See also* **FAST**; **SAST**; **SPEAR**. Continued as **TSER**

Monnet, Jean
One of the founding fathers of the EU. Monnet was the inspiration behind the Schuman Plan, which led to the creation of the European Coal and Steel Community (**ECSC**). He was the first President of the ECSC's **High Authority** (now the **European Commission**) and also devised the idea of the European Defence Community (**EDC**). He died in 1979

Monnet Project
See **Jean Monnet Project**

MONOFAST
Monolithic integration beyond 26.5 GHZ (**ESPRIT** project)

Monti Report
on taxation in the EU (**COM**(96)546)

Montreal Protocol
Decision 88/540/EEC on substances that deplete the ozone layer (**OJ** L297/88).
www.unep.org/ozone/montreal.shtml

MOP
Multifund operational programme

MORE
Marc optical recognition (project within Area 5 of the **Telematics Systems Programme**)

MORE
Mobile rescue phone (a Telematics for Disabled and Elderly People project within the **Telematics Applications Programme**)

More Europe
Slogan of the Spanish Presidency, January-July 2002

MOSAIC-HS
Modular system for application integration and clustering in home system (a Telematics for Disabled and Elderly People project within the **Telematics Applications Programme**)

MOSDT
MOMBSE for III-V semiconductor devices and technology (**ESPRIT** project)

MOSES
Development of a new generation of multi-media database services with integration of the multi-media features in the whole chain of equipment (**EUREKA** project)

MOU
Memorandum of understanding

MOVAID
Mobility and activity assistance systems for the Disabled (**TIDE** project)

MPD
Multi-lingual product description (**EUREKA** project)

MPP
Multi-annual policy programme

MRA
Mutual recognition agreement

MS
Member States

MST
Manufacturing science and technology for ICs production (within the **JESSI** programme)

MTC
Mediterranean **third countries**

MTCR
Missile technology control regime

MTFA
Medium-term financial assistance

MTFS
Medium-term financial support

MTN-T
Multimodal trans-European transport network

MTP
Managers training programme. A **Tacis** project developed in 1998 to continue the **PIP** programme for **NIS** managers

MTP
Mediterranean targeted project. Established in 1993 under **MAST**

MUA
Million units of account. *See also* **MECU**

MUCOM
Multisensory control of movement (**ESPRIT** project)

MUCPI
Monetary union consumer price index, based on the **HCPI**s of the **Member States** and produced by **EUROSTAT** (**OJ** C84/95)

MUICP
Monetary union index of consumer prices. Alternative form of **MUCPI**

Multi-APEL
Accreditation of prior experience and learning (**Leonardo da Vinci** project)

MULTICRAFT
Industrial fettling cell (**EUREKA** project)

Multifibre Agreement
See **MFA**

MULTIMED
Demonstration of functional service integration in support of professional user-groups (**RACE** project)

Multimedia Broker
Critical support tools for multimedia publishing (a Telematics Information Engineering project within the **Telematics Applications Programme**)

MULTIPLE
Multimedia education and training system (a Telematics for Disabled and Elderly People project within the **Telematics Applications Programme**)

MULTOS
Multimedia filing system (**ESPRIT** project)

Munich Convention
The 1973 Munich Convention created the European Patent Organisation (**EPO**)

MUNICIPIA
Multilingual urban network for the integration of city planners and involved local actors (a Telematics for Urban and Rural Areas project within the **Telematics Applications Programme**)

MUREX
Multi-purpose underwater remote expert system (**EUREKA** project)

MURIM
Multi-dimensional reconstruction and imaging in medicine (**AIM** project)

MUS
Monetary unit sampling. A method of statistical sampling undertaken by the **European Court of Auditors** to ensure that errors affecting the reliability of accounts do not exceed the selected reference amount

MUSA
Multilingual multimedia speech aid for hearing and language difficulties (**TIDE** project)

MUSE
Media Union Information Society and Education Network

MUSE
Multimedia distributed services environment (**ISIS** multimedia project)

MUSE
S/W quality and reliability metrics: safety management and clerical systems (**ESPRIT** project)

MUSIK
Project to give distributors, publishers and the public access to an electronic classical music catalogue (**TEDIS** project)

MUSIP
Multisensor image processor (**ESPRIT** project)

MUST
Next generation database management system (**ESPRIT** project)

MUSYC
Multi-media systems for customs (a Telematics for Administrations project within the **Telematics Applications Programme**)

MUTATE
Multimedia tools for advanced GIS training in Europe (**EMTF** project)

MUWIC
Multimedia for women in the cultural industries (**NOW** project).
www.miid.net/now/muwic.html

MVTET
Modernization of vocational and technical education in Turkey (under **MEDA**)

MWW
Mastering the wired world (a Telematics Information Engineering project within the **Telematics Applications Programme**)

N

N
Norway / Norwegian

NA
National accounts. Statistical domain on the **New Cronos** databank. *See* **NA_FINA**; **NA_MNAG**; **NA_SEC1**; **NA_SEC2**; **NA_SECT**

NA
Non-attached. *See also* **NI**

NABS
Nomenclature for the analysis and comparison of scientific programmes and budgets. Published by **EUR-OP** for **Eurostat**

NACE
Nomenclature générale des activités économiques dans la Communauté européenne (General industrial classification of economic activities within the European Community).
http://forum.europa.eu.int/irc/dsis/coded/info/data/coded/en/gl006813.htm

NADC
Non-associated developing countries

NAEEM
Network for Arab and European exchanges in management

NA_FINA
National accounts-financial accounts statistical domain on the **New Cronos** databank

NAFTA
North American Free Trade Agreement.
www.nafta-customs.org

Named directive
Term to describe a directive which is given a 'popular' name - usually unofficially, but occasionally as part of the formal title. The phrase 'short title' is used in a similar way

NA_MNAG
Candidate countries non-financial accounts statistical domain on the **New Cronos** databank

NANA
Novel algorithms for new real-time **VLSI** architectures (**ESPRIT** project)

NANOFET
Performance and physical limits of HFET transistors (**ESPRIT** project)

NANSDEV
Nanostructures for semiconductor devices (**ESPRIT** project)

NAOPIA
New architectures for optical processing in industrial applications (**ESPRIT** project)

NAP
National Awareness Partners. A network to raise awareness of the existence and availability of electronic information services. Created under the **IMPACT** programme

NAPPIES
Collective term for National Awareness Partners (**NAPs**)

NAPs
National action plans. *See* **Luxembourg Process**

NARCISSE
Network of art research computer image systems in Europe (**IMPACT** project)

NARIC
National Academic Recognition Information Centres. Established in 1982 and coordinated by the Education and Culture **DG** of the **European Commission** with national centres. Currently within the **Socrates** programme.
http://europa.eu.int/comm/education/programmes/socrates/agenar_en.html

NAS
Newly Associated States (Bulgaria, Cyprus, Czech Republic, Estonia, Hungary, Latvia, Lithuania, Malta, Poland, Romania, Slovakia, Slovenia)

NA_SEC1
National accounts aggregates statistical domain on the **New Cronos** databank

NA_SEC2
National accounts branches of production statistical domain on the **New Cronos** databank

NA_SECT
National accounts by sector statistical domain on the **New Cronos** databank

Natali Prize
The Natali Prize for Journalism: Excellence in Reporting Human Rights, Democracy and Development, is an annual award, established by the **European Commission** in 1992.
www.ejc.nl/files/awards/ifj/natalya/awards.html

NATASHA
Network and tools for the assessment of speech/language and hearing ability (a Telematics for Disabled and Elderly People project within the **Telematics Applications Programme**)

NATO
North Atlantic Treaty Organisation.
Blvd Leopold III, 1110 Brussels, Belgium.
www.nato.int

NAT-LAB
Natural learner acquisition (**DELTA** project)

Natura 2000
An ecological network of protected sites designated by **Member States** under the **Birds Directive** and **Habitats Directive**.
http://europa.eu.int/comm/environment/nature/natura.htm

NCAP
New cars assessment programme (1996-1997) to ensure safety testing of passenger cars

NCB
National central banks (of the **Member States**). List available at:
www.ecb.int

NCC
National Coordinating Committee

NCE
Non-compulsory expenditure

NCI
New Community Instrument. A financial mechanism managed by the European Investment Bank (**EIB**)

NCP
National contact points in **Member States**, which form part of the **CRAFT** initiative

NCPI
New commercial policy instrument

NCU
National coordination units

NDA
Non-differentiated appropriations

NDSNET
Harmonisation of nephrology data systems within regional networks (a Telematics for Healthcare project within the **Telematics Applications Programme**).
www.ehto.org/ht_projects/html/dynamic/88.html

NDWMU
Nuclear decommissioning and waste management unit. Part of the **JRC**

NEAPOL
Negotiated environmental agreements.
http://fetew.ugent.be/NeaPol

NEC
Network of employment coordinators (**OJ** C328/89)

NECs
National emission ceilings

NECTAR
Networked electronic storage and communication of telematics applications programme Results (a Telematics Engineering project within the **Telematics Applications Programme**)

NEDIES
Natural and environmental disaster information exchange system

NEF
New Economics Foundation. An independent research institute set up in 1986 to organise The Other Economic Summits (**TOES**).
3 Jonathan Street, London SE11 5NH, UK.
www.neweconomics.org

Negative Assent
Process by which the **European Parliament** can veto legislation by absolute majority in 14 policy areas. Introduced in the **Treaty on European Union**

Neighbourhood Policy
The idea that the EU can 'export' stability to neighbouring countries. Mentioned in a speech by Romano Prodi, 13 November 2001 (see SPEECH/01/531 on the **RAPID** database)

NEMESYS
Traffic and quality-of-service management for IBCN (**RACE** project)

NEPTUNE
New European programme for technology utilisation in education (**OJ** C187/87). Never formally adopted

NER
Network of European **Relays** (in the UK)

NERVES
Innovative architectures for neurocomputing machines and **VLSI** neuram networks (**ESPRIT** project)

NESC
Network for the evaluation of steel components. Established by the **JRC** with the **IAM** as the operating agent and the reference laboratory

NESSIE
Awareness environment. A **CSCW** project in the field of computers as a social medium (partially funded under the **Telematics Applications Programme**).
http://orgwis.gmd.de/projects/nessie

NESSTAR
Networked social science tools and resources (a Telematics Information Engineering project within the **Telematics Applications Programme**)

NEST
Part of the **Sixth Framework Programme**, NEST supports research on new potential

problems uncovered by science and helps to consolidate European efforts in emerging fields of research. It supports three specific actions: **ADVENTURE**, **INSIGHT**, **PATHFINDER**.
www.cordis.lu/nest/home.html

NET
Next European Torus

NET
Norme Européenne de Télécommunication. An approved technical specification of the **CEPT**

Netd@ys
Europe Commission initiative originally intended to promote the effective use of new media in education.
http://europa.eu.int/comm/education/netdays

NETLINK
Validation and coordination of implementation of interoperable data card systems and intranet solutions before nation wide implementation (a Telematics for Healthcare project within the **Telematics Applications Programme**).
www.ehto.org/ht_projects/html/dynamic/89.html

NETLOGO
The European educational interactive site (**EMTF** project)

NETMAN
Functional specification for IBC management (**RACE** project)

NETS
NETfor Nets (a Telematics for Administration project within the **Telematics Applications Programme**).
www.netfornets.org

NETS
See **TN-NETS**

NETT
Network for Environmental Technology Transfer

Network Europe
Term used in a speech by **European Commission** President Romano **Prodi**, May 2000. Looking forward to the publication of the **White Paper** on European Governance, he stated: "It will explore ways and means to achieve a more democratic form of partnership between the different levels of governance in Europe. A partnership I call 'Network Europe', with all levels of governance shaping, proposing, implementing and monitoring policy together." (See SPEECH/00/172 on the **RAPID** database)

Network of Excellence
Instrument under the **Sixth Framework Programme**, designed to strengthen scientific and technological excellence through networking of resources and expertise (sometimes referred to as NoE)

Network industries
... include energy, transport, telecommunications and post

NEUTRABAS
Neutral product definition database for large multi-functional systems (**ESPRIT** project)

NEVIS
Neural vehicle information system (**VALUE** project)

New Approach Directives
A Council **Resolution** on a new approach to technical harmonisation and standards (**OJ** C136/85) established a system under which "essential requirements" for products which are intended to be placed (or put into service) on the Community market are defined in a **Directive**, with more detailed technical specifications drawn up by one of the European

standards bodies (**CEN**, **CENELEC**, **ETSI**). This differs from an earlier approach under which technical details were included in the Directives themselves. The 'new approach' speeded up the standardisation process in the run-up to the Single Market (**SEM**).
www.newapproach.org

New Cronos
Eurostat database of over 160 million items of macroeconomic and social data. Previously Cronos

NFP
New Framework Programme. Term used for the **Sixth Framework Programme** prior to its adoption

NFPs
National Focal Points for the **Telematics for Libraries Programme**.
www.cordis.lu/libraries/en/nfp-list.html

NFS
Nuclear fission safety. 1998-2002: **Decision** 1999/175/Euratom (**OJ** L64/1999).
http://europa.eu.int/comm/dg12/fission/fission3.html

NGAA
National Grant Awarding Authority (within the **Erasmus** and **Socrates** programmes)

NGDO
Non-governmental development organisation

NGE
Net grant equivalent. Used by the **European Commission** in its assessment of aid schemes notified by the **Member States** for National Regional Aid.
http://europa.eu.int/scadplus/leg/en/lvb/g24214.htm

NGL
Nordic-Green Left group in the **European Parliament**. Seen also as **EUL/NGL** (European United Left / Nordic-Green Left)

NGO
Non-governmental organisation

NGO VOICE
Voluntary Organisations in Cooperation in International Emergencies.
43 av Louise, B-1050 Brussels, Belgium.
www.ngovoice.org

NI
Non-Inscrits. Group of Independents in the **European Parliament**. Also seen as NA - Non-Attached

NI
Northern Ireland

NIC
Nouvelle Instrument Communautaire (New Community Instrument - **NCI**)

NICE
Nitrogen cycling in estuaries (**ELOISE** project)

NICE
Nomenclature of the industries in the European Communities. *See* **NACE** Rev 1

Nice Treaty
See **Treaty of Nice**

NIGHTINGALE
Nursing informatics: generic high-level training in informatics for nurses; general applications for learning and education (a Telematics for Healthcare project within the **Telematics Applications Programme**)

Night of the long knives
Term used to describe an event associated with decisive / ruthless action, such as the allocation of portfolios to incoming **European Commissioners**

NIMEXE
Nomenclature of goods for the external trade statistics of the Community and statistics of trade between **Member States** (Nomenclature des marchandises pour les statistiques du commerce extérieur de la Communauté et du commerce extérieur entre les États membres). Replaced by the **CN**

Nineteen ninety two
Term used for the Single European Market (**SEM**), which was to be completed by the end of 1992

Ninth Summertime Directive
Directive 2000/84/EC of 19 January 2001 on summertime arrangements (**OJ** L31/01)

NIP
National Indicative Programme, negotiated by each **ACP** country

NIPRO
Common nomenclature of industrial products. Published by **OOPEC** in 1975

NIS
New Independent States (of the former Soviet Union): Armenia, Azerbaijan, Belarus, Georgia, Kazakhstan, Kyrgyzstan, Moldova, Russian Federation, Tajikistan, Turkmenistan, Ukraine, Uzbekistan and Mongolia

Nitrates Directive
Directive 91/676/EEC on the protection of waters against pollution caused by nitrates from agricultural sources (**OJ** L375/91)

NITREX
Nitrogen saturation experiments (**STEP** project)

NIVEMES
A network of integrated vertical medical services targeting ships and other vessels and remote populations (a Telematics for Healthcare project within the **Telematics Applications Programme**)

NJORD-TIDE
Methods for user sensitive evaluations of domotic environments (a Telematics for Disabled and Elderly People project within the **Telematics Applications Programme**). http://njord-tide.arch.kth.se/_hemsida/Content.htm

NL
Nederlands (Dutch) / The Netherlands

NLPAD
Natural language processing of patient discharge (**AIM** project)

NMP
New Mediterranean policy

NoE
Network of Excellence

NOHA
Network on humanitarian assistance diploma

NOISE
Electrical fluctuations and noise in advanced microelectronics... (**ESPRIT** project)

Noise Directive
Alternative name for **Environmental Noise Directive**

NONS
Notification of new substances

NORCAR-TRAMET
Development of a special off-road machine for soil preparation in reforestation (**EUREKA** project)

Norm
A standard, as in 'Euronorm'

NORM
Naturally occurring radioactive material

NOROS
Quantum noise reduction schemes in optical systems (**ESPRIT** project)

NORSPA
North Sea special action programme, to clean up coastal zones and coastal waters (**OJ** L370/91). Replaced by **LIFE**

NOSE
Nomenclature for sources of emissions. Developed by Eurostat to facilitate the description of emission sources. Manual published by **Eurostat**

NOW
New opportunities for women. Part of the **Community Initiative EMPLOYMENT** (1994-1999)

NPAA
National programme for the adoption of the acquis. Drawn up by **applicant countries**. *See also* **Acquis Communautaire**

NPCI
National Programme of Community Interest. Designated by the **ERDF** (1979-1999)

NPO
National patent offices

NQ
Non-quota programme

NRA
National regulatory authority

NRCVG
National Resource Centres for Vocational Guidance. *See* **Euroguidance**

NSI
National statistical institute. The organisation responsible for statistics within each **Member State**

NSIGHT
Vision systems for natural human environment (**ESPRIT** project)

NST/R
Revised uniform nomenclature of goods for transport statistics

NT
New technologies

NTB
Non-tariff barrier

NTM
New transatlantic marketplace

NTO
National **Tempus** office

Nuclear Suppliers Group
A "group of nuclear supplier countries which seeks to contribute to the non-proliferation of nuclear weapons through the implementation of Guidelines for nuclear exports and nuclear related exports." *See also* **Australia Group**, **Missile Technology Control Regime**, **Wassenaar Arrangement**, **Zangger Committee**. www.nsg-online.org

Numbering Directive
Directive 98/61/EC amending Directive 97/33/EC with regard to operator number portability and carrier pre-selection (**OJ** L268/98)

NUTOX
Testing the impact of human activities on the development of toxic algae blooms (**MAST III** project)

NUTS
Regions: nomenclature of territorial units for

statistics 1999. Published by **EUR-OP** for **Eurostat**

NVA
Net value added

O

OAA
Open aviation area. A free trade area for air transport between the EU and US, giving airlines freedom to serve any pair of airports in the EU and US and making it easier for them to enter into mergers and takeovers. *See also* **Brattle Group**, **TCAA**

OAR
Specification of an open architecture for reasoning (**AIM** project)

OAS
Organization of African States

OAS
Organization of American States.
17th Street & Constitution Ave, NW, Washington DC 20006, USA.
www.oas.org

OASIS
Open and secure information systems (**EUREKA** project)

OAT
Operational air traffic. Concerns organisation / management of military airspace

OAU
Organisation of African Unity. Now the **African Union**

Objectives
Priority Objectives within the **Structural Funds**. For 2000-2006 they are:
Objective 1: Regions whose development is lagging behind
Objective 2: Regions undergoing economic and social conversion
Objective 3: Education, training and employment

OBNOVA
Regulation 1628/96 for the rehabilitation and reconstruction of Bosnia and Herzegovina, Croatia, the Federal Republic of Yugoslavia and the Former Yugoslav Republic of Macedonia (**OJ** L204/96). From a Serbian/Croatian word that translates as 'revitalisation'. *See also* **EAFR**

Observatory
A team of experts, brought together by the **European Commission**, to advise on the situation regarding a particular topic, e.g. **EIRO**; **IMO**; **OEST**; **OETH**; **SME Observatory**; **SMO**

OCDS
Open control display system for industrial automation (**EUREKA** project)

OCHA
Office for the Coordination of Humanitarian Affairs (**UN**).
www.reliefweb.int

OCT
Overseas Countries and Territories. **Decision** 2001/822/EC on the association of the overseas countries and territories with the European Community (**OJ** L314/01).
http://europa.eu.int/comm/development/oct/index_en.htm

Octopus
Programme to help stamp out corruption in Central and Eastern Europe. Initially a joint programme of the **European Commission**

and the **Council of Europe**; now just the Council of Europe.
www.coe.int/T/E/Legal_affairs/Legal_cooperation/Combating_economic_crime/Programme_OCTOPUS

OCTS
Ocean colour and temperature sensor

OCVV
Office Communautaire des Variétés Végétales (Community Plant Variety Office - **CPVO**)

ODAS
Ocean data acquisition system (**COST** action project)

Ode to Joy
See **European Anthem**

ODIN
Origin-destination information versus traffic control (**DRIVE** project)

ODL
Open and distance learning (Enseignement Ouvert et à Distance - EOD). Within the **Socrates** programme

ODS
Ozone depleting substances

ODYSSEUS
A programme of training, exchanges and cooperation in the field of asylum, immigration and crossing of external borders, 1998-2002. Previously **SHERLOCK**; some elements continued within **ARGO**.
http://europa.eu.int/comm/justice_home/project/odysseus/index_en.htm

OEB
Office Européen des Brevets (European Patent Office - **EPO**)

OECD
Organisation for Economic Cooperation and Development.
2 rue André Pascal, F-75775 Paris Cédex 16, France.
www.oecd.org

OEDT
L'Observatoire européen des drogues et des toxicomanies (European Monitoring Centre for Drugs and Drug Addiction - **EMCDDA**)

OEE
Observatoire européen de l'emploi (European Employment Observatory - **EEO**)

OEEC
Organisation for European Economic Co-operation. Established in 1947 to implement the Marshall Plan

OEIL
A **European Parliament** database which shows the status of EU legislative proposals.
http:wwwdb.europarl.eu.int/dors/oeil/en/search.shtm

OEITFL
Organisation Européenne des Industries Transformatrices de Fruits et Légumes (Association of European Fruit and Vegetable Processing Industries - AEFVPI).
172 ave de Cortenberg, Boîte 6, B-1000 Brussels, Belgium.
www.oeitfl.org

OELs
Occupational exposure limits

OEM
Original equipment manufacturers

OESP
Office européen de sélection du personnel (European Communities Personnel Selection Office - **EPSO**)

OEST
Observatoire européen de la science et de la technologie (European Science & Technology Observatory - **ESTO**)

OETH
L'Observatoire Européen du Textile et de l'Habillement (European **Observatory** for Textiles and Clothing).
197 rue Belliard, box 9, B-1040 Brussels, Belgium

OFCA
Organisation de fabricants de produits cellulosiques alimentaires (Organisation of Manufacturers of Cellulose Products for Foodstuffs)

OFELIA
Optical fibres for electrical industry applications (**BRITE** project)

Official languages
The number of official languages can change as **Member States** join the Union. Since 1995 there have been 11 official languages: Danish, Dutch, English, Finnish, French, German, Greek, Italian, Portuguese, Spanish and Swedish. From May 2004, when **10** new countries join, the number will rise to 20, with the addition of: Czech, Estonian, Hungarian, Latvian, Lithuanian, Maltese, Polish, Slovak, Slovene.
http://europa.eu.int/comm/scic/thescic/multilingualism_en.htm

OFL
Office for Legislation. Body responsible for checking conformity with the **Acquis Communautaire**

OHIM
Office for Harmonization in the Internal Market (Trade marks and Designs). Set up under **Regulation** 40/94 (**OJ** L11/94).
4 av de Europa, E-03008 Alicante, Spain.
http://oami.eu.int

OHR
Office of the High Representative. *See also* **Dayton Accords**

Ohrid Agreement
Intended to prevent civil war in Macedonia. Signed 13 August 2001 following an international diplomatic initiative

OII
Open information interchange service. Part of **INFO 2000**

OIL
A database of prices of petroleum products, published by **Eurostat**

OISIN
Programme for the exchange and training of, and cooperation between, law enforcement authorities. Initially 1997-2000; OISIN II covers 2001-2002 (**Decision** 2001/13/JHA; **OJ** L186/01).
http://europa.eu.int/comm/justice_home/project/oisin_2_en.htm

OJ
Official Journal of the European Union. Published by the **Publications Office** every working day, in the Union's **official languages**. (The name changed from *Official Journal of the European Communities* on 1 February 2003). *See also* the following six entries.
http://publications.eu.int/general/en/oj_en.htm

OJ Annex
Official Journal of the European Communities: Annex of Debates in the **European Parliament** (ceased after the May 1999 session; information now available via **EUROPARL**)

OJ C
Official Journal of the European Union: C series: Information and notices. *See also* **OJ 'C E'**

OJ C E
Official Journal of the European Union: CE

series. An electronic version of OJ C which became available in 1999. Includes material no longer published in the paper version, such as proposals for legislation

OJEC
Term sometimes used for Official Journal of the European Communities (**OJ**)

OJ L
Official Journal of the European Union: L series: Legislation. Includes **Decision**s, **Directive**s, **Opinion**s, **Recommendation**s, **Regulation**s

OJ S
Official Journal of the European Union: S series: invitations for public tenders. No longer available in paper format; available online as **TED**

OLAF
Office européen de lutte antifraude (European Commission Anti-Fraud Office). **Decision** 99/352/EC (**OJ** L136/99). Operational 1 June 1999. Successor to **UCLAF**.
http://europa.eu.int/comm/dgs/olaf

OLDI
On-line data interchange. One of two **EUROCONTROL** standards adopted by **Directive** 97/15/EC which covers the specifications for the procurement of air management equipment and systems (**OJ** L95/97). *See also* **ADEXP**

OLE
Organisational learning in enterprises (**DELTA** project)

OLEW
Open learning experimental workshop (**DELTA** project)

OLIVES
Optical interconnections for **VLSI** and electronic systems (**ESPRIT** project)

OLMO
On-vehicle laser microsystem for obstacle detection (**INNOVATION** project)

OMAS
Office for Monitoring and Assessment

Ombudsman
See **European Ombudsman**

OMC
Open method of coordination (name used for exchange of good practice or experience between **Member States)**

OMEX
Ocean margin exchange. One of the four major regional **RTD** projects of **MAST III**. **OMEX** covers the Atlantic. *See also* **BASYS**; **CANIGO**; **MATER**

OMNI
Office wheelchair with high manoeuverability and navigational intelligence for people with severe handicap (**TIDE** project)

OMU
Observatoire du Marché unique (Single Market Observatory - **SMO**)

ONE
OPAC networking in Europe (**Telematics Applications** project)

ON LIVE
On-line interactive virtual educator (**EMTF** project)

ONP
Open network provision (in the telecommunications sector). **Directive** 90/387/EEC (**OJ** L192/90). No longer in force

OOPEC
Office for Official Publications of the European Communities (Office des publications officielles des Communautés

européennes - OPOCE). "The European Union's publisher." Adopted the unofficial name EUR-OP; now styles itself Publications Office.
http://publications.eu.int

OP
Official publications

OP
Operational programme (under the **Structural Funds**)

OPAC
Online public access catalogue

OPEN
Observatoire Permanent de l'Environment

OPEN
Orientation by personal electronic navigation (**TIDE** project)

OPENLABS
An open system architecture addressed to laboratories (**AIM** project)

Operation Concordia
The Union's military operation in the former Yugoslav Republic of Macedonia (FYROM), launched 31 March 2003. The EU's first military operation, Concordia took over a **NATO** operation, initially for six months, but later extended until 15 December 2003.
http://ue.eu.int/arym/index.asp?lang=EN

OPET
Organisations for the Promotion of Energy Technologies (previously Organisation for the Promotion of Energy Technology). Originally set up under the **THERMIE** programme, 1996-1999.
www.cordis.lu/opet/home.html

OPHTEL
Telematics in ophthalmology (a Telematics for Healthcare project within the **Telematics Applications Programme**)

Opinion
Opinions are produced by Community **Institutions**, including the **European Parliament**, **Council of the European Union**, **European Commission**, **Economic and Social Committee**, and **Committee of the Regions**. Although often defined as a type of legislative instrument, opinions are not legally binding, but are intended to influence decisions or actions of the institution or **Member States** to which they are addressed (e.g. by commenting on proposed legislation or by encouraging good practice). Also known by the French term 'avis'. *See also* **Own Opinion**, **Recommendation**

OPLAN
Operation plan

OPMODD
Operational modelling of regional seas and coastal waters (**EUREKA** project)

OPOCE
Office des publications officielles des Communautés européennes (Office for Official Publications of the European Communities - **OOPEC**)

Opt-out
An exemption from Treaty provisions

ORA
Opportunities for rural areas (project within Area 7 of the **Telematics Systems** and **Telematics Applications Programme**)

ORDIT
Development of a methodology for specifying non-functional requirements (**ESPRIT** project)

OREXPRESS
Logistical information and scheduling system

for the transportation of bulk materials on Europe's inland waterways (**EUREKA** project)

Organigramme
See **IDEA** (Inter-institutional directory of the EU)

ORIGIN
Organisation for an International Geographical Indications Network. First meeting held June 2003; see SPEECH/03/292 on the **RAPID** database. *See also* **PGI**.
www.origin-gi.com

ORNET
Origin network on customs and indirect taxation. Set up under the **IDA** programme

ORNIS
The ORNIS Committee was created to help implement the 1979 **Birds Directive**. Its work was supported by the 'ORNIS database', last updated in 1994

ORQUEST
A telematics system for oral health quality enhancement (a Telematics for Healthcare project within the **Telematics Applications Programme**)

ORTELIUS
Database on higher education in Europe. Set up in 1994; initially free, now subscription only

Ortoli Instrument
Alternative name for the **NCI**

OSA-TESMA
Open system architecture for telematics services in municipal applications (a Telematics for Urban and Rural Areas project within the **Telematics Applications Programme**)

OSCAR
Optical switching systems, components and applications (**RACE** project)

OSCE
Organization for Security and Cooperation in Europe.
Secretariat: 5-7 Kärntner Ring, 4th floor, 1010 Vienna, Austria.
www.osce.org

OSHA
See **EU-OSHA**

OSI
Open Society Initiative

OSIRIS
Open systems integrated roadfreight information services (**IMPACT** project)

OSIRIS
Optimal standards for successful integration of multi-media on-line services (**DELTA** project)

OSIS
One stop internet shop for business. Part of **Dialogue for Business**.
http://europa.eu.int/business

OSIS
Open shops for information systems (**COST** action project)

Oslo Declaration
Declaration by the Heads of Government of the **EFTA** countries on the strengthening of the association and relations with the EC. Signed March 1989 but not published in official sources. An unofficial translation is to be found in ***Agence Europe*** 4982 of 24 March 1989, and Documents Section 1549, 22 March 1989

Oslo Guidelines
Concerning the use of military and civil defence assets (MCDA) to support humanitarian assistance. Published 1994. http://www.reliefweb.int/mcdls/mcdu/oslo_guidelines/oslo_guidelines.html

Oslo Peace Process
Refers to negotiations between members of the Palestine Liberation Organization and Israel, 1994-2001, initially held in Oslo

OSSAD
Office support systems analysis and design (**ESPRIT** project)

OT
Overseas territories

OUSR
Operating unit status report. Part of **ERDS**

Outs
The three **Member States** which decided to opt out of Economic and Monetary Union (**EMU**): Denmark, Sweden, UK. Also referred to as 'Pre-ins'

OUVERTURE
A programme for cooperation between EU regions and regions in Central and Eastern Europe. Subsumed within **INTERREG**

Overseas Association Decision
Decision 2001/822/EC on the association of the overseas countries and territories with the European Community (**OJ** L314/01)

OVIDE/Epistel
Organisation du Videotex pour le Député Européen. **European Parliament** videotex service; replaced by **EUROPARL**

OVPIC
Office for Veterinary and Plant Health Inspection. Became the **FVO**

Own Opinion
Opinions submitted by the **European Parliament, Economic and Social Committee** and **Committee of the Regions** on subjects which they consider merit specific comment even if their views have not been requested by the **Council of the European Union**. *See also* **Opinion**

Own Resources
EU budget comprising **Member State** contributions for customs duties, agricultural levies, a fraction of **VAT** and a fraction of each Member State's **GNP**

OXODIPINE
Development of oxodipine pharmacological and clinical development of oxodipine (**EUREKA** project)

P

P
Portuguese / Portugal

P
Series of information memos issued by the Spokesman's group of the **European Commission**

PA
Payment appropriations

PABLI
Pages Bleues Information. A database of progress made by the EC's development projects. Sometimes called 'Blue pages'

PACA
Absorption heat pump (**EUREKA** project)

PACE
Programme d'Action Communautaire en vue d'améliorer l'efficacité de l'Electricité (Community Action Programme for the Efficient Use of Electricity). 1989-1992. (**OJ** L157/89). Incorporated into **SAVE II**

PACE
Perspectives for advanced communications in Europe (**RACE** project)

PACE
Prediction of aggregated-scale coastal evaluation (**MAST III** project)

PACE
Programme of advanced continuing education (**COMETT** project)

PACIFLOR
Development of a heat-resistant probiotic useful for animal productions (**EUREKA** project)

Packaging Waste Directive
Directive 94/62/EC on packaging and packaging waste (**OJ** L365/94)

PACOMA
Performance assessment of confinements for medium-level and alpha waste (part of the **EURATOM** research programme on the management and storage of radioactive waste)

PACT
PCTE - added common tools (**ESPRIT** project)

PACT
Promotion of combined transport (previously Pilot Actions for Combined Transport). Ended December 2001; replaced by **Marco Polo**

PACTE
Exchanges of experience between local and regional authorities in the **Member States** (under **Article 10** of the **ERDF**)

PADMAVATI
Parallel associative development machine for artificial intelligence (**ESPRIT** project)

Padoa-Schioppa Report
Published in 1987 as 'Efficiency, Stability and Equity', the report examined the economic impact of the Single Market (**SEM**) and of .Spain and Portugal joining the Community

PAG
Projects Advisory Group

Pagis
Performance assessment of geological isolation system (radioactive waste research programme)

PAIR
Process oriented agent based information retrieval (a Telematics Information Engineering project within the **Telematics Applications Programme**)

PALABRE
Integration of artificial intelligence, vocal input-output and natural language dialogue - application to directory services (**ESPRIT** project)

PALAVDA
Parallel architectures and languages for AIP - a **VLSI** directed approach (**ESPRIT** project)

PALIO
European standard qualification in the design, delivery, marketing and evaluation of multimedia open learning (**COMETT** project)

Palma Document
A report to the **European Council** on the lifting of controls at intra-EC borders

PAM-AID
Personal adaptive mobility aid for the frail and elderly visually impaired (a Telematics for Disabled and Elderly People project within the **Telematics Applications Programme**)

PAMELA
Pricing and monitoring electronically of automobiles (**DRIVE** project)

PAMINA
German-French border regions in Northern Alsace, Southern Palatinate and the Middle Upper Rhine (**INTERREG** project)

PANCAKE MOTORS
Axial low cost brushed axial flux DC motors with high energy pressed rare earth permanent magnets (**EUREKA** project)

PANDORA
Prototyping a navigation database of road network attributes (**DRIVE** project)

PANGLOSS
Parallel architecture for networking gateways linking OSI systems (**ESPRIT** project)

PAN(N5)
Manufacturer of pilot equipment to produce then prove the feasibility of manufacturing flow-line style, high pressure sub-sea pipes (**EUREKA** project)

Pannenborg Report
Report of the **ERB** to assess the progress of the **ESPRIT** programme (**COM**(85)616)

Panorama
Panorama of the **European Union**. Brief publication about the Union.
http://europa.eu.int/comm/publications/booklets/eu_glance/20/index_en.htm

Panorama
Panorama of EU Industry. Annual publication, 1989-1997. Previously Panorama of EC Industry. Replaced by European Business: Facts and Figures

PANORAMA
Perception and navigation system for autonomous mobile applications (**ESPRIT** project)

PAP
Policy advice programme

PAP
Prices of agricultural products (**CADDIA** project)

PAP
Priority action plan

PAQO
Plant availability and quality optimisation (**ESPRIT** project)

Paquet Delors
Delors Package. *See* **Delors I**

PARADI
Automatic production management system using **AI** developments (**EUREKA** project)

Parallel Convention
See **Lugano Convention**

PARASOL
ATM specific measurement equipment (**RACE** project)

PARCMAN
Parking management control and information systems (**DRIVE** project)

PARDOC
A **European Parliament** internal database which replaced **DOSE** and was later replaced by **EPOQUE**

Parental Leave Directive
Directive 96/34/EC on the framework agreement on parental leave concluded by **UNICE**, **CEEP** and **ETUC** (OJ L145/96)

PARIS
Project for the economic assessment of road transport and traffic information (**DRIVE** project)

Paris Summit
The 1974 Paris Summit founded the **European Council**

Paris Treaty
See **Treaty of Paris**

ParlEuNet
EMTF project which permits secondary school students to use networks and multimedia resources to learn about and to take part in collaborative projects on the **European Parliament**

PARNUTS
Directive 89/398/EEC on foodstuffs intended for particular nutritional uses (**OJ** L186/89)

PARQ
An internal **European Parliament** database of parliamentary questions, replaced by **EPOQUE**

PARTS
Performing Arts Research and Training Studios. An international contemporary dance school founded in 1994 (**Kaleidoscope** project).
164 ave Van Volxem, B-1190 Brussels, Belgium.
www.rosas.be

Pasqua-de Villiers
See **De Villiers List**

Passerelle
French term for 'footbridge'. A metaphor to describe the transfer of a policy area from one **Pillar** to another (e.g. under the **Amsterdam Treaty**, the subject of immigration, asylum and visas was moved from the Third Pillar to the First Pillar)

PASSYS
Passive solar components and systems testing (**JOULE I** project)

PATENT
Patent applications statistical domain on the **New Cronos** databank

PATHFINDER
Supported by **NEST**, PATHFINDER funding

"will enable European scientists to undertake pioneering work and establish expertise in new fields" with an emphasis on "clearly identified areas with substantial longer-term promise for Europe."
www.cordis.lu/nest/pathfinder.htm

PATINNOVA
A conference to promote the value of patents and patent information, organised jointly by the **European Commission** and the **EPO**.
www.european-patent-office.org/epidos/conf/eac2003/

PATLIB
A network of patent information centres throughout Europe.
www.european-patent-office.org/patlib

PATMAN
Patient workflow management systems (a Telematics for Healthcare project within the **Telematics Applications Programme**)

PATMOS
Power and timing modelling optimisation and specification (**ESPRIT** project)

PATRICIA
Proving and testability for reliability improvement of complex integrated architectures (**ESPRIT** project)

Paul Finet Foundation
To provide support for schooling and training the children of coal miners and steel workers killed by occupational disease or industrial accident.
Jean Monnet Building, Plateau du Kirchberg, L-2920 Luxembourg.
http://europa.eu.int/comm/secretariat_general/finet/index_en.htm

PAVE
PCTE and VMS environment (**ESPRIT** project)

PAXIS
Pilot action of excellence on innovative start-ups. A **DG** Enterprise initiative under the **Sixth Framework Programme**.
www.cordis.lu/paxis

PBKAL
Paris, Brussels, Köln, Amsterdam, London High Speed Rail Link (**TEN-Transport** project)

PBS
Passbook scheme. An export subsidy scheme, abolished and replaced on 1 April 1997 by the **DEPB**

PC
Programme Committee

PCA
Partnership and cooperation agreement

PCAD
Portable communication assistant for people with acquired dysphasia (a Telematics for Disabled and Elderly People project within the **Telematics Applications Programme**)

PCAOB
Public Company Accounting Oversight Board (of the United States). *See also* **Sarbanes-Oxley Act**

PCTE
A basis for a portable common tool environment (**ESPRIT** project)

PDB
Preliminary draft budget

PDCS
Predictably dependable computing systems (**ESPRIT** project)

PDO
Protected designation of origin. In the context

of **Regulation** 2081/92 on the protection of geographical indications and designations of origin for agricultural products and foodstuffs (**OJ** L208/92)

PDWEB
The public data web (a Telematics for Urban and Rural Areas project within the **Telematics Applications Programme**)

PE
Parlement européen (**European Parliament** - EP)

PEA
Positive economic agenda

PEA
Proposal expansion award (**Telematics Applications** project)

PEACE
Previously a **Community Initiative** for Peace and reconciliation in Northern Ireland and the border counties of Ireland. Now incorporated within **Objective** 1 of the **Structural Funds** (2000-2006)

PEACOCK
Software development using concurrently executable modules (**ESPRIT** project)

PEARL
Pan European competency assessment in rural and landbased industries (**EMTF** project)

PEARLE
European League of Employers' Associations in the Performing Arts / Ligue européenne des associations d'employeurs dans le secteur des arts du spectacle.
19/6 Sinctelettesquare, B-1000 Brussels, Belgium.
www.pearle.ws

PECA
Protocol to the Europe agreements on conformity assessment and acceptance of industrial products

PECH
European Parliament Committee on Fisheries

PECO
Pays d'Europe centrale et orientale (Central and Eastern European Countries - CEEC)

PECOS
Regulation 636/82 on outward processing arrangements applicable to certain clothing and textile products re-imported into the EU after working or processing in certain **Third Countries** (**OJ** L271/82). No longer in force

PEDACTICE
Educational multimedia in compulsory school: from pedagogical assessment to product assessment (**EMTF** project)

PEDAP
Programme spécifique de développement de l'agriculture au Portugal (Programme for the Development of Portuguese Agriculture). **Regulation** 3828/85 (**OJ** L372/85). No longer in force

PEDIP
Programme spécifique de développement industriel pour le Portugal (Programme for the Development of Portuguese Industry). **Regulation** 2053/88 on financial assistance for Portugal for a specific industrial development programme (**OJ** L185/88). 1988-1992. No longer in force

PEDRAA
Programme spécifique de développement da la Région Autonome des Açores (Development Programme for the Azores Region)

Peer Group
Established in February 2000 - in the context of the **Kinnock reforms** - to analyse the

European Commission's tasks and the human resources necessary to carry them out. The Group's findings were published in July 2000 as 'Matching the Commission's activities with its human resources - The means to achieve our objectives'. Members: Commission President Romano Prodi (chair), Vice-President Kinnock, Commissioners Fischler, Lamy, Schreyer

PEGASE
A **European Parliament** internal library management database containing the EP catalogue

Pegasus Foundation
A **European Parliament** initiative created in 1991 and operational under Parliament's Culture, Youth and Media Committee. It promotes the European identity to young people via educational projects in cultural heritage.
135 rue Belliard, EAS 2.59, B-1047 Brussels, Belgium

PENELOPE
Pan-European network of environmental legislation observatories for planning, education and research (a Telematics for Education and Training project within the **Telematics Applications Programme**)

Pension Funds Directive
Proposed **Directive** on the activities of institutions for occupational retirement provision (**COM**(2000)507; approved by the **Council of the European Union** in May 2003)

People's Europe
Reports prepared by a working party and chaired by Pietro Adonnino to encourage EC citizens to see themselves as Europeans (1st and 2nd reports published in *Bulletin of the EC* Supplement 7/85; further report published in *Bulletin of the EC* Supplement 2/88)

PEPA
Priority environmental programme for accession

PEPMA
Parallel execution of prolog on multiprocessor architectures (**ESPRIT** project)

PEPPER I & II
Reports on the Promotion of Employee Participation in Profits and Enterprise Results. PEPPER I published by **EUR-OP** as *Social Europe* Supplement 3/91. PEPPER II published as **COM**(96) 697

PEPs
Pre-accession economic programmes. Aim to identify appropriate economic policies and reforms needed to prepare **Applicant Countries** for EU accession. First submitted in 2001

PERF
Pan European Regulatory Forum for Pharmaceuticals.
http://perf.eudra.org

PERICLES
Protocol for the evaluation of residues in industrial contaminated liquid effluents (an Environmental Health and Safety Research project within the **ENVIRONMENT AND CLIMATE** programme)

PERIFRA
Régions périphériques et activités fragiles (peripheral regions and destabilised activities). A **European Parliament** initiative for special action in peripheral regions (1991-1992). Continued as **KONVER**

Perinorm
A bibliographic database of national, European and international standards, produced jointly by **BSI**, **DIN** and **AFNOR**. Launched in 1989.
www.perinorm.com

Periodic Report
on the social and economic situation of the regions of the Community (**COM**(80)816; COM(84)40; COM(87)230; COM(90)609; COM(94)322; COM(2001)24. Replaced by the triennial **Cohesion Report**. *See also* **Synthetic Index**

PERIPHERA
Telematics applications and strategies combating social and economic exclusion (a Telematics for Urban and Rural Areas project within the **Telematics Applications Programme**)

Perla
Performance calibration and training laboratory (**JRC** - fissile materials safeguards and management programme)

Personal Protective Equipment
See **PPE**
Directive

PES
Party of European Socialists (Group in the **European Parliament**).
www.socialistgroup.org

PES
Public employment services. A **European Commission** Communication on modernising PESs was published as **COM**(98)641.
http://europa.eu.int/scadplus/leg/en/cha/c10926.htm

PESC
Politique étrangère et sécurité européenne (Common Foreign and Security Policy - CFSP)

PESCA
Community Initiative to restructure the EU fishing industry (1994-1999) (Guidelines in **OJ** C180/94)

PETE
Portable educational tool environment (**DELTA** project)

Petersberg Declaration
Issued in June 1992, following a meeting of **WEU** Foreign and Defence Ministers. It has three parts: 1 - On WEU and European Security; 2 - On strengthening WEU's operational role; 3 - On relations between WEU and the other European **Member States** of the European Union or the Atlantic Alliance.
www.weu.int/documents/920619peten.pdf

Petersberg Tasks
As laid down in the **Petersberg Declaration**, the Petersberg tasks are: humanitarian and rescue tasks; peace-keeping tasks; tasks of combat forces in crisis management, including peace-making. They were incorporated into the **Treaty on European Union** by the **Treaty of Amsterdam**

PETI
European Parliament Committee on Petitions

Pet passport
A document to be provided under **Regulation** 998/2003 on the animal health requirements applicable to the non-commercial movement of pet animals (**OJ** L146/03), allowing pets to travel between **Member States**

PETI
European Parliament Committee on Petitions

PETrA
Pan European transport area developed in the Black Sea

PETRA
Project of equipment for the treatment of radioactive waste in **ADECO** (**JRC** - safety of nuclear materials programme)

PETRA
Programme d'action pour la formation et la préparation des jeunes à la vie adulte et professionnelle (Community action programme for the vocational training of young people and their preparation for adult and working life). 1992-1994 (**OJ** L214/91). Continued within the **Leonardo da Vinci** programme

PETS
Pricing European transport systems

PETs
Privacy enhancing technologies

Petten
A site of the Joint Research Centre (**JRC**). PO Box 2, 1755 ZG Petten, The Netherlands

PGI
Protected geographical indication. **Regulation** 2081/92 in connection with the origin of foodstuffs (**OJ** L208/92). *See also* **ORIGIN**.
http://europa.eu.int/comm/agriculture/qual/en/pdopgi_en.htm

Phare
Poland/Hungary aid for the reconstruction of the economy. **Regulation** 3906/89 (**OJ** L375/89). Extended to other **CEEC** by Regulation 2698/90 (OJ L257/90)

Phare Access
Programme to strengthen civil society and help **Applicant Countries** in Central and Eastern Europe prepare for accession. 2000-2002 (in two phases). Replaced **Phare LIEN**.
http://europa.eu.int/comm/enlargement/pas/phare/programmes/multi-bene/access2000.htm

Phare ACE
A programme to support academic and professional economists in Central and Eastern Europe. *See also* **ACE**, **ACE Quarterly**.
http://europa.eu.int/comm/economy_finance/publications/phare_ace/ace_en.htm

Phare AQ
Abbreviated form of **Phare ACE Quarterly**

Phare LIEN
Phare link inter European NGOs (**OJ** C29/98). Replaced by **Phare Access**

PHARMACOS
Pharmaceuticals and cosmetics

PHARMACOS
Website of the Pharmaceutical Unit of **DG** Enterprise.
http://pharmacos.eudra.org

PHASE
Physical forcing and biogeochemical fluxes in shallow coastal ecosystems (**ELOISE** project)

PHATOX
Pharmacological and toxicological data and information network

PHILOXENIA
Proposal for a multiannual programme on tourism, 1999-2002 (**OJ** C13/97), withdrawn April 2000. ('Philoxenia' is Greek for 'Welcome')

PHOEBUS
30mw solar demonstration plant (**EUREKA** project)

PHOENIX
Hierarchical integration of logic and functional paradigms (**ESPRIT** project)

PHOS
Phare operational service

PHOTON
Photonic communications (an **ACTS** project)

PHOTOTRONICS
Industrial development of amorphous silicon-based components for photoelectronic applications (**EUREKA** project)

PHOX
Extra interface processing of 3-D holographics images for analysis and control (**ESPRIT** project)

PHYSAN
Electronic system for national governments on **Phytosanitary Controls**. Set up under the **IDA** programme

Phytosanitary controls
A series of proposals contained in the Single Market (**SEM**) programme relating to plant health and the free movement of plants. *See also* **PHYSAN**

PIDEA
Packaging and interconnection development for European applications relating to the interconnection and assembly of electronic components (1998-2003) (**EUREKA** project)

Pillars
A metaphor commonly used to describe the structure of the **European Union**, the idea being that the Union rests on a number of supporting pillars. The first pillar comprises the **European Community** and is supranational in character, based on the **Community method**. The second pillar deals with the Common Foreign and Security Policy (**CFSP**). The third deals with Justice and Home Affairs (**JHA**). The second and third pillars are based on intergovernmental cooperation. Issues can be transferred between pillars via a 'footbridge' or **Passerelle**

PIMS
Project integrated management systems (**ESPRIT** project)

PIN
Pre-information notice / Periodic information notice. Issued by public bodies under EU procurement legislation to give advance notification of contracts to be awarded

PINC
Programmes Indicatifs Nucléaires Communs (Illustrative Nuclear Programme for the Community). Published by the **European Commission** in 1966, 1972, 1984 (updated 1990) and 1997

Pink Book
List of legislation for which **DG** Enterprise is responsible.
http://europa.eu.int/comm/dgs/enterprise/acquis.htm

PIP
Plant **Industry Platform**.
http://europa.eu.int/comm/dg12/biotech/ip2.html#PIP

PIP
Productivity initiative programme. A **Tacis** small-scale project to provide senior managers from the **NIS** with on-the-job training in companies in the EU. Continued as **MTP**

PIPA
Project for the improvement of public administration (part of **Phare**'s 1997 programme in the Czech Republic)

PIPE
EDI project under the **TEDIS** programme

PIPER
Project information prepared for exploitation and reference (a Telematics for

Administrations project within the **Telematics Applications Programme**)

PIR
Public Information Relay. A network of public libraries in the UK which provide EU information. Continued as European Public Information Centre (**EPIC**) network

PISC
Project for the inspection of steel components (**JRC** project)

PISG
Permanent Inter Service Group on refugees. A **European Commission** inter-departmental coordination body chaired by **ECHO**

PIU
Programme implementation unit

PJAECH
Preserving Jewish archives as part of the European cultural heritage (**Raphael** project)

PKI
Public key infrastructure

PLAIL
Public libraries and independent learners (project within Area 5 of the **Telematics Systems Programme**)

Plain Language Directive
Directive 93/13/EEC on unfair terms in consumer contracts (**OJ** L95/93)

PLANEC
Planning of the care of the elderly in the European Community (a Telematics for Healthcare project within the **Telematics Applications Programme**)

PLANET
European network for multimedia environmental education (**EMTF** project)

Planotheque
Computerised **European Parliament** document management system

PLASIC
Performance and reliability of plastic encapsulated CMOS (**ESPRIT** project)

Platform Europe
An award scheme for cultural events with a European profile. Replaced by **Kaleidoscope**

Plating Directive
Directive 76/114/EEC relating to statutory plates and inscriptions for motor vehicles and their trailers, and their location and method of attachment (**OJ** L24/76)

PLAY
Storage of various music input, conversion of different Braille syntax into sounds, graphics, Braille output and telematic access (a Telematics for Disabled and Elderly People project within the **Telematics Applications Programme**)

PLEASE
Permanent Liaison Committee of European Associations in Education.

Pleven Plan
... for the European Defence Community (**EDC**)

Plumber Regulations
Regulations 3/84, 1292/89 and 718/91 introducing arrangements for movement within the EC of goods sent from one **Member State** for temporary use in one or more other Member States (**OJ** L2/84, OJ L130/89 and OJ L78/91). No longer in force

p.m.
Pour Mémoire. A token entry in the EU budget - no money has been allocated but it is expected in due course

PME
Petites et Moyennes Entreprises (Small and Medium-sized Enterprises - **SME**)

PMG
Project management group

PMO
EU / Caribbean / US Maritime Cooperation Office

PMS
Project management services

PMU
Programme management unit

PNIC
Programme National d'Intérêt Communautaire (National Programme of Community Interest - **NPCI**)

PNR
Passenger Name Record.
http://europa.eu.int/comm/external_relations/us/intro/pnr.htm

POC
Point of contact

POCKET
EC economic data pocketbook statistical domain on the **New Cronos** databank

PODA
Piloting of the office document architecture (**ESPRIT** project)

POLINAT-2
Pollution from aircraft emissions in the North Atlantic flight corridor (**THESEO** project)

Polis
Cities and regions networking for innovative transport solutions (**DRIVE** project). 6 Rond-Point Schuman, box 8 (Scotland House), B-1040 Brussels, Belgium.
www.polis-online.org

POLIS
Parliamentary online indexing service. Used by the UK's House of Commons Library.
www.polis.parliament.uk

POLITeam
A tele cooperation system to support the cooperation of German ministries distributed between Bonn and Berlin (**CSCW** project).
http://orgwis.gmd.de/projects/POLITeam

POLLEN
Publishers on information highways (a Telematics for Education and Training project within the **Telematics Applications Programme**)

POLYGLOT
Multi-language speech-to-text and text-to-speech system (**ESPRIT** project)

Pompidou Group
Established in 1971 (within the **Council of Europe**) to combat drug abuse

PONTIFEX
Planning of non-specific transportations by an intelligent fleet expert (**ESPRIT** project)

POP
Programme d'Orientation Pluriannuelle (Multiannual guidance programme - **MAGP**)

POPCYCLE
Environmental cycling of selected persistent organic pollutants in the Baltic region (**ELOISE** project)

POPRAM
Multifund operational programme for the autonomous region of Madeira

POPs
Persistent organic pollutants

PORTICO
Portuguese road traffic innovations (**DRIVE** project)

POSEICAN
Programme d'options spécifiques à l'éloignement et à l'insularité des îles Canaries (Programme of options specific to the remote and insular nature of the Canary Islands). Became part of **REGIS II**

POSEIDOM
Programme d'options spécifiques à l'éloignement et à l'insularité des départements français d'outre-mer (Programme of options specific to the remote and insular nature of the French Overseas Departments). Became part of **REGIS II**

POSEIMA
Programme d'options spécifiques à l'eloignement et à l'insularité de Madere et des Acores (Programme of options specific to the remote and insular nature of Madeira and the Azores). Became part of **REGIS II**

Post-BCCI Directive
Directive 95/26/EC amending Directives 77/780/EEC and 89/646/EEC in the field of credit institutions, Directives 73/239/EEC and 92/49/EEC in the field of non- life insurance, Directives 79/267/EEC and 92/96/ EEC in the field of life assurance, Directive 93/22/EEC in the field of investment firms and Directive 85/611/EEC in the field of undertakings for collective investment in transferable securities (Ucits), with a view to reinforcing prudential supervision (**OJ** L168/95). BCCI was the Bank of Credit and Commerce International, which collapsed in a financial scandal

POST-DOC
Post graduate training for doctors in Europe (**EMTF** project)

Posted Workers Directive
Directive 96/71/EC concerning the posting of workers in the framework of the provision of services (**OJ** L18/97). Also known as the Subcontractors Directive

PostEurop
Association of European Public Postal Operators / Association des Opérateurs Postaux Publics Européens.
Centre Mercure, 100 rue de la Fusée, B-1130 Brussels, Belgium.
www.posteurop.org

Poverty
In 1993 the European Commission proposed establishing a medium-term action programme, 1994-1999, to combat exclusion and promote solidarity (**COM**(93)435). The proposal - popularly termed 'Poverty' or 'Poverty 4' - was rejected.
http://europa.eu.int/scadplus/leg/en/cha/c10613.htm

POVES
Portable opto-electronic vision enhancement system for visually impaired persons (**TIDE** project)

POWERMAG
Low cost brushless axial flux motor with a high energy rubber bonded rare earth permanent rotating magnet (**EUREKA** project)

PPE
Personal protective equipment. **Directive** 89/686/EEC relating to personal protective equipment (**OJ** L399/89)

PPE-DE
Parti Populaire Européen et Démocrates Européens (European People's Party and European Democrats - group in the **European Parliament**).
http://epp-ed.europarl.eu.int

PPF
Project preparation facility. Part of **Phare**'s investment strategy for Central Europe

PPG
Public procurement group

PPPs
Plant protection products

PPS
Purchasing power standard. An artificial currency used to improve data comparability, which allows for variations between national price levels not accounted for by exchange rates

PRACTITIONER
Support system for pragmatic re-use of software concepts (**ESPRIT** project)

PRAG
Agriculture prices and price indices statistical domain on the **New Cronos** databank

Preamble
Introductory part of a Treaty

Precautionary Principle
The **European Commission**'s February 2000 Communication on the precautionary principle (**COM**(2000)1) states that the Principle "covers those specific circumstances where scientific evidence is insufficient, inconclusive or uncertain and there are indications through preliminary objective scientific evaluation that there are reasonable grounds for concern that the potentially dangerous effects on the environment, human, animal or plant health may be inconsistent with the chosen level of protection."
http://europa.eu.int/comm/food/fs/pp/pp_index_en.html

PRECISE
Promoting and realising ELTA through communication and information strategies for Europe (**DELTA** project)

PRECISE
Prospects for extra-mural and clinical information systems environment (**AIM** project)

PREDICT
Pollution reduction by information and control techniques (**DRIVE** project)

PREDICT
Prediction and assessment of the acquatic toxicity of mixtures of chemicals (an Environmental Health and Chemical Safety Research project within the **Environment and Climate Programme**)

Pre-ins
See **Outs**

PREJEEMI
Bootstrap project for a multiple device file server (**ESPRIT** project)

Pre-JEP
Preparatory JEP. A compulsory first step before a proposal for a **JEP** can be submitted

PreLex
European Commission database on inter-institutional procedures, which provides details of current proposals and communications. Replaced the **APC** database.
http://europa.eu.int/prelex/apcnet.cfm?CL=en

PRES
Council of the European Union Press release, available via the **RAPID** database

Presidency
The Presidency of the **Council of the European Union** rotates between **Member**

States every six months (January-June, July-December). Scheduled holders are: 2004 - Ireland, The Netherlands; 2005 - Luxembourg, UK; 2006 - Austria, Finland. The country holding the Presidency is responsible for organising and chairing Council meetings and for reaching compromises on difficult issues. It also represents the Union in matters falling within the Common Foreign and Security Policy. The 2004 **IGC** is likely to propose changes to the Presidency.
http://ue.eu.int/en/presid.htm

PRESS
Press and Communications **DG** of the **European Commission**

Pressure Equipment Directive
Directive 97/23/EC concerning pressure equipment (**OJ** L181/97)

PREST
Working Party on Scientific and Technical Research Policy. Became **CREST**

PRESTIGE
Patient records supporting telematics and guidelines (a Telematics for Healthcare project within the **Telematics Applications Programme**)

PREXCO
Precursor exportation control. Database on precursors created in 1994

PRIAMOS
Validation and demonstration of GPRS protocol specifications for the mobile offices of the future (**ISIS** Teleworking project)

PRICE
Prices and purchasing power parities statistical domain on the **New Cronos** databank

Price Labelling
See **Unit Prices Directive**

Primarolo Group
Code of Conduct Group on Business Taxation, chaired by Dawn Primarolo. Established in response to the **ECOFIN** Council of 1 December 1997, to examine the 'tax-package', the Group submitted its report in November 1999

PRIMAVERA
Priority management for vehicle efficiency, environment and road safety on arterials (**DRIVE** project)

Prime-UP 12
Subscription service from **Eurostat**, offering e-mail delivery of selected statistics

PRINCE
Priority Information Activities. Programme to Inform Citizens about Europe (1995-). It initially comprised campaigns on: **Citizen's First**; the **euro**: one currency for all; **Building Europe Together**. Now covers enlargement; the euro; the future of the EU; the creation of an area of freedom, security and justice; and information activities in connection with specific policies

PRINT
Non-impact printer and plotter for Braille/Moon characters and tactile graphics (a Telematics for Disabled and Elderly People project within the **Telematics Applications Programme**)

PRISM
Progress Report on Initiatives in the Single Market. Established by the Economic and Social Committee under its **Single Market Observatory**.
www.ces.eu.int/Omu_Smo/prism

PRISMA
Preparing Regional Industry for the Single Market. A **Structural Funds** Initiative (1991-1993) (Guidelines in **OJ** C33/91). Continued in the **SME Community Initiative**

PROCAT-GEN
Product catalogues in the global engineering network (a Telematics Information Engineering project within the **Telematics Applications Programme**)

PROCIV-NET
Civil protection and environmental emergencies European network

PROCOS
Provably correct systems (**ESPRIT** project)

PRODCOM
Regulation 3924/91 for products of the **European Community**. A classification of industrial production in mining, quarrying, manufacturing, electricity, gas and water supply which is related to **NACE** Rev 1 (**OJ** L374/91)

PRODEC
EDI project under the **TEDIS** programme

PRO-DELTA
Portuguese research on **DELTA** (DELTA project)

PRODEP
Integrated operational programme in Portugal for the development of education (1990-1993)

Prodi, Romano
President of the **European Commission** since September 1999.
Prime Minister of Italy, 1996-1998.
http://europa.eu.int/comm/commissioners/prodi

PRODIS
Product development and innovation in shipbuilding (**Transport** project)

Product Liability Directive
Directive 85/374/EEC on the approximation of the laws, regulations and administrative provisions of the **Member States** concerning liability for defective products (**OJ** L210/85)

Pro-Eurojust
A provisional unit of **Eurojust**

PROFIL
Flexible fabrication of fresh fermented dairy products (**EUREKA** project)

PROGRESS
Term sometimes used for the **Poverty** programme

PROGUIDE
Promoting the development, dissemination and evaluation of guidelines of clinical practice (a Telematics for Healthcare project within the **Telematics Applications Programme**)

PROINNO
Promoting European innovation culture (**INNOVATION** project)

PROMETEUS
Promoting multimedia access to education and training in the European society (within the **IST** programme).
www.prometeus.org

PROMETHEUS
Programme for a European traffic system with highest efficiency and unprecedented safety (**EUREKA** project)

PROMIMPS
Process module integration in a multichamber production system (**ESPRIT** project)

PROMINAND
Extended office process migration with interactive panel displays (**ESPRIT** project)

PROMIS
Portable reception of multimedia information network (a Telematics Information

Engineering project within the **Telematics Applications Programme**)

PROMISE
Mobile and portable information system in Europe (**DRIVE** project)

PROMISE
Personal mobile traveller and traffic information (**Telematics Applications** project)

PROMISE
Pre-operational modelling in the seas of Europe (**MAST III** project)

PROMISE
Process operator's multi-media intelligent support environment (**ESPRIT** project)

PROMISE
Promoting the information society in Europe, 1998-2002. **Decision** 98/253/EC (**OJ** L107/98)

PROMISE
Promoting an information society for everyone. Project 1997-1998

PROMPT
Promotion of pedestrian traffic in Europe, an EESD project under the **Fifth Framework Programme**

PROMPT
Programme for MOS processing technology (**ESPRIT** project)

PROMPT
Protocols for medical procedures and therapies (a Telematics for Healthcare project within the **Telematics Applications Programme**)

PROMPT
Term used for Institute for Prospective Technological Studies - **IPTS**

PRONET
Multimedia computer based on-line training and support service for professionals (a Telematics for Education and Training project within the **Telematics Applications Programme**)

PROOF
Primary rate ISDN OSI office facilities (**ESPRIT** project)

PROREC
Promotion strategy for European electronic healthcare records (a Telematics for Healthcare project within the **Telematics Applications Programme**)

PROSIM
Process simulator development project (**EUREKA** project)

PROSIM
Propagation channel simulator (**MAST III** project)

PROSIT
Promotion of short sea shipping and inland waterways transport by use of modern telematics (**Transport** project)

PROSOMA
Service launched by the EU to help businesses benefit from the successes achieved in the **ACTS**, **ESPRIT** and **Telematics Applications** programmes, by facilitating access to and uptake of research results.
www.cordis.lu/esprit/src/pr_info0.htm

PROSPECTRA
Programme development by specification and transformation (**ESPRIT** project)

PROSPECTRA DEMO
Demonstration of **PROSPECTRA** methodology and system (**ESPRIT** project)

PROTEAS
ECHO database to assist organisations to promote and commercialise the results of their **R&D**. Now available on **CORDIS** as **RTD-RESULTS**

Protocol
See **Institutions**

PROTOS
Production and transport of organic solutes: effects of natural climatic variation (**TERI** project)

PROTOS
Prolog tools for building expert systems development of software tools in the programming language prolog, aimed at expert systems (**EUREKA** project)

PROTOWET
Procedures for the operationalisation of techniques for the functional analysis of European wetland ecosystems (a Water, Wetland and Acquatic Ecosystem Research project within the **Environment and Climate Programme**)

PROVE
Provision of verification (**RACE** project)

PROVERBS
Probabilistic design tools for vertical breakwater (**MAST III** project)

Provisional List
'Provisional list of Monetary Financial Institutions of the accession countries', published by the European Central Bank (**ECB**)

Proxima
European Union Police Mission in the Former Yugoslav Republic of Macedonia (FYROM). Set up by Joint Action 2003/681/ CFSP (**OJ** L249/03). Scheduled to start 15 December 2003, as a successor to **Operation Concordia**

PRT
Social protocol procedure regarding the passage of a **COM DOC**

PRTR
Pollutant release and transfer register. A database of potentially environmentally-harmful air, water and soil emissions and of wastes transferred off-site for treatment or disposal. Details of PRTRs can be found at: www.chem.unep.ch/prtr

PSC
Political and Security Committee (of the **Council of the European Union**)

PSC
Programme steering committee

PSCI
Proposed **SCI**

PSE
Parti des socialistes européens (Party of European Socialists - **PES**)

p.s.r.
Produced in specific regions. In relation to quality sparkling wines

PSU
Programme support unit

PT
Português (Portuguese)

PTF
Preliminary Task Force (of the **European Commission**)

Ptiers
ACP-ALA-MED/ Third Country statistical domain on the **New Cronos** databank

PTL
Phare topic link. The extension of **EIONET** to **CEEC**

PTL/AQ
PTL on Air Quality. Extends **EEA** work on air quality to the **Phare** countries

PTL/IW
PTL on Inland Waters

PTT
Post / telephone / telegraph

PubliCA
Concerted action for public libraries in Europe

Publications Office
'Popular' name adopted by **OOPEC**

Public Information Relay
See **PIR**

Publishers' Forum
See **European Union Publishers' Forum**

PULSAR
Parking urban loading unloading standards and rules (**DRIVE** project)

Push 2001
Project set up as part of **European Science Week** 2001.
www.poggio-imperiale.it/push2001

PUSHED
EDI project under the **TEDIS** programme

PUSSYCATS
Improvement of pedestrian safety and comfort at traffic lights (**DRIVE** project)

PWG
Permanent working group

Q

QMIS
Quality management information system (**EUREKA** project)

QMV
Qualified majority voting. A device whereby legislation is approved by the **Council of the European Union** on a majority weighted vote. In preparation for the 2004 **enlargement**, the **Treaty of Nice** allocated votes as follows (figures in parentheses are pre-enlargement votes):
Austria 10 (4), Belgium 12 (5), Denmark 7 (3), Finland 7 (3), France 29 (10), Germany 29 (10), Greece 12 (5), Ireland 7 (3), Italy 29 (10), Luxembourg 4 (2), The Netherlands 13 (5), Portugal 12 (5), Spain 27 (8), Sweden 10 (4), UK 29 (10).
Bulgaria 10, Cyprus 4, Czech Republic 12, Estonia 4, Hungary 12, Latvia 4, Lithuania 7, Malta 3, Poland 27, Romania 14, Slovakia 7, Slovenia 4

QOSMIC
QOS verification methodology and tools for integrated communications (**RACE** project)

QSGI
Inter-service Quality Support Group (**IQSG**)

QUAD Partners
Canada; the EU; Japan and the United States of America

Qualifed Majority
Voting *See* **QMV**

Quality
Decision 1999/167/EC adopting a specific programme for research, technological development and demonstration on the Quality of life and management of living resources (1998-2002) (**OJ** L64/99). One of the **Thematic Programmes** of the **Fifth Framework Programme**

QUANTUM
Quality network technology for user-oriented multi-media (a Telematics for Research project within the **Telematics Applications Programme**)

QUAMS
Quality assurance of medical standards (**AIM** project)

QUAMT
Qualitätssicherung medizintechnik (**COMETT** project)

QUATTRO
Quality approach in tendering / contracting urban public transport operations (**Transport** project).
www.cordis.lu/transport/src/quattro.htm

QUEST
Database of questions and answers on the **euro** and **EMU**.
http://europa.eu.int/euro/quest

QUEST
Quarterly European simulation tool. A modelling project of **DG** Economic and Financial Affairs to link quarterly econometric models for the individual **Member States** and Japan

QuickPick
An e-mail alerting service available from

CORDIS.
www.cordis.lu/en/src/i_014_en.htm

QUID
Quantitative ingredients declaration. In relation to foodstuffs; a percentage of certain key ingredients which must be declared, under **Directive** 2000/13/EC (**OJ** L109/00)

QUIRT
Real-time imaging and quality control in radiation therapy (**AIM** project)

QUOTA
Electronic control system involving national governments for the importation of goods from non-EU countries which are subject to quantity restrictions. Set up under the **IDA** programme

R

R3L
Regional Networks for Lifelong Learning. Launched April 2003, due to end December 2004. Brings together 120 regions in northern and southern Europe to promote life-long learning via 17 projects.
http://europa.eu.int/comm/education/policies/lll/life/regio/index_en.html

R&D
Renouveau & Démocratie. A trade union representing staff in the EU **Institutions**. www.renouveau.org

R&D
Research and development. *See also* **RTD**, **RDTD**

RACE II
R&D programme in advanced communications technologies for Europe (1990-1994) (**OJ** L192/91). Continued as **ACTS**

Race Directive
Directive 2000/43/EC implementing the principle of equal treatment between persons irrespective of racial or ethnic origin (**OJ** L180/00)

RA-D
Rig automation drilling (**EUREKA** project)

RADATT
Rapid damage assessment telematic tool (a Telematics for Environment project within the **Telematics Applications Programme**)

Radio Spectrum Decision
Decision 676/2002/EC on a regulatory framework for radio spectrum policy in the **European Community** (**OJ** L108/02)

RAID
Robot for assisting the integration of the disabled (**TIDE** project)

RAIL
Railway transport statistical domain on the **New Cronos** databank

RAINBOW
An object network for statisticians and administrations (a Telematics for Administrations project within the **Telematics Applications Programme**)

Rainbow Group
of the **European Parliament**. Seen also as ARC-Rainbow Group, where ARC stands for 'Arc-en-Ciel' - French for 'Rainbow'

RA-IQSE
An integrated quality support environment (**ESPRIT** project)

RAISE
Rigorous approach to industrial software engineering (**ESPRIT** project)

RALFH
Rotterdam, Antwerpen, Le Havre, Felixstowe, Hamburg. A group established in the context of **Customs 2002**

RAMON
Eurostat's classifications server.
http://europa.eu.int/comm/eurostat/ramon

Ramón y Cajal Scholarships
Post-graduate scholarships to familiarise students with the activities of the **European Parliament**. Formerly **STOA** Scholarships. *See also* **Robert Schuman Scholarships**

RAP
Research action programme

RAPEX
Rapid Exchange of Information System (Système d'Echange Rapide d'Information - SERI). Concerns «serious and immediate risk to the health and safety of consumers». Details in Annex to **Directive** 92/59/EEC on general product safety (**OJ** L228/92).
http://europa.eu.int/scadplus/leg/en/lvb/l32039.htm

Raphael
Community action programme in the field of cultural heritage, 1997-2000 (**Decision** 2228/97/EC, **OJ** L305/97). Activities now part of **Culture 2000**

RAPID
A database of press releases and similar communications from the Union's **Institutions**.
http://europa.eu.int/rapid/start/cgi/guesten.ksh

Rapid Reaction Facility
See **Rapid Reaction Mechanism**

Rapid Reaction Force
A military force of 60,000 intended to be in place by 2003. Also known as the European Rapid Reaction Force (ERRF) and sometimes (disparagingly) as the "EU army" or "European army". The RRF was first deployed on 31 March 2003 in **Operation Concordia**

Rapid Reaction Mechanism
Intended to allow the Community "to respond in a rapid, efficient and flexible manner, to situations of urgency or crisis or to the emergence of crisis". A non-military initiative under **Regulation** 381/2001, adopted February 2001 (**OJ** L57/01). Previously known as the Rapid Reaction Facility

RAPIDUS
Rapid delivery of updates on search-profiles. A **CORDIS** e-mail alerting service.
www.cordis.lu/en/src/i_014_en.htm

Rapporteur
A member of a committee or body appointed to act as author of, and spokesperson on, a report

RARE
See **TERENA**

RARP
Regional agricultural reform project (1995-1998) (**Tacis** project)

RASFF
Rapid alert system for food and feed. A **European Commission** system intended to inform **Member States** about risks concerning food which does not meet food safety requirements or which is improperly labeled so as to pose a risk to consumers. Also seen as Rapid alert system for foodstuffs.
http://europa.eu.int/comm/food/fs/sfp/ras_index_en.html

Raxen
Racism and Xenophobia Network. Set up and coordinated by the European Monitoring Centre on Racism and Xenophobia (**EUMC**)

RBW
Rainbow Group of the **European Parliament**

r.cade
Resource Centre for Access to statistical Data on Europe. Project started by the University of Durham. Ceased December 2001

RD
Regional **R&D** statistical domain on the **REGIO** database

RDE
Rassemblement des démocrates européens (European Democratic Alliance). Group of the **European Parliament**, 1988-1994

RDF
Regional Development Fund (short form of **ERDF**)

RDP
RACE definition phase

RDP
Regional development programme

RDTD
Research, demonstration and technological development

Re4view
Recycling electrical and electronic equipment environmental review. A newsletter from ERA Technology.
www.era.co.uk

REACH
Registration, evaluation and authorisation of chemicals. Proposed in the February 2001 **White Paper** on the Strategy for a future Chemicals Policy (COM(2001)88)

REACT
Real-time communication termina (a Telematics for Disabled and Elderly People project within the **Telematics Applications Programme**)

Readaptation Grants
for redundant workers in the coal and steel industries under Article 56 of the **Treaty of Paris**. Also known as redevelopment grants

REBUILD
Reusable energy in historic city centres (**RECITE** project)

REC
Regional environment centres. A **Tacis** initiative to help environmental interest groups and **NGOs** provide public access to environmental information

RECAP
Recycling of automobile plastics (**EUREKA** project)

RECEP
Russian-European Centre for Economic Policy (**Tacis** project).
www.recep.org

Reception Directive
Directive 2003/9/EC laying down minimum standards for the reception of asylum seekers (**OJ** L31/03)

RECERE
Réseau de Centres Européens de Ressources Educatives (Network of European Educational Regional Resource Centres)

RECHAR II
Reconversion des bassins Charbonnière (Conversion of coal mining areas). A **Community Initiative**, 1994-1999 (Guidelines in **OJ** C180/94)

RECITE
Regions and cities for Europe (set up under **Article 10** of the **ERDF**). Now within **INTERREG**

Recommendation
A non-binding legal measure used to put political and/or moral pressure on **Member States** (and occasionally on individual citizens). Recommendations have no legally binding effect (other than under the now

defunct **ECSC** legal system, where they were similar to a **Directive**). *See also* **Opinion**. http://europa.eu.int/eur-lex/en/about/abc/abc_20.html

RECOVER
Red Cross overall emergency resource management system (a Telematics for Healthcare project within the **Telematics Applications Programme**)

Redevelopment Grants
See **Readaptation Grants**

REDIS
R&D and innovation statistics (**Eurostat** project)

REDO
Maintenance reliability, reusability and documentation of software systems (**ESPRIT** project)

REDS
Registered excise dealers and shippers for **VAT** purposes

Red wastes
See **Wastes**

Reference price
A minimum price fixed according to EU producer prices for certain fruits and vegetables, wines and some fisheries products imported from non-Member States

REFLECT
Reflective expertise in knowledge-based systems (**ESPRIT** project)

REFLECT
A thematic network for teacher training in Europe (**TSER** project)

Reflection Group
A group of people established to examine a specific issue, e.g. 1996 **IGC** Reflection Group, comprised mainly of Foreign Ministers, and the **Amato Reflection Group**

Reform Correspondent Network
In the context of the **Kinnock reforms**, every Commission **DG** has a Reform Correspondent, appointed to liaise with the **Reform Task Force**

Reform Task Force
Group of 10 officials charged with researching and developing proposals for change in the context of the **Kinnock reforms**

Reform Group of Commissioners
Meets to discuss proposals concerning the **Kinnock reforms**. Members: Vice-President Kinnock (Chair), Vice-President de Palacio, Commissioners Fischler, Lamy, Monti, Nielson, Schreyer, Vitorino

Refrigerator Directive
Directive 96/57/EC on energy efficiency requirements for household electric refrigerators, freezers and combinations thereof (**OJ** L236/96)

Reg
Regulation

REGEN
Regional network policy for energy transmission and distribution networks in the Union's peripheral areas. A **Structural Funds** initiative (1990-1993) (Guidelines in **OJ** C326/90). Continued within **INTERREG II**

REGI
European Parliament Committee on Regional Policy

REGIE
Réseau européen des GEIE (European network of **EEIG**s).

REGIO
Regional Policy **DG** of the **European Commission**

REGIO
A regional statistical domain on the **New Cronos** databank

REGIOMAP
Statistical and topographical information on the EU regions up to level III of **NUTS**, published by **OOPEC**

Regional Fund
Short form of European Regional Development Fund -**ERDF**

REGIONET
Integrated multimedia services via a regional telematics information system - a cross-sectoral application pilot project (a Telematics for Urban and Rural Areas project within the **Telematics Applications Programme**)

REGIOSTAT
A database of selected regional statistics from the **REGIO** database loaded on **EUROCRON**

REGIS II
Régions Isolées (Isolated Regions). A **Community Initiative** for the isolated regions of the Azores, Canaries, Madeira and the French Overseas Departments (1994-1999) (Guidelines in **OJ** C180/94). Previously **IRIS**

Regulation
A form of EU legislation which automatically becomes law in all the **Member States**. Other forms of legislation are **Decision** and **Directive**. Sometimes used as a generic term meaning any type of EU legislation. In the UK, Statutory Instruments, which are often used to implement EU Directives, are also known as 'Regulations'

REITOX
Réseau Européen d'Information sur les Drogues et les Toxicomanies (European Information Network on **Drugs** and Drug Addiction). A European information network on drugs and drug addiction at the **EMCDDA**. Set up under the **IDA** programme by **Regulation** 302/93 (**OJ** L36/93).
www.emcdda.org/partners/reitox.shtml

RELA
European Parliament Committee on External Economic Relations

Relay Centre
Innovation Relay Centre -**IRC**

Relay Europe
A European affairs consultancy company providing services for the London **Representation** of the **European Commission**.
Charlemagne House, 2 Enys Rd, Eastbourne BN21 2DE, UK

Relays
Networks of EU information providers with priority access to the EU **Institutions** and publications. For those set up by **IRNU** *see* **Carrefour**; **DEP**; **EDC**; **EIP**; **LUIC**. For those set up by the Enterprise **DG** *see* **EIC**. For those set up by the Health and Consumer Protection DG *see* **Euroguichet**. For those set up by the Research DG *see* **IRC**. For those set up by the UK Commission **Representation** *see* **EPIC**; **ERC**; **Euro Units**; **Sectoral Relays**. *See also* **Stoke Rochford Conferences**

RELEX
External Relations **DG** of the **European Commission**

RELEX
Commission for External Relations, of the Committee of the Regions (**CoR**)

REM
Radioactivity Environmental Monitoring. A database of radioactivity measurements made in EU countries.
http://java.ei.jrc.it

REM
Réseau d'Enseignement Multimedia (Collaborative multimedia learning environments). A Telematics for Education and Training project within the **Telematics Applications Programme**

REMAIN
Modular system for reliability and maintainability management in European rail transport (**Transport** project)

Remedies Directive
Directive 89/665/EEC on the coordination of the laws, regulations and administrative provisions relating to the application of review procedures to the award of public supply and public works contracts (**OJ** L395/89). Amended by Directive 97/52/EC (OJ L328/97)

REMIE
Specification and development of an isolating electrical mineral coating on metal support (**EUREKA** project)

REMOT
Remote experiment monitoring and control (a Telematics for Research project within the **Telematics Applications Programme**)

REMSSBOT
Regional environmental management support based on telematics (a Telematics for Environment project within the **Telematics Applications Programme**)

REMUS
Reference models for useability specifications (**RACE** project)

RENAVAL
Reconversion des zones de chantiers navals. Reconversion Programme for former Shipbuilding Areas. A **Community Initiative**, 1988-1993 (**OJ** L225/88)

REPA
Regional economic partnership agreements

REPLAY
Replay and evaluation of software development plans using higher-order metasystems (**ESPRIT** project)

Representations
European Commission offices in **Member States**. *See also* **Delegations**.
http://europa.eu.int/comm/represent_en.htm

REQUEST
Reliability and quality of European software (**ESPRIT** project)

RES
Integrated development of renewable natural resources (**FAST** programme)

RES
Renewable energy sources

RESAM
Remote expert support for aircraft maintenance (**RACE** project)

Research and Technological Development Programme
See **Framework Programme**

RESEAU
European environmental, agricultural and urban development monitoring network. A database of environmental statistics within the **CADDIA** programme

Réseaubib
Network of libraries of the Commission's

DGs and departments.
http://europa.eu.int/comm/libraries/bibliotheques_en.htm

RESIDER II
Reconversion des zones sidérurgiques. A **Community Initiative** to assist the conversion of steel areas, 1994-1997 (Guidelines in **OJ** C180/94)

RESIGMUR
Development of geographic information systems (**RECITE** project)

RESMA
Reseau des marques. An electronic network used by **OHIM**

Resolution
A non-binding legislative instrument used by the **European Council**, the **Council of the European Union** and the **European Parliament** to express their views and intentions on particular issues

RESORT
Remote service of rehabilitation technology (a Telematics for Disabled and Elderly People project within the **Telematics Applications Programme**)

RESPECT
Requirements engineering and specification in telematics (a Telematics Engineering project within the **Telematics Applications Programme**)

RET
Renewable energy technologies (within the **ALTENER** programme)

RETEX
Régions fortement dépandantes du secteur Textile - habillement. A **Community Initiative** to support areas with a declining textile industry, 1992-1997 (Guidelines in **OJ** C142/92 and OJ C180/94)

RETI
Régions Européennes de Technologie industrielle (European Industrial Regions Association - EIRA).
36-38 rue Joseph II, B-1000 Brussels, Belgium.
www.association-reti.org

RETRANSPLANT
Regional and international integrated telemedicine network for medical assistance in end stage disease and organ transplant project (a Telematics for Healthcare project within the **Telematics Applications Programme**).
www.ehto.org/ht_projects/html/dynamic/104.html

RETT
European Parliament Committee on Regional Policy, Transport and Tourism

REVOLVE
Regional evolution planning for IBC (**RACE** project)

REWARD
Recycling of waste **R&D** (subprogramme of the Raw Materials and Recycling programme) (1990-1992) (**OJ** L359/89). Continued as **BRITE/EURAM II**

REX
European Parliament Committee on External Economic Relations

REX
Reconfigurable and extensible parallel and distributed systems (**ESPRIT** project)

RFLP
Genetic improvement of corn by restriction fragment length polymorphisms (**EUREKA** project)

RGMG
Representatives of the governments of the **Member States**

RICA
A system to transfer data under the **FADN** (**CADDIA** project)

RICE
Regional information centre. Developed out of **ESATT** and **INDIS**

RICHE
European information and communication networks for hospitals (**ESPRIT** project)

RIDDLE
Rapid information display and dissemination in a library environment (project within Area 5 of the **Telematics Systems Programme**)

Right of Initiative
The **European Commission** is the only EU body formally able to propose (initiate) legislation. Under the **Treaty on European Union** the **European Parliament** has powers to request the Commission to propose legislation in areas of relevance to the EU

RIMES
Road information and management Euro-system (**DRIVE** project)

RINNO
Resource for regional innovation & technology transfer.
www.rinno.com

Rio Group
Argentina, Bolivia, Brazil, Chile, Colombia, Ecuador, Mexico, Panama, Paraguay, Peru, Uruguay, Venezuela

RIPARIUS
Risk of inundation - planning and response interactive user system (a Telematics for Environment project within the **Telematics Applications Programme**)

RIPE
RACE integrity primitives evaluation (**RACE** project)

RIS
Regional innovation strategies (part of the **INNOVATION/SMEs** programme). *See also* **RITTS**; **RITTS/RIS NETWORK**

RISC
Réseau d'information du secteur de la chimie (Chemical Sector Information Network). An initiative of the **European Commission**'s Enterprise **DG**. *See also* **ChimEre**; **ChimStat**; **ComLégi**; **Légichim**.
http://europa.eu.int/comm/enterprise/chemicals/competiv/risc/db_en.htm

RISE
Caring for the elderly in the information society era (a Telematics for Disabled and Elderly People project within the **Telematics Applications Programme**)

RISE
Regional innovation strategies in Europe.
http://meritbbs.unimaas.nl/jan/rise.html

RISI
Regional Information Society Initiative (under **Article 10** of the **ERDF** and Article 6 of the **ESF**). *See also* **IRISI**.
http://europa.eu.int/ISPO/risi/main.html

Risk Assessment
Regulation 1488/94 laying down the principles for the assessment of risks to man and the environment of existing substances in accordance with Regulation 793/93 (**OJ** L161/94 and *Guidance* published in 4 vols in 1996 by EUR-OP)

RITTS
Regional innovation and technology transfer

infrastructures and strategies (part of the **INNOVATION/SMEs** programme). *See also* **RIS; RITTS/RIS NETWORK**

RITTS/RIS Network
A network to support all **RIS** and **RITTS** projects in order to facilitate the exchange of experience and to disseminate relevant information

R-LAN
Radio local area networks

RMC
RACE Management Committee

RMP
RACE main phase

ROAD
Road transport statistical domain on the **New Cronos** databank

ROADACOM
En route applied data communications development of an integrated system for on-based electronic data collection and processing… (**EUREKA** project)

Robert Schuman Project
An action programme to improve awareness of EU law for the legal profession (1998-2001) under **Decision** 1496/98/EC (**OJ** L196/98). *See also* **Schuman, Robert**.
http://europa.eu.int/comm/justice_home/project/schuman/en/index_en.htm

Robert Schuman Scholarships
Post-graduate scholarships in economics, law and political science for work experience in the **European Parliament**'s **DG** for Research. Formerly **STOA Scholarships**. *See also* **Ramon y Cajal Scholarships**; **Schuman, Robert**

ROBOSCOPE
Ultrasound-image-guided manipulator - assisted system for minimally invasive endo-neurosurgery (a Telematics for Healthcare project within the **Telematics Applications Programme**).
www.ehto.org/ht_projects/html/dynamic/105.html

ROBOTRAC
Development of a new vehicle drive gear technology for use in inaccessible terrain… (**EUREKA** project)

ROCK STADIUM
Public halls in rock (PHIR) (**EUREKA** project)

ROC NORD
Transfer of economic planning / environmental technology from Nordjylland to Crete (**RECITE** project)

ROCOCO
Real-time monitoring and control of construction site manufacturing (**ESPRIT** project)

RoHS
Restriction of hazardous substances

RoHS Directive
Directive 2002/95/EC on the restriction of the use of certain hazardous substances in electrical and electronic equipment (**OJ** L37/03)

Rome II
Popular term for a proposed **Regulation** on the law applicable to non-contractual obligations (**COM**(2003)427)

Rome Convention
Council Convention on contractual obligations (OJ L266/80)

Rome Declaration
Joint Declaration on Political Dialogue between the **European Union** and the

Andean Community. Issued following a meeting in Rome on 30 June 1996. http://europa.eu.int/comm/external_relations/andean/doc/decl_rome_en.htm

Rome Declaration
WEU statement issued in November 1998. www.esteri.it/eng/archives/arch_events/weu/dec17nov98.htm

Rome Treaty
Establishing the European Economic Community and European Atomic Energy Community. *See* **Treaty of Rome**

Rome Treaty
Establishing the International Criminal Court. *See* **ICC**

ROPS
Roll-over protective structures relating to wheeled agricultural or forestry tractors

ROS
Research in Official Statistics. An international journal published twice a year by **Eurostat**

ROSA
New conception of a very high stability miniature frequency source for applications in navigation, telecommunications and metrology (**EUREKA** project)

ROSA
RACE open services architecture (**RACE** project)

ROSAL
Robot for rose plants handling and grafting (**EUREKA** project)

ROSAMES
Road safety management expert system (**DRIVE** project)

ROSE
Research open systems for Europe (**ESPRIT** project)

ROSES
Road safety enhancement system which takes into account road and weather conditions (**DRIVE** project)

Route map for reform
Timetable for the **Kinnock reforms**

Royaumont Process
The Royaumont Process or Initiative is associated with the 1995 **Stability Pact** and the **Dayton Accords**. It focuses on building and strengthening civic structures and establishing effective channels of communication across national boundaries.
Secretariat of the Council of Ministers of the European Union, 175 rue de la Loi, B-1048 Brussels, Belgium.
http://royaumont.lrf.gr

R-Phrases
Standard phrases on the nature of specific risks under the **Dangerous Substances Directive**

RPPF
Romanian Post-Privatisation Fund. Set up by the **European Commission** (under the **Phare** programme) and the **EBRD** to finance investments in the private sector in Romania

RRF
Rapid Reaction Force. Also seen as European Rapid Reaction Force **-ERRF**

RSG
Recreational Craft Sectoral Group

RSVP
RACE strategy for verification (**RACE** project)

RTD
Research **DG** of the **European Commission**

RTD
Research and technological development

RTD-ACRONYMS
A **CORDIS** database relating to EU **RTD** activities

RTD-COMDOCUMENTS
A **CORDIS** database providing details of **RTD**-related **COM** and **SEC** documents

RTD-CONTACTS
A **CORDIS** database of contact points for **RTD** information and advice at national and European level

RTDE
European Parliament Committee on Research, Technological Development and Energy

RTD Framework
See **Framework Programme**

RTD-NEWS
A **CORDIS** database giving news on all aspects of EU **RTD** activities

RTD-PARTNERS
A **CORDIS** database enabling researchers to identify partners for collaboration

RTD-PROGRAMMES
A **CORDIS** database containing information on all EU research and research-related programmes

RTD-PROJECTS
A **CORDIS** database covering individual contracts and studies within the EU-funded programmes

RTD-PUBLICATIONS
A **CORDIS** database of bibliographical information and abstracts of publications, reports and papers arising from EU research activities. Previously **EABS**

RTD-RESULTS
A **CORDIS** database of information on results from EU **RTD** research awaiting commercial exploitation

RTGS
Real-time gross settlement (linked to **TARGET**)

RTI
Road transport informatics (**DRIVE** project)

RTIS
Regional traffic information service (**EURET** project)

RTTS
Road transport telematic systems

RUBRIC
A rule-based approach to information systems development (**ESPRIT** project)

Ruding Report
of the Committee of Independent Experts on company taxation. Published by **EUR-OP** in 1992

RUE
Rational use of energy

RUEM
Regional and urban energy management. Incorporated into **SAVE II**

RULE
European Parliament Committee on the Rules of Procedure, the verification of credentials and immunities

RURALNET
On-line version of a directory which contained information on local (and primarily) rural development projects. Ceased 1989

S

S
Socialists. Alternative abbreviation for Party of European Socialists - **PES**

S
Spain

SAAs
Stabilisation and association agreements.
http://europa.eu.int/comm/external_relations/see/actions/sap.htm

SAARC
South Asia Association for Regional Cooperation.
www.saarc-sec.org

SABE
Strategy Advisory Body on Environment. Set up by **CEN**

SABINE
Système d'Accès à la Banque Informatique des Nomenclatures Européennes. Became **SIMONE**

SAC
Special areas of conservation, within the **Habitats Directive**

SACODY
A high-performance FMS robot with dynamic compensation (**ESPRIT** project)

SAD
Single administrative document. Introduced in 1988, when it replaced 150 existing customs documents. Since 1993 it has been mainly used in trade with **EFTA** countries

SAELN
Students across Europe language network (a Telematics for Education and Training project within the **Telematics Applications Programme**)

SAFE
Safety actions for Europe (1996-2000). Proposed programme of non-legislative measures to improve health and safety at work (Amended proposal in **OJ** C92/97)

SAFE
Standard authority facility environment (**DELTA** project)

SAFE
Support and training service for entrepreneurs

SAFE 21
Social alarms for Europe in the 21st century (a Telematics for Disabled and Elderly People project within the **Telematics Applications Programme**)

SAFETY-NET
Safety critical industries workplace learning telematic network (a Telematics for Education and Training project within the **Telematics Applications Programme**)

SAI
Space Applications Institute. Part of the **IPSC** at the **JRC**

SAIL
Strengthening academic and industrial links thematic network.
www.sail-eu.net

Sakharov Prize
The Sakharov Prize for Freedom of Thought, named after the Soviet dissident and Nobel Peace Prize winner, Andrei Sakharov, has been awarded by the **European Parliament** since 1988. It "honours individuals or organisations for their efforts on behalf of human rights and fundamental freedoms and against oppression and injustice." www.europarl.eu.int/comparl/afet/droi/sakharov/default_en.htm

SAM
Multi-lingual speech input/output assessment: methodology and standardisation (**ESPRIT** project)

SAMOVAR
Safety assessment monitoring on-vehicle with automatic recording (**DRIVE** project)

SANCO
Health and Consumer Protection **DG** of the **European Commission**

Santa Maria da Feira Summit
See **Feira Summit**

Santer, Jacques
Prime Minister of Luxembourg, 1984-1995, then President of the **European Commission**. Resigned in 1999, following investigation by a **Committee of Independent Experts**

SAP
Stabilisation and association process

SAPARD
Special accession programme for agriculture and rural development. Pre-accession aid for countries in **CEE**. Information can be found via http://europa.eu.int/comm/agriculture/external/enlarge/back/index_en.htm

Sapir Report
See **Agenda for a Growing Europe**

SAPPHIRE
PCTE portability (**ESPRIT** project)

SARA
Simulation of reactor accident

SARA
Structural adjustment and reform assistance (part of the 1997 **Phare** programme)

Sarbanes-Oxley Act
US legislation introduced in 2002 in the wake of financial scandals "to protect investors by improving the accuracy and reliability of corporate disclosures ..." Contentious in EU-US relations, because it requires European audit companies to register with the United States Public Company Accounting Oversight Board (PCAOB)

SARS
Severe acute respiratory syndrome. Details of its impact and of EU responses can be found at: http://europa.eu.int/comm/health/ph_threats/com/sars/sars_en.htm

SAST
Strategic analysis in science and technology programme (part of the **MONITOR** programme)

SATDOC
Satellite mediated controlled experiment for continuing education and monitoring doctors (**DELTA** project)

SATURN
Smart card and terminal usability requirements and needs (**TIDE** project)

SAVE
Specific actions for vigorous energy efficiency. Initially 1991-1995, but extended 1996-2000 under SAVE II (**Decision** 96/737/EC, **OJ** L335/96), and then incorporated into the Energy Framework Programme, 1998-2002.

http://europa.eu.int/comm/energy/en/pfs_save_gen_en.html

SAVE ART
EC-funded project to develop an environmentally friendly way of conserving old books, textiles and antiquities

SAVIE
Support action to facilitate the use of videoconferencing in education (a Telematics for Education and Training project within the **Telematics Applications Programme**)

SBIP
Structural Biology **Industrial Platform**.
http://europa.eu.int/comm/dg12/biotech/ip2.html# SBIP
www.sbip.org

SBS
Structural business statistical domain on the **New Cronos** databank

SC
Scientific committee

SC
Standing committee

SCA
Shared-cost action

SCA
Special Committee on Agriculture

SCAD
Automated central documentation service of the **European Commission**

SCAD
Système Communautaire d'Accès à la Documentation (Community system for accessing documentation). A print and web-based bibliographical database of EU legislation, official publications and periodical articles. Discontinued and records transferred to **ECLAS**. *See also* **SCADPlus**

SCADPlus
A series of web pages providing summaries of EU policies and legislation.
http://europa.eu.int/scadplus

Scaffolding Directive
Directive 2001/45/EC amending Directive 89/655/EEC concerning the minimum safety and health requirements for the use of work equipment by workers at work (**OJ** L195/01)

SCAHAW
Scientific Committee on Animal Health and Animal Welfare. *See also* **SSC**

SCALE
Small countries improve their audiovisual level in Europe (**MEDIA** project)

SCAN
Scientific Committee on Animal Nutrition. *See also* **SSC**

SCAN
Subcontracting assistance network. A project to improve the communication of information on subcontracting exchanges and databases in Europe, 1994-1997.
http://europa.eu.int/comm/enterprise/entrepreneurship/supply/community_initiatives.htm

SCAR
Standing Committee on Agricultural Research.
http://europa.eu.int/comm/research/agriculture/era/scar.html

SCCNFP
Scientific Committee on Cosmetic Products and Non-Food Products. *See also* **SSC**

SCE
Societas Cooperativa Europaea. *See* **European Co-operative Statute**

SCE
Standing Committee on Employment. Established 1970, reformed 1999.
http://europa.eu.int/scadplus/leg/en/cha/c10233.htm

SCENT
System customs enforcement network (**CADDIA** project)

SCENT-CIS/FISCAL
Management of tariff application for imports and exports of goods from and to **Third Countries**

SCF
Scientific Committee for Food. *See also* **SSC**

SCG
Space Coordination Group. Set up by the **European Commission** in 1996.
http://europa.eu.int/comm/jrc/space/index_en.html

SCHEMA
Social cohesion through higher education in marginal areas (**EMTF** project)

Schengen Acquis
A body of rules relating to the relaxation of border controls between a number of EU **Member States** originating in the **Schengen Agreement**. The rules were incorporated into the framework of the EU as a Protocol to the **Treaty of Amsterdam**. The acquis was published in **OJ** L239/2000

Schengen Agreement
Signed in the village of Schengen, Luxembourg, on 14 June 1985 by Belgium, Luxembourg, The Netherlands, Germany and France, the Agreement abolished border controls between signatories as from 26 March 1995. Other EU **Member States** joined later: Italy (1990), Spain and Portugal (1991), Greece (1992), Austria (1995), Sweden, Finland and Denmark (1996). In 1999, Iceland and Norway also became parties to the Agreement. The text has apparently never been officially published. *See also* **Schengen Acquis**; **Schengenland**; **SIS**

Schengenland
Term used to describe the area of free circulation within the EU created by the signatories to the **Schengen Agreement**

Schuman, Robert
One of the founding fathers of the **European Union** who, as French Foreign Minister, proposed the creation of the European Coal and Steel Community (**ECSC**). In 1958 he became the first President of the Joint Assembly - now the **European Parliament**. *See also* **Europe Day**; **Robert Schuman Project**; **Robert Schuman Scholarships**; **Schuman Declaration**.
www.europarl.eu.int/ppe/tree/schuman/en/biography.htm

Schuman Day
See **Europe Day**

Schuman Declaration
A Declaration of 9 May 1950 by the French Foreign Minister Robert Schuman on the formation of the ECSC. Reprinted in *European Documentation* 3/1990. *See also* **30th May Mandate**; **Schuman, Robert**; **Europe Day**

SCI
Site of Community Interest, within the **Habitats Directive**. *See also* **PSCI**, **SAC**

SCIC
Service Commun Interprétation Conférences (Joint Interpreting and Conference Service - of the **European Commission**)

SCIENCE
Programme to stimulate the international cooperation and interchange needed

by European research scientists (1988-1992) (**OJ** L206/88). Previously **Science Stimulation** programme. Continued as the **HCM** programme

Science Stimulation Programme
Action to stimulate the efficacy of the EEC's Scientific and Technical potential (1985-88) (**OJ** L83/85). Continued as **SCIENCE**. *See also* **BRAIN**

SCIMITAR
Support and coordination for integrated multimedia telematics applications for researchers (a Telematics for Research project within the **Telematics Applications Programme**)

SCIT
Standing Committee on Information Technology

SCMPMD
Scientific Committee on Medicinal Products and Medicinal Devices. *See also* **SSC**

SCOOP
Common Services Unit of the **European Commission**, set up to improve the coordination of sections of **DG**'s 1 and VIII

SCOPE
Software certification on programs in Europe (**ESPRIT** project)

SCOPE
Support of Commission objectives and the environment for administrations and urban and rural areas (a Telematics for Administrations project within the **Telematics Applications Programme**)

SCP
Scientific Committee on Plants. *See also* **SSC**

SCP
Single cell protein (**COST** action project)

SCP-ECG
Standard communication protocol for computerised electrocardiography (AIM project)

SCR
Security Council Resolution (of the **UN** Security Council)

SCR
Service commun des Relations extérieures (Common Service for External Relations; also seen as Joint Relex Service or Common Relex Service). A Commission **DG**, now part of **EuropeAid**

SCREEN
Internal (confidential) database on RTD programmes and results, used by the Information Society **DG**

Screwdriver plants
Factories which assemble products from parts imported from another country, primarily to avoid restrictions on **Local Content**

SCRIBO
Secure card reader in bank communication (**EUREKA** project)

SCRIPT
Support for creative independent production talent (**MEDIA** project)

SCTEE
Scientific Committee on Toxicity, Ecotoxicity and the Environment. *See also* **SSC**

SCVPH
Scientific Committee on Veterinary Measures relating to Public Health. *See also* **SSC**

SD
Special Directive

SDR
Special drawing rights

SDT
Service de traduction (Translation Service) of the **European Commission**.
http://europa.eu.int/comm/sdt/en/index.html

SE
Societas Europea (European Company). **Regulation** 2001/2157/EC adopted October 2001 (**OJ** L294/2001).
http://europa.eu.int/comm/internal_market/en/company/company/news/ecompanyfaq.htm

SE
Sverige (Swedish) / Sweden

SEA
Single European Act. Signed by the 12 **Member States** in February 1986. The first comprehensive review of the **Treaties of Rome**, the SEA came into force in July 1987. Amongst other things, it: formally recognised the **European Council**; gave the **European Parliament** increased legislative powers via the **Cooperation Procedure**; established the Court of First Instance (**CFI**); launched the Single Market (**SEM**); extended the use of qualified majority voting (**QMV**); and made environment policy a legitimate Community interest

SEA
Strategic environmental assessment

SEAFO
South-East Atlantic Fisheries Organisation

SEAHORSE
Support, empowerment and awareness for HIV/AIDS; the on-line research and self-help exchange (a Telematics for Healthcare project within the **Telematics Applications Programme**). Followed by SEAHORSE II:
www.seahorse.oxi.net/nu

SEALINK
Improved maritime transport connections (**RECITE** project)

SEALOOK
R&D for new real-time underwater acoustic optic systems (**EUREKA** project)

SEAMOS
Sea environmental monitoring system (**EUREKA project)**

Seattle
Venue for the **WTO** Millennium Round of trade negotiations, December 1999, which attracted large anti-capitalist demonstrations. The meeting failed to reach agreement on the new Round

SEC
Système européen de comptes économiques intégrés (ESA - European System of (Integrated Economic) Accounts)

SEC
Usually in SEC Doc - a document of the Secretariat-General of the **European Commission**. Historically not generally available to the public, but with the move towards greater transparency and openness, more SEC docs are being issued as **COM** documents

SECFO
Systems engineering and consensus formation office (**DRIVE** project)

Second Chance Schools
A pilot project, 1996-2000, intended to provide new education and training opportunities to young excluded people.

http://europa.eu.int/comm/education/archive/2chance/home_en.html

Second Pillar
See **Pillars**

Second Railway Package
COM(2002)18: 'Towards an integrated European railway area'. Proposals adopted in January 2002 intended to revitalise the Union's railways.
http://europa.eu.int/comm/transport/rail/package/reaction_en.htm

Sectoral Relays
EU information providers in the UK from various organisations which have national sectoral coverage. *See also* **Relays**

SED
SETL experimentation and demonstrator (**ESPRIT** project)

SEDESES
Selective deposition of silicides and epitaxail silicon (**ESPRIT** project)

SEDOC
Système européen de diffusion des offres et des demandes d'emploi enregistrées en compensation internationale (European System for the International Clearing of Vacancies and Applications for Employment). Set up under **Regulation** 1612/68 (**OJ** L257/68); replaced by **EURES**

SEDODEL
Secure document delivery for blind and partially sighted people (a Telematics for Disabled and Elderly People project within the **Telematics Applications Programme**)

SEDOS
Software environment for the design of open distributed systems (**ESPRIT** project)

SEDOS DEMO
SEDOS Estelle demonstrator (**ESPRIT** project)

SEER
Social, Economic and Environmental Research (Area D III of the **Environment and Climate Programme**)

SEISCAN
A project to rescue early seismic reflection profiles that exist only as paper records, by computer scanning and archiving to a CD-ROM (**MAST III** project).
http://www.soc.soton.ac.uk/CHD/seisweb/SEISCAN.html

SEISMED
Security questions in medical information systems (**AIM** project)

SELECT
Feasibility and definition of integrated measurement, databases and computer-aided design for orthopaedic footwear (**EUREKA** project)

SELECT
Rating and filtering of scientific, technical and other network documents (a Telematics for Research project within the **Telematics Applications Programme**)

SEM
Single European Market. An initiative to achieve an internal market without trade or fiscal barriers and to enable the free movement of people throughout the **Member States** by the end of 1992. Now often referred to as the 'Internal Market'. *See also* **Cecchini Report**, **Cockfield White Paper**, **Four freedoms**, **Single Market Review**.
http://europa.eu.int/scadplus/leg/en/lvb/l70000.htm

SEM
South and Eastern Mediterranean countries

SEM 2000
Sound and Efficient Management 2000. Set up in 1995 to improve the **European Commission**'s administration and financial management.
http://europa.eu.int/comm/budget/evaluation/pdf/fullsemreport_en.pdf

SEMAGRAPH
Semantics and pragmatics of generalised graph rewiring (**ESPRIT** project)

SEMANTIQUE
Semantics-based program manipulation techniques (**ESPRIT** project)

SEMDOC
Statewatch European Monitoring and Documentation Centre ("a primary source of information on justice and home affairs in the EU").
www.statewatch.org/access.htm

SEMPER
Socio-economic analysis (**ACTS** project)

SEMRIC
Secure medical record information communication (**ISIS** healthcare network project).
www.ramit.be/semric

SENIOR ONLINE
Use of networks for reducing the isolation of elderly people and people with mobility impairments (a Telematics for Disabled and Elderly People project within the **Telematics Applications Programme**)

SENSE
Solid enforcement of substances in Europe. A project, which ended in 1997, concerning the implementation of **Directive** 67/548/EEC on the classification, packaging and labelling of dangerous substances

SEPLIS
Secrétariat Européen des Professions Libérales et Intellectuelles (European Secretariat for the Liberal Professions).
70 Coudenberg, B-1000 Brussels, Belgium

SERG
European system of geographical references (**COST** action project)

SERI
Système d'Echange Rapide d'Information (Rapid Exchange of Information System - **RAPEX**)

SERIS
State of the environment reporting information system. A gateway to information about the state of the environment in European countries and regions. Part of the **EEA**.
http://countries.eea.eu.int/SERIS

SERT
Business statistics and telematics networks for the collection and dissemination of data

SERV
Service activities and technological change (**FAST** project)

SERVICE 2000
Project based on the concept of the one-stop-shop framework for integrated services on a community level (a Telematics for Disabled and Elderly People project within the **Telematics Applications Programme**)

Services
Specific units within the **European Commission**. Divided into 'Internal Services' and 'General Services'. Often used in the context 'Directorates-General and Services', but also used more loosely to mean Commission staff or officials.
General Services: European Anti-Fraud Office, Eurostat, Press and Communication,

Publications Office, Secretariat General.
Internal Services: Budget, Group of Policy Advisers, Internal Audit Service, Joint Interpreting and Conference Service, Legal Service, Personnel and Administration, Translation Service.
See also **DG**.
http://europa.eu.int/comm/dgs_en.htm

SERVIVE
Service for integrated virtual environments (a Telematics for Education and Training project within the **Telematics Applications Programme**)

SES
Structure of earnings statistical domain on the **New Cronos** databank

SESAME
Derivation of the relationship between land use, behaviour patterns and travel demand for political and investment decisions (**Transport** project)

SESAME
Online database of innovative energy technology projects supported by the EU. Closed December 1999

SESAME
Standardisation in Europe on semantical aspects in medicine (**AIM** project)

SESEFA
Self-service facilities architecture (**ESPRIT** project)

SESPROS
Social protection statistical domain on the **New Cronos** databank

Set-aside
A voluntary scheme set up in 1985 to encourage farmers to 'set-aside' arable land (i.e. take it out of production), in order to reduce the amount of produce grown. The establishment of a support system for producers of certain arable crops was covered by Article 7 of **Regulation** 1765/92 (**OJ** L181/92) - no longer in force

Seventh Company Law Directive
Directive 83/349/EEC on consolidated accounts (**OJ** L193/83). One of the '**Accounting Directives**'

Seveso I , Seveso II
See **COMAH**

Seville
One of the locations for the **JRC**

Seville Conference
A conference held in Seville in November 1995 launched the Transatlantic Business Dialogue - **TABD**

Seville Strategy
Adopted by **UNESCO** in 1995, the Seville Strategy makes recommendations for the development of biosphere reserves in the 21st century.
www.unesco.org/mab/docs/stry-1.htm

SFAC
Social Fund Advisory Committee

SFINX
Software factory integration and experimentation (**ESPRIT** project)

SFOR
Stabilisation Force in Bosnia and Herzegovina. Also known as Operation Joint Guard / Operation Joint Forge. The **NATO**-led SFOR replaced **IFOR**. See also **Dayton Accords**.
www.nato.int/sfor

SG
Secretariat-General (e.g of the **European Commission**)

SG
Secretary-General

SGEI
Services of general economic interest. Commercial services of general economic utility, such as transport, energy and communications services, which are subject to public service obligations. Not the same as **SGI**.
http://europa.eu.int/scadplus/leg/en/lvb/l26087.htm

SG/HR
Secretary General/High Representative

SGI
Services of general interest. Includes services of both general economic and non-economic interest, including: energy, postal services, transport, telecommunications, health, education, social services. A **Green Paper** on SGI was issued in May 2003 (**COM**(2003)270). A broader concept then **SGEI**.
http://europa.eu.int/comm/secretariat_general/services_general_interest/index_en.htm

SGM
Standard gross margin

SH
Système harmonisé (Harmonised system - **HS**)

Shadow Directive
An unofficial text produced to serve as a model for an officially-produced **Directive**. An example is the Shadow Directive on Gender, produced by the European Women's Lobby (www.womenlobby.org)

SHERLOCK
Joint Action 96/637/JHA for a programme of training, exchanges and cooperation in the field of identity documents (1996-2000) (**OJ** L287/96). Replaced by **Odysseus**

SHIFT
System for animal health inspections at frontier posts. Set up under the **IDA** programme

Short title
See **Named directive**

SHOW
Standards for home working (**ISIS** teleworking project).

SIC
Standards Implementation Committee

SICAMOR-ED
Information system and coordinated action in favour of the rural community (**CADDIA** project)

SIDRI
Sustainable intra-district return initiative, under **CARDS**

SIERRA
Support for the implementation of the Europe agreement. A Polish programme set up under **Phare**

SIG
Special interest group

SIGLE
An electronic system involving national governments for licence administration. Set up under the **IDA** programme

SIGLE
On-line system for information on grey literature in Europe. A product of **EAGLE**. Details from: www.ovid.com (use the 'search' facility) or www.cas.org/ONLINE/DBSS/sigless.html

SIGMA
Support for improvement in governance and management in Central and Eastern European Countries. An EU and **OECD** joint programme to support reforms in public administrations in **CEEC**. Financed mainly by **Phare**.

SIGMA
Integrated and global support system for environmental management and monitoring (a Telematics for Environment project within the **Telematics Applications Programme**)

SIGMA
A statistical magazine from **Eurostat**.
www.datashop.org/en/publications/sigma.html

SIGNBASE
Development of multimedia signed language database (**TIDE** project)

SIGNING BOOKS
Signing books for the deaf (a Telematics for Disabled and Elderly People project within the **Telematics Applications Programme**)

SII
Integrated information systems. Previously **CIRCE**

SILC
Statistics on income and living conditions

SILMAG
Thin film magnetic heads on silicon (**EUREKA** project)

SIMAP
Système d'Information pour les Marchés Publics (Information System for Public Procurement). To promote, coordinate and manage change in public procurement. Set up under the **IDA** programme to access international procurement databases.
http://simap.eu.int

SIMBIOSE
Scientific improvement of biofilters and sensors (**EUREKA** project)

SIMET
Smart inter-modal transfer (**EURET** project)

SIMONE
A **Eurostat** database containing nomenclatures and the relationships between them. Previously **SABINE**; replaced by **RAMON**

SIMPR
Structured information management processing and effective retrieval (**ESPRIT** project)

SIMULAB
On-line simulations on the web (a Telematics for Education and Training project within the **Telematics Applications Programme**)

SINAPSE-EUROCIM
Flexibile automated factory for the production of electronic equipment (**EUREKA** project)

SINDAVE
Support for Investors in the Region of Vale do Ave, Portugal, 1992-1993

Single Act
Short form of Single European Act - **SEA**

Single Currency
See **euro**

Single Document
See **SAD**

Single European Act
See **SEA**

Single European Market
See **SEM**

Single Market
See **SEM**

Single Market Observatory
See **SMO**

Single Market Review
Series of studies published in 1996. Summaries available online at:
http://europa.eu.int/comm/internal_market/studies.htm

SIP
Advanced algorithms and architectures for speech and image processing (**ESPRIT** project)

SIP
Sectoral impact programme and technical assistance for **SMEs** in Poland (**Phare** programme)

SIR
Système informatisé de réservation (Computerised reservation system - **CRS**)

SIRCH
Societal and institutional responses to climate change and climatic hazards (**Environment and Climate** project)

SIRE
System of infraregional data for Europe

SIREN
Security in regional networks (a Telematics for Healthcare project within the **Telematics Applications Programme**)

SIRENE
Energy statistical domain on the **New Cronos** databank

SIRENE MANUAL
See **SYRENE Manual**

SIRIUS
Sociopolitical implications on road transport informatics implementation and use strategies (**DRIVE** project)

SIS
Schengen Information System. A computerised network to collect information from police forces and justice systems within the **Schengen Agreement**. *See also* **SYRENE Manual**

SITC
Standard international trade classification. A **United Nations** classification

SITE
Computerised system for **VAT** exchanges set up under the VAT **Directive**s introduced by the Single Market (**SEM**)

SITYA
Sharing information on troubled young adults (a Telematics for Integrated Applications for Digital Sites project within the **Telematics Applications Programme**)

Sixth Framework Programme
for Research & Technological Development, 2002-2006. Covers seven key areas: genomics and biotechnology for health; information society technologies; nanotechnologies and nanosciences; aeronautics and space; food safety; sustainable development; and economic and social sciences. Budget □17.5 billion. *See also* **Framework Programme**.
http://europa.eu.int/comm/research/fp6/index_en.html

SJ
Service juridique (Legal Service). A **Service** of the **European Commission**

SKIDS
Signal and knowledge integration with decisional control for multi-sensory systems (**ESPRIT** project)

SLAPS
Spatial variability of land surface processes (**EPOCH** project)

SLIM
Simpler legislation for the Internal Market.
http://europa.eu.int/comm/internal_market/en/update/slim/

SLOM
Supplementary levy on milk

SLOM farmers
Dairy farmers who were not attributed a milk quota when the quota system was launched in 1984, because they had previously stopped producing milk on a voluntary basis

Small is beautiful
Project set up as part of **European Science Week** 2001.
www.micro-worlds.org

SMART
Electronic cards for travel and transport (**DRIVE** project)

SMART
System measurement and architectures techniques (**ESPRIT** project)

Smart Card Charter
Adopted at a 'Smart-Card Summit' held in Lisbon on 11 April 2000. Subsequently the eEurope Smart Cards initiative was established, intended to act as a catalyst for the development of smart cards, which include applications such as e-government, healthcare, transportation, payTV and digital signatures.
www.eeurope-smartcards.org

SMARTS
Socio-economic analysis (**ACTS** project)

SMCU
Single Market Compliance Unit. A UK initiative to help companies experiencing trade barriers in the **SEM**. Now called Action Single Market.
www.dti.gov.uk/europe/asm/04.htm

SME
A **Community Initiative** (1994-1999) which continued the assistance previously given to **SME**s under **PRISMA**, **STRIDE** and **TELEMATIQUE** in order to adjust to the **SEM**. Guidelines in **OJ** C180/94

SME
Small and medium-sized enterprise. Defined in **Recommendation** 2003/361/EC (**OJ** L124/03) and previously in Recommendation 96/280/EC (OJ L107/96).
http://europa.eu.int/comm/enterprise/enterprise_policy/sme_definition/index_en.htm

SME
Small and medium-sized enterprise statistical domain on the **New Cronos** databank

SMEAP
SME Action Programme. The Third Multiannual Programme for SMEs, 1997-2000, established by **Decision** 97/15/EC (**OJ** L6/97). Replaced by the Multiannual Programme for Enterprise and Entrepreneurship, 2001-2005 (Decision 2000/819/EC, OJ L333/00).
http://europa.eu.int/comm/enterprise/enterprise_policy/mult_entr_programme/overview.htm

SME-NARIO
Revitalisation of **SME**s: enabling management to formulate new telematics needs (a Telematics Engineering project within the **Telematics Applications Programme**)

SME Observatory
Officially 'The Observatory of European SMEs'. Established by the **European Commission** in 1992 to "improve the monitoring of the economic performance of **SME**s in Europe".
http://europa.eu.int/comm/enterprise/enterprise_policy/analysis/observatory.htm

SME TF
Small and Medium-Sized Enterprise Task Force (of the European Commission). Now the **European Commission**'s Enterprise **DG**

SME-WEB
Services and assistance for **SMEs** on the information highway (a Telematics Engineering project within the **Telematics Applications Programme**)

SMIE
Support measures and initiatives for enterprises. Project to set up an integrated information resource on business support measures. http://europa.eu.int/comm/enterprise/smie/

SMILE
A sign language and multimedia-based interactive language course for deaf for the training of European written languages (**EMTF** project)

SMILE
Technical feasibility of high volt smart power ICs for lighting applications (**ESPRIT** project)

SMILER
Short-wave microwave links (**DRIVE** project)

SMO
Single Market **Observatory**. Established in 1994 by the **Economic and Social Committee** to look into the impact and effectiveness of the **SEM** and to propose changes.
www.esc.eu.int/omu_smo/en/

SMP
Single Market Programme. *See* **SEM**

SMT
Standardisation, Measurement and Testing. Research programme 1994-1998, under **Decision** 94/803/EC (**OJ** L334/94). Previously **MEASUREMENTS AND TESTING**. Replaced by **GROWTH**.
www.cordis.lu/smt/home.html

SMU
Small and medium-sized undertaking - alternative for **SME**

SMUK
Supplementary measure in favour of the UK

SNA
System of National Accounts. A **Eurostat** publication containing macro-economic accounts

SNB
Special negotiating body. Responsible for negotiating the establishment of European Works Councils (**EWC**)

SNMT
Strategic niche management as a tool for transition to an environmentally sustainable transportation system (**Environment and Climate** project)

SOAG
Senior Officials Advisory Group - to assist the **European Commission** to define and implement measures for a common information market

SOC
Socialists - as in Party of European Socialists - **PES**

SOCI
European Parliament Committee on Social Affairs and Employment

Social Chapter
A Protocol on social policy annexed to the **Treaty on European Union**. The UK

Conservative government opted out, but the succeeding Labour administration joined in 1997

Social Charter
'Community Charter of the fundamental social rights of workers'. Published by **EUR-OP** in 1990. An action programme relating to the Charter was published as COM(89)568. Both the Charter and the action programme appeared in *Social Europe* 1/90. Details of the Charter via:
http://europa.eu.int/comm/archives/abc/cit1_en.htm

Social dialogue
defined by the **ILO** to include all types of negotiation, consultation or simply exchange of information between, or among, representatives of governments, employers and workers, on issues of common interest relating to economic and social policy

Social Fund
Short form of European Social Fund - **ESF**

Social Summit
Informal Social Summits were held in Stockholm (March 2001) and Barcelona (March 2002) before the initiative was formally recognised and the first meeting of the Tripartite Social Summit for Growth and Employment took place on 20 March 2003. The decision to hold a Social Summit before each Spring Summit was taken at the Nice **European Council** in December 2000, when EU leaders invited the social partners to participate in the implementation of the EU's Social Agenda and to present their contributions at an annual meeting

Social Summit
The 1995 World Summit for Social Development, held in Copenhagen under the aegis of the **United Nations**.
www.iisd.ca/linkages/wssd95.html

Societas Cooperativa Europaea
See **European Co-operative Statute**

SOCKER
Search and retrieval origin communication kernel (project within Area 5 of the **Telematics Systems Programme**)

SOCOMAT
Development, production and investigation of new soft coating materials into heavy duty slide bearings for tribological applications... (**EUREKA** project)

SOCPOL
Proposal for a Community Programme for Older People (1995-1999) (**OJ** C115/95)

Socrates
The European Community action programme in the field of education. Initially 1995-1999 (**Decision** 819/95/EC, **OJ** L87/95), but extended 2000-2006 (Decision 253/2000/EC, OJ L28/00). Combines **ARION**; **COMENIUS**; **Erasmus**; **EURYDICE**; **GRUNDTVIG**; **LINGUA**; **MINERVA**; **NARIC**; **ODL**.
Technical Assistance Office: 59-61 rue de Trèves, B-1000 Brussels, Belgium.
http://europa.eu.int/comm/education/programmes/socrates/socrates_en.html

Socrates
System of cellular radio for traffic efficiency and safety (**DRIVE** project)

SODA
Superoxide dismutase analogues - free radical scavengers (**EUREKA** project)

SOE
State-owned enterprise

SOEC
Statistical Office of the European Communities. Now known as **Eurostat**

SOGITS
Senior Officials Group for Information Technology Standardisation. A committee composed of representatives of **Member State** administrations which assists the **ISIS** initiative

SOG-T
Senior Officials Group on Telecommunications

SOHO
Small office, home office

SOIA
Système d'Observation et d'Information des Alpes (Alps Observation and Information System - **AOIS**)

Solana Coup
Term coined to describe the actions of the **Council of the European Union** during July and August 2000, when changes to **Decision** 93/731/EC on public access to Council documents were adopted unilaterally - without reference to the **European Parliament** as legally required. The move was attributed to Javier Solana, Secretary-General of the Council

Soloniki 8
Term coined by Statewatch for eight people arrested during the Thessaloniki Summit in June 2003.
www.statewatch.org/news/2003/jul/28greece.htm

Solidarity Fund
The European Union Solidarity Fund (EUSF) was established in November 2002 by **Regulation** 2012/2002 (**OJ** L311/02), with the aim of enabling the Union to provide assistance to **Member States** or **Applicant Countries** which have suffered a major natural disaster.
http://europa.eu.int/scadplus/leg/en/lvb/g24217.htm

Solidarity Funds
Previous name for the **Structural Funds**

SOLVIT
Problem Solving in the Internal Market. Seen also as 'Effective Problem Solving in the Internal Market' and as 'the Internal Market Problem Solving Network'. A network of national centres established in 2001 to help solve problems arising from the "possible misapplication of Internal Market Rules by a public administration in another Member State". Based on national Coordination Centres set up in response to the 1997 **SMEAP**.
http://europa.eu.int/comm/internal_market/solvit/

SOM
Senior Officials Meeting.
http://europa.eu.int/comm/external_relations/asem/cluster/process.htm

SOMIW
Secure open multimedia integrated work-station (**ESPRIT** project)

SOMTI
Senior Officials' Meeting on Trade and Investment. Meetings held since 1996 between the EU and ASEM.
www.tni.org/asem/asemdoc/econ.htm

Sorensen Report
On the fight against trafficking in women

SOS-Europe
Statewatch Observatory on Surveillance in Europe.
www.statewatch.org/soseurope.htm

SOUR-CREAM
Software use and re-use: computerised requirements and methodology (**EUREKA** project)

Southern Cone Common Market
See **MERCOSUR**

SPA
Special protection area, within the **Birds Directive**

SPACE
Signal processing for auditory communication in noisy environments (a Telematics for Disabled and Elderly People project within the **Telematics Applications Programme**)

SPACE
Single point of access for citizens of Europe (a Telematics for Administrations project within the **Telematics Applications Programme**)

SPAN
Parallel computing systems for integrated symbolic numeric processing (**ESPRIT** project)

SPAN
Regional promotion of electronic commerce standards for **SME**s (**ISIS** SME promotion project)

SPAN
Safe passage and navigation. **BRITE/EURAM** project to design safer and more efficient ships, coordinated by **NETS**

SPARTACUS
System for planning and research in towns and cities for urban sustainabilty (**Environment and Climate** project)

SPC
Statistical Programme Committee

S-PCS
Satellite-personal communication services. **Decision** 710/97/EC on a coordinated authorization approach in the field of satellite personal-communication services in the Community (**OJ** L105/97)

SPD
Single programming document (under the **Structural Funds**). *See also* **IDO**

SPEAR
Support programme for a European assessment of research (1988-1992) (Part of the **MONITOR** programme)

Spearhead
A database of information on Single Market (**SEM**) legislation and other EU legislation relevant to the operation of businesses in the EU, compiled by the UK Department of Trade and Industry. Discontinued by the DTI in June 2000, but still produced by some commercial publishers - details at:
www.dti.gov.uk/support/spear.htm

SPEC
Formal methods and tools for the development of distributed and real-time systems (**ESPRIT** project)

SPEC
Statistical programme of the European Community

SPEC
Support programme for employment creation. A **European Parliament** initiative

SPECS
Specification environment for communication software (**RACE** project)

SPECTRA
Sustainability, development and spatial planning (**Environment and Climate** project)

SPECTRE
Submicron CMOS technology (**ESPRIT** project)

SPECTRUM
Strategies for preventing road traffic congestion (**DRIVE** project)

SPEECH
Text of speeches given by **European Commissioners**, made available on the **RAPID** database

SPEL/EU
Agricultural data relating to prices, quantities and values of agricultural output statistical domain on the **New Cronos** databank

SPEM
Software production evaluation model (**ESPRIT** project)

SPES
Stimulation plan for economic science (1989-1992) (**OJ** L44/89). Continued as **TMR**

SPHERE
Small/medium sized ports with harmonised, effective re-engineered processes (**Transport** project)

S-Phrases
Standard safety precaution phrases under the **Dangerous Substances Directive**

Spierenburg Report
Proposals for the reform of the **European Commission**, 1979

SPIN
Speech interface at office workstations (**ESPRIT** project)

Spinelli Treaty
A Draft Treaty establishing the **European Union**, drawn up by a committee of MEPs, with Altiero Spinelli MEP acting as rapporteur. The text was adopted by the European Parliament on 14 February 1984 and is seen as the basis of the European Union. *See also* **Crocodile Group / Club**

SPIRIT
High performance technical workstation (**ESPRIT** project)

SPMMS
Software production and maintenance management support (**ESPRIT** project)

SPNET
Science parks networks

SPOT
Signal processing for optical and cordless transmissions (**RACE** project)

SPP
Strategic planning and programming

SPP-ESF
Special preparatory programme for European Structural Funds. To prepare Applicant Countries for the administration of the **Structural Funds** (part of the **Phare** programme)

Spring Day in Europe
On 21 March 2003, pupils from more than 5,000 schools from 32 European countries discuss the future of Europe, in an event developed by national education ministries and supported by the **European Commission**.
http://futurum-21.eun.org/index_spring.cfm

SPRINT
Signal processor using innovative III/V technologies (**ESPRIT** project)

SPRINT
Software programme for research in telecommunications (**RACE** project)

SPRINT
Speech processing and recognition using integrated neuro-computing techniques (**ESPRIT** project)

SPRINT
Strategic programme for the promotion of innovation and technology transfer (1989-

1993-1994) (**OJ** L112/89 and OJ L6/94). Continued as **INNOVATION**

SPRINTEL
Speedy Retrieval of Information on the Telephone (project within Area 5 of the **Telematics Systems Programme**)

SPRITE
Storage processing and retrieval of information in a technical environment (**ESPRIT** project)

SPRITE-S2
Pilot action in the area of support and guidance in the procurement of ICT systems and services. Launched in July 1997. Replaced **EPHOS**

SPS
Sanitary and phyto-sanitary

SRAFAS
Strategic restructuring and financial advisory services. **Phare** project

SRV
Sustainability reference value

SSC
Scientific Steering Committee. Coordinates the work of the Scientific Committees run by the **European Commission**'s Health and Consumer Protection **DG**. Created June 1997, ceased April 2003; previously the Multidisciplinary Scientific Committee (MDSC). Responsibilities passed to the European Food Safety Authority - **EFSA**. *See also* **CSTEE**; **SCAHAW**; **SCAN**; **SCCNFP**; **SCF**; **SCMPMD**; **SCP**; **SCTEE**; **SCVPH**; **STFC**.
http://europa.eu.int/comm/food/fs/sc/ssc/index_en.html

SSE
Système statistique européen (European statistical system - ESS)

SSID
Specialised service for documentary data processing

SSS-CA
Concerted action on short sea shipping. To oversee the implementation of **Transport RTD** projects

SSV
Short study-visits (1977-1987). Incorporated into the **Erasmus** programme

St Malo Statement
Joint statement following discussions between France and the UK held in St Malo, in December 1998, concerning the Union's Common Foreign and Security Policy (**CFSP**)

STA
Science and Technology Agency. A Japanese Government Agency which runs a Fellowship programme to enable young European scientists to carry out research in Japan's national laboratories and non-profit making institutions.

STABEX
(System of) stabilisation of export earnings of agricultural products under the **Lomé Convention**

Stability and Growth Pact
Adopted in 1997, with the aim of ensuring budgetary discipline in the context of Economic and Monetary Union (**EMU**).
http://europa.eu.int/comm/economy_finance/about/activities/sgp/sgp_en.htm

Stability Pact
The Stability Pact for South Eastern Europe, adopted on 10 June 1999, was intended to bring peace, stability and economic development to the region. Parties to the Pact include the EU, the **European Commission**, the Balkan countries, Japan, Russia, Turkey

and the US.
50 rue Wiertz, B-1050 Brussels, Belgium.
www.stabilitypact.org

STABINE
Development of an advanced power generation system, compounding a diesel cycle to that of an industrial gas turbine (**EUREKA** project)

STACCIS
Support for telematics cooperation with the Commonwealth of Independent States - CIS (a Telematics for Education and Training project within the **Telematics Applications Programme**)

STADIUM
Statistical data interchange universal monitor (**CADDIA** project)

Stage
Short form of **Stagiare**

Stage 1 Directive
Directive 94/63/EC on **VOC** emissions resulting from the storage and distribution of petrol (**OJ** L365/94). *See also* **Stage 2 Directive**

Stage 2 Directive
Directive 1999/13/EC on the limitation of emissions of **VOC**s due to the use of organic solvents in certain activities and installations (**OJ** L85/99). *See also* **Stage 1 Directive**

Stagiaire
A graduate given training within the **European Commission** in order to gain experience of the workings of the EU - possibly before taking up a career in the Commission. Often shortened to 'Stage' - which is also used to describe the placement process

STAMMI
Definition of standards for in-vehicle man-machine interface (**DRIVE** project)

STANORM
Statistical normalisation to study the standardisation of data exchange between various types of data processing environments (**CADDIA** project)

STAPLE
Development of an efficient functional programme system for the support of prototyping (**ESPRIT** project)

STAR
Comité des Structures Agricoles et du Développement Rural (Committee for Agricultural Structures and Rural Development). A **European Commission** committee. Details of meetings (in French only) are at: http://europa.eu.int/comm/agriculture/minco/othco/star/index.htm

STAR
Seamless telematics across regions (a Telematics for Healthcare project within the **Telematics Applications Programme**)

STAR
Special telecommunciations action for regional development in certain less-favoured regions (1986-1991) (**OJ** L305/86). Continued under **Telematique**

STAR
Standardisation of interoperable road tolling systems based on dedicated short range communications (DSRC) (**ISIS** Transport project)

STAR
Sustainability targets and references value database. An **EEA** database of current environmental policy targets and **SRV**s.
http://star.eea.eu.int

STARCM
Support to agrarian reform communities in Central Mindanao

STARLAB
Self-sustaining tele-media applications research laboratory (a Telematics Information Engineering project within the **Telematics Applications Programme**)

STARS
Database for business on legislation and advisory services relevant to the **SEM**. Replaced by **Inforules**

Starter
Projects funded under the **LIFE**-Nature programme.
http://europa.eu.int/comm/environment/life/news/life-coop_projects02.htm

START-UP
Suppliers for technological advanced requirements through users protocols (**DELTA** project)

State aid
Assistance granted by a government or via state resources aimed at giving particular companies or products favourable treatment in relation to their competitors. Examples of state aid include: state grants, interest relief, tax relief, provision by the state of goods and services on preferential terms. State aid that distorts - or threatens to distort - competition is prohibited by the EC Treaty.
http://europa.eu.int/scadplus/leg/en/s12002.htm and
http://europa.eu.int/comm/competition/citizen/citizen_stateaid.html

STATEL
Statistics telematics. Common interfaces for statistics applications (**IDA** project)

STATEL
Statistiques Télétransmission. Electronic data exchange between the **SOEC** and institutions in the **Member States** (**CADDIA** project)

STAT-LEX
A **Eurostat** database of secondary legislation on statistics. Available on CD in two volumes: up to 1997, and 1998-2000

Statewatch
A pressure group focusing on issues concerning the state and civil liberties in the **European Union**.
PO Box 1516, London N16 0EW, UK.
www.statewatch.org

STATONIS
Insurance services statistical domain on the **New Cronos** databank

STC
Scientific and Technical Committee (**EURATOM**)

STC
Scientific and technical cooperation

STD III
Science and technology for developing countries. **R&D** programme 1990-1994 (**OJ** L196/91). Continued as **INCO I**

STECLA
Standing Technological Conference of European Local Authorities

STEELCAL
Computer-aided learning in structural steelwork design (**EMTF** project)

STELCI
Short-term earnings and labour costs indices statistical domain on the **New Cronos** databank

STEM
Sustainable telematics for environmental management (a Telematics for Environment project within the **Telematics Applications Programme**)

STEMM
Strategic European multi-modal modelling (**Transport** project)

STEP
Science and technology for environmental protection (1989-1993) (**OJ** L359/89). Continued in the **Environment and Climate Programme**

STEPS Handbook
'Solutions for telematics between European public services', published 1994

STFC
Scientific and Technical Fisheries Committee. *See also* **SSC**

STI
Safety Technology Institute. Part of the **JRC** at **Ispra**

STID
Scientific and technical information and documentation

STI-ERA
Science and technology indicators for the European Research Area.
http://europa.eu.int/comm/research/era/sti_en.html

STIG
Telematic systems of general interest. *See* **Telematics Systems Programme**

STILMED
Safety technology in laser medicine (**EUREKA** project)

Stimulation Programme
See **Science Stimulation Programme**

STM
Supplementary trade mechanism

STMS
Short-term monetary support under the **EMS**

STOA
Scientific and Technical Options Assessment. A unit in the **European Parliament**'s Research **DG** which provides expert scientific and technical advice to MEPs and EP Committees. *See also* **EPTA**; **ETAN**; **STOA Scholarships**.
www.europarl.eu.int/stoa

STOA Scholarships
For first degree level young scientists and engineers to obtain work experience in the **European Parliament** Research **DG**. Replaced by **Ramon y Cajal Scholarships**. *See also* **Robert Schuman Scholarships**; **STOA**

Stoke Rochford Conferences
Held at Stoke Rochford in January 1993 and January 1994 to establish the decentralisation of EU information provision in the UK. The concept of **Relays** and the **NCC** were set up as a result

STOP
Programme, initially 1997-2000, to promote training, information, study and exchange programmes for people responsible for combating trade in human beings and the sexual exploitation of children, under Joint Action 96/700/JHA (**OJ** L322/96). Extended 2001-2002, as STOP II.
http://europa.eu.int/comm/justice_home/funding/stop/funding_stop_en.htm

STORM
Process modelling and device optimisation for submicron technologies (**ESPRIT** project)

STORMS
A European agreement on the radio access system for third generation multi-media mobile communications (**ACTS** project)

STP
Scientific Training Programme in Japan. Set up in 1986 to create an exchange scheme for young scientists

STRADA II
Standardisation of traffic data transmission and management (**DRIVE** project)

STRATA
Strategic analysis of specific political issues. www.cordis.lu/improving/science/home.htm

Strategic Planning
Assistance to small and medium-sized cities in the area of strategic planning (**RECITE** project)

STRC
Scientific and Technical Research Committee (Comité de la recherche scientifique et technique - **CREST**)

STREAM III
Stratosphere - troposphere experiments by aircraft measurements III (**THESEO** project)

Stresa Conference
Held in Stresa, Italy, in July 1958, the Conference laid the basis for the development of the Common Agricultural Policy - **CAP**

STRETCH
Extensible KBMS for large knowledge base applications (**ESPRIT** project)

STRIDE
Science and technology for regional innovation and development in Europe (1990-1993). A **Structural Funds** Initiative (Guidelines in **OJ** C196/90). Continued in the **Community Initiative 'SME'**

STRIDE
Speech-analytical hearing aids for the profoundly deaf in Europe (**TIDE** project)

STRIKES
Industrial disputes statistical domain on the **New Cronos** databank

STRINGS
Statistical report integrated generation service (**CADDIA** project)

Structural Funds
There are four Structural Funds: European Regional Development Fund (**ERDF**), European Social Fund (**ESF**), European Agricultural Guidance and Guarantee Fund (**EAGGF**), Financial Instrument for Fisheries Guidance (**FIFG**). Funds for the period 2000-2006 have their legal basis in **Regulation** 1260/99 laying down general provisions on the Structural Funds to strengthen the economic and social cohesion of the EU (**OJ** L161/99). *See also* **Community Initiatives**; **Objectives**. http://europa.eu.int/comm/regional_policy/funds/prord/sf_en.htm

STRUDER
Structural development in selected regions (in Poland) (under the **Phare** programme)

Stuttgart Declaration
Concerning the Institutions and policies of the EC. Issued by the **European Council** meeting in Stuttgart on 19 June 1983. Published in the *Bulletin of the European Communities* 6/83 p24-29

SUAW
Stand up and walk (**BIOMED** project)

Subcontractors Directive
Name sometimes used for the **Posted Workers Directive**

Sub-GATE
Submarine groundwater-fluxes and transport-processes from methane rich coastal sedimentary environments (**ELOISE** project)

Subsidiarity
The principle of decision-making at the lowest possible level so that the EU only becomes involved in issues which cannot be dealt with at national or regional level

SUBSOITEC
High performance submicron SOI-CMOS technologies (**ESPRIT** project)

SUITE
Sulfonates in terrestrial environments (**TERI** project)

Summit
See **European Summit**

SUM-PROJECT
Shoe upper material project (**EUREKA** project)

SUNDIAL
Speech understanding and dialogue (**ESPRIT** project)

SUNSTAR
Integration and design of speech understanding interfaces (**ESPRIT** project)

SUPERDOC
Set of software tools for a document workstation (**ESPRIT** project)

SUPERNODE
Development and application of a low cost high performance multiprocessor (**ESPRIT** project)

SUPERNODE II
Operating systems and programming environments for parallel computers (**ESPRIT** project)

Super Regions
Listed as follows:
I. Alpine regions
II. Atlantic Arc
III. Northern arc
IV. Central capitals
V. Diagonal Continental
VI. Central Mediterranean
VII. West Mediterranean
VIII. New German Länder

SUPERSMOLT
Production system for salmonids at elevated temperatures using sterile supermolts (**EUREKA** project)

SUPER SUBSEA
Project to develop standardised modular subsea production systems, under **EUREKA**

SUPRADYNAMICS
Lattice dynamics of high TC single crystal superconductors (**ESPRIT** project)

SURE
To promote safety in the nuclear sector especially within countries participating in the **Tacis** programme (1998-2002)

SUSCOM
Sustainable communities in Europe (**Environment and Climate** project)

Sutherland Report
on the operation of the Community's Internal Market after 1992; issued as **SEC**(92)2277

SV
Svenska (Swedish)

SVC
Standing Veterinary Committee

SWIFT
Specification for working positions in future air traffic control (**EURET** project)

SWIFT
User oriented and workflow integrated

federation of service providers for the elderly (a Telematics for Disabled and Elderly People project within the **Telematics Applications Programme**)

SWPI
Standing Working Party on Investment

SYMBIOSIS
Short-lived information network of non-profit-making organisations on People's Europe to inform citizens of the advantages of the Single Market (**SEM**). Established 1992 (**OJ** C293/91), halted for review 1994 and not restarted

SYMBOL
Multilingual and multiple lexical learning on CD-I environment (**TIDE** project)

SYN
See **Cooperation Procedure**

SYNAPSES
Federated healthcare record serve (a Telematics for Healthcare project within the **Telematics Applications Programme**)

SYNERGY
Decision 99/23/EC adopting a multi-annual programme to promote international cooperation in the energy sector (1998-2002) (**OJ** L7/99; no longer in force).
www.cordis.lu/synergy/home.html

Synthetic Index
of regions, measuring the relative intensity of regional problems in the **European Community** (**COM**(84)40 Table 7.1.1.; COM(87)230 p23; COM(90)609 Statistical Annex p35; COM(94)322 Table A.25; COM(96)542 p133). *See also* **Cohesion Report**; **Periodic Report**

SYRECOS
Systeme Regional d'echange de Competences et des Services (a Telematics for Urban and Rural Areas project within the **Telematics Applications Programme**)

SYRENE Manual
Defines procedures to exchange information under the **SIS**

SYSDEM
Systeme Européenne de Documentation sur l'Emploi (European System of Documentation on Employment). Now part of the European Observatory on Employment - **EEO**.
www.eu-employment-observatory.net

SYSMIN
System of stabilisation of export earnings from mining products. A trade provision within the **Lomé Convention**

SYSTRAN
System translation. The multilingual machine translation system used by the **European Commission**.
Produced by SYSTRAN S.A., 1 rue du Cimetière, 95230 Soisy-sous-Montmorency, France.
www.systransoft.com

T

T3
Telematics for teacher training (a Telematics for Education and Training project within the **Telematics Applications Programme**)

T3E
Drug addiction-Europe-exchange-training. Part of the five-year Community programme for the prevention of drug dependence (1996-2000)

T4D
Telemployment for the disabled (a Telematics for Urban and Rural Areas project within the **Telematics Applications Programme**)

TABD
Transatlantic Business Dialogue - "an informal process whereby European and American companies and business associations develop joint EU-US trade policy recommendations, working together with the European Commission and US Administration."
www.tabd.org

TAC
Technical Advisory Committee

TAC
Total allowable catch [of fish]. Specified annually, as under e.g. **Regulation** 2340/2002 of 16 December 2002 fixing for 2003 and 2004 the fishing opportunities for deep-sea fish stocks (**OJ** L356/02) and Regulation 2341/2002 of 20 December 2002 fixing for 2003 the fishing opportunities and associated conditions for certain fish stocks and groups of fish stocks, applicable in Community waters and, for Community vessels, in waters where catch limitations are required (OJ L356/02). Details of other TACs available via:
http://europa.eu.int/comm/fisheries/doc_et_publ/pub_en.htm

TACD
Transatlantic Consumer Dialogue. A United States-EU consumer forum, launched in September 1998.
www.tacd.org

TACIS
Tactile acoustic computer interaction system (**TIDE** project)

Tacis
Technical assistance to the Commonwealth of Independent States. Launched in 1991. Tacis II spanned 1996-1999 (**OJ** L165/96). **Regulation** 99/2000 "concerning the provision of assistance to the partner States in Eastern Europe and Central Asia" extended the programme 2000-2006 (OJ L12/00).
http://europa.eu.int/comm/external_relations/ceeca/tacis/index.htm

Tacis ACE
Tacis action for co-operation in economics. Modelled on **Phare ACE**

Tacis ACE Quarterly
Magazine published under **Tacis ACE**, along the lines of **Phare ACE Quarterly**

Tacis AQ
Abbreviated form of **Tacis ACE Quarterly**

Tacis Bistro
See **Bistro**

Tacis IBPP
Tacis institution building partnership programme. Aimed at supporting "the development of non-profit organisations from civil society, local & regional authorities and public institutions in the New Independent States (NIS) and Mongolia". Previously **Tacis LIEN**.
http://europa.eu.int/comm/europeaid/projects/ibpp/index_en.htm

Tacis LIEN
Tacis link inter European NGOs (**OJ** C29/98). Replaced by **Tacis IBPP**.
http://europa.eu.int/comm/europeaid/projects/tacis_lien/index_en.htm

TAFI
Textile antifraud initiative

TAFKO
Task Force for Kosovo. **European Commission**'s Task Force for the Reconstruction of Kosovo. Established in Pristina on 1 July 1999, it was responsible for the programming and implementation of the first phase of the EU's reconstruction programme. Replaced on 5 February 2000 by the European Agency for Reconstruction (**EAR**)

TAIE
Design and assessment of a vessel traffic management system (**EURET** project)

TAIEX
Technical Assistance and Information Exchange. Set up by the Commission in 1996 to help the EU applicant countries in the **CEEC**s.
Charlemagne Building, 170 rue de la Loi, Brussels, Belgium.
http://taiex.be

Takeover Directive
Proposal for a **Directive** on takeover bids (**COM**(2002)534). Also known as the 13th Directive on company law concerning takeover bids

TALAT
Training for aluminium applications technologies (**COMETT** project)

TALON
Testing and analysis of local area optical networks (**ESPRIT** project)

TAMCRA
Telematics applications to create alternative marketing channels for **SME**s (a Telematics for Urban and Rural Areas project within the **Telematics Applications Programme**)

TANIT II
Telematics for anaesthesia and intensive therapy II (a Telematics for Healthcare project within the **Telematics Applications Programme**)

TANKER
Ecological economical European tanker (**EUREKA** project)

TAO
Technical assistance office

TAP
Telematics Applications Programme

TAPPE
Telematics for administrations: public procurement in Europe (a Telematics for Administrations project within the **Telematics Applications Programme**)

TARDIS
Total traffic management environment (**DRIVE** project)

TARGET
Telematics applications in radiation and general oncology (a Telematics for Healthcare

project within the **Telematics Applications Programme**)

TARGET
Trans-European automated real-time gross settlement express transfer system - "an EU-wide system for euro payments", introduced on 1 January 1999 to regulate transactions between commercial banks and the **ECB**.
www.ecb.int/target

Target price
The price which it is estimated an agricultural producer should receive for a product sold on the open market

TARIC
Tarif Intégré de la Communauté (Integrated Tariff of the Community). Established under **Regulation** 2658/87 on the tariff and statistical nomenclature and on the Common Customs Tariff (**OJ** L256/87). "The TARIC contains a nomenclature in all 11 official languages with about 15,000 tariff lines. It shows all third country and preferential duty rates actually applicable as well as all commercial policy measures."
http://europa.eu.int/comm/taxation_customs/databases/taric_en.htm

TASBI
Transatlantic Small Business Initiative. Set up as a result of recommendations in 1996 by the **SME** Working Group of the Trans Atlantic Business Dialogue (**TABD**). TASBI exists to promote partnerships between small and medium sized enterprises in the EU and US

TASC
Telematics applications supporting cognition (a Telematics for Disabled and Elderly People project within the **Telematics Applications Programme**)

TASQUE
Tool for assisting software quality evaluation (**EUREKA** project)

TASTE
Technology assessment in tele-neuro-medicine (a Telematics for Healthcare project within the **Telematics Applications Programme**)

TAU
Technical assistance unit

Tax Package
European Commission Communication: Towards tax co-ordination in the **European Union** - A package to tackle harmful tax competition (**COM**(97)495). Includes proposals to introduce a code of conduct for business taxation; regulate the taxation of savings; and exempt interest and royalty payments from withholding tax

TAXUD
Taxation and Customs **DG** of the **European Commission**

TAYLOR
Transputer based APD/INMOS language and operating system research (**EUREKA** project)

TBR
Trade Barriers Regulation, laying down Community procedures in the field of the common commercial policy in order to ensure the exercise of the Community's rights under international trade rules, in particular those established under the auspices of the World Trade Organization - **WTO** (**Regulation** 3286/94 l , **OJ** L349/94).
http://europa.eu.int/comm/trade/issues/respectrules/tbr/index_en.htm

TBT
Technical Barriers to Trade. Technical regulations, standards, testing or certification procedures which can create barriers for manufacturers and exporters.
http://trade-info.cec.eu.int/tbt/index.cfm

TC
Technical committee

TCAA
Transatlantic Common Aviation Area. The June 2003 EU-US Summit agreed to open negotiations on air transport liberalisation between the two (also referred to as an 'open aviation area' - **OAA**). *See also* **Brattle Group**.
http://europa.eu.int/comm/press_room/presspacks/eu_us/pp_eu_us_en.htm

TCEU
Translation Centre for the Bodies of the European Union. *See* **CdT**

TCI
European Parliament Temporary Committee of Inquiry

TCNs
Third Country Nationals

TCT
Technical Committee on Transport (**COST**)

TDDS
Tariff data dissemination system. A series of databases managed by the **European Commission** concerning customs and taxation.
http://europa.eu.int/comm/taxation_customs/databases/database.htm

TDHS
Technological developments in the hydrocarbons sector scheme

TDI
Groupe Technique des Députés Indépendants (Technical Group of Independents - TGI) in the **European Parliament**. The group was not recognised by Parliament and was dissolved when it lost an appeal to the Court of First Instance (**CFI**) in Willy Rothley and Others v European Parliament (Case T-17/00, **ECR** 2002 Page II-579)

TDI
Tolerable daily intake

TDSP
Training and dissemination schemes projects (part of **INNOVATION**).
www.cordis.lu/tdsp

TEAC HEALTH
Towards evaluation and certification of health care telematics services in Europe (a Telematics for Healthcare project within the **Telematics Applications Programme**)

TEAM
Techno-economic-analysis network in the Mediterranean. Joint initiatives and strategies between the science and technology communities of Europe and the Mediterranean (an **IPTS** initiative)

TEAM 92
See **Team Europe**

Team Europe
A team of speakers from the **Member States** who are available for conferences, training sessions and so on, covering all EU policies and activities. Started in the run-up to the Single European Market (**SEM**) and initially called Team 92.
Contact: **TECIS** (Team Europe, Carrefours and Info-Points Service), c/o Intrasoft, Montoyer 40, B-1000 Brussels, Belgium.
http://europa.eu.int/comm/dg10/teameurope/index_en.html

TECAR
Training network for the European car industry (a Telematics for Education and Training project within the **Telematics Applications Programme**)

TECDOC
Portable information devices for technical documentation (**IMPACT** project)

Technology Marketplace
European technology market place: "a free on line service where you can find research and technological development results and search for innovative business opportunities on emerging technologies."
www.cordis.lu/marketplace

Technology Transfer
Electronic communication and exchange of data in order to facilitate the search for target **SME**s in partner regions (**RECITE** project)

TECIS
Team Europe, Carrefours and Info-Points Service. A support service (Helpdesk) for Carrefours, Info Points Europe and Team Europe, which started in October 2001.
c/o Intrasoft, 40 Montoyer, B-1000 Brussels, Belgium.
www.tecis.be

TECLA
Multilingual glossary of head-words used for **ECJ** case-law. 4 volumes 1994-1995, published by **EUR-OP**

TECS
The Europol computer system

TED
Tenders Electronic Daily. Electronic version of the **OJ S**, giving details of public contracts. *See also* **TED - Alert**.
http://ted.publications.eu.int

TED Alert
A commercial service alerting subscribers to relevant tenders listed on **TED**.
www.tenders.com

TEDIS II
Trade electronic data interchange systems. Phase two, 1991-1994. **Decision** 91/385/EEC (**OJ** L208/91) - no longer in force.
http://europa.eu.int/scadplus/leg/en/lvb/l24122.htm

TEISS
Telematics - European industry standards support (a Programme Support Actions project within the **Telematics Applications Programme**)

TELEFARMS
Telematics multimedia application for farmers support (a Telematics for Administrations project within the **Telematics Applications Programme**)

TELEFLEUR
Telematics-assisted handling of flood emergencies in urban areas (a Telematics for Environment project within the **Telematics Applications Programme**)

TELEFLOW
Telematics supported workflow analysis and business process enhancement (a Telematics Engineering project within the **Telematics Applications Programme**)

TELE-INSULA
Telematic services for islands (a Telematics for Urban and Rural Areas project within the **Telematics Applications Programme**)

TeleInViVo
3D ultrasound telematics medical emergency workstation (a Telematics for Healthcare project within the **Telematics Applications Programme**).
http://www.ehto.org/ht_projects/html/dynamic/121.html

TELEMAN
Research into remote-controlled handling in nuclear hazardous and disordered environments (1989-1993) (**OJ** L226/89)

TELEMAN
Teleteaching and training for management of **SMEs** - studies (a Telematics for Education and Training project within the **Telematics Applications Programme**)

TELEMART
Telematics marketing of teleworkers (a Telematics for Urban and Rural Areas project within the **Telematics Applications Programme**)

TELEMATE
Telematic multidisciplinary assistive technology education (a Telematics for Disabled and Elderly People project within the **Telematics Applications Programme**)

Telematics Applications Programme
Under the **Fourth Framework Programme**, 1994-1998. Established by **Decision** 94/801/EC (**OJ** L334/94). *Successor to* the **Telematics Systems Programme**. Continued as **IST**

Telematics for Libraries Programme
Part of the **Fourth Framework Programme**, 1994-1998.
www.cordis.lu/libraries

Telematics Systems Programme
Telematic systems in areas of general interest, 1990-1994 (**OJ** L192/91). Incorporated **AIM**; **DELTA**; **DRIVE**; **LRE**; **ORA**. Continued as **Telematics Applications Programme**

Telematique
A **Structural Funds** initiative for regional development services and networks related to data communication (1991-1993) (Guidelines in **OJ** C33/91). Continued as the **'SME' Community Initiative**

TELENURSE
Telematic applications for nurses in Europe (a Telematics for Healthcare project within the **Telematics Applications Programme**)

TELEPLANS
Telemedicine for citizens (a Telematics for Healthcare project within the **Telematics Applications Programme**).
www.ehto.org/ht_projects/html/dynamic/124.html

TELEPROMISE
Telematics to provide for missing services (a Telematics for Urban and Rural Areas project within the **Telematics Applications Programme**)

TELER
Telematics for enterprise reporting (a Telematics for Administrations project within the **Telematics Applications Programme**)

TeleRegions SUN2
Teleapplications for European regions (a Telematics for Integrated Applications for Digital Sites project within the **Telematics Applications Programme**).
www.faw.uni-linz.ac.at/cgi-pub/e_showprojekt.pl?projektnr=182

TeleSCAN
Telematic services in cancer. The first European internet service for cancer research, treatment and education (**MARIA** project).
http://telescan.nki.nl

TELETEENS
Methods and services to provide diseased European teenagers with usual access to telematics (a Telematics for Urban and Rural Areas project within the **Telematics Applications Programme**).
www.if.insa-lyon.fr/if/teltnet2/tindexa.html

Television Without Frontiers Directive
See **TWF Directive**

TELEXPER
Dissemination action on telematics experiences (a Programme Support Actions

project within the **Telematics Applications Programme**)

TELI
The European Language Initiative. UK-based organisation which produces language learning materials in EU official languages for local government.
PO Box 1901, Wicken, Milton Keynes MK19 6DN, UK

TELOS
Telematics enhanced language learning and tutoring systems (a Telematics for Education and Training project within the **Telematics Applications Programme**)

TEMBLOR
Bioinformatics research project, funded under the **Quality** programme of the **Fifth Framework Programme**

TEMPLE
Telematic employment engine (a Telematics for Urban and Rural Areas project within the **Telematics Applications Programme**)

TEMPORA
Integrating database technology, rule-based systems and temporal reasoning for effective software (**ESPRIT** project)

Tempus
Trans-European mobility scheme for university studies. Tempus II, 1994-1998 (**Decision** 93/246/EEC, **OJ** L112/93); Tempus III 2000-2006 (Decision 1999/311/EC in OJ L120/99). Incorporated **MED-Campus**.
http://europa.eu.int/comm/education/programmes/tempus/index_en.html

Tempus Phare
Initiative to extend **Tempus** awards to new **Applicant Countries**

Tempus Lien
Initiative to extend **Tempus** awards to the **NIS** and Mongolia

TEMSIS
Transnational environmental management support and information system (a Telematics for Environment project within the **Telematics Applications Programme**)

TEN(s)
Trans-European network(s). Transport, energy and telecommunications infrastructures which are of EU-wide significance, linking people and businesses in the Single European Market (**SEM**). TENs projects are eligible for EU funding.
See also TEN-Energy; TEN-Telecommunications; TEN-Transport.
http://europa.eu.int/comm/ten/index_en.html

TEN
Trans-European tele-education network (a Telematics for Education and Training project within the **Telematics Applications Programme**)

TEN-34
Trans-European network interconnect at 34 Mbps (a Telematics for Research project within the **Telematics Applications Programme**)

TEN-E
TEN-Energy

TEN-Energy
Trans-European energy networks. Also called TEN-E, it „concerns the main transportation/transmission networks for electricity and natural gas, excluding distribution networks." **Decision** 1229/2003/EC laying down a series of guidelines for trans-European energy networks (**OJ** L176/03). *See also* **TENs**.
http://europa.eu.int/comm/energy/ten-e/en/index.html

TEN-T
See **TEN-Transport**

TEN-Telecommunications
Now called eTEN. "Programme designed to help the deployment of telecommunication networks based services (e-services) with a trans-European dimension." **Decision** 1336/97/EC on a series of guidelines for Trans-European Telecommunications Networks (**OJ** L183/97). Amended by Decision 1376/2002/EC (OJ L200/02). *See also* **TENs**.
http://europa.eu.int/information_society/programmes/eten/index_en.htm

TEN-Transport
Trans-European transport networks - "comprises roads, railways, inland waterways, airports, seaports, inland ports and traffic management systems which serve the entire continent". **Decision** 1692/96/EC (**OJ** L228/96, but see additional legislation at the website below). *See also* **TENs**.
http://europa.eu.int/comm/ten/transport/index_en.htm

TEP
Territorial employment pacts. Also seen as Territorial pacts for employment.
http://europa.eu.int/scadplus/leg/en/cha/c10230.htm

TEPIT
EDI project under the **TEDIS** programme

TEP
Transatlantic Economic Partnership. Initiated at the May 1998 EU-US Summit.
http://europa.eu.int/comm/trade/bilateral/usa/1109tep.htm

TEPSA
Trans European Policy Studies Association.
11 rue d'Egmont, B-1000 Brussels, Belgium.
www.tepsa.be

TERA
Development and manufacture of high performance, high capacity optical disc storage systems for data library applications (**EUREKA** project)

TERENA
Trans-European Research and Education Networking Association. Formed in 1994 by the merger of RARE (Réseaux Associés pour la Recherche Européenne) and EARN (European Academic and Research Network).
466-468 Singel, NL-1017 AW Amsterdam, Netherlands.
www.terena.nl

TERES
European Renewable Energy Study, published (together with 3 Annexes) for the Commission's **DG** XVII by **EUR-OP** in 1994

TERI
Terrestrial ecosystems research initiative (part of the **Environment and Climate Programme**).
http://europa.eu.int/comm/dg12/teri/teri-pro.html

TERICA
Concerted action for coordination of TERI (**TERI** project)

TERM
Transport and environment reporting mechanism

Terminals Guide
ECHO database giving descriptions of terminals with the addresses of suppliers and service operators in Europe

TERN
Trans-European road network

TERRA
Networks of local/regional authorities to carry out innovative and/or demonstration

pilot projects on spatial planning (under **Article 10** of the **ERDF**)

TERRACE
TMN evolution of reference configurations for RACE (**RACE** project)

TES/IOT
Tableaux entrées-sorties / Input-output tables. A database of input-output tables of the national accounts of the **Member States**

TESCO
Test on cooperative driving (**DRIVE** project)

TESEMED
Telematics in community pharmacies for responsible self-medication (a Telematics for Healthcare project within the **Telematics Applications Programme**)

TESS/SOSENET
Telematics for social security/social security network to exchange information about insured persons. Set up under the **IDA** programme

TESTA
Trans-European services for telematics between administrations, funded under the **IDA** programme

TESTLAB
Testing systems using telematics for library access for blind and visually handicapped readers (a Telematics for Libraries project within the **Telematics Applications Programme**)

TESUS
Telesurgical staff (a Telematics for Healthcare project within the **Telematics Applications Programme**)

TET
Technology, employment and labour (**FAST** project)

TET-ADAPT
Adaptation of techno-economic evaluation tools for RACE (**RACE** project)

TETJAPAN
Telematics for education and training in Japan (a Telematics for Education and Training project within the **Telematics Applications programme**)

TETRISS
Telematics for education and training - intermediate support structure (a Telematics for Education and Training project within the **Telematics Applications Programme**)

TEU
Treaty on European Union

TEXATWORK
Textile application of teleworking (a Telematics for Urban and Rural Areas project within the **Telematics Applications Programme**)

TF
Task Force. Established on an ad-hoc basis to examine or deal with some specific issue. Six Research-Industry Task Forces were launched by the **European Commission** in 1995, covering Car of the future; Multimedia educational software; New generation of aircraft; Vaccines and viral illnesses; Train of the future; Transport intermodality. Two others were later set up on Environmentally-friendly water technologies, and Maritime systems.
http://europa.eu.int/comm/research/tf-ini.html

TFAN
Task Force for Accession Negotiations. Set up by the **European Commission** in 1998. Now merged with the services responsible for pre-accession in the Commission's Enlargement **DG**

TFAP
Trade Facilitation Action Plan. Adopted at **ASEM** 2, TFAP was intended to promote trade between the EU and Asia by reducing non-tariff barriers and transaction costs

TF-HRETY
Task Force Human Resources, Education, Training and Youth (of the **European Commission**). Became the Commission's Education and Culture **DG**

TFTS
Terrestrial flight telecommunications service (**EUREKA** project) (**OJ** C222/92)

TGI
Technical Group of Independents (Groupe Technique des Députés Indépendants - **TDI**) in the **European Parliament**

THEATRON
Theatre history in Europe: architectural and textual resources on-line (**EMTF** project)

Thematic Network
See **TN**

Thematic Programmes
Focused programmes to implement **Key Actions**, **RTD** activities of a generic nature and activities in support of research infrastructures. A component of the **Fifth Framework Programme**. *See* **EESD**; **GROWTH**; **IST**; **QUALITY**. *See also* **Horizontal Programmes**

THERMIE II
The demonstration component of the Non-Nuclear **RTD** programme **JOULE-THERMIE**. Continued as **ENERGIE** within the **EESD** programme.
http://europa.eu.int/comm/energy/en/pfs_55_en.html

THESAURI
An online analytical inventory of current structured vocabularies which have appeared in at least one of the official EU languages.
www.iopsys.ru/rice/echo/te86.html

THESEO
Third European stratospheric experiments on ozone. A campaign to monitor and study the ozone loss over Europe, 1998-99 (**Environment and Climate** project).
http://europa.eu.int/comm/dg12/envsc/theseo.html

Thessaloniki 8
See **Soloniki 8**

THETIS
A data management and data visualisation system for supporting coastal zone management for the Mediterranean Sea (a Telematics for Research project partly funded by the **Telematics Applications Programme**)

THIN
Travel health information network (a Telematics for Healthcare project within the **Telematics Applications Programme**)

Third Country / Countries
Any country or countries which are not EU **Member States**

Third Framework Programme
for research, covering 1990-1994. *See also* **Framework Programme**

Third Pillar
See **Pillars**

Thirtieth May Mandate
See **30th May Mandate**

THORN
The obviously required name server (**ESPRIT** project)

Three E's
Employment, enlargement, environment (priorities of the 2001 Swedish **Presidency**)

Three Pillars
See **Pillars**

Three Wise Men Report
on air transport, chaired by De Croo and published in 1994 by **EUR-OP** for the Commission's **DG** VII as 'Expanding horizons: Civil aviation in Europe, an action programme for the future'

Three Wise Men Report
on EC steel policy (**OJ** C9/88)

Three Wise Men Report
on the European Institutions. Published by the Council of Ministers in 1979

Three Wise Men Report
on the institutional implications of enlargement, 18 October 1999 (the Dehaene-von Weizsäcker-Simon Report).
http://europa.eu.int/igc2000/repoct99_en.htm

Threshold price
The minimum price at which agricultural produce from **Third Countries** can enter the EU

THTPs
Transnational high-technology projects

TIAH project
Total income for agricultural households. A **EUROSTAT** project to provide a measure of the aggregate disposable income of farmers. Published 1992-1995. Superseded by Income of the agricultural households sector

TIBIA
Technology initiative in BICMOS for applications (**JESSI/ESPRIT** project)

TICQA
Database of conformity assessment services in Europe, developed by the **European Commission**, the **EOTC** and **EFTA**.
www.ticqa.eotc.be

T-IDDM
Telematic management of insulin dependent diabetes mellitus (a Telematics for Healthcare project within the **Telematics Applications Programme**)

TIDE
Technology initiative for disabled and elderly people (1993-1994) (**OJ** L240/93). Continued in the **Telematics Applications Programme**

TIERRAS
Trans-European research on telematics applications for regional administration development strategies (a Telematics for Urban and Rural Areas project within the **Telematics Applications Programme**)

TII
European Association for the Transfer of Technologies, Innovation and Industrial Information.
3 rue Aldringen, L-1118 Luxembourg.
www.tii.org

TINA
Transport infrastructure needs assessment. A transport initiative to identify the infrastructure requirements of the **Applicant Countries** (part of the **Phare** programme)

Tindeman Report
on **European Union**. Published in *Bulletin of the EC* Supplement 1/76

TIP
Technology implementation plan. Information submitted by **R&D** contractors at the end of a project, describing the results and plans for using them. The electronic form is known as **eTIP**

TIP
Technology integration project (within the **ESPRIT** programme)

TIP
TEMPUS Information Point (in **TEMPUS** and **Tacis** partner countries)

TIPPS
Transnational innovation pilot programme in **SMEs** (**INNOVATION** project)

TIRONET
Interconnected broadband islands between Northern Ireland and the Republic of Ireland: a fibre interconnection initiative to prepare for **TEN-Telecommunications**

TIS
Terminological information system, of the General Secretariat of the **Council of the European Union**.
http://tis.consilium.eu.int

TITAN
Tactical integration of telematics applications across intelligent networks (a Telematics for Integrated Applications for Digital Sites project within the **Telematics Applications Programme**)

TMIE
Tutoring and monitoring intelligent environment (**DELTA** project)

TMPF
Tacis micro-project facility

TMR
Decision 94/916/EC on the Training and Mobility of Researchers: Activity 4 of the **Fourth Framework Programme** (**OJ** L361/94). Previously **HCM**; **SPES**. Continued as **IMPROVING**.
http://europa.eu.int/comm/dg12/tmr1.html

TN
Thematic network. A means of **RTD** coordination and cooperation, bringing together technologies around specific on-going and complementary fields throughout the EU. This ensures the exchange of information and resources between partners

TNG
Thematic Network Group. Established by **EU-OSHA**

TN-NETS
The **BRITE/EURAM** thematic network: new concepts and technologies for the next century maritime transport

TOAD
Transfer of administrative documents. A Committee of the Regions (**CoR**) database.
www.toad.cor.eu.int

TOBIAS
Tools for object-based integrated administration of systems (**ESPRIT** project)

Tobin Tax
A tax on foreign exchange transactions intended to reduce volatility in world financial markets by deterring financial speculation. Originally proposed by US economist James Tobin. Discussions have taken place at EU level.
http://tobintaxcall.free.fr

TODOS
Automatic tools for designing office information systems (**ESPRIT** project)

TOES
The Other Economic Summits. *See also* **NEF**

TOM
Territoires d'outre-mer. *See* **FOD**

ToMeLo
Towards a strategic alliance between developers of medical terminology and health care record systems (a Telematics for Healthcare project within the **Telematics Applications Programme**)

TOMPAW
A totally modular prosthetic arm with high workability (a Telematics for Disabled and Elderly People project within the **Telematics Applications Programme**)

TOOL-USE
Advanced support environment for method driven development and evolution of packaged software (**ESPRIT** project)

TOOTSI
Telematic object oriented tools for services interfaces (**ESPRIT** project)

TOPILOT
To optimise the individual learning process of occupational travellers (a Telematics for Education and Training project within the **Telematics Applications Programme**)

TOPMUSS
Tools for processing of multi-sensorial signals for plant monitoring and control (**ESPRIT** project)

TOPOZ-2
Towards the prediction of stratospheric ozone (**THESEO** project)

TOPP
Transverse optical patterns (**ESPRIT** project)

TOROS
Tinto Odiel river ocean study (**ELOISE** project)

TOSAFES
Treatment of obstructive sleep apnea with functional electrical stimulation (a Telematics for Disabled and Elderly People project within the **Telematics Applications Programme**)

Tosca
A **CSCW** project to provide an organisational knowledge base.
http://orgwis.gmd.de/projects/TOSCA/

TOSKA
Tools and methods for a sophisticated knowledge-based content free authoring facility (**DELTA** project)

TOUR
Tourism statistical domain on the **New Cronos** databank

TOUR-R
Tourism statistical domain on the **REGIO** database

Toy Safety Directive
Directive 88/378/EEC on the approximation of the laws of the **Member States** concerning the safety of toys (**OJ** L187/88)

TPA
Third party access (in the context. For example, of national gas and power grids)

TPC
Technical progress committee

TPF
Technology performance financing, set up under the **SPRINT** programme to strengthen the innovative capacity of **SME**s in Europe

TPF
Third party financing

TQC
Total quality control in the production industry (**COMETT** project)

TRA
Targeted research action. Set up by the Commission at the end of the **Third Framework Programme** in 1994 under **BRITE/EURAM**. *See also* **TRA NESS**

TRACE
Employment access routes. Mentoring programme for young people in France under a **CEDEFOP** three year plan

TRACE
Trade cooperation and economic policy reform in South-Asia. Part of the Union's cooperation with Asia

TRACECA
Transport corridor Europe-Caucasus-Asia

TRACIT
Transponders for R/T activity control of manufacturing links to CIM IT systems (**ESPRIT** project)

TRADE
EDI project under the **TEDIS** programme

TRADE
Trade **DG** of the **European Commission**

TrainCom
Train-ground communication infrastructure. An "Integrated Communication System for Intelligent Train Applications". Part funded by the **Information Society Technologies Programme**.
www.traincom.org

TRAINING
Vocational training in enterprises statistical domain on the **New Cronos** databank

TRAIN-IT
Training of IT innovators (**ESPRIT** programme)

TRAINS
Carriage of goods statistical domain on the **New Cronos** databank

TRAN
European Parliament Committee on Transport and Tourism

TRAN
Regional transport statistical domain on the **REGIO** database

TRAN
European Parliament Temporary Committee of Inquiry into the Community Transit Regime

TRA NESS
New ship concept in the framework of short sea shipping. A project to group together seven Community-funded RTD projects. Part of **TRA**

TRANS
Transport **DG** of the **European Commission**

Transfers Directive
Alternative name for the **Acquired Rights Directive**

TRANSIT
An electronic system for national governments on customs clearance for goods in transit between the EU and **EFTA** countries. Set up under the **IDA** programme

TRANSMETE
Seminars for training SMEs in the use of telematics (a Telematics for Education and Training project within the **Telematics Applications Programme**)

Transparency
A term used to mean openness, especially with regard to public access to information, in which context **Regulation** 1049/2001 regarding public access to **European**

Parliament, **Council of the European Union** and **European Commission** documents (**OJ** L145/01) is relevant. Often used in the phrase 'openness and transparency'

Transparency Directive
Directive 80/723/EEC on the transparency of financial relations between **Member States** and public undertakings (**OJ** L195/80)

Transport
RTD programme in the field of transport (**Decision** 94/914/EC, **OJ** L361/94) under the **Fourth Framework Programme**. Previously **EURET**.
www.cordis.lu/transport/home.html

TRANSPOTEL
A worldwide reproduceable concept for physical distribution centres, where central facilities are offered of which the major provision is an integral data and communications processing system (**EUREKA** project)

TRANSTEC
Internet-based multimedia knowledge transfer for innovative engineering technologies (**EMTF** project)

TRANSWHEEL
Transportation wheelchair with high impact safety and advanced sensor comfortability for people with mobility problems (a Telematics for Disabled and Elderly People project within the **Telematics Applications Programme**)

TRAPCA
Risk assessment of exposure to traffic-related air pollution for the development of inhalent allergy, asthma and other chronic respiratory conditions in children (an Environmental Health and Chemical Safety Research project within the **Environment and Climate Programme**)

Treaty of Accession
See **Accession Treaty**

Treaty of Amsterdam
Signed by the 15 **Member States** at Amsterdam on 2 October 1997, it entered into force on 1 May 1999, making significant changes to the **Treaty on European Union**. Amsterdam emphasised citizenship and individual rights, gave more powers to the **European Parliament**, promoted the **area of freedom, security and justice** and the **common foreign and security policy**.
http://europa.eu.int/abc/obj/amst/en/index.htm

Treaty of Nice
Adopted at the Nice **European Council**, 7-11 December 2000, and signed in Nice on 26 February 2001 (published in **OJ** C80/01). Agreed new rules for qualified majority voting (**QMV**) and decided that new EU members should join before the 2004 **European Parliament** elections.
http://europa.eu.int/eur-lex/en/treaties/

Treaty of Paris
See **EDC** - European Defence Community

Treaty of Paris
The European Coal and Steel Community (**ECSC**) Treaty. Signed by Belgium, France, Germany, Italy, Luxembourg and The Netherlands on 18 April 1951. Came into force 23 July 1952; expired 23 July 2002

Treaties of Rome / Treaty of Rome
The Treaty establishing the European Economic Community (EEC) and the Treaty establishing the European Atomic Energy Community (Euratom). The term 'Treaties of Rome' means both these Treaties; but 'Treaty of Rome' is invariably used to mean the EEC Treaty. Both were signed by France, Germany, Italy, the Netherlands, Belgium and Luxembourg on 25 March 1957, and entered into force 1 January 1958. The EEC Treaty (later renamed EC Treaty) expanded the scope of cooperation agreed under the **Treaty of Paris** (ECSC) to include

common policies in areas such as agriculture, transport, competition and economics. It also set the goal of creating "an ever closer union among the peoples of Europe", and set up both the Joint Parliamentary Assembly (now the **European Parliament**) and the European Court of Justice (**ECJ**). The Euratom Treaty was intended to promote the "speedy establishment and growth of nuclear industries"

Treaty on European Union
Signed by the - then **12** - **Member States** at Maastricht on 7 February 1992, and came into force 1 November 1993. Often referred to as the Maastricht Treaty, it amended the texts of the ECSC Treaty and EEC Treaty, set a date for Economic and Monetary Union (**EMU**), established a Common Foreign and Security Policy, introduced the **Codecision procedure**, and established the principle of **Subsidiarity** and the concept of citizenship of the Union

TREES
Tropical ecosystem environment observations by satellites (a **European Commission** / **ESA** project)

TREMOR
Development and validation of new assistive devices for the treatment of disability caused by tremor (a Telematics for Disabled and Elderly People project within the **Telematics Applications Programme**)

TREMOVE
A simulation model developed to support policy making concerning emission standards for vehicles and fuel specifications. Calculates costs of different transport scenarios for nine European countries from 1996 to 2020. Initially developed within the second **Auto-Oil** programme.
www.tremove.org

TREND
An **ECHO** database to monitor trends in the development of computer hardware and software

Trend Chart
The European trend chart on innovation - "a practical tool that offers valuable information for innovation policy makers and scheme managers in Europe."
http://trendchart.cordis.lu

TRENDS
Training educators through networks and distributed systems (a Telematics for Education and Training project within the **Telematics Applications Programme**)

TRESHIP
Technologies for reduced environmental impact from ships. One of the **TN**s supported by the **Transport** programme relating to short sea shipping

TRESMED
A **European Commission**-funded project, carried out by the Economic and Social Council of Spain, on the consultative role of economic and social agents and its contribution to the Euro-Mediterranean Partnership.
www.ces.es/trabajo/docus/tresmed.htm

TREVI Group
Member States' Interior Ministers meeting to discuss terrorism, radicalism, extremism and violence

Trialogue
See **Trilogue**

TRIDISMA
Three-dimensional sediment transport measurements by acoustics (**MAST III** project).
www.uea.ac.uk/~e470/www_trid.htm

Trilogue
Term denoting a meeting between the

Council of the European Union, **European Commission** and **European Parliament**. Sometimes seen as 'Trialogue'

TRIM
Main aggregates of the national accounts statistical domain on the **New Cronos** databank

TRIMS
Trade-related investment measures - within the **GATT** and subsequent negotiations

Triple bottom line
Expression used to denotes the need for businesses to take account of the social, economic and environmental impact of their actions

TRIPS
Trade-related aspects of intellectual property rights - within the **GATT** and subsequent negotiations

TRITON
Training material and courses on the technology for environmental protection in water resources management (**COMETT** project)

Troika
The Troika originally comprised the Foreign Ministers of the previous, current and forthcoming Presidencies of the **Council of the European Union**. The **Treaty of Amsterdam** altered its composition and the Troika now comprises the Foreign Minister of the **Member State** holding the **Presidency** of the EU, the **High Representative** for the Common Foreign and Security Policy (CFSP), and a representative of the **European Commission** (usually the Commissioner for External Relations). The Foreign Minister of the next Member State to hold the Presidency can also be involved, but need not be

TROPICS
Transparent object-oriented parallel information computing system (**ESPRIT** project)

TRUST
Testing and consequent reliability estimation for real-time embedded software (**ESPRIT** project)

TrustHealth
Trustworthy health telematics (a Telematics for Healthcare project within the **Telematics Applications Programme**). Followed by TrustHealth II

TS
Technology stimulation actions

TSE
Transmissable spongiform encephalopathies

TSE IP
Transmissable spongiform encephalopathies **Industrial Platform**

TSER
Targeted Socio-economic Research, within the **Fourth Framework Programme** under **Decision** 94/915/EC (**OJ** L361/94). Previously **MONITOR**. Continued as **IMPROVING**.
www.cordis.lu/tser/home.html

TSIs
Technical specifications for interoperability of the trans-European high-speed rail system. Drawn up by the **AEIF**

TSME
Technology stimulation measures for **SME**s

TSPF
Tacis small project facility

TSPs
Trailing spouses and partners

TSSP
Telecommunications sector support programme

TSUNAMI II
Technology in smart antennas for the universal advanced mobile infrastructure Part II (**ACTS** project)

TTA
All terrain amphibious vehicle (**EUREKA** project)

TTA
Time-triggered-architecture. Development of a new concept in on-board automotive electronic systems (**ESPRIT** project)

TT-CNMA
Testing technology for communications networks for manufacturing applications (**ESPRIT** project)

TTE
Transport, Telecommunications and Energy **Council of the European Union**

TTER
Two-tier exchange rate

TTNet
Community training of trainers network. Set up in 1998 by **CEDEFOP**

TTP+TVP
Technology transfer and technology validation projects (**INNOVATION** project).
www.cordis.lu/tvp/home.html

TT-RT-SMEIRT
Business-opportunity creation for **SME**s (**TIDE** project)

TUDOR
Usability issue for people with special needs (**RACE** project)

TUNICS
Tunnel integrated control system (**DRIVE** project)

TUPE
Transfer of Undertakings (Protection of Employment). Regulations which introduced the **Acquired Rights Directive** into the UK

TURA
Telematics for urban and rural areas.
www.tweuro.com

TUTB
European Trade Union Technical Bureau for Health and Safety.
5 blvd du Roi Albert II, B-1210 Brussels, Belgium.
www.etuc.org/tutb/index_en.html

TV Signals Directive
Directive 95/47/EC on the use of standards for the transmission of television signals (**OJ** L281/95). No longer in force

TVA
Taxe sur la valeur ajoutée (Value Added Tax - VAT)

TV-Anytime
Home storage multimedia systems based on standards (**ISIS** Multimedia systems project)

TWE
The relationship between technology, work and employment (**FAST** programme)

Twenty-One
Multimedia information transaction and dissemination tool (a Telematics Information Engineering project within the **Telematics Applications Programme**)

TWEURO
Telework Europa. A Commission-funded project to support the **Telematics Applications Programme**. Ended December 1999. Also seen as ‘TWEUROPA’.
www.tweuro.com

TWEUROPA
See **TWEURO**

TWF
Television without frontiers. In the context of **Directive** 89/552/EEC on the coordination of certain provisions laid down by Law, Regulation or Administrative Action in **Member States** concerning the pursuit of television broadcasting activities (**OJ** L298/89)

TWG-DFO
Technical Working Group on Data Exchange and Forecasting for Ozone Episodes in Northwest Europe. Set up in 1996 and coordinated by the **ETC/AQ**

U

u.a.
Unit of account

UAA
Utilised agricultural area. Sometimes seen as Usable agricultural area

UAC
Users Advisory Council. Set up by the **European Commission** in 1994 to encourage the dissemination of information on EU affairs

UACES
University Association for Contemporary European Studies.
c/o King's College, Strand, London WC2R 2LS, UK.
www.uaces.org

UAM
Union of the Arab **Maghreb** countries

U-CARE
Unexplained cardiac arrest registry of Europe (**BIOMED** project)

UCITS
Undertakings for collective investment in transferable securities. Subject to **Directive** 85/611/EEC (**OJ** L375/85) on the coordination of laws, regulations and administrative provisions relating to UCITS

UCLAF
Unité de Coordination de la Lutte Anti-Fraude (EU Anti-Fraud Coordination Unit). Replaced by **OLAF**

UCOL
Ultra wideband coherent optical LAN (**ESPRIT** project)

UEA
Union Européenne de l'Ameublement (Federation of European Furniture Manufacturers).
www.ueanet.com

UEAPME
European Association of Craft, Small and Medium-Sized Enterprises. Merged secretariats with EUROPMI, 1999.
4 rue Jacques de Lalaing, B-1040 Brussels, Belgium.
www.ueapme.com

UEN
Union for Europe of the Nations group (groupe Union pour l'Europe des Nations) in the **European Parliament**. Previously **EDN**, **UPE**.
www.europarl.eu.int/uen

UETP
University-enterprise training partnership (Strand A in the **COMETT** programme, continued in the **Leonardo da Vinci** programme)

UFE
Union for Europe (Union Pour l'Europe - UPE). Group in the **European Parliament**, 4th parliamentary term 1994-1999

UHP
Unit of homogeneous production

UK
United Kingdom

UK CEE
United Kingdom Centre for European Education. Merged with the Central Bureau for Educational Visits and Exchanges.
CBEVE, 10 Spring Gardens, London SW1A 2BN, UK

UKREP
United Kingdom Permanent Representation to the European Union.
10 av d'Auderghem, B-1040 Brussels, Belgium.
www.ukrep.be

UKRHEEO
UK Research and Higher Education European Office. Now **UKRO**

UKRO
UK Research Office. Previously **UKRHEEO**.
83 rue de la Loi, BP10, B-1040 Brussels, Belgium.
www.ukro.ac.uk

ULIC
Urban local initiative centres. Also seen as Local urban initiative centre - **LUIC**

ULISIS
Ultrasonic images of system interfaces (**EUREKA** project)

ULTRA
Exposure and risk assessment for fine and ultrafine particles in ambient air (Environmental Health and Chemical Safety research project within the **Environment and Climate Programme**)

ULYSSES
Urban lifestyles, sustainability and integrated environment assessment (**Environment and Climate** project)

UN
United Nations. The **European Union** has established a website dedicated to its relations with the UN:
http://europa-eu-un.org

UNCTAD
United Nations Conference on Trade and Development.
www.unctad.org

UNDCP
United Nations Drugs Control Programme, under the aegis of the **UNODC**

UNECE
United Nations Economic Commission for Europe. Also seen as UN/ECE.
Palais des Nations, CH-1211 Geneva 10, Switzerland.
www.unece.org

UNEMP
Unemployment statistical domain on the **REGIO** database

UNEMPLOY
Unemployment statistical domain on the **New Cronos** databank

UNEP
United Nations Environment Programme.
www.unep.org

UNESDA
Union of the EC Soft Drinks Associations. Now UNESDA-CISDA (Confederation of International Soft Drinks Associations).
77-79 blvd Saint-Michel, B-1040 Brussels, Belgium.
www.unesda-cisda.org

UNESCO
United Nations Educational, Scientific and Cultural Organization.
www.unesco.org

Unfair Commercial Practices Directive
Proposed **Directive** concerning unfair

business-to-consumer commercial practices in the Internal Market and amending directives 84/450/EEC, 97/7/EC and 98/27/EC (**COM**(2003)356).
http://europa.eu.int/comm/consumers/cons_int/safe_shop/fair_bus_pract/index_en.htm

UNGASS
United Nations General Assembly Special Session

UNICE
Union of Industrial and Employers' Confederations of Europe / **Union des Confédérations de l'Industrie et des Employeurs d'Europe**.
168 av de Cortenbergh, B-1000 Brussels, Belgium.
www.unice.org

UNIPOS
A UNIX-like parallel operating system (**EUREKA** project)

UNISTOCK
Union des Stockeurs Professionnels de Céréales dans la CEE / Union of Cereal Storage Firms in the EEC.
68 Michelangelolaan, B-1000 Brussels, Belgium.
www.unistock.be

UNITED
High-T superconducting thin films and tunnel junction devices (**ESPRIT** project)

UNITEL
Unified architectural specification for the set-top box (**ISIS** multimedia project). Extended by UNITEL-2: set-top functionalities in the multimedia chain

Unit Prices Directive
Directive 98/6/EC on consumer protection in the indication of the prices of products offered to consumers (**OJ** L80/98). Also known as 'Dual Pricing Directive'

UNIVERSE
Large sale demonstrator for global, open distributed library services (a Telematics for Libraries project within the **Telematics Applications Programme**)

UNIXIM
CT and Planar image acquisition by means of solid state linear x-ray image detector for slit scan digital radiology (**EUREKA** project)

UNMIK
United Nations Interim Administration in Kosovo

UNODC
United Nations office on Drugs and Crime.
www.unodc.org

UPE
Union pour l'Europe des Nations (Union for Europe of the Nations - **UEN**) group in the **European Parliament**

UPI
User validation best practice manual for information engineering (a telematics information engineering project within the **Telematics Applications Programme**)

UPP
Urban pilot programme / Urban pilot projects, under **Article 10** of the **ERDF** (1979-1999). Details at the **URBAN** website

URB-AL
See **URB-LA**

URBAN
A **Community Initiative** for integrated programmes concerned with economic, social and environmental problems in depressed urban areas. Initially 1994-1999, extended 2000-2006 as URBAN II.
http://europa.eu.int/comm/regional_policy/urban2/index_en.htm

Urban Observatory
Contraction of European Urban Observatory - **EUO**

URB-LA
A programme to develop cooperation between local authorities in Latin America and EU **Member States** (1996-1999). Based on **Asia Urbs**. Also seen as URB-AL

UROP
Universal roadside processor (**DRIVE** project)

Uruguay Round
Multilateral trade negotiations established in 1986 in the context of **GATT** (now the **WTO**)

US
Union Syndicale. "European Public Service" / "Service Public Européen". One of a number of trades unions operating within the EU institutions.
av. des Gaulois, 36, B-1040 Brussels, Belgium.
www.unionsyndicale.org

US
United States [of America]

USA
United States of America

UseDHE
User-group on the architecture of healthcare information systems (a telematics for healthcare project within the **Telematics Applications Programme**)

Use MARCON
User-controlled generic MARC convertor (project within Area 5 of the **Telematics Systems Programme**)

USER
Usability requirements elaboration for rehabilitation technology (**TIDE** project)

UTE
Union des Théâtres de l'Europe. Founded in 1990 to develop cultural cooperation across national borders (**Kaleidoscope** project).
8 blvd Berthier, F-75017 Paris, France.
www.ute-net.org

Utilities Directive
Directive 93/38/EEC on the procurement procedures of entities operating in the water, energy, transport and telecommunications sectors (**OJ** L199/93)

Utilities Remedies Directive
Directive 1992/13/EEC coordinating the laws, regulations and administrative provisions relating to the application of Community rules on the procurement procedures of entities operating in the water, energy, transport and telecommunications sectors (**OJ** L76/92)

UVECOS
Effects of UV-B radiation on sensitive European ecosystems (Environmental Health and Chemical Safety Research project within the **Environment and Climate Programme**)

V

V
Vertes (Green group of the **European Parliament**). *See also* **Greens/EFA**

V4
Visegrad Four

VALASPI
Developing and evaluating culture and language-learning multimedia telematics for primary school pupils (**EMTF** project)

Val Duchesse
Château near Brussels where a number of high-level discussions have taken place. Gave its name to the 1985 Val Duchesse Social Dialogue Process. Limited information from: www.europarl.eu.int/factsheets/4_8_6_en.htm

VALID
Validation methods and tools for knowledge-based systems (**ESPRIT** project)

VALIDATA
Validated databank and dissemination for prescribers (**AIM** project)

VALOREN
Programme for exploitation of indigenous energy potential in certain less-favoured regions, 1987-1991 (**OJ** L305/86)

VALUE II
Dissemination and exploitation of results from research valorisation and utilisation for Europe (1989-1992-1994) (**OJ** L200/89 and OJ L141/92). Continued as **INNOVATION**

Value Relay Centres
A network intended to promote information about innovation. Renamed Innovation Relay Centres (**IRC**)

VALUES@WORK
European conference on the prospects of the social economy within the context of sustainable development, held November 2001.
www.socialeconomy.be

VAMAS
International scientific and technical collaboration on advanced materials and standards (**COM**(84) 642)

VAMOS
Requirements and system specification for dynamic traffic messages (**DRIVE** project)

Van Eyck
Visual arts network for the exchange of cultural knowledge (project within Area 5 of the **Telematics Systems Programme**)

VAP
Vision as process (**ESPRIT** project)

VAs
Voluntary approaches

VASARI
Visual arts system for archiving and retrieval of images (**ESPRIT** project)

VAT
Value added tax (Taxe sur la valeur ajoutée - TVA)

VATAM
Validation of telematics applications in medicine (a Telematics for Healthcare

project within the **Telematics Applications Programme**)

VEDILIS
Vehicle discharge light system (**EUREKA** project)

VEGETATION
An Earth observation system launched March 1998 on the SPOT4 satellite. Co-financed by the **European Commission**.
http://spot4.cnes.fr/waiting.htm

VEINS
Variability of exchanges in the northern seas (**MAST III** project)

VENICE
Virtual enterprises nurtured using intelligent collaborative environment (a Telematics for Urban and Rural Areas project within the **Telematics Applications Programme**)

Venice Commission
European Commission for Democracy through Law. A **Council of Europe** body, established 1990.
www.venice.coe.int

VERTS/ALE
Verts/Alliance Libre Européenne (Greens/ European Free Alliance - **Greens/EFA**) group in the **European Parliament**

VES
Virtual European school (**EMTF** project)

VET
Vocational education and training

Vibrations Directive
Directive 2002/44/EC on the minimum health and safety requirements regarding the exposure of workers to the risks arising from physical agents (**OJ** L177/02)

VIC
Vehicle inter-communication (**DRIVE** project)

VICH
International Cooperation on Harmonisation of Technical Requirements for Registration of Veterinary Medicinal Products. An EU-Japan-USA initiative launched in April 1996.
http://vich.eudra.org

VICO
Cultural values in information and communication technology (a Telematics for Healthcare project within the **Telematics Applications Programme**)

VIDIMUS
Generic vision system for industrial applications (**ESPRIT** project)

VIE
Virtual information exchange

Vienna Convention
for the Protection of the Ozone Layer, signed 1985; precursor to the **Montreal Protocol**.
www.unep.org/ozone/vienna.shtml

VIES
VAT information exchange system. An electronic system for national governments. Set up under **IDA**

VIEWS
Visual inspection and evaluation of wide-area scenes (**ESPRIT** project)

VILAR
Landscape virtual gallery (**Raphael** project)

VIMP
Vision based on-line inspection of manufactured parts (**ESPRIT** project)

VIN
Vehicle identification number

VIP
VDM onterface for PCTE (**ESPRIT** project)

VIPS
Scientific press service designed to disseminate the results of EU-funded research to the media. Ceased May 2000

VIROS
Virtual Institute for Research in Official Statistics "designed and developed by Eurostat to co-ordinate research activities in official statistics and dissemination of their results, with a view to improving their exploitation."
http://europa.eu.int/comm/eurostat/research/

VIRTUOSO
Virtual simulation and treatment via telematics applications in clinical radio oncology (a Telematics for Healthcare project within the **Telematics Applications Programme**)

VIS
Visa information system

VISA
Universal access to WIMP-software for partially sighted and blind users (**TIDE** project)

Visegrad Agreements
Poland (**OJ** L348/93); Hungary (OJ L347/93); Czech Republic (OJ L360/94); Slovak Republic (OJ L359/94)

Visegrad Four
Czech Republic, Hungary, Poland, Slovakia. Details at:
www.v-4.sk/may/history-of-visegrad.html

VISILOG
Advanced data processing for management support (**EUREKA** project)

VISIMAR
Visualisation and simulation of marine environmental processes (**EUREKA** project)

VISIOBOARD
Gaze control system to provide services and applications to severely handicapped citizens (a Telematics for Disabled and Elderly People project within the **Telematics Applications Programme**)

Vision Book
An initiative to develop a series of 'future concepts' relating to people, information technology, and culture over the next five to 25 years. Initially web-based, but "planned to be printed in 2004."
http://europa.eu.int/information_society/topics/research/visionbook/index_en.htm

Vista
The **European Commission** Secretariat General's internal database of Commission documents including minutes of meetings. **Pre-Lex** is a limited, publicly-available version

VISTEL
Visual impaired screen based telephony (a Telematics for Disabled and Elderly People project within the **Telematics Applications Programme**)

VITAL-Home
Vital signs monitoring from home with open systems (**ISIS** Bioinformatics project)

VITAMIN
Visualisation standard tools in manufacturing industry (**ESPRIT** project)

Vitorino II
COM(2002)350: Communication on an information and communication strategy for the **European Union** (named after **Commissioner** António Vitorino, responsible for Communication Policy)

VIVA
Validation initiative for vital application

(**ISIS** bioinformatics project)

VLSI
Very large scale integrated [circuits]

VOCs
Volatile organic compounds. *See* **Stage 1 Directive** and **Stage II Directive**

VOICE
Giving a voice to the deaf, by developing awareness of voice to text recognition capabilities (a Telematics for Disabled and Elderly People project within the **Telematics Applications Programme**)

VOICE
See **NGO VOICE**

VOICE
Voluntary Organisations in Cooperation in Emergencies.
www.ngovoice.org

VOILA
Variable object identification, location and acquisition (**ESPRIT** project)

Volet Social
A series of measures intended to recognise the significance of the social dimension in the **European Commission**'s (reformed) personnel policy

Volkswagen law
Name given to a German law which the **European Commission** believes protects the eponymous car manufacturer from hostile or foreign takeovers. A legal challenge was launched by the Commission in March 2003

Vredeling Initiative
Proposal for a **Directive** on procedures for informing and consulting the employees of undertakings with complex structures (originally published in *Bulletin of the EC* Supplement 3/1980, with a revision in Supplement 2/1983 and a Council Conclusion in **OJ** C203/86)

VREPAR
Virtual reality environments for psycho-neuro-physiological assessment and rehabilitation (a Telematics for Healthcare project within the **Telematics Applications Programme**)

VRLEARNERS
Virtual reality learning environment for network of advanced educational multimedia resource centres, museums and schools (**EMTF** project)

VSB
Very small businesses

VSOP
Voice supported optical publisher (**EUREKA** project)

VULCANUS
A training programme to help Japanese students, business people and companies learn about European industrial companies.
www.eu.emb-japan.go.jp/interest/vulcanus.htm

VUSEC
Voluntary work and employment. A **European Commission** study published in 1986 in the *Document* series by **OOPEC** and entitled *The extent and kind of voluntary work in the EEC…*

W

WAI
Web accessibility initiative (a Telematics for Disabled and Elderly People project within the **Telematics Applications Programme**)

WAI-DA
Web accessibility initiative-design for all

WALCYNG
How to enhance walking and cycling instead of shorter car trips and to make these modes safer (**Transport** project)

WAMM
Water management model. Involves the application of a new satellite-based technology to improve flood forecasting in the Venice lagoon (**INNOVATION** project)

Washington Treaty
Founding document of **NATO**, signed in 1949 by 12 countries: Belgium, Canada, Denmark, France, Iceland, Italy, Luxembourg, the Netherlands, Norway, Portugal, UK, USA

WASP
Wadden Sea project (**MAST I** project)

Wassenaar Arrangement
on export controls for conventional arms and dual-use goods and technologies. *See also* **Australia Group**, **Missile Technology Control Regime**, **Nuclear Suppliers Group**, **Zangger Committee**.
www.wassenaar.org

WasteBase
Database launched by **ETC/W** containing detailed data and information on all relevant waste management issues covered by the ETC/W.
www.hull.ac.uk/cwpr/html/body_database.html

Waste Directive
Directive 75/442/EEC on waste (**OJ** L194/75)

Wastes
Regulation 259/93/EEC on the supervision and control of shipments of wastes within, into and out of the EU (**OJ** L30/93). Categories of Green, Amber and Red wastes are listed

WATCH-CORDIS
Windows access to Commission host - CORDIS. A Windows application to provide easy access to **CORDIS** (**INNOVATION** project)

WATER
Wetland and Aquatic Ecosystem Research. A **TN**, launched formally in 1998, to assemble projects covering a wide spectrum of water and wetland related tasks

Water Framework Directive
Directive 2000/60/EC establishing a framework for Community action in the field of water policy (**OJ** L327/00). Also known as **WFD**

Water Quality Directive
Directive 80/778/EEC relating to the quality of water intended for human consumption (**OJ** L229/80)

WATERNET
Distributed water quality monitoring

using sensor networks (a Telematics for Environment project within the **Telematics Applications Programme**)

WATIS
Work and training information system (a Telematics Information Engineering project within the **Telematics Applications Programme**)

WEAG
Western European Armament Group, within the Western European Union (**WEU**). Members: Austria, Belgium, Czech Republic, Denmark, Finland, France, Germany, Greece, Hungary, Italy, Luxembourg, Netherlands, Norway, Poland, Portugal, Spain, Sweden, Turkey, UK.
www.weu.int/weag

WEB4GROUPS
Transfer of knowledge between research, education, business and public administration through world wide web extended for group communication (a Telematics for Research project within the **Telematics Applications Programme**)

WebCDS
Catalogue of environmental locators pointing to environmental information sources in Europe.
www.mu.niedersachsen.de/cds/webpages/52.htm

WED
World Environment Day. Organised by the **United Nations** Environment Programme.
www.unep.org/wed/2003/

WEEE
Waste electrical and electronic equipment. Covered by both **Directive** 2002/96/EC on waste electrical and electronic equipment (**OJ** L37/03) and Directive 2002/95/EC on the restriction of the use of certain hazardous substances in electrical and electronic equipment (OJ L37/03).
http://europa.eu.int/comm/environment/waste/weee_index.htm

WEEN
Women's Enterprises Electronic Networks. Centre for Higher Education and Development (HEAD), University of North London, 236-250 Holloway Road, London N7 6PP, UK.
www.unl.ac.uk/head/ween

Weimar Three
France, Germany and Poland - specifically, meetings between their leaders, held since 1991. Also called the Weimar Triangle

WEPRO
Women Entrepreneurs Project

Werner Report
on monetary union. Published in the *Bulletin of the EC* Supplement 11/1970. *See also* **EMU**

Westendorf Group
Reflection Group report on Institutional reform which was issued in December 1995 in preparation for the **IGC**. Published in *Bulletin of the EU* 12/1995, p46-51

WETO
World energy, technology, and climate policy outlook. A study presented in May 2003 by the **European Commission**, highlighting energy, technological and environmental trends over the next 30 years.
http://europa.eu.int/comm/research/energy/pdf/weto_final_report.pdf

WETS
Worldwide emergency telemedicine services (a Telematics for Healthcare project within the **Telematics Applications Programme**).
www.ehto.org/ht_projects/html/dynamic/137.html

WFD
Water Framework Directive

WGCS
Working Group on Codes and Standards

WHDC
World harmonised duty cycle

White Paper
A proposal issued by the **European Commission** for Community action in a specific area. Published in the **COM** document series, often as a follow-up to a **Green Paper**.
http://europa.eu.int/comm/off/white/index_en.htm

WIDE
Network Women in Development Europe.
10 rue de la Science, B-1000 Brussels, Belgium.
www.eurosur.org/wide

Widening
The idea of increasing the number of **Member States**, through enlargement of the Union. Often seen as a concept opposed to that of **Deepening**, as it can be argued that more members will lead to greater fragmentation of policy and thus to less integration

Wild Birds Directive
See **Birds Directive**

Williamson Report
Report of the Reflection Group on Personnel Policy, November 1998.
www.renouveau.org/en/cedocse/willrpte.doc

WIR
Women in Industrial Research.
www.europa.eu.int/comm/research/science-society/women/wir/index_en.html

WISDOM
Wireless information services for deaf people on the move

WISE
Women's International Studies Europe.
2 Heidelberglaan, NL-3584 Utrecht, Netherlands.
http://women-www.uia.ac.be/women/wise

WISE
Working in synergie for Europe (a Telematics for Healthcare project within the **Telematics Applications Programme**).
www.ehto.org/ht_projects/html/dynamic/138.html

WISECARE
Workflow information systems for European nursing care (a Telematics for Healthcare project within the **Telematics Applications Programme**).
www.ehto.org/ht_projects/html/dynamic/139.html

WITTY
Wireless traffic and transport information system for urban areas (**ISIS** Transport project)

WOMAN
Intelligent telematics services for women care by a European network (a Telematics for Healthcare project within the **Telematics Applications Programme**).
www.ehto.org/ht_projects/html/dynamic/140.html

WOME
European Parliament Committee on Women's Rights

Work Equipment Directive
Directive 89/655/EEC concerning minimum safety and health requirements for the use of work equipment by workers at work (**OJ** L393/89)

Workers' Charter
Name sometimes used for the **Social Charter**

Working Hours Directive
Alternative name for **Working Time Directive**

Working Time Directive
Directive 93/104/EC on certain aspects of the Directive organisation of working time (**OJ** L307/93)

Works Council Directive
Short form of European Works Council Directive - **EWC**

WorldDAB
World Forum for Digital Audio Broadcasting: "an international non-governmental organisation whose objective is to promote, harmonise and co-ordinate the implementation of Digital Radio services based on the Eureka 147 DAB system".
5th Floor, 7 Swallow Place, London W1B 2AG, UK.
www.worlddab.org

WOW
Women on Work.
35 Via di S.Spirito, 50125 Florence, Italy.
www.wow-womenonwork.it

WSI
Wafer scale integration (**ESPRIT** project)

WTO
World Trade Organisation. Established 1995 as a successor to **GATT**.
Centre William Rappard, 154 rue de Lausanne, CH-1211 Geneva 21, Switzerland.
www.wto.org and
http://europa.eu.int/comm/trade/issues/newround/eu_wto/index_en.htm

X-Y-Z

X-by-wire
Project to develop a safety-related fault-tolerant system in vehicles (supported by the **BRITE/EURAM** programme)

XML/EDI
European XML (extensible markup language) / **EDI** pilot project (**ISIS** Electronic Commerce project)

YB_1999
Regions statistical yearbook 1999 statistical domain on the **REGIO** database

YEE
Youth and Environment Europe. A group "of 61 European youth organisations that study nature or are active for environment protection."
Ekologicke centrum Toulcuv Dvur, 1/32 Kubatova, 102 00 Prague 10 - Hostivar, Czech Republic.
www.ecn.cz/yee

YES
Youth Exchange Scheme. Now **Youth for Europe**

YES for Europe
Young Entrepreneurs for Europe. European Confederation of Young Entrepreneurs.
1 av de la Joyeuse Entrée, B-1040 Brussels, Belgium.
www.yes.be

YFE
Youth for Europe

YIP
Yeast **Industry Platform**.
http://europa.eu.int/comm/dg12/biotech/ip2.html#YIP

YIP
Youth initiative projects (within the **PETRA** programme)

Young Workers' Exchange Programme
Incorporated into **PETRA**

YOUTH
Community action programme on mobility and non-formal education, for young people aged between 15 and 25 years. Established by **Decision** 1031/2000/EC (**OJ** L117/00). Incorporates **Youth for Europe** and **EVS**.
http://europa.eu.int/comm/education/youth/youthprogram.html

Youth for Europe
A programme for the promotion of youth exchanges, 1995-1999, under **Decision** 818/95/EC (**OJ** L87/95). Now part of **YOUTH**

YOUTHSTART
Part of **EMPLOYMENT**, a **Community Initiative** for the promotion of access to work and continuing education for the under 20s, 1994-1999

YWU
Year-work-unit

Zangger Committee
Set up to establish guidelines for implementing the export control provisions of the Nuclear Nonproliferation Treaty. *See also* **Australia Group**, **Missile Technology Control Regime**, **Nuclear Suppliers Group**, **Wassenaar Arrangement**.
www.fas.org/nuke/control/zangger

ZPA1
Agricultural products statistical domain on the **New Cronos** databank

ZPA1_CC
Agricultural production in **Candidate Countries** statistical domain on the **New Cronos** databank

ZRD1
Government **R&D** statistical domain on the **New Cronos** databank

ZRD2
Regional data statistical domain relating to government **R&D** on the **New Cronos** databank

Non-alphabetical entries

.com Summit
«dot com Summit» - a term sometimes used for **Lisbon Summit**

.eu
See **dot.EU**

3 Pillars
See **Pillars**

3SNET
Short Sea Shipping Network. Project to improve the direct information and communication links between the different participants in the transport chain (**Transport** project)

3 Wise Men
See **Three Wise Men Report**

4FP
Fourth Framework Programme

4th Motor Insurance Directive
See **Fourth Motor Insurance Directive**

5FP
See **Fifth Framework Programme**

5mail
An e-mail newsletter launched by the Employment and Social Affairs **DG** of the **European Commission** in 1999 (then DG V) to give a short overview of the latest news on employment, industrial relations and social affairs. Replaced by **ESmail**

6
The six original members of the European Coal and Steel Community (**ECSC**): Belgium, France, Germany, Italy, Luxembourg, Netherlands

6EAP
Sixth Environment Action Programme
- **EAP**

6FP
See **Sixth Framework Programme**

9
The members of the **European Community** following the first enlargement i.e. the original **6**, plus Denmark, Ireland and the United Kingdom

9 May
See **Europe Day**

10
Members of the **European Community** following the accession of Greece in 1981

10
The new **Member States** from 1 May 2004: Czech Republic, Cyprus, Estonia, Hungary, Latvia, Lithuania, Malta, Poland, Slovakia, Slovenia

12
Members of the **European Community** between 1986 and 1995, i.e. after Portugal and Spain joined the **10**-member Community

13th Directive on company law
See **Takeover Directive**

15
Members of the **European Union** from 1995: Austria, Belgium, Denmark, Finland, France, Germany, Greece, Ireland, Italy, Luxembourg, Netherlands, Portugal, Spain, Sweden, United Kingdom

25
The Members of the **European Union** from 1 May 2004, i.e. the **15**, plus the **10**

30th May Mandate
Declaration following the Congress of Europe (organised by the **European Movement**) held in Paris in May 1980 to celebrate the 30th anniversary of the **Schuman Declaration**. Published in *Bulletin of the EC* Supplement 1/81

48 Hour Directive
See **Working Time Directive**

1992
Synonym for Single European Market **(SEM)**

XIII Magazine
See **I&T Magazine**